Introduction to Quantitative
Aspects of Social Phenomena

Introduction to Quantitative Aspects of Social Phenomena

ELLIOTT W. MONTROLL

and

WADE W. BADGER

Department of Physics
University of Rochester
New York

GORDON AND BREACH SCIENCE PUBLISHERS

New York   London   Paris

Copyright © 1974 by

Gordon and Breach, Science Publishers, Inc.
One Park Avenue
New York, N.Y. 10016

Editorial office for the United Kingdom

Gordon and Breach, Science Publishers Ltd.
42 William IV Street
London W.C.2.

Editorial office for France

Gordon & Breach
7–9 rue Emile Dubois
Paris 75014

Library of Congress catalog card number 72-96824. ISBN 0 677 04070 9. All rights reserved. No part of this book may be reproduced or utilized in any form or by any means, electronic or mechanical, including photocopying, recording, or by any information storage or retrieval system, without permission in writing from the publishers. Printed in Scotland by Bell and Bain Limited, Glasgow.

Preface

THE AIM of this book is to present and discuss a collection of mathematical models of social phenomena and to introduce a number of strategies which might be considered when attempting to model complex phenomena. Some of the models are to be found scattered through a literature of several hundred years' extent while others are original to the authors. An historical introduction generally precedes the systematic exposition of each topic to provide some perspective to certain current social problems.

Since controlled social experiments are difficult and rare, models must be based on observations and therefore frequently on historical data. In the collection of material for this book the authors have become impressed with the wealth of excellent relevant data, some old and some new, available to motivate and test various models. A significant part of this data has been collected over the past three centuries by leisured eccentrics, without academic affiliation, who devoted long hours to their projects and published their works of love without the threat of perishing academically.

It has been interesting to discover how many of the early physical scientists observed and wrote about social phenomena as a hobby. One of the authors (EWM) has to some degree tried to follow in this tradition. He has written about traffic and population growth and competition. However, his published work does not reflect his old and deep fascination with the history and mechanism of the development of countries and of industrial and agricultural technology, and with the dilemmas faced by high level planners who have the responsibility of making preparations and policies which minimize the effect of future natural and man-made disasters.

Several years ago, Dean Kenneth Clark asked one of us (EWM) to give an informal course to a small number of Freshman Science students on some topic which might interest them. This opportunity was seized upon to furnish an excuse to organize the random thoughts and accidental literature findings of many years into a more systematic outline of quantitative aspects of social phenomena. The second author (WWB) was invited to be the graduate assistant in the course. It was his notes on the lectures which provided the seed from which the book has developed.

A number of other lecture series were given, one being an intense set of daily lectures continuing for two weeks to advanced undergraduates, graduate students, and physics faculty members at Simon Fraser University, and another being a one-semester course for upper class students at the University of Rochester. This course was most instrumental in setting the final mathematical level and the style of the book. Numerous colloquium talks based on various parts of the book have been delivered at a variety of institutions. The audience response to these has been very helpful in structuring the exposition.

Our first chapter is an historical survey of some selected items. The second is a combination of a presentation of the rate equation style for constructing models and of the analyses of some aspects of population growth. The third is a collection of statistical styles and techniques with socially oriented examples of each. The remaining chapters are more exhaustive treatments of the following subjects: speculation, traffic, air pollution, and the development of countries and the growth of cities.

Since the present state of understanding of these topics varies, as does the authors' expertise, there is some unevenness in the exposition. In preparing the manuscript, a compromise had to be made between reasonably early publication and completeness. The large number of requests we have received for copies of the lecture notes of the courses mentioned above, at various stages of completion, has provided considerable pressure toward the option of early publication at the expense of forgoing a more thorough literature search of some of the fields considered. We feel, however, that even though some important ideas and references may have been neglected, we have included a sufficiently broad bibliography so that anyone who wishes to delve more deeply into any of the subjects presented can start with the literature cited.

Since an unbalanced feature of the book evident to the authors is the large space devoted to speculation and the small space devoted to problems of the city, some words of justification of this situation are perhaps warranted. Social phenomena are generally a reflection of the interaction of people. If one wishes to develop an intuition about this type of interaction in a quantitative way, he must find examples in which daily numerical records exist which depend on these interactions. Investment in the stock market is one of the few phenomena which involve many interacting people and about which there is an easily available daily (and even hourly) record of the effects of their interaction. Furthermore, the overall economy and the political actions of a country are often strongly influenced by investment and speculation. For these reasons, and, it must be admitted, for the sheer entertainment in following the lore of the market, we let ourselves get carried away by this subject. The unraveling of the myriad statistical records of problems of the city would postpone the completion of the book indefinitely.

The narrative parts of Chapter IV on speculation represent the portion of the book which is farthest from the authors' usual style of presentation. For that material we are especially indebted to the authors of the following books: *Extraordinary Popular Delusions and the Madness of Crowds* by Charles MacKay (1841), *The Panic of 1837* by Reginald McGrane (1924), *Only Yesterday* by Frederick Allen (1931), and *The Great Crash* by John Galbraith (1954). All these books are strongly recommended to the reader who is interested in this type of material.

We have derived considerable satisfaction in assembling the material in the book. However, at times we have had an uneasy feeling which we believe to be common to mathematical model makers who have been educated in a more disciplined branch of science such as physics. We can have excellent agreement between observations and the theory of a model but most of these results remain isolated, standing alone from the others. Almost all branches of a disciplined subject such as physics are connected. A clear, peculiar observation if followed through to its logical consequences might eventually threaten the foundations of the whole subject. This creates some excitement so that it is regarded critically by a number of persons who eventually resolve the paradox or find a mistake, or attempt to reformulate the subject. At present this type of criticism can not be made about our models. As our subject becomes better understood it will be desirable to develop a set of broad principles from which our various results can be deduced. We feel that the time will not be ripe for such generalizing and systematizing until a richer collection of special results is acquired.

Two extreme attitudes may be taken of our endeavor. One would be in the spirit of Lord Kelvin who stated that he could not understand anything until it was expressed with numbers. The other is embodied in the remark of Nietzsche "No more fiction for us, we calculate; but that we may calculate, we had to make fiction first." The reader has his choice. We have committed ourselves.

Before proceeding with our main text, several acknowledgements are in order. First we wish to thank the U.S. Air Force Office of Scientific Research and the New York State Education Department for supporting some of our early researches on some of the topics reported on in the book. We appreciate the continued interest of William J. Price and Paul J. Daily of OSR in that research. We are grateful for the aid of Shirley A. Montroll in compiling the author index and in correcting proofs. We thank Shirley MacDonnell for her excellent typing of many versions of the original lecture notes and of the final manuscript. Finally we thank the copyright holders of figures which we are reprinting in the book for allowing us to use their figures. The authors and publishers of the figures are generally identified in the references at the end of each section.

ELLIOTT W. MONTROLL
WADE W. BADGER

Contents

A*

CHAPTER I

Some Introductory Historical Remarks

MAN'S EXISTENCE on this planet has always been beset with problems. He has had to defend himself against beasts, pestilence, forces of nature, and, sometimes, his fellowmen as well as his own hallucinations. Progress and security have developed from a combination of improved understanding, lucky accidents, better planning, and, on occasion, belligerent action against other species or his fellows. In early times he was often forced to face events which he could neither comprehend nor combat. The situation for many is not significantly different today.

A partial listing of ancient man's fears is well presented in the Jewish Passover services. The motivation for the Israelites for leaving Egypt was to escape from slavery, one of the cruelest afflictions experienced by man. God's punishment of the Egyptians, as stated in the service, consisted of ten plagues:

Blood	Boils	Frogs
Hail	Vermin	Locusts

Murrain (an infection of mucous membrane of intestines of sheep and
cattle)

Pestilence	Slaying of first born	Darkness

which might be considered as representative of the worst disasters one could wish on his enemies. These can be categorized as:

(a) Diseases of man and important domesticated animals.

(b) Annoyance by other species.

(c) Weather problems.

(d) Attacks by opponents.

Perhaps a third to one-half of the items on the plague list no longer bother us.

Pollution does not appear on the list, but it is conjectured that the "rivers turning to blood" might have been a rapid growth of red or brown algae in polluted waters, or, perhaps, of purple sulphur bacteria.[1]

1

While overcrowding was not mentioned, it apparently did bother some at an even earlier era. One believes that the first metropolitan area in the western world was the city of Uhr, the residence of Abraham until he dropped out seeking a more nomadic and ascetic life. It is estimated from recent excavations that Uhr covered an area of four square miles and contained a population of 500,000 with a density of 125,000 per square mile. Abraham's descendants who lived in the Bronx or Brooklyn in 1960 were immersed in a population of density 34,000/sq. mile while their more recent forebears who were squeezed into the Lower East Side of New York in 1900 lived under one of the highest densities recorded in the Western world, 350,000 per square mile. The density in that region has diminished considerably in the past seventy years.

Problems associated with overcrowding were evident in the Rome of Julius Caesar, a city with a population between 800,000 and a million. One of Caesar's important actions was to reduce the 320,000 persons on the dole at the beginning of his tenure to 150,000 at the time of his assassination.[2]

The non-returnable bottle was already a nuisance in Roman times. One of the largest "monuments" of Rome, known as Monte Testaccio, was a mound of some 40 million broken clay jars which were piled behind the ancient docks. It had the form of a cone about 140 feet high with a diameter of 1200 feet. By the second century, A.D., cheap Spanish wine had captured the popular Roman market.[2] It was shipped in large clay jars which weighed about 95 Roman pounds empty and about 215 pounds filled. Since it was more profitable to load the galleys returning to Spain with Italian goods than with empty wine casks, Monte Testaccio grew steadily.

During the sacking of Rome by the Barbarians, the organization and facilities of the city collapsed, epidemics were common and the population dropped to about 500,000. This drop continued during the Middle Ages. The population was 175,000 in 1850, rose to 300,000 by 1890, and today stands at about 2,560,000.

It seems that smog was first mentioned officially in the reign of Edward I in England about 1300 A.D. when members of the nobility drew up a petition concerning the offensive coal smoke in London. Within a hundred years Henry V established a commission to supervise and restrict the movement of coal into the London area.[3]

Certain minor annoyances were alleviated in the Middle Ages by a slowly developing technology; others persisted until rather recent times. The invention of spectacles is attributed to a Florentine at about 1300 A.D. with their adoption being popularized by certain Monks to help "poor blind men." While it is clear from an examination of fine detail on Greek and Roman coins that magnifying glasses must have been commonly used by ancient artisans, their simple transition into spectacles was an exceedingly slow process. Many strange "visions" seen by people in the Middle Ages no doubt were the effect of faulty, uncorrected eyes. Spectacle production led to the discovery of lens systems and the invention of the telescope and microscope which stimulated the rapid growth of the physical and biological sciences.

Famines and food shortages were encountered almost every year somewhere in Europe until the great railroad network was constructed in the 1840's and 1850's. The absence of fresh meat and vegetables during the winter months was responsible for a low resistance to bacterial attack. To the very young and the very old, March was the killer month. After a winter diet of dried food and salt meat, scurvy was common as well as bronchial infection. This condition has only been corrected in the past hundred years through the cultivation of corn and roots of the turnip family as animal food which can be stored easily and cheaply in the winter. Until their introduction, few farmers could afford to keep more than a few animals alive through the winter.

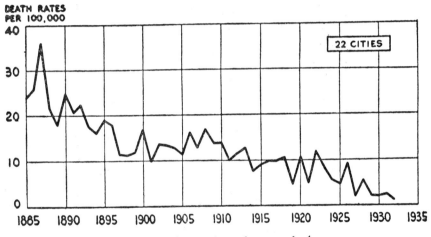

Figure 1   Death rate from measles.[4]

As is evident[4] in Figures 1, 2, and 3, certain common dangerous diseases have been eliminated only in the authors' lifetimes. In 1948 the death rate per 100,000 from the combined causes of whooping cough, diphtheria, measles, and scarlet fever was only 1.8 in the U.S. so that the measles point would hardly show on a continuation of Figure 1 into recent decades. While Figure 2 represents a triumph of public health measures, it was partly to the detriment of the purity of Lake Michigan. The data in Figure 3 since 1920 is quite representative of the U.S. generally. The death rate per thousand since 1920 has hovered around ten even though a number of important new

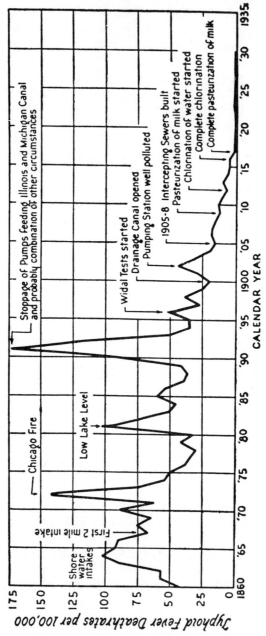

Figure 2   Conquest of typhoid fever[4] in the city of Chicago, 1860–1930

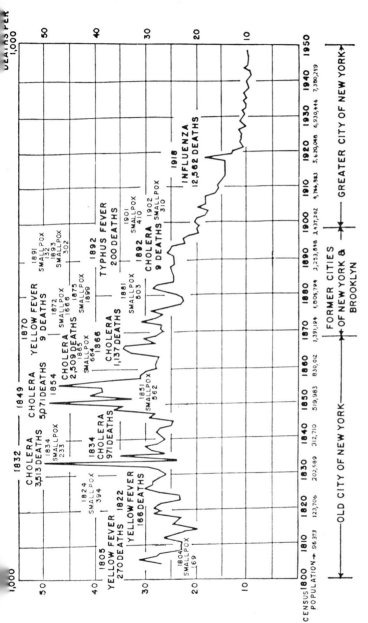

Figure 3 Trends in disease: Mortality and epidemics in New York City, 1804–1948.

The trends in mortality and epidemics in New York City since the beginning of the nineteenth century illustrate changes in large cities in all modern nations.

The first half of the nineteenth century saw no substantial improvement in the security of health and life; conditions at the mid-century were indeed disastrous. After that time epidemics became less frequent, although typhus and smallpox continued to invade the city from time to time and an effective weapon against diphtheria was not forged until near the end of the century. The progress in health is evident not only from the decline in general mortality but also from the flattening of the peaks that once marked periodic outbreaks of epidemics.[15]

medical discoveries have been made. The numbers for 1940, 1950, and 1960 were respectively 10.8, 9.6, and 9.5. In 1965 the region with the best record was Utah with 7.1 and the worst, the District of Columbia 12.5 with New York State having a slightly above average death rate of 10.2 per thousand.

Undoubtedly the most mortal enemy of Europeans in the Middle Ages was the Bubonic Plague. The Black Death carried away a quarter of the population of Europe during the 1348–49 epidemic. Even as late as the eighteenth century, it still cast its deathly shadow with about forty percent of the residents of Copenhagen and Danzig dying in the epidemic of 1709–10, and with 40,000 out of 90,000 being victims at Marseilles in 1720. The constant threat of death during plague years led to the disappearance of all moral conventions in some places, while it turned people into religious fanatics in others. Considerable improvement of the lot of weavers in the early industrial enterprises of Europe came immediately after plague epidemics. If a large number of weavers died in a given weaving town, the survivors in a neighboring town were recruited with promises of better wages and working conditions.

In a period when half of a young Italian's friends might be carried off by the plague while the other half was hounded by the Inquisition, the world must have looked hopeless. It would have been hard to convince one so affected that both of these scourges would disappear through the development of science and the understanding of biological and natural phenomena.

While the modern scientific method was born in Italy, the enthusiasm for its broad application caught on more rapidly in the Protestant countries of England and the Dutch Netherlands than it did in the Catholic south which was still influenced by the Inquisition. The Royal Society of England provided a forum for those who had sufficient leisure to participate in the scientific adventure. Regular meetings encouraged the membership to report their observations and theories, and social as well as physical and biological observations were presented.

Most of the experimenters and observers were men of means or professors who did not have to grub for a living. One of the exceptions, John Graunt (1620–1674), haberdasher of small-wares, obtained his leisure by ". . . rising early in the morning to his study before shop time. He wrote shorthand dextrously. He was a man with an excellent working head, was very facetious and fluent in his conversation, and understood Latin and French."[8]

Said haberdasher was the founder of the subject of our lectures. His little pamphlet[9] "Natural and Political Observations Made Upon the Bills of Mortality", 1662, was the first collection and interpretation of vital statistics and represented the first quantitative examination of the affairs of man. The "Bills of Mortality" which furnished Graunt the required raw data were the parish records of births and deaths (with their cause). Graunt's work made such an impression on Charles II that he proposed him as an original member of the newly incorporated Royal Society . . . "his majesty gave this particular charge to his society, that if they found any more such tradesmen, they should be sure to admit them all without any more ado."[7]

Before briefly presenting some of Graunt's detailed statistics, it is revealing to note some of the observations which appeared in the covering letter of the copy of his pamphlet which was delivered to the king . . .

that London, the metropolis of England, is perhaps a Head too big for the Body and possibly too strong; that this head grows three times as fast as the Body to which it belongs . . . that old streets are unfit for the present frequency of Coaches . . . that the fighting men about London are able to make three great Armies as can be of use in this Island. . . . [9]

A typical page of Graunt's statistics is given here as Table I. The most striking point is the small difference between the number of births and deaths. With only 49 more births than deaths, London was barely holding its own.† At that rate it took considerable rural population influx to compensate for each plague year. In a non-plague year such as 1632, childhood diseases and consumption caused half the deaths. The cancer figure of ten deaths seems to be very low. Probably some deaths listed under other headings were actually a form of cancer. Heart attacks as such are not listed, but some of the 62 "suddenly" may be attributed to that cause as well as some of the "dead on the street", and perhaps others.

In a period when violence was common on the continent, the 7 "murthered" is indeed remarkable. Graunt[9] makes a special comment to the effect that of the 229,250 deaths which occurred in the period of the twenty years 1603–1624, only 51 are starved and . . .

there but few are murthered, viz. not above 86 of 229,250 which have died of other diseases, and casualties; whereas in Paris few nights scape without their tragedie. . . . The reason of this we conceive to be two; one is the Government and guard of the City by Citizens themselves, and that alternately. No man settling into a trade for that employment. And the other is, the natural and customary abhorrence of that inhumane Crime, and Bloodshed by most Englishmen; for of all that are Executed, few are for Murther.

It was estimated that 36% of the deaths in the twenty-year period considered occurred before the age of six. Of the 229,250 deaths, about 50,000 were of acute diseases and 70,000 of chronic ones. Graunt[9] also observes that

---

† The number of burials in London generally exceeded the number of baptisms throughout the 18th Century. For each thousand burials there were the following number of baptismals in successive twenty-year periods: 1680–1700, 681; 1700–1720, 721; 1720–1740, 649; 1740–1760, 638; 1761–1765 (four years) 644.

TABLE I

The Diseases, and Casualties this year being 1632.

ABortive, and Stilborn ..	445	Grief	11
Affrighted	1	Jaundies	43
Aged	628	Jawfaln	8
Ague	43	Impostume	74
Apoplex, and Meagrom	17	Kil'd by several accidents..	46
Bit with a mad dog	1	King's Evil	38
Bleeding	3	Lethargie	2
Bloody flux, scowring, and flux	348	Livergrown	87
Brused, Issues, sores, and ulcers,	28	Lunatique	5
		Made away themselves	15
Burnt, and Scalded	5	Measles	80
Burst, and Rupture	9	Murthered	7
Cancer, and Wolf	10	Over-laid, and starved at nurse	7
Canker	1	Palsie	25
Childbed	171	Piles	1
Chrisomes, and Infants	2268	Plague	8
Cold, and Cough	55	Planet	13
Colick, Stone, and Strangury	56	Pleurisie, and Spleen	36
Consumption	1797	Purples, and spotted Feaver	38
Convulsion	241	Quinsie	7
Cut of the Stone	5	Rising of the Lights	98
Dead in the street, and starved	6	Sciatica	1
		Scurvey, and Itch	9
Dropsie, and Swelling	267	Suddenly	62
Drowned	34	Surfet	86
Executed, and prest to death	18	Swine Pox	6
Falling Sickness	7	Teeth	470
Fever	1108	Thrush, and Sore mouth	40
Fistula	13	Tympany	13
Flocks, and small Pox	531	Tissick	34
French Pox	12	Vomiting	1
Gangrene	5	Worms	27
Gout	4		

Christened { Males....4994 / Females..4590 / In all....9584 } Buried { Males....4932 / Females..4603 / In all....9535 } Whereof, of the Plague.8

Increased in the Burials in the 122 Parishes, and at the Pest-house this year.. 993

Decreased of the Plague in the 122 Parishes, and at the Pest-house this year................................... 266

the vast numbers of Beggars, Swarming up and down this City, do all live, and seem to be most of them healthy and strong, whereupon I make this question, whether, since they do all live by Begging, it were not better for the State to keep them, even although they earned nothing; that so they might live regularly, and not in that Debauchery, as many Beggars do; and that they might be cured of their bodily Impotencies, or taught to work, each according to his condition or capacity.

In his conclusion he says[9]:

It may be now asked, to what purpose tends all this laborious buzzling, and groping? To know,

1. The number of the People?
2. How many *Males*, and *Females*?
3. How many Married, and Single?
4. How many *Teeming* Women?
5. How many of every *Septenary*, or *Decad* of years in *age*?
6. How many *Fighting* Men?
7. How much *London* is, and by what steps it has increased?
8. In what time the housing is replenished after a *Plague*?
9. What proportion die of each general and perticular *Casualties*?
10. What years are Fruitfull, and Mortal, and in what Spaces, and Intervals, they follow each other?
11. In what proportion Men neglect the Orders of the *Church*, and *Sects* have increased?
12. The disproportion of Parishes?
13. Why the Burials in *London* exceed the Christenings, when the contrary is visible in the Country?

To this I might answer in general by saying, that those, who cannot apprehend the reason of these Enquiries, are unfit to trouble themselves to ask them.

I might Answer; That there is much pleasure in deducing so many abstruse, and un-expected inferences out of these poor despised Bills of *Mortality*; and in building upon that ground, which hath lain waste these eighty years. And there is pleasure in doing something new, though never so little, without pestering the World with voluminous Transcriptions.

But, I Answer more seriously; by complaining, That whereas the Art of Governing, and the true *Politiques*, is how to preserve the Subject in *Peace*, and *Plenty*, that men study onely that part of it, which teacheth how to supplant, and over-reach one another, and how, not by fair outrunning, but by tripping up each other's heels, to win the Prize.

Now, the Foundation, or Elements of this honest harmless *Policy* is to understand the Land, and the hands of the Territory to be governed.

I conclude, That a clear knowledge of all these particulars, and many more, whereat I have shot but at rovers, is necessary in order to good, certain, and easie Government, and even to balance Parties, and factions both in *Church* and *State*. But whether the knowledge thereof be necessary to many, or fit for others, then the Sovereign, and his chief Ministers, I leave to consideration.

Unlike Graunt, Edmund Halley (1656–1742), had a wealthy father who encouraged him to pursue the sciences by supporting his education at Oxford and supplying him liberally with astronomical instruments. Halley was an FRS at the age of twenty-two and later became secretary of the Society. It was he who persuaded Newton to publish his work on the orbits of the planets, as well as to write the Principia. Halley corrected the proofs and wrote the Latin verses which stand at the beginning of the work. He discovered the comet which bears his name and predicted the years of its return. He also mapped the earth's magnetic lines of force and motion of the trade winds.

Halley constructed the first mortality tables based on the records of births and of deaths at various ages in the city of Brestlau. These tables and their extensions and improvements form the basis of life insurance practice. It was from these tables that De Moivre made the hypothesis that the decrements of human life are nearly equal at all ages such that out of 86 persons born, one dies every year until all are gone. As we shall see later, this hypothesis is certainly not valid now.

Halley died at the age of eighty-six. He was a generous, easygoing person, "free from rancor or jealousy," who spoke and acted with an "uncommon degree of sprightliness and vivacity." He enjoyed his work, had excellent health and owned a large circle of friends, among them Peter the Great of Russia to whose table he always had access. Bishop Berkeley thought Halley an "infidel," and it is true that in 1691 he was refused the Savilian professorship of astronomy at Oxford because of his alleged "materialistic views." The evidence is that he was a sensible man who spoke his mind freely—a dangerous practice in any age.[7]

Halley's concern with the "curious tables" of Brestlau was one of his lesser diversions. This Silesian city had, for more than a century before his entry into the problem, kept regular records of its births and deaths. Dr. Caspar Neumann, a scientist and clergyman of Brestlau had analyzed some of these data, "disproving certain current superstitions with regard to the effect of the phases of the moon and the so-called 'climacteric' years, on health." His results were submitted to Leibniz who sent them to the Royal Society. It was at about this time that the Society resumed publication of the Transactions after a lapse of several years. Halley promised to furnish five sheets in twenty of the forthcoming issues. He was never hard up for ideas, nor for the energy and ingenuity to express them. His Brestlau papers may therefore be regarded as a kind of filler for the Transactions, to keep his word until something better came along. Nevertheless, the analysis reflects the exceptional power of his mind.[7]

The phenomenal successes of Newtonian mechanics and optics and the exciting observations made by Leeuwenhoek and Hooke with their primitive microscopes encouraged the growing scientific community to pursue the physical and biological sciences to the neglect of the social and economic ones.

SOME INTRODUCTORY HISTORICAL REMARKS

Newton himself, however, when master of the Mint, did give considerable thought to one of the basic and most frustrating economic problems of his tenure. England, as well as the Continental countries, operated on a double gold and silver monetary standard; each country established its own price ratio with, for example, France choosing a ratio which gave preference to silver and England one which favored gold. These differences led to a continuing flow (usually illegal) of coins from one country to another where a more favorable ratio made it profitable to melt down and sell as bullion the coins recently minted at great expense.

Newton's report[11] on the criteria for the choice of a ratio led to the establishment of the 21 silver shilling level for the gold guinea (a coin later replaced by the 20-shilling gold sovereign) by the proclamation of 22 December 1717. While his report was a brilliant, logical analysis, he did not fully appreciate that continuing fluctuations in supply and demand of the two precious metals made the establishment of a constant ratio impossible; and that the adherence to a double standard was basically an unstable practice. While every money changer in the ports and markets of Europe had for hundreds of years made many a quick ducat or guinea on these fluctuations, it was not until the act of 1816 that England showed an official understanding of this mechanism and established the single gold standard.[12] Other countries followed later.

The tendency for money that is overvalued to drive undervalued money out of circulation was called (first by H. D. MacLeod in 1857) Gresham's Law after Sir Thomas Gresham (1519–1579), financial advisor to Queen Elizabeth I. The principle was, in fact, set forth in earlier economic writings of Oresme, and Copernicus, the astronomer. At an especially critical time, Copernicus served on the finance committee of the King of Poland. He gave the following expression of the law

when rulers . . . try to make a profit . . . when they add a new coin to . . . the current . . . while imperfect in grain or cut and yet valued equally, they are like a stingy farmer who sows bad seeds in order to save good ones, and then there will be even more produced than he sowed. This destroys the value of coins, just as the weeds destroy the grain, when the former win the upper hand.[13]

The present paucity of silver coins in one's pocket change is evidence of the effectiveness of the law. A cursory survey of the literature did not provide any statistical indication of how fast bad money drives out the good. To obtain a rough indication of the rate, almost a thousand dimes were withdrawn from circulation and sampled in March 1969. Twenty-six silver Roosevelt dimes were found (dates 1946–1964) and 903 clad copper dimes dated 1965–68. Two silver liberty dimes (minted before 1946) and perhaps a half-dozen 1969 clad dimes were also found, but these are irrelevant in the calculations below. The number of silver Roosevelt dimes minted in the period 1946–64 (inclusive) was 5.137×10^9 while the number of clad dimes minted in 1965, '66, '67, '68 was 6.757×10^9. Hence, if the silver coins had not been removed from circulation in the manner predicted by Gresham's Law, the fraction of silver Roosevelt dimes circulating should have been $(5.137/11.894) = 0.432$ instead of the $(26/929) = 0.02798$ observed. On the basis of our sampling, it is estimated that only

$$(26/903)(6.757 \times 10^9) = 1.945 \times 10^8$$

silver dimes remained in circulation.

Now let us assume $N(t)$ is the number of silver coins remaining in circulation and N^* the number at time $t = 0$, March 1965, when clad dimes first appeared in significant numbers. Then, if we postulate an exponential decay in the number in circulation

$$N(t) = N^* \exp(-\lambda t)$$

where λ is to be determined from the data given above and $N^* = 5.137 \times 10^9$. Since $t = 4$ years,

$$\lambda = -t^{-1} \log(N(t)/N^*)$$
$$= -(1/4 \text{ yr}) \{\log 1.945 - \log 51.37\}$$
$$= 0.82/\text{year}$$

The constant λ probably depends on the denomination and on the difference in value between the "good" and the "bad" money.

Not only has our coinage been debased, but we are also living in an inflationary period. This is not an unusual state. From ancient to modern times, monarchs and parliaments alike have habitually kept their people in debt, usually through overextending their military commitments, their explorations abroad, and/or their domestic construction programs. Thus the debasement of coinage and creeping or galloping inflations which are stimulated by such overextensions have plagued both their poor and the rich subjects from time immemorial. About the year 300 A.D. prices were soaring to such an extent that the emperor Diocletian issued his famous decree on price and wage control. The preamble to the decree reads:

Who is of so hardened a heart and so untouched by a feeling for humanity that he can be unaware, that in the sale of the wares which are exchanged in the market, or dealt with in the daily business of the cities, an exhorbitant tendency in prices has spread to such an extent that the unbridled desire of plundering is held in check neither by abundance nor by seasons of plenty. . . .

The restrictions themselves are in Table II and are compared with more recent figures.[14] The 1970 data is our own.

TABLE II

	Diocletian's	1906	1970
Bushel of salt	$0.74.5		
Bushel of rye	0.45.	$0.79	0.97 to 1.07
Bushel of beans, ground	0.74.5	0.45	
Bushel of beans, not ground	0.45.		
Bushel of lentils	0.74.5		
Bushel of oats	0.22.5		
Bushel of poppy seeds	0.01.12		
Bushel of mustard	0.01.12		
Bushel of wheat	0.33.6	1.19	1.22 to 1.39
Quart wine (Picenum, Tibur, Falernum)	0.22.		3.75 to 5.00
Quart wine, common variety	0.06.		1.59 to 1.99
Quart beer	0.01.5		0.43 to 0.55
Quart oil, first quality	0.30.3		0.62 to 0.68
Quart oil, second quality	0.18.		
Quart vinegar	0.04.3	0.05 to 0.07	0.31 to 0.37
Quart honey, first quality	0.30.3		
Pound pork	0.07.3		0.69 to 0.79
Pound beef	0.04.9	0.15 to 0.18	0.49 to 1.59
Pound mutton	0.04.9	0.13 to 0.16	0.89 to 1.49
Pound ham	0.12.	0.18 to 0.25	0.89 to 1.69
Goose, artificially fed	0.87.		
Goose, not artificially fed	0.43.5		
Pair fowls	0.26.		
Pair pigeons	0.10.5	0.14 to 0.18 lb	
100 oysters	0.43.5		
5 artichokes	0.04.3		0.49
5 heads of lettuce	0.01.7		1.75 to 1.95
5 cabbages	0.01.7		1.45 to 1.95
10 turnips	0.01.7		0.28 to 1.85
25 asparagus	0.02.6		
20 large snails	0.01.7		
Pair trousers	0.08.7		
Felt horse blanket, weight 3 lbs.	0.43.5		
Cover, 1st quality, weight 3 lbs., with embroidery	$1.09.		
Women's slippers	0.21.7		
Men's slippers	0.26.		
Boots, first quality, per pair	0.52.		
Soldiers' boots, without nails	0.43.		
Knight's shoes	0.30.5		
Senatorial shoes	0.43.		
Patrician's shoes	0.65.		
Sewing needle	0.01.7		
Military mantle, first quality	$17.40.		
Undergarment, first quality	$8.70.		
British mantle and cowl	$26.08.		
African mantle and cowl	$6.52.		
Storm coat, first quality	$21.76.		
Gallic soldier's cloak	$43.78.		
White bed blanket, weight 12 lbs.	$6.96.		
Ordinary cover, weight 10 lbs.	$2.18.		
White silk, per pound	$52.22.		
Genuine purple silk, per pound	$652.20.		
Genuine purple wool, per pound	$217.40.		
Butter	0.09.8	0.26 to 0.32	0.79 to 0.83
Fish, river	0.07.3	0.12 to 0.15	1.79 to 2.29
Fish, sea	0.09 to 0.14.	0.08 to 0.14	0.99 to 1.49
Fish, salt	0.08.3	0.08 to 0.15	
Eggs, per doz.	0.05.1	0.25 to 0.30	0.49 to 0.69
Wages per Day			
Barber, per shave	0.9		
Gymnastic teacher, per pupil per month	0.21.6		
Employee to watch children, per month	0.21.6		
Advocate or council presenting case	$1.09.		
Advocate for finishing case	$4.35.		
Unskilled workman	0.10.8	$1.20 to 2.24	34.00 to 36.00
Bricklayer	0.21.6	$4.50 to 6.50	48.00 to 50.00
Carpenter	0.21.6	$2.50 to 4.00	46.50 to 48.50
Stone mason	0.21.6	$3.70 to 4.90	48.00 to 50.00
Painter	0.32.6	$2.75 to 4.00	44.00 to 46.00
Transportation, 1 person 1 mile	0.9		
Rent for wagon, 1 mile	0.05.		
Freight charges (for 1200 lbs.) per mile	0.08.7		
Writer, 100 lines, best writing	0.10.9		
Writer, 100 lines, ordinary writing	0.08.7		
Writer, 100 lines, documents	0.04.3		

The individual prices and wages are not as interesting as their relative levels. Fish and meat were very dear so that the average unskilled workman must have seldom eaten them.

The interpretation of the statement "born to the purple" is clear from an examination of the table.

REFERENCES

1. Louis Klein, *River Pollution*, Vol. II, p. 83 (London 1965–67, Butterworth Press).
2. Helen J. Loane, *Industry and Commerce of The City of Rome*, The Johns Hopkins University Studies in Historical and Political Science LVI (1938).
3. Maynard E. Smith, *The Use and Misuse of The Atmosphere*, Brookhaven Lecture Series No. 24 (1963).
4. Louis I. Dublin and Alfred J. Lotka, *Length of Life* (New York, 1936).
5. Johannes Nohl, *The Black Death* (Ballantine Books, New York, 1960).
6. Daniel Defoe, *A Journal of The Plague Year* (Reprint Edition, Signet Classics, New York, 1960).
7. James R. Newman, *The World of Mathematics*, Vol. III (Simon and Schuster, 1956).
8. *Aubrey's Brief Lives* (Reprint Edition, Ann Arbor Paperbacks, 1962).
9. John Graunt, *Natural and Political Observations Mentioned in a Following Index and Made Upon the Bills of Mortality* (London, 1676; Reprint Edition, Johns Hopkins, 1936).
10. Edmond Halley, Phil. Trans. of Roy. Soc., XVII (1693).
11. John Craig, *Newton at The Mint* (Cambridge, 1946).
12. J. Laurence Laughlin, *Money, Credit and Prices* (Chicago, 1931).
13. Herman Kestin, *Copernicus and His World* (Secker and Warburg, London, 1945).
14. Edward T. Newell, The Numismatist, May 1916 (reprinted in *Selections from The Numismatist, Ancient and Medieval Coins* (Whitman, Racine, Wisconsin, 1960)).
15. W. S. Woytinsky and E. S. Woytinsky, *World Population and Production* (20th Century Fund, New York, 1953).

CHAPTER II

Populations, their Growth and Competition, and Vital Statistics

1 Europe's Initial Population Explosion and the Potato[1]

BEFORE THE mid-eighteenth century, the growth of Europe's population had been slow and fitful. 1750 was about the time that Europe's so-called initial population explosion began. This is dramatically illustrated by examining the variation of Europe's population over the 150-year period 1750–1900, as given below:

$$
\begin{array}{ll}
1650\text{—}100 \times 10^6 \text{ people} & 1800\text{—}188 \times 10^6 \text{ people} \\
1700\text{—}110 \times 10^6 \text{ people} & 1850\text{—}266 \times 10^6 \text{ people} \\
1750\text{—}140 \times 10^6 \text{ people} & 1900\text{—}401 \times 10^6 \text{ people} \\
\multicolumn{2}{c}{1950\text{—}559 \times 10^6 \text{ people}}
\end{array}
$$

It is commonly assumed that this rapid increase was due primarily to a drastic decline in the death rate which, in turn, resulted from (1) fewer wars, (2) a reduction in the number and severity of famines, (3) an improvement in the food supply and, finally, (4) advanced medical knowledge leading to improved general health.

Strong counter arguments tend to contradict the above points. While it is true that the frequency of wars decreased during the period in question, it is generally agreed that nations usually recover quickly from the manpower losses of war. Were this not so, the bloody conflicts of the French revolutionary and Napoleonic periods should have significantly retarded the growth of the European population which, in fact, they did not. Famines continued to be common until the mid-19th century when the railroads were first able to facilitate rapid, large scale distribution of foodstuffs. Improved agricultural techniques such as rotation of crops, systematic manuring, etc., were not generally employed until the same period and grain yields per acre rose only slowly during the entire 150-year period. The disappearance of the Black Plague by the early 1800's certainly contributed to the improvement in the condition of European life, but, as we already pointed out, other diseases (among them smallpox, tuberculosis, scarlet fever, cholera, and typhus) took over where the plague had left off. The largest smallpox epidemic hit Europe in 1871–72 causing 23,062 deaths in England and Wales, 56,826 in Prussia in 1871 and 61,109 in 1872. During the cholera epidemic of 1836, Polermo lost 24,000 out of 173,000 while Russia in 1848–49 registered over 1,000,000 dead. It was not uncommon for diphtheria to carry off all children under six in a village during an epidemic.

Aside from disease, we must also consider what Malthus called the "bad nursing of children", but which might more properly be termed infanticide. It was common practice in the cities to entrust babies to old women nurses. The least offensive of these "Angel makers" kept the children quiet with gin. Certain other popular elixirs which were not meant for children were more often fatal.

The number of illegitimate children was very high in the middle and late 18th century. The state maintained foundling hospitals at which both married and unmarried women could dispose of their unwanted children without question. The majority of these children were sent to peasant nurses in the provinces within the first year of their life (if they had not already died of disease or lack of care!). Many of the small minority that actually began this trip died from exposure on the long stagecoach ride or from further lack of care upon arrival. The magnitude of this practice was truly shocking. The number of children being abandoned, smothered, or otherwise disposed of became so great that as a humanitarian measure Napoleon decreed in 1811 that foundling homes should have a turntable device, not unlike that used in ticket windows of European railroad stations but with an opaque wall separating the depositor and the receiver so that babies could be left without interrogation or recognition of the parent.

In Paris in the middle of the 18th century, about 20% of all the children born were left in the Foundling Hospitals and over 30% of those dying died in these hospitals. The figures are[2]

Year	Christenings	Left in Foundling Hospitals
1751	19,231	3,783
1752	20,227	4,127
1753	19,729	4,329

Year	Burials	Deaths in Hospitals
1751	16,673	5,517
1752	17,762	5,829
1753	21,716	7,167

The practice continued well into the 19th century. Twenty to thirty percent of all children born in France were abandoned, the number reaching 127,000 in 1833. Many spoke out against the inhuman but well-known operation of this system. Some even suggested that a sign reading "Children Killed at Government Expense" should be posted at the entrance to all foundling hospitals. With the above statistics it is clear that infanticide was a major factor in holding down the population in a period when the population was rising rapidly.[1]

Recently some researchers have come to the conclusion that increased birth rates and not declining death rates were characteristic of Europe's population explosion. In attempting to explain these increased birth rates, it was at first thought that the industrial revolution with its attendant emphasis on child labor might have promoted larger families. However, statistics show that Western urbanized populations have generally had lower birth rates than their rural counterparts; their rapid growth being a result of population movement from rural areas. Furthermore, nonindustrialized nations such as Russia experienced the population "explosion" in parallel with the rest of Europe. To explain the rising birth rates, one is forced to conclude that a larger proportion of the young adults married and that they married at an earlier age. The latter is particularly important because it not only lengthened the total possible childbearing period, but also increased the ease with which the children could be borne as women are most fecund in the 17–21 year-old age range. Thus only a small shift in marriage customs could produce a large shift in birth rates. The breaking down of old regulations such as the forbidding of men entering guilds to marry until they had finished their apprenticeship helped to hasten these trends, but they do not appear to explain the full effect. Some of the German states tried to stem the rise in population by refusing to issue marriage licenses to men younger than thirty and even then only provided the license if they could show that they had learned a trade and had a job waiting for them. These restrictions undoubtedly were instrumental in promoting the German emigration of the mid-1800's.

It has been proposed by Langer[1] (see also Salaman[3]) that the introduction and widespread acceptance of the potato led to earlier marriages and higher birth rates. In short, more food brings more mouths. This general proposition is well substantiated by countries such as Sweden which have kept exceptionally good records. The annual excess of births over deaths in eighteenth-century Sweden was only two per thousand after a poor harvest, but 6.5 after an average harvest, and 8.4 after an exceptionally good one.[4] The introduction of the potato had the same effect as a bumper crop. It was extremely nutritious, could be grown on poor or marginal land, and had a yield per acre in nutritional value that was two to four times higher than grain. An acre of poor soil planted in potatoes could support a family of six or even eight. Young people married early, rented an acre or less for growing potatoes and had large families.

Ireland[1, 5] is an excellent example because it did not experience many of the developments affecting the rest of Europe. It had no wars, no industrial revolution, and the pattern of famine and disease remained unchanged. It was, and continued to be, a very poor country. The potato was introduced into Ireland in about 1600 and by 1800 little else was eaten by the common man. According to K. H. Connell, "Day after day, three times a day, people ate salted, boiled potatoes, probably washing them down with milk, flavouring them, if they were fortunate, with an onion or a bit of lard, with boiled seaweed or a scrap of salted fish." This diet was not restricted to the Irish. It became standard throughout the impoverished population of Europe and is graphically portrayed in the marvelous painting by Van Gogh entitled "Aardappeleters" (the potato eaters). The potato seemed clearly to be the cause of the fantastic rise in the Irish population as shown in Figure 4. The

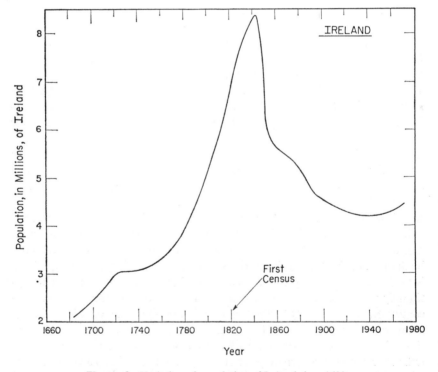

Figure 4 Variation of population of Ireland since 1680.

mean marriage age dropped from about 26 to 19 or 20. The sudden population drop was due to the disastrous potato famine of 1845 and the emigration which followed it. Since the emigrants were predominantly younger people, the birth rate dropped and the population continued to diminish until about 1940.

The potato became the principal food in the Scottish Highlands by 1740 with a corresponding rise in population. It was suspect in the Scottish Lowlands because it was not mentioned in the Bible and there the population growth was not so rapid.

Frederick the Great was a potato enthusiast, but he could not sell it to the German peasants until after the crop failures of 1770 and 1772. The peasants ". . . were impressed by the fact that the potato thrived in wet seasons, when the wheat crop suffered, and that the potato did well in sandy soil. They also realized that it would make an excellent salad. . . ."[1] Austria followed Germany and even in France the potato production increased from 21×10^6 hectoliters in 1815 to 117×10^6 in 1840, a period when the French population was still increasing. The great population growth in Russia during the nineteenth century paralled the widespread cultivation of the potato.

In 1844 the eminent German agronomist, Baron August von Haxthausen, noted that the introduction of the potato 'has undoubtedly produced immense effects upon Europe, in the moulding and culture of which it has probably operated more powerfully than any other material object.' A few years later the equally authoritative German economist, Wilhelm George Roscher, declared without qualification that the adoption of the potato had resulted in a rapid growth of population.[1]

REFERENCES

1. W. L. Langer, *Amer. Hist. Rev.* **LXIX**, 1 (1963).
2. M. Dorothy George, *London Life in The Eighteenth Century* (reprint edition Capricorn Books, New York 1965), p. 334.
3. Redcliffe N. Salamon, *The History and Social Influence of the Potato* (Cambridge, 1949).
4. E. E. Heckscher, *Econ. Hist. Rev.*, 2nd Ser. II, 266 (1950).
5. K. H. Connell, *The Population of Ireland* 1750–1845 (Oxford Press, 1950).

2   Malthus vs. Saturation and The Logistic Curve

1, 2, 3, 4, 5, 6, 7, 8, . . .   Arithmetic progression.

1, 2, 4, 8, 16, 32, 64, 128, . . .   Geometric progression.

In 1798, when the effects of Europe's population explosion were already quite apparent, Thomas Robert Malthus first published (anonymously) *An Essay on the Principle of Population As It Affects the Future Improvement of Society.*

Malthus noted that an unrestrained population could double itself every twenty-five years or less. Indeed this is just what had been occurring in the United States during the one hundred and fifty years prior to the *Essay*, and Malthus predicted the following ultimate result of this geometrical increase.

If the United States of America continue increasing, which they certainly will do, though not with the same rapidity as formerly, the Indians will be driven further and further back into the country, till the whole race is ultimately exterminated and the territory is incapable of further extension.[1]

As Malthus could not foresee food production increasing by more than a fixed amount every year (an arithmetic increase), he thus envisioned a situation in which the world's population would soon outstrip its means of support.

As he thought it highly unlikely that men would give up their habit of early attachment to one woman and he did not foresee contraceptives, he was led to the pessimistic conclusion that population must necessarily be limited by the "positive checks" of vice and misery. Under the former category, he primarily considered the promiscuous attachment of many men to one woman who, with frequent abortions and contacts with venereal disease, would soon become sterile. In the latter category, he included such things as extreme poverty, bad nursing of children, great towns, the whole train of common diseases and epidemics, wars, plague, and famine.

Under conditions of unlimited resources then, Malthus proposed that the rate of increase of the population was proportional to the size of that population—a geometrical increase. This can be expressed mathematically as

$$dn/dt = kn \tag{1}$$

where n is the number of people and k is some proportionality constant. The solution to this equation is obtained straightforwardly by integration. We find

$$n(t) = n(0)e^{kt} \tag{2}$$

Verhulst,[2] inspired by his teacher Quetelet, proposed a modification of Malthus' mechanism which would take into account the limited (usually food) resources in a given area. He postulated that the rate of population growth was proportional to the product of the existing population and the difference between the total available resources and the resources used by the present population. Under these conditions the population would at first grow exponentially (as Malthus proposed), and then decrease its rate as the food limitations become important. As the total population approaches the fixed maximum imposed by the limited resources, we say the population reaches "saturation." We then let

θ = fixed maximum population

A = amount of resources needed per person to survive

$A\theta$ = total existing resources

Then

$[A\theta - An(t)]$ = total amount of resources left for the "new" people

The Verhulst differential equation for population growth then becomes

$$dn/dt = An(t)[\theta - n(t)] \tag{3}$$

Certainly when the population $n(t)$ is very small compared to θ, the factor $[\theta - n(t)]$ is almost equal to θ and equation (3) reduces to the Malthus equation

$$dn/dt = (A\theta)n(t) \tag{3a}$$

However, as $n(t)$ approaches the saturation population θ, $[\theta - n(t)]$ approaches zero and the rate of population increase decreases rapidly.

Let us now divide both sides of equation (3) by θ

$$\frac{n}{\theta}\left(1 - \frac{n}{\theta}\right)$$

and, after letting $k \equiv A\theta$, we find

$$df/dt = kf(1-f) \quad \text{with } f = n(t)/\theta \tag{4}$$

which puts the Verhulst formulation in a more convenient form. Clearly

$$(df/f) + df/(1-f) = k\,dt$$

which follows from the identity $1/f(1-f) = 1/f + 1/(1-f)$.

Integrating through the range $(0, t)$ we obtain

$$\log f(t)/f(0) - \log [1 - f(t)]/[1 - f(0)] = t$$

or

$$\frac{f(t)}{f(0)} \frac{[1 - f(0)]}{[1 - f(t)]} = e^{kt}$$

Solving for $f(t)$ we find

$$f(t) = \frac{f(0)e^{kt}}{1 - f(0)(1 - e^{kt})}$$

$$f(t) = f(0)/\{f(0) + [1 - f(0)]e^{-kt}\} \tag{5}$$

B

This is the equation of the so-called logistics curve which has a characteristic S-like shape as shown in Figure 5. In order to assure that this solution makes sense, the limiting values of $f(t)$ for $t = 0$ and $t = \infty$ should be investigated. In the first case, $f(0) = f(0)$ (so we are at least self consistent) and, in the second case $f(\infty) = 1$ (so we have reached saturation, just as expected). It should be noted that three parameters other than the independent variable t must be specified in order that the above equation be well defined. To see this, note that $f(0) = n_0/\theta$ and $k = A\theta$. Thus specification of n_0 (the initial population) to give us a starting point, A (the amount of resources needed per person to survive), tells us something about how rapidly the population will increase, and θ (the saturation population) gives us the limit of population growth. Equation (5) is often called the Pearl-Reed equation, having been rediscovered by these two authors.

In practice we would generally have at our disposal a time sequence of population data (for example, the total U.S. population in 1970, 1800, 1810, etc.), and would desire to find that logistic curve which fits these points. The earliest census figure would give n_0, e.g., $n_0 = n(1790)$, and any two later figures would suffice to specify A and θ. To see this, rewrite equation (5) as

$$n(t) = \theta n_0/\{n_0 + (\theta - n_0) \exp(-A\theta t)\}$$

Since we are given (for example) $n(1800)$ and $n(1810)$, we can write

$$n(1800) = \frac{\theta n(1790)}{n(1790) + [\theta - n(1790)]e^{-A\theta(1800 - 1790)}} \qquad (6)$$

$$n(1810) = \frac{\theta n(1790)}{n(1790) + [\theta - n(1790)]e^{-A\theta(1810 - 1790)}} \qquad (7)$$

We thus have two equations in the two unknown A and θ which we can solve for in terms of the known figures $n(1790)$, $n(1800)$, and $n(1810)$. This is straightforward but a little lengthy.

As any three census figures will determine a logistics curve (see, for example, Figure 5), we would hope that our other data falls on or very near this same curve. If it does, we begin to have some faith in the model of population growth embodied in equation (3). If it does not, or if sizeable fluctuations from the basic curve are noticed, we must re-examine our ideas or at least elaborate on them.

Notice that the Pearl-Reed, or logistic curve fits the U.S. population data remarkably well for the period 1790–1930. Comments on the post-1930 period will be made later. A similar analysis of European data would start with points around 1750 when, as discussed earlier, the Malthus-Verhulst mechanism began. Adjustments would have to be made in equation (5) so that any resulting formula would reflect the fact that the population varied little over the preceding period of several hundred years. Raymond Pearl,[3] in his book *Studies in Human Biology*, found that the population variation of a number of European countries could be expressed almost perfectly by the formula

$$n(t) = c_0 + c_1/[1 + c_2 e^{-\alpha t}] \qquad (8)$$

over the range ~ 1800–1910 for which valid census data existed. The constant c_0 for a given country represents its stable population before Europe's first population explosion.

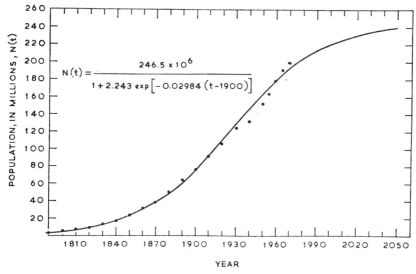

Figure 5 Population of U.S. Logistic curve fitted so that observed points at 1840, 1900 and 1960 are exact.[4] Points represent census data.

Of the countries which followed (8), Austria, Belgium, Denmark, England and Wales, Hungary, Norway, Serbia, Scotland, Sweden and France, France had the special characteristic that the inflection point on its logistic curve appeared at 1789 (at the eve of the French Revolution), while that of most of the others listed, as well as that of U.S., came during the interval 1910–1930 (also a period of crisis).

We have compared Pearl's predictions in millions (made in 1924) for 1960 with 1960 census data for those of the countries listed above which preserved their identity of 1924.

Country	Pearl	Census 1960
Sweden	6.9	7.5
Belgium	11.0	9.1
Denmark	4.4	4.6
England and Wales (1961)	52.1	46.1
France	41.4	46.5
Norway	3.2	3.6
Scotland	6.2	5.2

Pearl's prediction for the sum of these populations 125.2×10^6 exceeds the census report figure of 122.6×10^6 by only 2.6×10^6.

There is no set of basic principles which imply the Verhulst equation (3), which we write in an alternative form

$$dn/dt = kn[1-(n/\theta)] \qquad (9a)$$

where θ is the saturation level. Two other possibilities are

$$dn/dt = -kn \log (n/\theta) \qquad (9b)$$

$$dn/dt = kn[1-(n/\theta)^\nu]/\nu \qquad (9c)$$

Form (9b) is known as the Gompertz equation.[16] It was first proposed (with $k < 0$) in connection with mortality analyses of elderly people, an application which employs a different interpretation of n. But it was also applied to population growth statistics by several other authors. Equation (9c) is a generalization of the Verhulst and Gompertz equations which correspond respectively to the cases $\nu = 1$ and 0.

All of the models proposed are of the form

$$d \log (n/\theta)/dt = kG(n/\theta) \qquad (10)$$

where

$$G(1) = 0 \qquad (11)$$

and, if $\nu > 0$

$$G(0) = 1/\nu \qquad (12)$$

If we define V by

$$V = \log (n/\theta), \qquad (13)$$

then
$$dV/dt = kG(e^V)$$
so that if
$$V_0 = \log [n(0)/\theta],$$
$$kt = \int_{V_0}^{V} dV/G(e^V)$$

In the Gompertz case
$$kt = -\log V + \log V_0$$

from which one finds that if
$$f(t) = n(t)/\theta$$
$$f(t) = \exp \{e^{-kt}[\log f(0)]\} = [f(0)]^{\exp(-kt)} \tag{14}$$

which approaches saturation θ as $t \to \infty$. The same is true for the generalized Verhulst equation for which

$$kt = v \int_{V_0}^{V} \frac{dV}{1-\exp(Vv)} = -\int_{V_0}^{V} \frac{v \exp(-vV)dV}{[1-\exp(-vV)]}$$

$$= -\log \left\{ \frac{\exp(-vV)-1}{\exp(-vV_0)-1} \right\}$$

or
$$f(t) = f(0)\{[f(0)]^v + e^{-kt}[1-[f(0)]^v]\}^{-1/v} \tag{15}$$

which reduces to (5) when $v = 1$. We have plotted $f(t)$ as a function of kt for several values of $f(0)$ and v in Figure 6.

A given one of these saturation curves may fit population data better than others, but such fits are empirical even though useful. An interesting older review of this subject is given in reference (13) and a modern guide to the methods of population prediction is given in reference (14). It is interesting and informative to investigate some of the more basic mechanisms in the population growth problem. We examine some of these in the remainder of this section and others in the next one.

Three fundamental elements in the generation of population curves are annual birth rates, annual death rates, and immigration rates. One clearly has the conservation equation (increase in population in time Δt) = (births in time Δt)+(immigrants in time Δt)−(deaths in time Δt). Births and deaths are generally discussed in terms of birth rate (or death rate) per thousand population.

The record of the variation of these two quantities for the past 55 years in the U.S. is given in Figure 7. The low birth rate in the period 1925–1945 is responsible for the dropping of the population curve below the logistic curve at that time while the abnormally high birth rate in 1948–60 caused the population to rise above the logistic. The U.S. record low birth rate of 17.4 per 1000 was attained in 1968. If the birth rate curve is extrapolated, one finds that it will cross the death rate by 1985 so that the U.S. population would level off at about 220×10^6 (see Figure 5). This is quite different from the enormous growth predictions which are made on the basis of extrapolating the line connecting the 1950 and 1960 census points. Now which of these extrapolations is correct? Probably neither, but we would be inclined to give the birth rate extrapolation more weight because of the following observations.

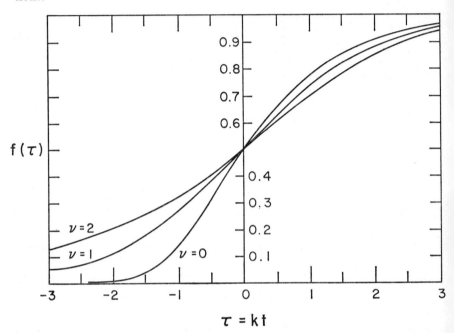

Figure 6   A family of growth curves which saturate. The case $\nu = 0$ is the Gompertz growth curve, and the case $\nu = 1$ is the Verhultz growth curve.

There has been a general trend toward reduced birth rates in western Europe and the United States for a long time. The French data which is exhibited in Figure 8 is an example of this. The largest fluctuations from the steady downward trend appear during wars when the decrease is more rapid and after wars when there is an increase. The 1811–13 dip, the 1870–71 dip, the 1914–1920 dip and the 1939–43 dip are associated respectively with the drive of Napoleon to occupy Europe, the Franco-Prussian War, World War I, and World War II. The peaks at 1814, 1872, 1920, and 1946 correspond to recovery periods. The 1946–1955 baby boom decade was more pronounced than usual (see U.S. curve, as well) because there was a period of great optimism after the long period of economic depression and war (1929–1945). The downward trend seems again to be the current mode. A small new bulge may develop since the babies of the post-World II War boom are now becoming parents. We feel that the pill, legal abortion, and the present inflation will prevent the bulge from becoming very large.

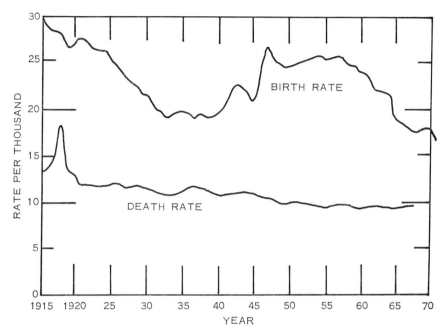

Figure 7 Variation in birth and death rates per thousand per year in the U.S. during the period 1915–1970.

Russia has had a remarkable birth rate history. Its birth rate was 52 per 1000 in 1851 which is one of the highest ever recorded. On the other hand, the 1970 figure is one of the lowest of any major country.

The average number of children born per family in England in marriages which took place in 1925–29 was 2.19. From the British birth rate of 16.1 of that period and the observations that 8% of the children born at that time did not live to a marriageable age and that another 5–10% would never marry, it was deduced that the population of England, Scotland and Wales

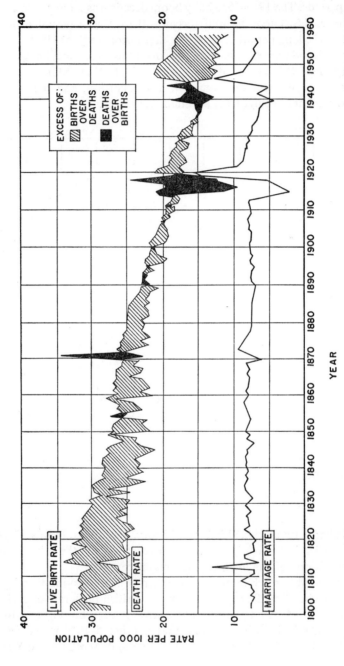

Figure 8   France: Crude rates of birth, death, and marriage from 1801–1958. (*Annuaire Statistique*, 1951, pp. 35–37; *Population*, 1953, p. 754, and 1959, p. 106.) Overall graph from *Marriage and the Family in France since the Revolution*, W. D. Camp (Bookman Associates, N.Y., 1961).

would diminish as follows (a situation which was prevented by the baby boom of the period 1945–60):

1931	44,800,000
1941	44,840,000
1951	42,670,000
1961	39,670,000

English books written in 1935–50 on economic development and population problems were deeply concerned with the economic and political stability of a country with a decreasing population (cf. Refs. 10, 11, and 15). For example, in a welfare state a decreasing number of young adults would have to provide for an increasing number of elderly persons and perhaps pay the debts incurred by a larger population. It is interesting that while our birth rate is diminishing fairly rapidly, we are worrying about population explosions while when the British were in the same mode, they were concerned about a possible population drop.

TABLE III

Some selected birth rates circa 1950 and circa 1969

Country	∼1950	∼1969	Country	∼1950	∼1969
UK	16.1	16.6	Argentina	24.9	20.8
Sweden	16.4	13.4	Japan	28.4	18.6
Hungary	19.1	15.0	USSR	23('60)	14.2('68)
Italy	19.6	17.3	Chile	32.4	29.2
Netherlands	22.7	18.6	Colombia	35.3	31.0
Australia	22.3	20.0	India	39.0	37.0
US	23.4	17.7	Mexico	45.7	41.0

A collection of birth rates in selected countries around 1950 is compared with more recent ones in Table III. Notice that there is a general trend to lower birth rates. As a group, the Latin-American countries have showed the least tendency to change. Death rates in developed countries change very slowly. However, new hygienic measures yield remarkable results in developing areas. One of the most dramatic events occurred in Ceylon in 1946–47 when the death rate dropped 34% as a result of malaria control achieved by the spraying of fields with DDT[13].

Raymond Pearl's book contains numerous population graphs which resemble the U.S. curve of Figure 5. Whether on purpose or through an

B*

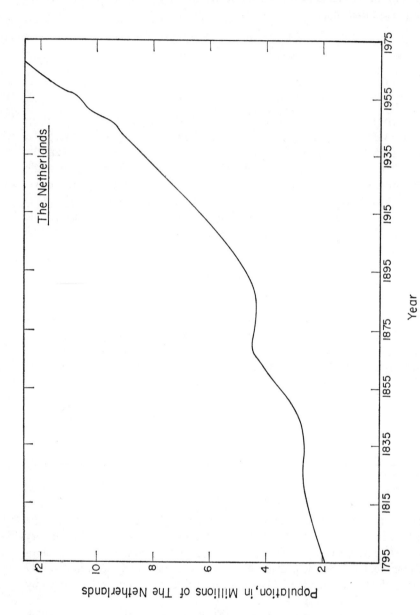

Figure 9   The variation of population of the Netherlands since 1795.

oversight, Pearl seemed to neglect two of the most interesting cases, Ireland and the Netherlands. Clearly by no stretch of the imagination could a logistic curve be fitted to the data shown in Figures 4 and 9 for these countries.

Reliable census figures for Ireland date back to about 1820. Since there is some disagreement between various authorities for estimates prior to 1800, the "corner" near 1730 may be a slight exaggeration. There is no exaggeration in the character of the catastrophic drop at 1846, which of course corresponds to the potato famine during which 700,000 died and a million emigrated mainly to the U.S. Since most of the emigrants that year, and in the twenty or thirty years which followed were young adults, the birth rate per thousand population declined to a point such that it was overcome by the death rate (plus the declining emigration rate). This effect continued unabated until the local as well as the world economy improved in the 1940's when the Irish birth rate rose somewhat as did that in the rest of Europe. By now the minimum has been passed and again the population of Ireland is rising.

The Dutch curves reflect a number of interesting national events. Until 1947, the Netherlands controlled large colonies abroad (especially the Dutch East Indies) and had considerable economic interest in areas they did not control (especially in South Africa). In the 1860's when the industrial revolution demanded raw materials, a flood of young Dutchmen sought their fortunes in these economically favorable areas. It was also a period in which the rural population had reached such a level that little farm land was available for younger sons. Traditionally The Netherlands increases its area by recovering land from the sea through the construction of dikes. The improvement of mechanical techniques in the early 1900's produced polders more rapidly, making more farm land available. These events are well reflected in Figure 9. The increased slope starting at 1945 reflects the post World War II baby wave.

The Netherlands was one of the first countries to accept a form of the Protestant faith and had only a small minority of Catholics by 1650. For 400 years the Catholic favoring of large families gradually changed the ratio until, by 1950, it was noticed that among school children a state of almost numerical equality was achieved. Since the Netherlands is such a small country all faiths have now become concerned with the rapid population growth so that the Dutch Catholic Clergy have been the leaders of the opposition to Papal pronouncements on birth control.

In order to give some idea of trends in the Orient, the Chinese population statistics since 1931 are given in Table IV. Some remarks about India will be made in Section 9. The approval of low cost abortions in the early 1950's changed population trends radically in Japan. The abortion was the most commonly practiced operation in Japanese hospitals. The birth rate has declined steadily since the new laws went into effect; now there is some concern about whether something should be done to decelerate the decline.

The logistic curve characterizes the early stages of other time-dependent phenomenon besides population growth. For example, the growth of industries, railroad networks, numbers entering new professions, sales of new products, the development of a technology, etc., follow the logistic curve at their early states. In some of these, records exist which are long enough so that significant deviations have been observed.

TABLE IV

Population of China 1931–58

Year	Population $\times 10^{-3}$	Year	Population $\times 10^{-3}$
1931	485,000	1945	529,573
1932	486,940	1946	534,339
1933	488,887	1947	539,148
1934	491,820	1948	543,730
1935	495,854	1949	548,080
1936	500,316	1950	553,627
1937	504,818	1951	561,309
1938	507,330	1952	571,132
1939	509,886	1953	582,555
1940	512,925	1954	594,255
1941	515,002	1955	606,734
1942	518,348	1956	619,475
1943	521,718	1957	631,864
1944	525,370	1958	643,237

Sometimes oscillatory fluctuations about a logistic curve begin to develop. There are very striking examples of this behavior in the production curves of copper or zinc during the last century as exhibited in Figure 10. These oscillations appear at about the time the logistic curve is near or a little beyond the inflection point, i.e., when the process in question begins to deviate significantly from an exponential growth. Glancing at the curve for copper production we might say that the increase around 1915 was due to the demands of World War I so that it was no surprise; the sharp drops in 1921 and the 1930–33 period are due to depressions, etc. However, it is not so clear that it was not the competition in production and, especially marketing (e.g., in Afro-Asian colonies), that was one of the causes of World War I as all

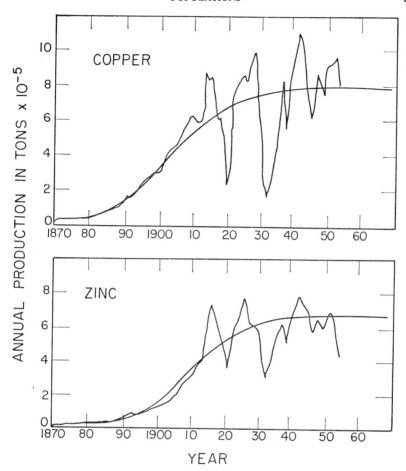

Figure 10 Logistic growth of raw material production, showing oscillation on attaining ceiling conditions (Data from S. G. Lasky, *Eng. Mining J.*, 156 (Sept., 1955).)

nations attempted to maintain exponential increases in their economic activities in the face of limited opportunities. In short it is not clear which is the cause and which the effect.

If a growing rat colony is given only a fixed daily food supply, it also displays population oscillations about a logistic curve. This happens because the larger, more aggressive, rats begin hoarding food (and attracting females) when food begins to get scarce. The more timid rats huddle together, do not reproduce, and eventually die. The population thus decreases until only the aggressive rats are left. They then propagate rapidly until an over-populated condition exists which will, in turn, be followed by another round of hoarding by superaggressive rats or by a decline to extinction.

If technology changes so that the maximum attainable population assumes a new level, a saturating logistic curve might "escalate" to new saturation levels. Figures 11 and 12 show extremely good examples of technological development. The plot of the rate of discovery of the elements was taken from Derek de Sola Price's book,[6] *Big Science, Little Science*. The basic data in Figure 12 was constructed from case histories in reference 7.

In view of various observed deviations from the predictions of the Verhulst and other growth toward saturation equations, we must reinterpret them and suggest some changes in them. One way of improving population predictive powers is to introduce age distributions, fertility rates as a function of age, and death rates as a function of age. Some discussion of this type of analysis will be given in the next section and an excellent review of it, as well as of the history of population growth analysis, is given in reference 14. An equation such as one of the set (9a)–(9c) might be considered to be analogous to Newton's first law of mechanics which states that in the absence of any forces, a body will continue to move in a straight line with a constant velocity. Then in the second law, a force is characterized by the manner in which it affects a violation of the first law. The postulate would be made that in a closed region in the absence of any "forces" or changes, economic, technical, weather-wise, etc., a population would develop according to one of the saturation equations. The character of applied forces would be established by changes in the population curve.

Some population disturbing forces are clear. For example, if people enter or leave an area, the rate of transfer should be included. Fluctuations in birth rate can also be considered. For simplicity we use the Gompertz law as the basic saturation inducing form and assume that perturbing forces are described by the function $F(t)$ so that

$$n_t = -kn \log (n/\theta) + nF(t). \tag{16}$$

The function $F(t)$ might depend on the population n. The factor n is associated with the perturbing force to set the scale of perturbation. Generally the rate of growth due to the perturbation will be small compared with the unperturbed rate kn. Hence we can assume that $F(t)$ is proportional to some small parameter ε. Then (16) can be written as

$$d \log (n/\theta)/dt = -k \log (n/\theta) + \varepsilon\alpha(t). \tag{17}$$

where we define

$$F(t) \equiv \varepsilon\alpha(t). \tag{18a}$$

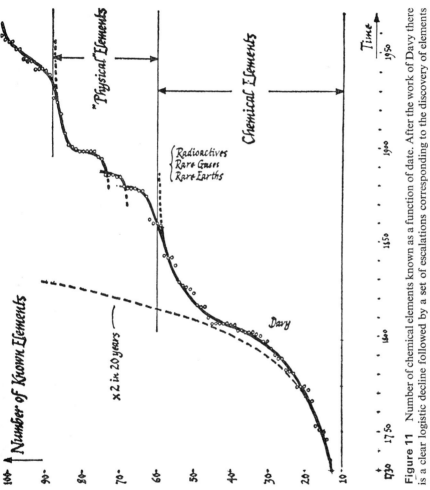

Figure 11 Number of chemical elements known as a function of date. After the work of Davy there is a clear logistic decline followed by a set of escalations corresponding to the discovery of elements by techniques that are predominantly physical. Around 1950 is the latest escalation produced by the manufacture of trans-uranic elements.[6]

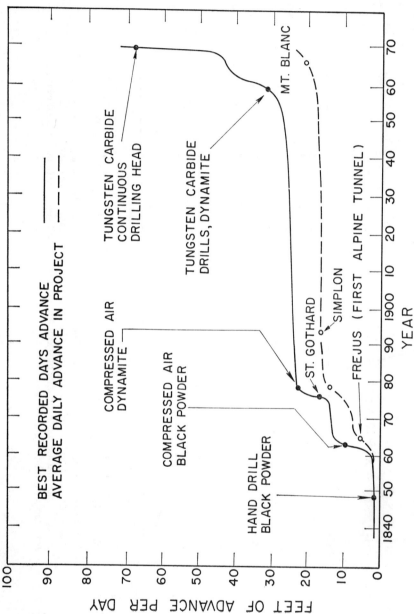

Figure 12 Progress in tunnel drilling in hard rock. All drilling records before 1965 were taken from alpine tunnels so that conditions were essentially the same. While there were great days in the Mt. Blanc tunnel digging with the latest tools, the average rate of advance was not significantly higher than in tunnel construction at the turn of the century, due to various unexpected hold-ups. The 72 ft. per day record of 1967 was made in a water tunnel under St. Louis with the latest continuous drilling machine. We have no data on the average rate. The automatic boring machine is now being used near Baden, Switzerland, for soft sandstone

Now let

$$v = \log(n/\theta) \qquad (18b)$$

Then

$$\varepsilon\alpha(t) = v_t + kv$$

$$= e^{-kt} d(ve^{kt})/dt$$

so that

$$v(t) = v(0)e^{-kt} + \varepsilon \int_0^t \alpha(\tau)e^{-(\tau-t)k} d\tau \qquad (19a)$$

or

$$v(t) = v(0)e^{-kt} + \varepsilon \int_0^t \alpha(t-\tau)e^{-\tau k} d\tau \qquad (19b)$$

The response of the population to a pulse with

$$\alpha(\tau) = \delta(\tau - t_0) \qquad (20)$$

is

$$v(t) = v(0)e^{-kt} + \varepsilon e^{-(t-t_0)k}$$

$$= \{v(0) + \varepsilon e^{kt_0}\}e^{-kt} \qquad (21)$$

This is equivalent to changing $v(0)$ to $[v(0) + \varepsilon \exp kt_0]$ or the initial population $n(0)$ to $n^*(0)$ with

$$n^*(0) = n(0) \exp\{\varepsilon \exp[-kt_0]\} \qquad (22)$$

Hence a pulse of population has a stronger effect at an early time long before saturation than at a late time close to saturation. The reader might experiment with various other driving forces to understand the nature of those which have led to various observed population fluctuations.

One of the most interesting driving forces which might be investigated is that in which $F(t)$ is a random variable. This is studied in Section 5 of Chapter III. Instead of trying to predict a population at a given time, one seeks a distribution function, i.e., the probability that the population will achieve a preassigned level in a specified time.

Populations not only grow with time, but they also spread in a special way. An interesting and fairly well documented example of this process is the diffusion of muskrats through Europe as plotted in Figure 13. Six muskrats escaped from a cage in Prague in 1907. The curves labeled by years show the most distant points from Prague at which muskrats were observed during those years. Notice that regions which have lines close to each other represent mountainous regions through which the muskrats diffuse very slowly.[16]

R. A. Fisher introduced a generalization of the Verhulst equation which allows for population diffusion

$$\frac{\partial n(r, t)}{\partial t} = An(r, t)[N - n(r, t)] + D\nabla^2 n(r, t) \qquad (23)$$

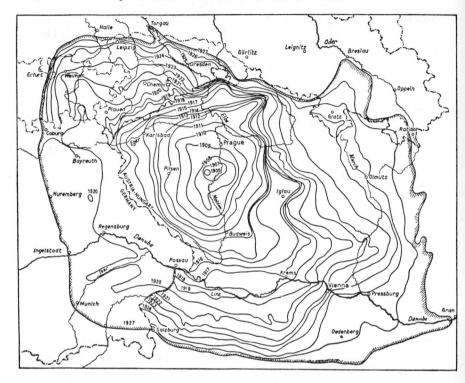

Figure 13   Spread of the muskrat, *Ondatra zibethica*, up to 1927, from five individuals introduced into Bohemia in 1905. Data was originally taken by J. Ulbrich, 1930, and the figure was obtained from reference 16.

where $\nabla^2 n$ is the two-dimensional Laplacian

$$\nabla^2 n = \partial^2 n/\partial x^2 + \partial^2 n/\partial y^2$$

with $n(r, t)$ corresponding to the population per unit area at $r = (x, r)$ at time t. The dynamics of the growth of a new colony on an uninhabited area might be represented by (23). The equation was proposed by Fisher to describe the manner in which a virile mutant starting at one point in a population would generate his progeny through the population.

The flow of population from one country to another through emigration might be described by a set of coupled equations

$$\frac{dn_i}{dt} = k_i n_i \{1 - (n_i/\theta_i)\} + \sum F_{ij} \qquad (24)$$

where F_{ij} represent the rate at which population of the jth country or region flows into the ith. Some exploration would have to be made to determine F_{ij} which would certainly have to depend on $n_j(t)$ and $n_i(t)$, perhaps with time lags. Of course (23) is a special case of (24) where i is chosen to be a continuously varying position. The quantity k_i (or A in (23)) might be taken to be very small in areas where life is hard to sustain or even negative where it is not suitable for population growth.

We have noted earlier that population growth is correlated with the economy. It would be interesting to couple the population growth equations with equations which represent the state of the economy. There is also a feedback in the sense that the economy depends on the population as it effects home construction, automobile sales, agriculture, etc.

REFERENCES

1. Thomas Robert Malthus, *An Essay on The Principle of Population As It Affects the Future Improvement of Society*, 1798.
2. P. F. Verhulst, *Mem. Acad. Roy. Bruxelles*, **28**, 1 (1844).
3. Cf. Raymond Pearl, *Studies in Human Biology* (Baltimore, 1924).
4. Elliott W. Montroll, *Lectures in Theoretical Physics*, University of Colorado, **XA**, 531 (1967).
5. K. H. Connell, *The Population of Ireland 1750–1845* (Oxford, 1950).
6. Derek J. de Sola Price, *Little Science, Big Science* (New York, 1967).
7. Gosta E. Sondstrom, *The History of Tunnelling* (Barrie, London, 1963).
8. *Statistical Abstracts of the U.S., 1968*, U.S. Bureau of Census (Washington, D.C.)
9. W. S. Thompson, *Population Problems* (McGraw, 1953).
10. G. Harrison and F. C. Mitchell, *The Home Market, A Handbook of Statistics* (Allen and Unwin, London, 1935).
11. Eva M. Hubback, *The Population of Britain* (Pelican Book, 1947).
12. R. A. Fisher, *Ann. Eugenics* **7**, 355 (1937).
13. H. T. Davis, *Theory of Econometrics* (Principia Press, Bloomington, 1941).
14. D. V. Glass, *Proc. Roy. Soc.* **B168**, 119 (1967).
15. J. M. Keynes, *Eugen. Rev.* (April 1937).
16. C. S. Elton, *The Ecology of Invasions by Plants and Animals* (Methuen, London, 1958).

3 Age Distributions of Population and Mortality Curves

Social planners, economists, public health officials, insurance executives and even the more curious non-professionals are not satisfied with population statistics which are restricted to the variation of the total population with time. Educators require information on the number of children of various ages, insurance actuaries want to know the probability that a person of a given age will remain alive for a specified number of years. Merchandising policies of department stores change as the maximum in the population age distribution changes. This section is concerned with various ways in which population data can be presented and with inferences that can be made from the data.

The Romans were apparently the first to be concerned with life expectancy data. They frequently bequeathed annuities, the equivalent lump value of which had to be determined by computation. Life expectancy tables for this purpose were proposed by Praetorian Praefect Ulpian and Jurisconsult Aemilius Macer at about the 3rd century, A.D. These tables, which are summarized in Table V were still used in Northern Italy until the late 18th century.[1]

TABLE V

Ulpians life expectancy table (~200 A.D.)

Age	Expectations in years	Age	Expectations in years
0–20	30	44–45	15
20–25	27	45–46	14
25–30	25	46–47	13
30–35	22	47–48	12
35–40	20	48–49	11
40–41	19	49–50	10
41–42	18	50–55	9
42–43	17	55–60	7
43–44	16	60–and up	5

As was mentioned earlier, Edmond Halley published a life expectancy table based on the mortality experiences in Breslau in the period 1687–1691. It is summarized in the table opposite and, when compared with the above data, indicates a small amount of medical or public health improvement over a period of 1400 years.

At frequent intervals since Halley's time, updated tables appear. As the world becomes more and more social security oriented, such tables increase in importance. Traditionally insurance rates were based on such tables. As social security and retirement programs become more universal, they become important to every company and country which must properly budget for its retirement plans. Significant changes which represent responses to medical progress are especially watched. While life insurance companies which pay death benefits to survivors would increase their profits if a common form of cancer would be cured, governments whose planning for retirement benefits is based on a certain life expectancy after retirement would suffer from such a cure. The younger active workers would have to be taxed in order to pay benefits for the extra years of life of those retired.

Several bits of life expectancy data are plotted in Figure 14. The Roman Egypt curve was estimated by Karl Pearson who in 1902 in collaboration with W. C. Macdonell analyzed the ages of death recorded on a number of mummy cases from North Africa. These cases were about 2,000 years old. The most

TABLE VI

Halley's table (1693)

Age	Expectations in years	Age	Expectations in years
0	33.50	45	19.22
5	41.55	50	16.81
10	39.99	55	14.51
15	36.86	60	12.09
20	33.61	65	9.73
25	30.38	70	7.53
30	27.35	75	5.99
35	24.50	80	5.74
40	21.78		

recent data is taken from reference 4. One might question the observation that the life expectancy at 80 was greater in Roman times than it is today. Clearly the number of cases examined was limited in that age range and the data in general was hardly good enough to warrant such a conclusion. However, the crossing of the life expectancy curves associated with two different populations is not uncommon. For example, the U.S. white male 1967 curve is above the U.S. non-white male 1967 curve until the age of 66, at which age the white male curve goes below that for non-whites.

An explanation sometimes given for this process is that, in order for a member of the population with the lower curve at early ages to survive to old age, he must be basically stronger and more vigorous. Therefore, would have a longer expectancy at old age if he survives.

An exhibition of mortality data which is more illuminating from the public health standpoint is that of Figure 15, in terms of human survival curves. The curves of survivors tell us what would happen to a given group of people (cohorts) as a function of time if the mortality conditions that were prevalent when they were born persisted until the last cohort died. The curves are a convenient abstraction from real life statistics which simply give us the number and age distribution of all people dying within a given year. By

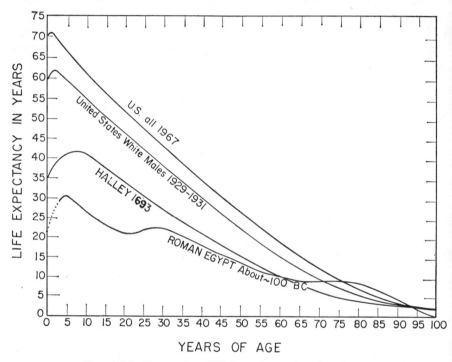

Figure 14   Expectation of life in ancient and modern times.

examining the set of curves in Figure 15, we can see the consequence of improvement in mortality conditions in the U.S. in the period 1900–1940. While there exist countries in which conditions are better, e.g., New Zealand, conditions in many others, e.g., Mexico and India, are much, much worse. While the maximum life span for all groups has stayed approximately the same (about 100 years), the percentage of people living to any given age except the oldest has increased impressively in the more advanced societies; medical science has done wonders for the young and middle-aged, but has

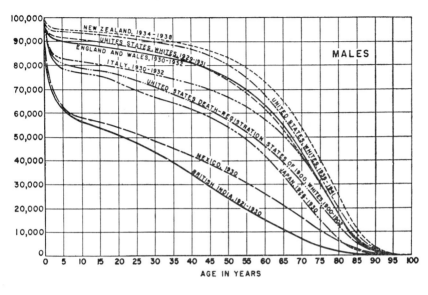

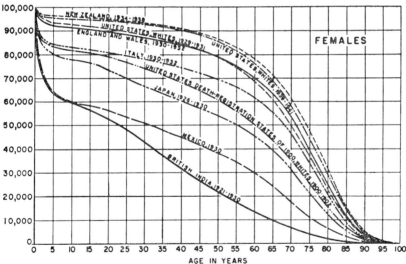

Figure 15   Life tables: proportion of live born surviving to a given age.[12]

been of considerably less help to the elderly. The probability of a baby born today living until his eighty-fifth birthday is not much greater than it was fifty years ago. A comparison of survival curves of various countries can be suggestive in the planning of public health programs in those countries whose records are not as good as others.

Given annual birth rates and curves of survivors for successive groups of cohorts, we can calculate the age structure of the population at any given time provided we know that structure at some particular time in the past. The Swedish demographer Sundbärg was the first to characterize societies by their age structures. He characterized a population as consisting of the "class of children"—0 to 14 years old, "the class of parents"—15 to 49 years old, and, "the class of grandparents"—50 years old and up. Sundbärg called a society progressive, stationary, or regressive, if it had the appropriate one of the following proportions:

Proportion of	Progressive	Stationary	Regressive
Children	40%	27%	20%
Parents	50%	50%	50%
Grandparents	10%	23%	30%

Since the proportion of parents in all the societies he studied was within ±1.5% of being exactly half of the entire population, Sundbärg put forth his "law of age structure balance" which postulated the constancy of the percentage of adults in any population. Subsequent demographers have found this law to be violated occasionally, but variations from it seldom exceed ±4% (the proportion of parents almost always being between 46% and 54%).

Let us now consider how the age structure of the United States population has changed over the last eighty years. In 1870 the age structure of the U.S. looked almost exactly like the progressive structure shown in Figure 16. By 1940 (see Figure 17), there were proportionately fewer people in the lowest age brackets and more in the parent age group. This was due, in large measure, to the drop in the birth rates which started in the late twenties and lasted until the onset of World War II. By 1935 birth rates almost equaled death rates and the population structure took on the bell-shape characteristic of stationary populations. By 1950 the base of the structure again broadened as the effects of the war-time "baby boom" manifested themselves. By 1960 the progressive structure had almost returned except for the "constriction"

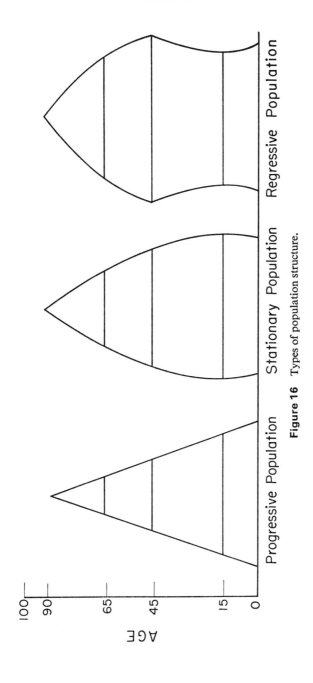

Figure 16 Types of population structure.

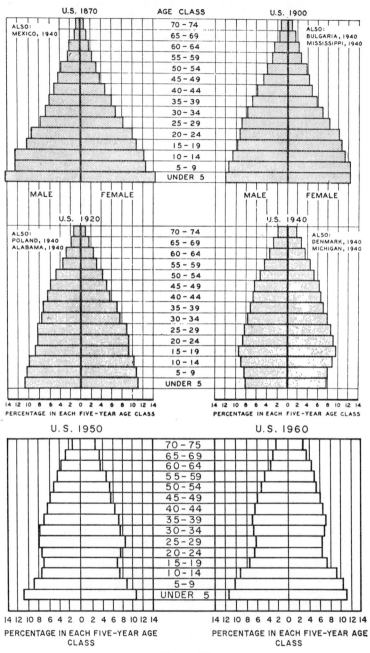

Figure 17

in the twenty-to-thirty year old age range. The "constriction", due to the low birth rates during the 1930's, will continue to propagate upward through the age structure as years roll on.

French population structure curves are plotted in Figure 18. The catastrophic character of World War I is evident in the pyramid of 1956. The war casualties produced the scarcity of males relative to females in the birth years 1870–1900. The abnormally low birth rates in the World War I and World War II periods are also clearly indicated.

An alternative form for mortality data is in terms of age dependence rates, i.e. age-specific death rates as a function of age. The age-specific death rate is the percentage of a certain population living under the health conditions characteristic of a given period who reach a specified age and then die within the next year; it is the probability $p(x)$ that having reached a specified age x a person will die during the next year. A typical example of a curve of mortality rates is given in Figure 19. We can give age-specific death rates due to all causes or due to particular diseases such as heart disease. Using this kind of curve, we can, for example, show that our ability to treat diseases such as cancer is improving while the number of people dying of cancer per 1000 population is increasing. The key lies in the fact that while age-specific death rates due to cancer are going down, proportionately many more people are living long enough to reach ages at which cancer takes a high toll.

If one examines the age-specific death rates for the higher ages, he notes that they seem to be exponentially increasing (see Figure 20a). Indeed, if we plot the log of the age-specific death rate as a function of age, the graph becomes a straight line at the higher ages (see Figure 20b). It is just in this region that we say the aging process has set in; indeed, we might define aging as that deteriorative process which leads to a continually higher probability that an individual will die. Advancing one step further, we can say that the

---

Figure 17 Population pyramids for the United States, 1870, 1900, 1920, 1940, 1950 and 1960.

Population pyramids for the United States in periods from 1870–1960 illustrate successive phases in the development of the country. Similar phases can be observed currently in other countries.

The population pyramid for Mexico and other comparatively underdeveloped agricultural countries is like that of the United States in 1870. That for southeastern Europe (exemplified by Bulgaria) is about the same as that of the United States at the turn of the century. In 1920 the population of the United States had the same age composition as Poland in 1940. The 1940 population pyramid of the United States was like that of Denmark.[12]

Similar comparisons can be made between the population pyramids for various states in 1940 and for the United States as a whole in different years.

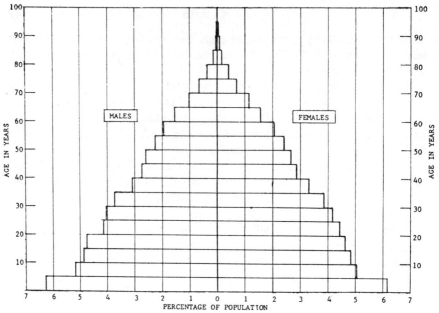

Figure 18a   French age pyramid estimated for 1786.[14]

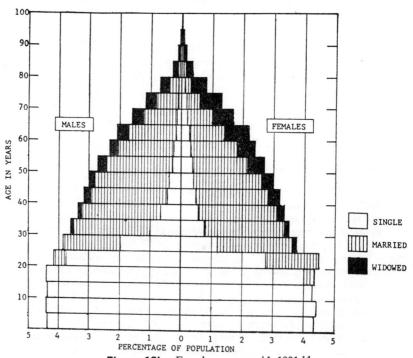

SINGLE

MARRIED

WIDOWED

Figure 18b   French age pyramid, 1891.[14]

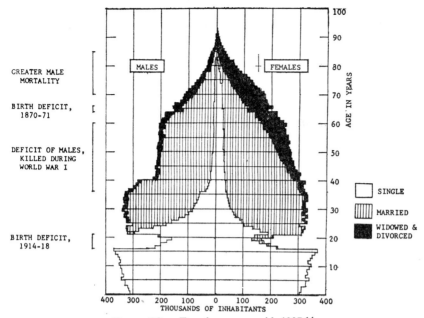

Figure 18c French age pyramid, 1937.[14]

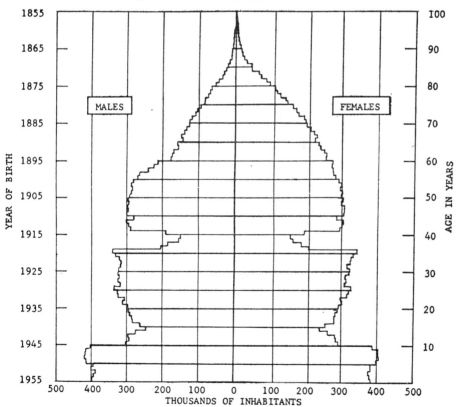

Figure 18d French age pyramid, 1956.[14]

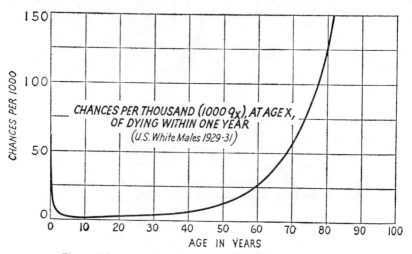

Figure 19 Typical example of the ''curve of mortality rates''.

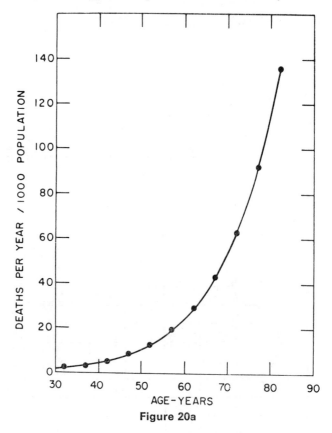

Figure 20a

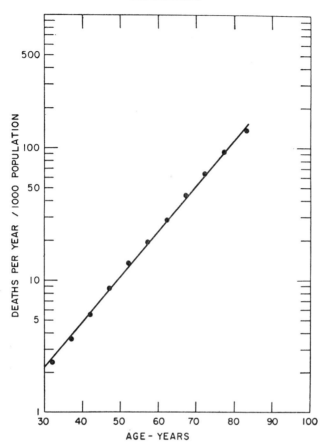

Figure 20b Age-specific death rate from all causes as a function of age for U.S. males, 1949 (data from Jones).[10] Figure 20b is plotted on a logarithmic scale.

age-specific death rate is a very good measure of physiologic age. Thus, for example, a man who reached seventy-one under the health conditions prevalent in 1950 was the same physiologic age as a man who reached sixty-six under the conditions prevalent in 1900. As the average man lived to be seventy-one in 1950 while he only lived to be fifty-five in 1900, sixteen years have been added to the average life span in the last half century. However, five of these years should really not count toward his physiologic age on the 1900 scale of aging. In general, each succeeding generation is physiologically more youthful than its predecessor at any age of comparison (see Figure 21).

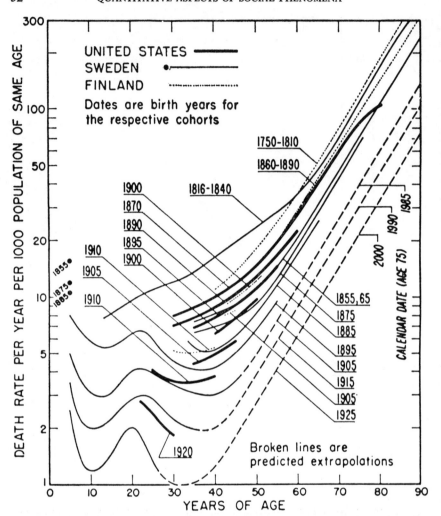

Figure 21 The age-specific death rates expressed as population cohorts having the approximate-same birth date. Note the common tendency for the progression of the death rates to have a slope of 8.5 years doubling time on this semi-logarithmic plot. The age-specific death rates are shown to be receding to relatively lower age-specific rates; this change has accompanied a lowering of the death rates in earlier life of these same cohorts. Each cohort continues to die on its own death pattern in spite of the fact that these individuals are living in association with younger cohorts of a more favorable resistance to disease.[10]

Broken lines show the predicted age-specific death rates for current cohorts of young Swedes.

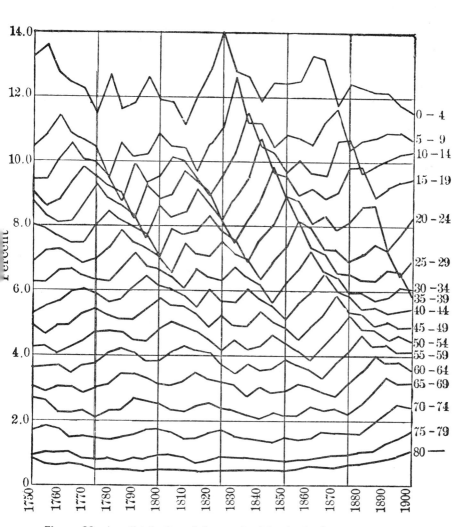

Figure 22 Age distribution of the people of Sweden by five-year groups: 1750–1900.[11]

Figure 21 gives a time sequence of curves of mortality rates for the U.S. and Sweden. From these curves we see that the age-specific death rates have decreased with time for all age groups although the exponential increase in these rates eventually becomes so great at old age that no one who reaches 60 lives very much longer than his ancestors did, if they survived to that age. The "bump" in this sequence of curves centered at age 20 is getting proportionally larger, probably due to the fact that fatal accidents have not been reduced to the same degree as deaths due to other major causes in this age range. Automobile accidents make the main contribution to the peak at 20 years today, a hundred years ago it was probably accidents at sea, fifty five years ago World War I took its toll. Traditionally in every period youth finds ways of probing the system in manners which tempt fate. "A calculation was made by M. de Lomenie, in the year 1607, that since the accession of Henry IV (of France) in 1589, no less than four thousand French gentlemen had lost their lives in duels."[16] Most of these were under 30.

The exponential increase in death rate sets in at an earlier age with each succeeding curve, but at progressively lower absolute values. This occurs in such a way that successive curves appear shifted to the right, although unchanged in slope. This means that death rates are increasing at the same rate, although the magnitude of said rate is getting lower with each successive curve for all ages. The doubling time, the number of years that must pass before the probability of dying doubles, is about 8.5 years for the exponentially increasing portions of the curves in Figure 21. The latest Swedish data indicates that the doubling time has actually decreased to 7 years. This offsets the fact that the exponential growth of the age-specific death rate begins at lower and lower values and lends further weight to the idea that there is some maximum life span beyond which it is extremely improbable that anyone will survive.

We close this section with a mode of presentation which on one figure gives a population history of a country over an enormous time span. We have plotted, in Figure 22, the age distribution of people of Sweden by five-year groups. The manner in which peaks in the birth rate are propagated as "waves" through the years is emphasized in this type diagram. Note, for example, how the 1825 peak propagates on, even beyond 1900.

REFERENCES

1. L. I. Dublin and A. J. Lotka, *The Length of Life* (Roland Press, 1936).
2. J. S. Elston "Sources and characteristics of the principal mortality tables," *Trans. Actuarial Soc. Amer.* **27**, 471 (1926).
3. E. W. Kopf, *Proc. Casualty Actuarial Soc.* **13** (part II), 232 (1927).

4. *Statistical Abstracts of the United States, 1968*, U.S. Bureau of Census (Washington. D.C.).
5. A. Comfort, *Scientific American* **205** (No. 2), 114 (1961).
6. W. S. Thompson, *Population Problems* (McGraw-Hill, 1953).
7. P. M. Hauser, *Scientific American* **205** (No. 1), 44 (1961).
8. G. Sundbärg, *Int. Congress of Hygiene and Demography, Berlin, 1907*.
9. H. J. Curtis, *The Biology of Aging*, Brookhaven Lecture Series No. 34 (1964).
10. H. B. Jones, *Advan. Bio. and Med. Phys.* **4**, 285 (1956).
11. G. C. Whipple, *Vital Statistics* (Chapman Hall, 1923).
12. W. S. Woytinsky and E. S. Woytinsky, *World Population and Production* (20th Century Fund, New York, 1953).
13. K. Davis, *Amer. Econ. Rev.* **46**, 307 (1956).
14. W. D. Camp, *Marriage and the Family in France Since the Revolution* (Bookman Ass., New York 1961).
15. D. W. Thomas, *Social and Economic Aspects of Swedish Population Movements 1750–1933* (MacMillan, 1941).
16. C. Mackay, *Extraordinary Popular Delusions and The Madness of Crowds* (London, 1841; Reprinted edition, Noonday Press, New York, 1932).

4 Relationship Between Birth Rates, Death Rates, and Age Distributions and Conditions for Zero Population Growth

The previous two sections contained statistics of age distributions, population pyramids, birth rates, death rates, etc. In this section we show how some of these quantities are connected. We also discuss conditions for stationary population pyramids, as well as requirements if one is to plan a zero population growth society.

Let us consider a sequence of time intervals..., $n-2$, $n-1$, n, $n+1$, $n+2$, ... each of duration Δ years. If anyone was born in the nth interval, we state that they are of age 0 in that interval; age 1 in the next interval, $n+1$; age 2 in the interval $n+2$, etc. Hence anyone whose age is j in the kth interval was born in interval $(k-j)$. We define $P_j(n)$ to be the number of persons of age j at the beginning of the nth interval so that the total population at the beginning of the nth interval is

$$P(n) = \sum P_j(n) \tag{1}$$

If we postulate our population to be geographically isolated so that emigration and immigration are both impossible, then any time variation in the population is a consequence of births or deaths or both. We must now introduce age specific death and birth rates.

We define $f_j(n)$ to be the fraction of those of age j during the nth time interval who survive alive to the $(n+1)^{st}$ time interval (into which they arrive with age $j+1$). We also define $b_j(n)$ to be the probability that a woman of age j will give birth to a child during the interval n which survives until the $(n+1)^{st}$ interval.

$$P_1(n+1) = \Sigma \tfrac{1}{2} P_j(n) b_j(n) \tag{2}$$

For simplicity we have postulated half the persons of any age to be females and we neglect multiple births. It is easy to proceed differently with males and females by introducing $P_j^{(i)}(n)$ with $i = 1$ for males and 2 for females, but we avoid that complication here.

The number of individuals of a given age alive in the nth time interval is the same as the survivors from the previous interval $(n-1)$ of age one interval younger. Thus

$$P_j(n) = f_{j-1}(n-1)P_{j-1}(n-1) \quad \text{if} \quad j = 2, 3, \ldots \tag{3a}$$

$$P_1(n) = \tfrac{1}{2} \sum_{j>0} P_j(n-1) b_j(n-1) \tag{3b}$$

These equations also have the matrix form

$$
\begin{bmatrix} P_1(n) \\ P_2(n) \\ P_3(n) \\ P_4(n) \\ \vdots \end{bmatrix}
=
\begin{bmatrix}
b_1(n-1) & \tfrac{1}{2}b_2(n-1) & \tfrac{1}{2}b_3(n-1) & \cdots \\
f_1(n-1) & 0 & 0 & \cdots \\
0 & f_2(n-1) & 0 & \cdots \\
0 & 0 & f_3(n-1) & \cdots \\
& \cdots & &
\end{bmatrix}
\begin{bmatrix} P_1(n-1) \\ P_2(n-1) \\ P_3(n-1) \\ P_4(n-1) \\ \vdots \end{bmatrix}
\tag{4}
$$

The above set of equations and the associated matrix can either be considered as finite or infinite. To make it finite one considers the last age group to be composed as all those individuals whose age is $> N$. Then

$$P_N(n) = f_{N-1}(n-1)P_{N-1}(n-1) + f_N(n-1)P_N(n-1) \tag{5a}$$

If, for example, $N = 4$

$$
\begin{bmatrix} P_1(n) \\ P_2(n) \\ P_3(n) \\ P_4(n) \end{bmatrix}
=
\begin{bmatrix}
\tfrac{1}{2}b_1(n-1) & \tfrac{1}{2}b_2(n-1) & \tfrac{1}{2}b_3(n-1) & \tfrac{1}{2}b_4(n-1) \\
f_1(n-1) & 0 & 0 & 0 \\
0 & f_2(n-1) & 0 & 0 \\
0 & 0 & f_3(n-1) & f_4(n-1)
\end{bmatrix}
\begin{bmatrix} P_1(n-1) \\ P_2(n-1) \\ P_3(n-1) \\ P_4(n-1) \end{bmatrix}
\tag{5b}
$$

The development of the population with time can thus be followed by repetition of the above matrix operation. Suppose that the various b_j's and f_j's are independent of n so that $b_j(n) = b_j(n+1) = b_j(n+2) = \ldots$ and $f_j(n) = f_j(n+1) = f_j(n+2) = \ldots$. Then, equation (5) has the form

$$P(n) = MP(n-1) \tag{6a}$$

or

$$P(n) = M^n P(0) \tag{6b}$$

We can seek the initial population distribution which is stable, so that the fraction of individuals in any age interval is a constant. Let the vector ψ with elements $\psi_1, \psi_2, \ldots$ represent that distribution. Then

$$\lambda\psi = M\psi \tag{7a}$$

Then if $P(0) \equiv \psi$

$$P(n)\psi = \lambda^n\psi \tag{7b}$$

There are three possibilities, $\lambda > 1$, $\lambda = 1$, $\lambda < 1$. In the first case the population grows while the age distribution remains invariant; in the second case the total population remains constant, as does the distribution, while, in the third case, the total population drops.

Let us suppose that the element ψ_1 of ψ is given. Then the others can be expressed in terms of it since

$$\psi_2 = (f_1/\lambda)\psi_1$$
$$\psi_3 = (f_2/\lambda)\psi_2 = (f_1 f_2/\lambda^2)\psi_1$$
$$\psi_4 = (f_3/\lambda)\psi_3 = (f_1 f_2 f_3/\lambda^3)\psi_1$$

.

.

.

$$\psi_j = (f_1 f_2 \ldots f_{j-1}/\lambda^{j-1})\psi_1 \tag{8}$$

If the ψ's are normalized so that ψ_j is the fraction of the population of age j at the beginning of a given time interval

$$\psi_1 + \psi_2 + \ldots = 1 \tag{9a}$$

or

$$\psi_1\{1 + f_1\lambda^{-1} + f_1 f_2\lambda^{-2} + f_1 f_2 f_3\lambda^{-3} + \ldots\} = 1 \tag{9b}$$

so that

$$\psi_1 = \Psi \equiv \{1 + f_1\lambda^{-1} + f_1 f_2\lambda^{-2} + f_1 f_2 f_3\lambda^{-3} + \ldots\}^{-1} \tag{9c}$$

Hence the fraction of population of age j at beginning of a new interval is

$$\psi_j = f_1 f_2 \ldots f_{j-1}\lambda^{-j+1}\Psi \tag{10}$$

The possible values of the characteristic values λ are roots of the characteristic equation which is obtained from

$$2\lambda\psi_1 = b_1\psi_1 + b_2\psi_2 + b_3\psi_3 + \ldots$$

or

$$2\lambda = b_1 + f_1 b_2 \lambda^{-1} + f_1 f_2 b_3 \lambda^{-2} + f_1 f_2 f_3 b_4 \lambda^{-3} + \ldots \tag{11}$$

Since the age of fecundity is limited, all b_j's beyond a certain point vanish so that the right hand side of this equation is a polynomial in λ^{-1}. If our time interval's Δ are of one year duration, we note that since the period of fecundity in women extends from about 12 to 55 at the extremes (with an almost negligible number of births coming from those outside the range 16–50), the first term on the right hand side of (11) would be $f_1 \ldots f_{11} b_{12} \lambda^{-12}$ and the last $f_1 f_2 \ldots f_{54} b_{55} \lambda^{-55}$.

A zero population growth policy would be associated with setting $\lambda = 1$ and would be satisfied only if

$$2 = b_1 + f_1 b_2 + f_1 f_2 b_3 + f_1 f_2 f_3 b_4 + \ldots, \tag{13}$$

a condition that would seldom be satisfied unless rather drastic measures were instituted. A control policy which meddled into the affairs of all women would be costly and oppressive. Statistics on the b_j's and f_j's are generally known and change by only a small amount from year to year. A single age group might be chosen, say 23-year-olds, as a control group. The required number b_{23} would be obtained in terms of the f's and the other b's from (13) such that (13) is satisfied. A control policy which might not be too oppressive would be one in which 23-year-olds would be drafted, intimidated, or encouraged to make b_{23} come out right. All 23-year-olds might be required to report their intentions relative to becoming pregnant during their 24th year. If too many showed such an interest, a random choice of the excess number might be made and forbidden to become pregnant that year, with threats of penalties which might range from the payment of a fine to an abortion.

The above ideas are to be taken only semi-seriously because (13) is based on the assumptions that the f's and b's do not change, that half of the population in any age group is female, and that there is no emigration or immigration. These points can be taken into account without too much difficulty, but the same kinds of problems would exist if a national population policy were to be instituted.

When the b's and f's are constants, $P(0)$ can be expressed as a linear combination of the characteristic vectors of M. For this purpose we use the finite form of M, the generalization of equation (5b). Let

$$P(0) = \sum_\mu c_\mu \psi^{(\mu)}, \tag{14}$$

$\psi^{(\mu)}$ being the μ's characteristic vector of the matrix M (and corresponding to the characteristic value λ_μ). Then, from (7a)

$$M^n\psi^{(\mu)} = M^{n-1}\lambda_\mu\psi^{(\mu)} = \lambda_\mu^n\psi^{(\mu)},$$

$$P(n) = \sum c_\mu\lambda_\mu^n\psi^{(\mu)} \tag{15}$$

If we introduce the left hand characteristic vectors of M, say ϕ such that

$$\phi M = \lambda\phi \tag{16}$$

Then it is well known that the $\phi^{(\mu)}$ is orthogonal to $\psi^{(\nu)}$ if $\lambda_\mu \neq \lambda_\nu$ and that normalization is possible so that

$$\phi^{(\mu)}\cdot\psi^{(\nu)} = \delta_{\mu\nu} \tag{17}$$

Following standard methods we note then that

$$\phi^{(\nu)}\cdot P(0) = \sum c_\mu(\phi^{(\nu)}\cdot\psi^{(\mu)}) = \sum_\mu c_\mu\delta_{\mu\nu} = c_\nu \tag{18}$$

Hence

$$P(n) = \sum \lambda_\mu^n\{\phi^{(\mu)}\cdot P(0)\}\psi^{(\mu)}. \tag{19}$$

The characteristic values λ of the finite form of the matrix M are those which cause the following characteristic determinant to vanish.

$$\begin{vmatrix} \tfrac{1}{2}b_1-\lambda & \tfrac{1}{2}b_2 & \tfrac{1}{2}b_3 & \cdots & \tfrac{1}{2}b_{N-1} & \tfrac{1}{2}b_N \\ f_1 & -\lambda & 0 & \cdots & 0 & 0 \\ 0 & f_2 & -\lambda & \cdots & 0 & 0 \\ \cdot & \cdot & \cdot & \cdot & \cdot & \cdot \\ 0 & 0 & 0 & \cdots & f_{N-1} & f_{N-\lambda} \end{vmatrix} = 0 \tag{20}$$

This determinant can be expanded to obtain the characteristic equation of which are characteristic values are the roots $\lambda_1, \lambda_2, \ldots, \lambda_N$ of

$$(f_N-\lambda)\{(b_1-2\lambda)(-\lambda)^{N-2}-f_1 b_2(-\lambda)^{N-3}+f_1 f_2 b_3(-\lambda)^{N-1}$$

$$-\ldots+(-1)^N f_1 f_2 f_3\ldots f_{N-2}b_{N-1}\}+(-1)^{N+1}f_1 f_2\ldots f_{N-1}b_N = 0 \tag{21}$$

The components of the right hand characteristic vector ψ satisfy the occurrence formulae (we omit the subscript μ on λ_μ and the superscript μ on $\psi^{(\mu)}$)

$$\lambda\psi_j = f_{j-1}\psi_{j-1} \quad j = 2, \ldots, N-1 \tag{22}$$

$$\lambda\psi_N = f_{N-1}\psi_{N-1}+f_N\psi_N$$

so that

$$\psi_j = f_1 f_2 \cdots f_{j-1}/\lambda^{j-1})\psi_1 \quad \text{if } j = 2, \ldots, N-1$$

$$\psi_N = (f_1 f_2 \cdots f_{N-2}/\lambda^{N-2})\psi_1/(\lambda-f_N) \tag{23}$$

The components of the left hand characteristic vector ϕ satisfy

$$f_j\phi_{j+1} = \lambda\phi_j - b_{j-1}\phi_1 \qquad j = 2, \ldots, N-1$$

$$f_N\phi_N = \lambda\phi_N - b_N\phi_1 \tag{24}$$

so that

$$\phi_j = \tfrac{1}{2}\{2\lambda^{j-1} - \lambda^{j-2}b_1 - f_1 b_2\lambda^{j-3} - f_1 f_2 b_3\lambda^{j-4}$$

$$-\ldots-f_1 f_2 \ldots f_{j-2}b_j\}(f_1 f_2 \ldots f_{j-1})^{-1}\phi_1 \tag{25a}$$

$$\Phi_N = \tfrac{1}{2}b_N\phi_1/(\lambda-f_N) \tag{25b}$$

The normalization condition

$$\phi^{(\mu)}\cdot\psi^{(\mu)} = \sum_{j=1}^{N}\phi_j^{(\mu)}\psi_j^{(\mu)} = 1 \tag{26}$$

can be carried out in various ways. From (23) and (25); (26) becomes a relationship between $\phi_1^{(\mu)}$ and $\psi_1^{(\mu)}$. If, for example, one chooses $\psi_1^{(\mu)}$ so that

$$\sum_{j=1}^{N}\psi_j^{(\mu)} = 1$$

then $\psi_1^{(\mu)}$ would be defined and (26) would yield the appropriate value of $\phi_1^{(\mu)}$.

Sequences of vectors such as $P(n)$ in equation (66) whose components are probabilities, and which are connected by a matrix such as M in (6a), are called Markoff chains, and the matrix elements are called transition probabilities.[1,2] The general equations which relate the probability of being in state j at an nth time interval, $P_j^{(n)}$ is related to the probabilities of being in other states $\{P_k(n-1)\}$ at intervals $(n-1)$ are

$$P_j(n) = \sum_k a_{jk}P_k(n-1)$$

so that (6) is valid with

$$M = \begin{bmatrix} a_{11} & a_{12} & a_{13} & \cdot & \cdot \\ a_{21} & a_{22} & a_{23} & \cdot & \cdot \\ \cdot & \cdot & \cdot & \cdot & \cdot \end{bmatrix}$$

A. Rogers[3] has applied Markoff chain theory to the investigation of population movement. The transition probability a_{jk} would represent the probability of a resident of region k moving to region j in a given year.

A. Lopez[4] has discussed the relationship between population growth and age specific birth and death rates on a continuous time basis. The general mathematical theory of this type of process is called renewal theory. It is also applicable to the planning of preventive maintenance programs. The deterioration of components is analogous to the death process in individuals.

E. G. Lewis[5] and P. H. Leslie[6] were the first to develop the type of analysis which we have used in this section.

REFERENCES

1. M. B. Hostinsky, "Methodes generales du calcul de Probabilities," *Memorial de Sciences Mathematiques*, fasc. LII (Guthier-Villars 1931).
2. W. Feller, *An Introduction to the Theory of Probability* (Wiley, New York 1950).
3. Andrei Rogers, *Matrix Analysis of Interregional Population Growth and Distribution* (Univ. of Cal. Press, 1968).
4. Alvaro Lopez, *Problems in Population Theory* (Princeton, 1961).
5. E. G. Lewis, *Sankhyā*, **6**, 93 (1942).
6. P. H. Leslie, *Biometrica*, **33**, 183 (1945); **35**, 213 (1948); **45**, 16 (1958).

5 Competition Between Species

Numerous examples exist of competition and cooperation between species. Ecology is the science of competition between various plants and animals. The rise and fall of political parties, businesses and countries furnish other cases. The theory of chains of chemical reactions which occur in the atmosphere, in bodies of water, and in organisms, has a structure not unlike that of the processes mentioned above. Air and water pollution are the consequence of introducing foreign species into formerly stable population distributions. This section is concerned with some examples of such competition (the Volterra-Lotka model) between two species.

Cyclic oscillations have been observed in the population of two species which influence each other. One of the classical cases reported is the change in the abundance of the lynx and snowshoe hare as indicated in Figure 23a. Considerable fluctuation seems to exist in the number of arctic fox skins taken annually by the Hudson Bay Company, as indicated in Figure 23b.

The classical theory of two interacting species is that due to Volterra and Lotka in which it is assumed one of the species must eat the other in order to survive. The model was motivated by a statistical study by D'Ancona of Adriatic fish catches of the period 1905–1923. It appeared that the survival of a certain species of big fish depended on a plentiful supply of small fish. As the population of the big fish increased, a time would come when the available small fish was insufficient to support the large ones, causing some of the large ones to starve and leading to a decrease in their number. Without being

C*

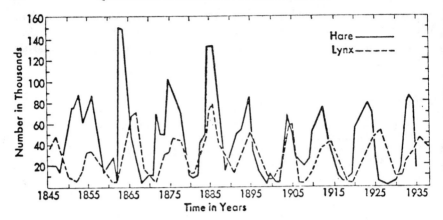

Figure 23a Changes in the abundance of lynx and snowshoe hare (from D. A. MacLuich, University of Toronto Studies, *Biological Science* **43**, 1937).

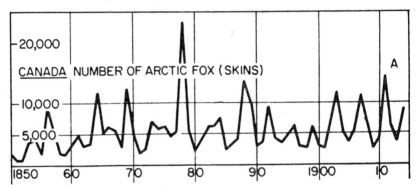

Figure 23b Number of Arctic Fox skins taken annually by the Hudson Bay Company.

preyed upon, the population of the small fish could increase. With more food available, the larger fish could again multiply and grow, repeating the cycle outlined above.

Let $N_1(t)$ be the number of Species 1 (the small fish) at time t which would increase in the absence of Species 2 (the large fish) of which there are $N_2(t)$. We follow Volterra by characterizing the competition through the equations

$$dN_1/dt = k_1 N_1 - \lambda_1 N_1 N_2 \qquad dN_2/dt = -k_2 N_2 + \lambda_2 N_1 N_2 \qquad (1)$$

The population of Species 1 is postulated to grow in the Malthusian manner in the absence of Species 2, k_1 being the rate constant while that of Species 2 is postulated to die out with rate constant k_2 in the absence of Species 1. The two interaction terms, $\lambda_1 N_1 N_2$ and $\lambda_2 N_1 N_2$ are proportional to the number of possible binary encounters $(N_1 N_2)$ between Species 1 and Species 2. The constant λ_1 tells us how rapidly these encounters will lead to decreases in the number of Species 1 and λ_2 tells us how rapidly these encounters will lead to increases in the population of Species 2.

For convenience we define

$$f_1(t) = \lambda_2 N_1(t)/k_2 \quad \text{and} \quad f_2(t) = \lambda_1 N_2(t)/k_1 \tag{2}$$

By substituting these into equation (1) we find

$$df_1/dt = k_1 f_1(1 - f_2) \tag{3}$$

$$df_2/dt = -k_2 f_2(1 - f_1) \tag{4}$$

so that

$$df_1/[k_1 f_1(1 - f_2)] = dt = -df_2/[k_2 f_2(1 - f_1)] \tag{5}$$

$$(1 - f_1)df_1/k_1 f_1 = -(1 - f_2)df_2/k_2 f_2$$

$$[f_1 - \log f_1]/k_1 + [f_2 - \log f_2]/k_2 = c$$

where c is the constant of integration.

Taking antilogarithms of both sides of equation (5) we find

$$(f_1 e^{-f_1})^{1/k_1}(f_2 e^{-f_2})^{1/k_2} = \text{constant} \tag{6}$$

which is the solution of the system of equation (2) which relates f_1 to f_2. The periodic character of this solution can be seen in terms of the relation between f_1 and f_2, as given by equation (6) through the aid of the four diagrams in Figure 24.

If we let

$$u_1 = (f_1 e^{-f_1})^{1/k_1}; \quad u_2 = (f_2 e^{-f_2})^{1/k_2} \tag{7}$$

then equation (6) becomes the equation of a hyperbola

$$u_1 u_2 = \text{constant} \tag{8}$$

which is plotted in Figure 24. Figures 24c and 24b show the behavior of u_1 and u_2 as functions of f_1 and f_2, respectively. An important feature of these two figures is that u_1 and u_2 attain maximum values which are identified by M_1 and M_2 in these figures. Hence the relevant region of the hyperbola in Figure 24a is bounded by points A and B. Note that a typical point 0 between A and B corresponds to two values of f_2 (a and b), and to two values of f_1, a' and b'. Hence, on Figure 24d which relates f_1 and f_2, the point 0 corresponds to the four points C, D, E, F. As one goes from points A to B in Figure 24a, one traces out the closed curve in Figure 24d. The end points A and B correspond respectively to extrema in f_2 and f_1 on Figure 24d.

Equations (3) and (4) imply that the initial conditions $f_1(0) = 0$ and $f_2(0) = 0$, or $f_1(0) = 1$, and $f_2(0) = 1$, yield species populations which will remain at their initial values forever. While the first set of conditions are of no interest, the second represents a true equilibrium state. Any other set of initial populations yield periodic population variations which periodically trace out a closed curve about the equilibrium point in a counterclockwise direction. There is, of course, a whole family of these curves, each member

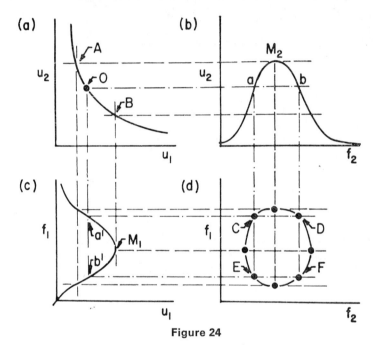

Figure 24

depending upon the initial conditions. Curves which lie close to the equilibrium point are essentially ellipses, whereas those which are further away begin to look like lopsided eggs (see Figure 25).

It is interesting to note that the average values of f_1 and f_2 for any member of this family of curves are $\bar{f}_1 = 1$ and $\bar{f}_2 = 1$, the equilibrium values. This follows from writing equation (3) as

$$d \log f_1/dt = k_1(1 - f_2)$$

By letting T be the duration of a cycle we find

$$k_1 \int_0^T (1 - f_2) dt = \int_0^T d \log f_1(t)$$
$$\log f_1(T) - \log f_1(0) = k_1 T - k_1 \int_0^T f_2 dt$$

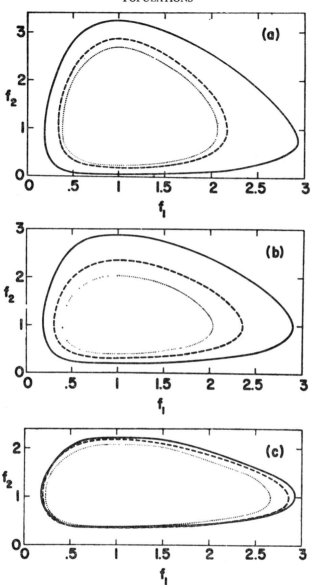

Figure 25 Variation of f_1 with respect to f_2 for various values of the para meters and initial values $f_1(0)$ and $f_2(0)$. (a) $(\alpha_1/\alpha_2) = \frac{1}{2}$ with the values of $f_1(0)$ and $f_2(0)$: ———, 0.2 and 0.8; – – –, 2.0 and 0.5; ..., 0.5 and 2.0. (b) (α_1/α_2) = 1 with the values of $f_1(0)$ and $f_2(0)$; ———, 0.2 and 0.8; – – – ; 0.5 and 2.0; ..., 1.0 and 0.8. (c) $(\alpha_1/\alpha_2) = 2$ with the values of $f_1(0)$ and $f_2(0)$: ———, 0.2 and 0.8; – – –, 0.2 and 2.0; ..., 2.0 and 0.5.

Since, by definition

$$\bar{f}_2 = \frac{1}{T}\int_0^T f_2\,dt$$

we have

$$\log f_1(T) - \log f_1(0) = T[k_1 - k_1\bar{f}_2]$$

Since $(0, T)$ is a complete cycle, we must have $f_1(T) = f_1(0)$. Hence $\bar{f}_2 = 1$ as required. In a similar manner it can be shown that $\bar{f}_1 = 1$.

For each set of initial values $f_1(0)$ and $f_2(0)$, one finds a solution of (6) (for fixed k_1 and k_2). The points on closed curves such as those in Figure 25 can be identified with the time by integrating (3)

$$t = \int_{f_1(0)}^{f_1(t)} df_1/k_1 f_1(1-f_2) \tag{9}$$

Since f_2 is given as a function of f_1 on the curve in Figure 25, one could start at the initial values $[f_1(0), f_2(0)]$, integrate numerically along the curve a short distance to a prechosen point $f_1(t)$ and from the value of t determined from (9), one would identify the time appropriate for that value of $f_1(t)$. This process could be continued until a full oscillation would be completed.

We have plotted in Figure 26 the variation of both f_1 and f_2 with time for a variety of initial conditions and values of the parameters k_1 and k_2. When $f_1(0)$ and $f_2(0)$ are close to the stationary values (1, 1), the functions $f_1(t)$ and $f_2(t)$ vary sinusoidally with time. When the initial f values are far from (1, 1), the growth and decline of both species show a sharp rise as well as a sharp fall in a spike-like manner.

REFERENCES

1. C. S. Elton, *Animal Ecology* (London, 1927); *Volls, Mice and Lemmings* (Oxford, 1942).
2. A. J. Lotka, *Elements of Mathematic Biology* (Johns Hopkins, 1924; Dover Reprint, 1956).
3. V. Volterra, *Lecons sur la theorie mathematique de la lutte pour la vie* (Paris, 1931)i.
4. H. T. Davis, *Introduction to Nonlinear Differential and Integral Equations* (Dover, 1962).
5. V. D'Ancona, *The Struggle for Existence* (Brill, Leiden, 1954).
6. E. W. Montroll, *Lectures in Theoretical Physics*, Univ. of Colorado XA, 531 (1967).
7. N. Goel, S. Maitra and E. Montroll, *Rev. Mod. Phys.*, **43**, 231 (1971).
8. G. F. Gause, *The Struggle for Existence* (Williams and Wilkins, Baltimore (1934)).
9. J. G. Kemeny and J. L. Snell, *Mathematical Models in the Social Sciences* (New York, 1962).
10. E. C. Pielou, *An Introduction to Mathematical Ecology* (Wiley-Interscience, New York, 1969).

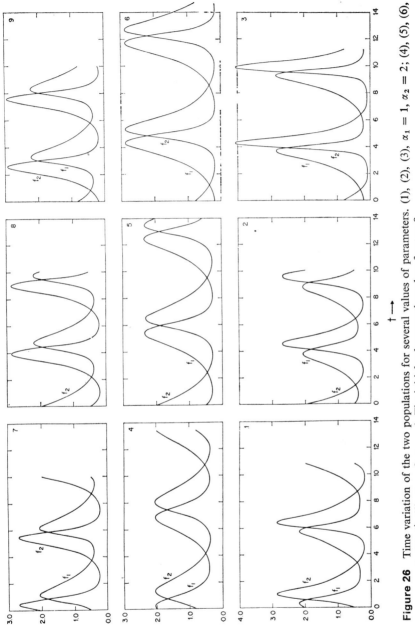

Figure 26 Time variation of the two populations for several values of parameters. (1), (2), (3), $\alpha_1 = 1$, $\alpha_2 = 2$; (4), (5), (6), $\alpha_1 = \alpha_2 = 1$; (7), ('), (9), $\alpha_1 = 2$, $\alpha_2 = 1$. The initial values are the values for $t = 0$.

6   Interaction Between Three or More Species

The pair of equations which represent the interaction between two species (5.1) has been generalized by Volterra to a set for n interacting species:

$$\frac{dN_i}{dt} = k_i N_i + \beta_i^{-1} \sum_{j=1}^{n} a_{ij} N_i N_j \tag{1}$$

The first term describes the behavior of ith species in the absence of others; when $k_i > 0$, the ith species is postulated to grow in an exponential Malthusian manner with k_i as the "rate constant". When $k_i < 0$ and all other $N_j = 0$, the population of the ith species would die out exponentially. The quadratic terms in equation (1) describe the interaction of the ith species with all the other species. The ith term in the quadratic sum is proportional to the number of possible binary encounters $N_i N_j$ between members of the ith species and members of the jth species. The constants a_{ij} might be either positive, negative, or vanish. A positive a_{ij} tells us how rapidly encounters between ith and jth species will lead to an increase in N_i, and a zero a_{ij} simply denotes the fact that ith and jth species do not interact. If, during a collision between ith and jth species, jth species are gained, then ith species are lost. Hence a_{ij} and a_{ji} have opposite signs. The positive quantities β_j^{-1} have been named "equivalence" numbers by Volterra. During binary collisions of species i and j, the ratio of i's lost (or gained) per unit time to j's gained (or lost) is $\beta_i^{-1}/\beta_j^{-1}$. With this definition,

$$a_{ij} = -a_{ji} \tag{2}$$

We sometimes abbreviate,

$$b_{ij} = \beta_i^{-1} a_{ij}. \tag{3}$$

Except under certain conditions which we discuss below,

$$a_{ii} \equiv 0 \qquad \text{for all } i. \tag{4}$$

We define the steady state of our assembly to be characterized by that set of populations $\{N_j\}$ for which $dN_j/dt = 0$ for all j. The quantity q_j is defined to be the value of N_j under this condition so that the defining equations for $\{q_i\}$ are

$$q_i[k_i\beta_i + \sum_j a_{ij}q_j] = 0. \tag{5}$$

When none of the q's vanish, they satisfy

$$k_i\beta_i + \sum_{j=1}^{n} a_{ij}q_j = 0 \qquad i = 1, 2, \ldots, n \tag{6}$$

It is important to note, as was first shown by Volterra, that there is a constant of the motion which depends on the $\{q_j\}$ for our assembly. We define

$$v_j = \log (N_j/q_j) \quad \text{or} \quad N_j = q_j \exp v_j \tag{7}$$

Clearly, as $N_j \to q_j$, $v_j \to 0$ so that v is a measure of the deviation from equilibrium. The rate equation (1) is easily expressed in terms of the v_j (by expressing $k_i \beta_i$ through equation (6)),

$$\beta_j dv_j/dt = \sum_i a_{ji} q_i (e^{v_i} - 1) \tag{8}$$

If we multiply both sides of this equation by $q_j(e^{v_j} - 1)$ and sum over all j, we find

$$(d/dt) \sum_j \beta_j q_j (e^{v_j} - v_j) = \sum_{ij} a_{ji} q_i q_j (e^{v_i} - 1)(e^{v_j} - 1) = 0,$$

the double sum vanishing because the summand is antisymmetrical in i and j. Let us now restrict ourselves to the stable case of physical interest with all $q_j > 0$.
Then

$$G = \sum_j \beta_j q_j (-v_j + \exp v_j) = \text{constant} = \sum G_j \tag{9}$$

so that G is our desired constant of the motion. Every individual term in G is positive since, in case a) $v_j > 0$ implies $\exp v_j > v_j$ and, in case b), $v_j < 0$, $-v_j > 0$ and the exponential is positive whether v_j is positive or negative. Hence, $G > 0$. Since $\sum \beta_j q_j$ is constant, one also finds that

$$G_0 = -\sum \beta_j q_j (1 + v_j - \exp v_j) = \text{constant} \tag{10}$$

In the special case $n = 2$, these results can be reduced to those obtained in the last section by setting

$$\alpha_1 = k_1, \qquad \alpha_2 = -k_2$$
$$\lambda_1 \beta_1 = -a_{12} = a_{21} = \lambda_2 \beta_2.$$

Then (10) implies (5.6).

It is useful to introduce "graphs" which describe the manner in which various species interact with each other. We represent each of the species by a point and, for each nonvanishing a_{ij} in (1), we connect points i and j by a bond. An example which involves 12 species is given in Figure 27a. Further information can be placed on the graph to indicate the direction of flow of matter. If i feeds on j, $(a_{ij} > 0)$, we direct the bond connecting i and j by an arrow pointing from j to i. Those species, i, for which $k_i > 0$, would continue to multiply in the absence of other enumerated species. Their growth in number depends on the existence of a large ecological bath of unenumerated species which exist in such an enormous quantity that their extent is unaffected by the growth of species i. Generally the ecological bath survives on the waste and decomposition products of many species. The graph associated with two competing species is given in Figure 27b.

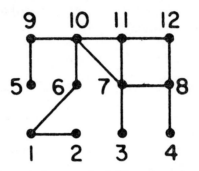

Figure 27a　The graph of an example of a 12-species ecology. If species i either feeds on species j or is eaten by j, a bond connects points i and j.

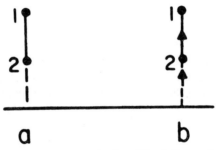

Figure 27b　Two-species graph. The dotted line indicates that species 2 feeds of the large natural reservoir and species 1 feeds only on 2. The arrows indicate the direction of mass flow.

When resources are limited, one sometimes changes the Volterra equations by adding Verhulst type saturation inducing terms for those species whose k_i is positive (species whose population would grow exponentially in the absence of other species). Then (if sign $x = 1$ with $x > 0$ and zero otherwise),

$$\frac{dN_j}{dt} = k_j N_j (\theta_j - \tfrac{1}{2}[1 + \text{sign } k_j] N_j)/\theta_j + \beta_j^{-1} N_j \sum_{i=1}^{n} a_{ji} N_i. \qquad (11)$$

It can be shown that with the inclusion of these saturation terms, populations do not oscillate indefinitely about their stationary values, but eventually achieve them.

Let us investigate the calculation of steady state populations and the conditions under which no species vanish in the steady state. The steady state populations $\{q_j\}$ of an assembly of n species satisfy equation (5). We drop the Verhulst terms in (11) unless the system becomes unstable in the $\theta_j \to \infty$ limit.

We start our systematic discussion of equilibrium values of species populations by examining the case of three species. Then equation (6) has the form

$$q_1[\beta_1 k_1 \qquad\qquad +a_{12}q_2+a_{13}q_3] = 0 \qquad\qquad (12a)$$

$$q_2[\beta_2 k_2+a_{21}q_1 \qquad\qquad +a_{23}q_3] = 0 \qquad\qquad (12b)$$

$$q_3[\beta_3 k_3+a_{31}q_1+a_{32}q_2 \qquad\quad] = 0 \qquad\qquad (12c)$$

If one of the species vanishes, say $q_1 \equiv 0$, then the other equilibrium populations are given immediately with $q_3 = \beta_2 k_2/a_{32}$ and $q_2 = \beta_3 k_3/a_{23}$. Since the only interesting case is one which q_3 and q_2 are non-negative, k_2/a_{32} must have the same sign as k_3/a_{23}. Hence, k_2 and k_3 must have opposite signs.

Let us seek a solution of (12) for which none of the q_j's vanish. Then the q_j factors on the left of each equation can be dropped. In order for this type of solution to exist, the determinant of the coefficients of the q_j's must not vanish. That determinant is

$$\begin{vmatrix} 0 & a_{12} & a_{13} \\ a_{21} & 0 & a_{23} \\ a_{31} & a_{32} & 0 \end{vmatrix} = a_{12}a_{23}a_{31}+a_{13}a_{32}a_{21}$$

In view of the anti-symmetry of the a_{ij}'s, this determinant vanishes so that we have the interesting result (already known to Volterra) that there is no equilibrium population distribution between three species such that the population of all the species is finite and non-vanishing.

Since in this discussion we postulated that no species vanished at equilibrium, one way we can avoid having an equilibrium with a finite population of each species is to allow at least one to become infinite. When such a situation arises, one can no longer neglect the Verhulst term in (11). Let us suppose that species 3 is the only one for which k_j is positive. Then equation (12c) becomes

$$\beta_3 k_3(1-q_3/\theta_3)+a_{31}q_1+a_{32}q_2 = 0. \qquad\qquad (13)$$

Now consider the diagrams of Figures 27c, i–iv. Clearly, in Figure 27c–i species 1 would vanish because it is eaten by 2 with no source to supply it. Hence the problem would reduce to a two-species problem and the discussion below (12) would apply.

In Figure 27c–i, $a_{31} = a_{13} = 0$ so that our full set of equations would be:

$$\beta_3 k_3 (1 - q_3/\theta_3) + a_{32} q_2 = 0 \tag{14a}$$

$$k_1 \beta_1 + a_{12} q_2 = 0 \tag{14b}$$

$$k_2 \beta_2 + a_{21} q_1 + a_{23} q_3 = 0 \tag{14c}$$

with

$$a_{32} < 0, a_{12} > 0, k_1 \beta_1 < 0 \quad \text{and} \quad k_2 \beta_2 < 0, k_3 \beta_3 > 0 \tag{15}$$

We then have the equilibrium population

$$q_2 = k_1 \beta_1/a_{21} > 0 \tag{16a}$$

$$q_3 = \theta_3 (1 - a_{32} k_1 \beta_1/a_{12} k_3 \beta_3) \tag{16b}$$

$$q_1 = -(k_2 \beta_2/a_{21}) + (a_{23}/a_{12}) \theta_3 (1 - a_{32} k_1 \beta_1/a_{12} k_3 \beta_3) \tag{16c}$$

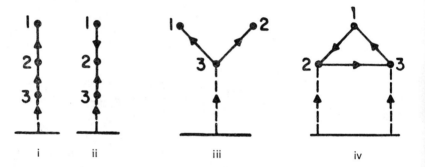

Figure 27c   Some graphs involving three interacting species.

If

$$(a_{32} k_1 \beta_1/a_{12} k_3 \beta_3) < 1, \tag{17}$$

then $q_3 > 0$. The second term in q_1 is also positive while the first term is negative. The ultimate fate of species 1 then depends on whether or not

$$(a_{23}/a_{12}) \theta_3 (1 - a_{32} k_1 \beta_1/a_{12} k_3 \beta_3) > (k_2 \beta_2/a_{21}) \tag{18}$$

If it is, then species 1 survives. If it is not satisfied, then the equilibrium population of species 1 is negative so that, from any initial distribution, it will pass zero, the point of the vanishing of the species in its trajectory toward the equilibrium point.

The ecology of Figure 27c–iv can be discussed in a similar way. The basic equations for equilibrium are (13) and

$$k_2\beta_2 + a_{23}q_3 = 0 \tag{19a}$$

$$k_1\beta_1 + a_{13}q_3 = 0 \tag{19b}$$

with

$$k_2\beta_2 < 0;\, k_1\beta_1 < 0;\, a_{23} > 0,\quad \text{and}\quad a_{13} > 0 \tag{20}$$

Hence,

$$q_3 = k_2\beta_2/a_{32} > 0 \quad \text{and} \quad q_3 = k_1\beta_1/a_{31} \tag{21}$$

Generally these two equations are inconsistent; hence the hypothesis that there exists an equilibrium solution in which no species vanishes is false so that at least one has to vanish. In the *special* case,

$$k_2\beta_2 a_{31} = k_1\beta_1 a_{32} \tag{22}$$

the two species 1 and 2 behave as though they are a single species and can form an equilibrium system with 3. Under this special condition, the system is equivalent to a two-species system.

Qualitatively it is not surprising that the ecology corresponding to Figure 27c–iii is generally unstable.

Both "1" and "2" nibble on "3" in a manner that is generally uncorrelated. Let us suppose that the death rate constant of 1 is smaller than that of 2. In the absence of 1, the population of 2 and 3 would oscillate. But now, when the population of both 3 and 2 are both low in a state such that 3 would start to recover in the absence of too many preying 2's, 1 with its smaller time constant would continue to attack 3 until either 2 or 3 disappeared. If 2 disappeared first, then 1 and 3 would form an oscillating 2-species ecology. If 3 disappears, then both 1 and 2 would also die out. The reader might find it interesting to make an analysis of the graph 27c–iv.

It can be shown that the determinant of any antisymmetrical matrix of an odd order vanishes. This is related to the fact that the eigenvalues of an antisymmetric matrix are purely imaginary and they occur in pairs, one being the complex conjugate of the other. In the case of an odd order matrix, the only way this condition can be satisfied is to have one eigenvalue zero. Since the determinant of the matrix is the product of all the eigenvalues, it must then vanish. This means that in every Volterra ecology of an odd number of species, at least one must eventually die out or that at least one species would grow indefinitely in the absence of the Verhulst term. In the latter case, the Verhulst saturation term would have to be included in the manner discussed above for the three-species case. We develop the general theory after we complete our discussion of the ecology of an even number of species. We first examine in special cases the necessary condition for the existence of stable populations in the absence of a Verhulst term.

When n is even, say $2N$, the necessary condition for the existence of a set of finite non-vanishing solutions of (6) is

$$D_{2N} = \begin{vmatrix} 0 & a_{12} & a_{13} & \cdots & a_{1,2N} \\ a_{21} & 0 & a_{23} & \cdots & a_{2,2N} \\ \cdot & \cdot & \cdot & & \cdot \\ a_{N1} & a_{N2} & a_{N3} & \cdots & 0 \end{vmatrix} \neq 0 \qquad (23)$$

The determinant of an antisymmetric matrix A is a perfect square and, indeed, its square root is an object called a Pfaffian with

$$(D_{2N})^{\frac{1}{2}} = PfA = \begin{vmatrix} a_{12} & a_{13} & a_{14} & \cdot & \cdot & a_{1,2N} \\ & a_{23} & a_{24} & \cdot & \cdot & a_{2,2N} \\ & & & & & \cdot \\ & & & & & a_{2N-1,2N} \end{vmatrix} \qquad (24a)$$

$$= \sum \delta_p a_{p_1 p_2} a_{p_3 p_4} \cdots a_{p_{2N-1}, p_{2N}} \qquad (24b)$$

$$p_1 < p_2, p_3 < p_4, p_5 < p_6, \ldots \quad \text{and} \quad p_1 < p_3 < p_5 < \ldots \qquad (24c)$$

where the summation extends over all permutations of the integers $1, 2, \ldots, 2N$ which satisfy conditions (24c). The signature δ_p is $+1$ if $(p_1, p_2, \ldots, p_{2N})$ is an even permutation of the first $2N$ integers, and -1 if it is an odd permutation. When $N = 2$ (4-species),

$$D_4 = (PfA)^2 = (a_{12}a_{34} - a_{13}a_{24} + a_{14}a_{23})^2 \qquad (25)$$

The equilibrium numbers in the case $n = 4$ are easily shown to be

$$q_1 = (k_2\beta_2 a_{34} + k_3\beta_3 a_{42} + k_4\beta_4 a_{23})/PfA = \begin{vmatrix} k_2\beta_2 & k_3\beta_3 & k_4\beta_4 \\ & a_{23} & a_{24} \\ & & a_{34} \end{vmatrix}/PfA \quad (26a)$$

$$q_2 = (k_1\beta_1 a_{43} + k_3\beta_3 a_{14} + k_4\beta_4 a_{31})/PfA \qquad (26b)$$

$$q_3 = (k_1\beta_1 a_{24} + k_2\beta_2 a_{41} + k_4\beta_4 a_{12})/PfA \qquad (26c)$$

$$q_4 = (k_1\beta_1 a_{32} + k_2\beta_2 a_{13} + k_3\beta_3 a_{21})/PfA \qquad (26d)$$

Similar expressions can be derived for the general case of an even number of species. All q_j's can always be expressed as a ratio of two Pfaffians.

All possible diagrams (without arrows) which involve four connected species are given in Figure 27d. Equation (25) tells us which of these diagrams corresponds to the vanishing of one species. In cases $a-f$, respectively, the Pfaffians, $Pf\,A$, are

(a) $-a_{13}a_{24}$ (b) 0

(c) $a_{12}a_{34}-a_{13}a_{24}$ (d) $-a_{13}a_{24}+a_{14}a_{23}$ (27)

(e) $a_{12}a_{34}-a_{13}a_{24}$ (f) $a_{12}a_{34}-a_{13}a_{24}+a_{12}a_{23}$

Hence, with the exception of case (b), there is some possibility that there exist appropriate non-vanishing a_{jk} such that non-vanishing finite equilibrium populations exist for all species, even in the absence of the Verhulst terms.

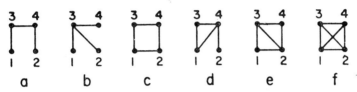

Figure 27d All the connected graphs involving four interacting species.

In order for physically reasonable non-vanishing solutions to exist for the basic equilibrium equation, all equilibrium populations q_j must be non-negative. This puts certain restrictions on the ranges of the a_{jk}'s. Let us first consider case (a). Then from (26) with $a_{12} \equiv a_{23} \equiv a_{14} \equiv 0$,

$$q_1 = (k_2\beta_2 a_{34}+k_3\beta_3 a_{42})/a_{31}a_{24} \qquad (28a)$$

$$q_2 = (k_1\beta_1 a_{43}+k_4\beta_4 a_{31})/a_{31}a_{24} \qquad (28b)$$

$$q_3 = k_1\beta_1/a_{31} \quad \text{and} \quad q_4 = k_2\beta_2/a_{42} \qquad (28c)$$

There are a number of diagrams which express the manner in which graph (a) is applicable. One or more of our four species can feed on the nutrient reservoir and there are a number of possibilities of whether i eats j or j eats i. Some of these possibilities are exhibited in Figure 27e. Consider, first, case (i). We ask for a set of conditions such that each $q_j > 0$. Our arrangement of arrows imply

$$k_1 > 0, k_2 < 0, k_3 < 0, \quad \text{and} \quad k_4 < 0$$

$$a_{31} > 0, a_{43} > 0, \quad \text{and} \quad a_{24} > 0.$$

From these conditions it is clear that $q_3 > 0$, $q_4 > 0$, and, $q_1 > 0$. The stationary population q_2 of species 2 can be positive only if

$$k_1\beta_1 a_{43} > k_4\beta_4 a_{13} \qquad (29)$$

Hence once the diagram with the arrow arrangement (i) is presented to us, an equilibrium population distribution exists as long as (29) is satisfied.

A discussion of the other graphs involving four species can be found in reference 5 as well as general remarks on graphs of many species.

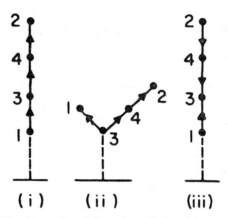

Figure 27e   Examples of directed graphs involving four species.

An analysis of the time dependent behavior of more than two competing species can be developed in detail only through a high speed computer. However, if the initial deviations from equilibrium are small, one can use small vibration theory to follow the time development of the various populations.

We write

$$N_i(t) = q_i[1 + \delta_i(t)] \tag{30}$$

where q_i is the steady state population of species i. Then, if each δ_i is small, (1) becomes

$$\beta_i \delta_i = \sum_{j=1}^{n} a_{ij} q_j \delta_j \tag{31}$$

If we let

$$x_i = \delta_i (q_i \beta_i)^{\frac{1}{2}} \tag{32}$$

$$C_{ij} = (q_i/\beta_i)^{\frac{1}{2}} a_{ij} (q_j/\beta_j)^{\frac{1}{2}} = -C_{ji} \tag{33}$$

then (4.3) becomes

$$\dot{x}_i = \sum_j C_{ij} x_j \tag{34}$$

or

$$\dot{x}(t) = Cx(t) \tag{35}$$

where $x(t)$ is a column vector with components $x_j(t)$ and C is a $n \times n$ anti-symmetric matrix with C_{ij} as elements.

It is well known that the characteristic values of an antisymmetric matrix such as C are purely imaginary and they occur in pairs so that, if one is $i\omega_l$, another is $-i\omega_l$. Let A_{il} be the ith element of the lth characteristic vector (corresponding to the characteristic value λ_l) of C, i.e.,

$$\sum_k C_{ik}A_{kl} = \lambda_l A_{il} \tag{36}$$

Let A be the matrix whose elements are A_{il} and $A^\dagger$ one whose elements are A_{li}^*. If we normalize the characteristic vectors properly, we can choose

$$A^\dagger A = I \quad \text{i.e.,} \quad \sum_i A_{li}^* A_{lj} = \delta_{ij} \tag{37a}$$

where A^* is the Hermitian conjugate of A, and I is the identity matrix. Taking the complex conjugate of (36) and using the identity $\lambda_l^* = -\lambda_l$, we get

$$\sum_k C_{ik}A_{kl}^* = -\lambda_l A_{il}^* \tag{37b}$$

Thus A_{kl}^* is the kth element of the characteristic vector which corresponds to the characteristic value $-\lambda_l$. Further, using the identity $C_{ij} = -C_{ji}$, we get

$$\sum_k (A^\dagger)_{lk}C_{ki} = \lambda_l (A^\dagger)_{li} \tag{38}$$

Therefore $(A^\dagger)_{il}$ is the ith element of the lth characteristic row vector corresponding to the characteristic value λ_l.

The solution of (34) can now be written as

$$x_i(t) = \sum_l \alpha_l A_{il} \exp t\lambda_l \tag{39}$$

where α_l are constants to be determined from the application of the orthogonality relationship (37) to $x_i(0)$, i.e.,

$$\sum_i x_i(0)A_{im}^* = \alpha_m \tag{40}$$

Substituting (40) into (39), we get

$$x_i(t) = \sum_{lj} A_{jl}^* A_{jl} x_j(0) \exp t\lambda_l \tag{41}$$

This equation thus gives the time evolution of the population near equilibrium. Since q_i's are functions of k_i and a_{ij}, from (33) the C_{ij}'s are functions of k_i, β_i and a_{ij}, the parameters describing the growth and interaction of the various species. Thus, in principle, A and λ_l, and from (32) for the given initial values of N_i, $x_i(t)$ too can be expressed in terms of k_i, β_i and a_{ij}.

Further discussion and application of these results will be given later when we discuss statistical aspects of competitive processes.

REFERENCES

1. V. Volterra, *Leçons sur la theorie mathematique de la lutte pour la vie* (Paris, 1931).
2. V. D'Ancona, *The Struggles for Existence* (Brill, Leiden 1954).
3. E. Cainiello, *Nuovo Cimento* (*Suppl.*) **14**, 177 (1959).
4. E. Montroll, in *Applied Combinatorial Mathematics* (edited by E. Bechenbach (Wiley, 1964)).
5. N. Goel, S. Maitra, and E. Montroll, *Rev. Mod. Phys.* **43**, 231 (1971).

7   Some Remarks on Arms Races

Most engineers would not dream of designing a structure without introducing a safety factor into the calculations. Factors of two and even ten are not unheard of. Theory is fine, but when the engineer bets his job on success, he plays it safe. As a class, the aeronautical engineers, the designers of one of the most risky devices, were among the first to be forced to believe in their own plans. Suppose that one wished to put a larger than necessary safety factor in wing strength, then the engine would have to be more powerful, and, if a larger than necessary safety factor were put into the power of the larger engine, the fuel-carrying capacity would have to be increased, etc. Unless some careful trimming is made in the safety factor, the plane might never get off the ground. Such trimming requires tremendous confidence in one's calculations.

Now consider Nation A's main defense planner, a man who must perform properly under the great responsibility which had been thrust upon him. He must decide on next year's military procurement policy. He pours over intelligence data, listens to his advisors and makes a best estimate of the force strength of various other nations, especially that of Nation B with whom Nation A is not on the best of terms. In a certain category of arms, say offensive missiles, it seems that B will have x units. Our planner, like a good engineer, decides that his beloved country should take no chances and he introduces a safety factor α into his analysis and proposes that his country should be prepared to defend itself with αx missiles. In the course of events, our planners counterpart in B is confronted with reports of the behavior of A. His intelligence sources tell him that A is expanding its missile production and seems to be working toward a number αx. Not being too confident in his sources and wanting to do right by his country, he also applies a safety factor (it might even be α) and recommends a missile force of $x\alpha^2$, which should act as a deterrent even to A. A year goes by and the new budget cycle starts in A, etc., etc. If the international climate does not change and if a butter-not-guns campaign does not start in A or B, the arms race is on and arms procurement exponentiates.

The British physicist and meteorologist, Lewis Fry Richardson, expressed the basis of this exponentiation (which is described below) in a somewhat different but essentially equivalent manner. His major work was concerned with atmospheric eddies (a topic which will be important later in our discussions of air polution) and with weather prediction. As a Quaker he hated war, but believed it to be difficult to cope with a menace if one has no understanding of it.

In his essay on Mathematics of War and Foreign Politics, Richardson reviews the defense budgets of France, Germany, Russia and the Austria-Hungarian empire for the pre-World War I years. Since France and Russia were close allies, their defense expenditures are linked together (and called U) while, for a similar reason, those of Germany and Austria-Hungary are combined (and called V). The data is tabulated in Table VII. The rate of increase in $(U+V)$ with time, $\Delta(U+V)/\Delta t$, was plotted as a function of $(U+V)$ and Richardson's curve is reproduced in Figure 28.

TABLE VII

Defense budgets in £10^6 sterling

Country		1909	1910	1911	1912	1913
x	France	48.6	50.9	57.1	63.2	74.7
	Russia	66.7	68.5	70.7	81.8	92.0
y	Germany	63.1	62.0	62.5	68.2	95.4
	Austria–Hungary	20.8	23.4	24.6	25.5	26.9
	Total	199.2	204.8	214.9	238.7	289.0
	Rate of increase		5.6	10.1	23.8	50.3

The linear relationship between the two quantities plotted in Figure 28 is an exhibition of the exponentiation of arms expenditure. Richardson proposed that the rate at which the arms budget of A increases is proportional to that of B. Indeed, if both groups use the same proportionality constant

$$dU/dt = kV \quad \text{and} \quad dV/dt = kU \tag{1}$$

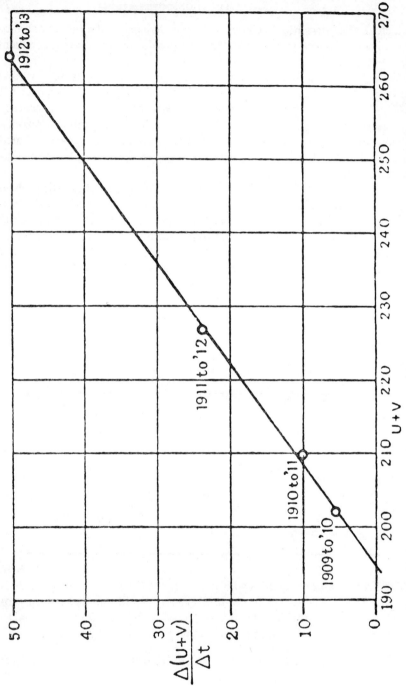

Figure 28 Rate of increase of total armament expenditures vs. expenditures in the arms race preceding World War II.[1]

Adding these two equations we find that

$$d(U+V)/dt = k(U+V) \qquad (2)$$

which corresponds to the linear relationship in Figure 28. Furthermore,

$$U(t)+V(t) = [U(0)+V(0)] \exp kt \qquad (3)$$

which is just our exponential growth rate.

As in our population growth discussion, we know that this law cannot continue forever. The declaration of war would put one in a different planning mode and, in the absence of a war, the defense expenditures would eventually become competitive with other items. One should then couple these equations to others which involve non-defense spending. However, for simplicity we introduce the internal competition factor into (1) by stating that as the armament expenditures in A increases, there is a pressure on the defense planners to decrease their rate of spending by an amount which is proportional to the total size of the defense establishment. A reasonable generalization of (1) would then be

$$dU/dt = k_1 V - l_1 U \qquad (4a)$$

$$dV/dt = k_2 U - l_2 V \qquad (4b)$$

where we have made A and B unsymmetrical.

There is another contribution which might also be added to the rates of spending. Suppose that the world is peaceful and that A has no special enemy nor does B. There would still be the tendency to purchase arms as an exhibition of national pride and prestige and as a bit of insurance against the unexpected. It is even a message to the world that the arms purchaser will be no pushover to anyone who has covetous ideas. He argues that military lore and skills must be preserved since they cannot be developed hastily in a crisis. Finally, some leaders like parades, traditions, shows, and costumes. They feel that their positions internally would not be respected without a military force to keep order at home. The significance of these reasons for arms purchase vary from country to country but, at a given time, any country would have a term in its arms growth equation which would be independent of U and V. It would probably vary slowly with time depending on internal politics and general world politics so that we would generalize (4) to

$$dU/dt = Vk_1 - Ul_1 + \alpha_1(t) \qquad (5a)$$

$$dV/dt = Uk_2 - Vl_2 + \alpha_2(t) \qquad (5b)$$

Over a long period of time, certain statistical properties might be assigned to $\alpha_i(t)$.

Finally, there is another refinement which might be added. The arms purchases of A at time t might depend on those of B at some earlier time $t-\tau$ since there is a time lag between the observation of B's intent and A's response. Such time lags and their influence in interacting systems will be discussed in considerable detail in our analysis of traffic flows. An integral formulation of our problem is more suitable to the introduction of time lags. One might express $U(t)$ and $V(t)$, the arms production functions at time t through memory functions $F_{ij}(t-\tau)$ which indicates the response of A and B to each others and their own past programs:

$$U(t) = \int_{-\infty}^{t} F_{11}(t-\tau)U(\tau)d\tau + \int_{-\infty}^{t}F_{12}(t-\tau)V(\tau)d\tau \qquad (6a)$$

$$V(t) = \int_{-\infty}^{t}F_{21}(t-\tau)U(\tau)d\tau + \int_{-\infty}^{t}F_{22}(t-\tau)V(\tau)d\tau \qquad (6b)$$

The quantity $F_{12}(t-\tau)V(\tau)d\tau$ is the response A makes at time t to B's arms construction program during the time interval $d\tau$ at a time τ earlier. Similar interpretations can be given to the other terms. By examining the detailed history of both the A and B armament program over a long period, one might determine the functions U and V. We do not attempt such an analysis here; we merely show that if the memory functions F_{12} and F_{21} decay exponentially, and if $F_{11} = F_{22} = 0$, we recapture the Richardson's equations.

Let

$$F_{12}(t) = k_1 \exp(-l_1 t) \quad \text{and} \quad F_{21}(t) = k_2 \exp(-l_2 t). \qquad (7)$$

Then

$$U(t) = k_1 \int_{-\infty}^{t} V(\tau) \exp\{-l_1(t-\tau)\} d\tau \qquad (8a)$$

$$V(t) = k_2 \int_{-\infty}^{t} U(\tau) \exp\{-l_2(t-\tau)\} d\tau \qquad (8b)$$

so that

$$dU/dt = k_1 V - l_1 k_1 \int_{-\infty}^{t} V(t) \exp\{-l_1(t-\tau)\} d\tau \qquad (9)$$

$$= k_1 V - l_1 U$$

which is equation (4a). Equation (4b) is obtained by differentiation (8b). Our basic equations (6a) and (6b) are stimulus-response equations and are in a form which would allow one to investigate empirically the stimulus-response characteristics of nations. A random term could be added to both (6a) and (6b).

A more sophisticated theory would include the influence of the economy, unemployment, and other domestic variables on arms construction.

Richardson and several other authors have made extended investigations of equations such as (5) and compared the solutions with more data than has been presented above. An elaborate discussion of various components including defense, of the British budget for the period 1890 to 1955 has been made by Peacock and Wiseman. Similar work should be done for the other major powers so that the influence between budgets of different countries could be better understood. An interesting narrative account of arms races has been given by S. P. Huntington in Reference 5.

REFERENCES

1. Lewis Fry Richardson, *Arms and Insecurity; A Mathematical Study of the Causes and Origins of War*, edited by Nicolas Rashevsky and Ernesto Trucco (Pittsburgh, 1960).
2. A. Rapoport, *J. Conflict Resolution* **1**, 249 (1957).
3. R. P. Abelson, *J. Conflict Resolution* **7**, 13 (1963).
4. Alan T. Peacock and Jack Wiseman, *The Growth of Public Expenditures in The United Kingdom; A Study by The National Bureau of Economic Research* (Princeton, 1961).
5. Samuel P. Huntington, *Public Policy* **8**, 41 (1958).

8 Propagation of Information by Exponentiation

Some of our previous discussions have laid the blame for various troubles in the world to the process of exponentiation. In this section we discuss an exponentiation mechanism through which useful information can be rapidly disseminated. In preparation for this discussion, let us consider the mechanism of the chain letter.

The chain letter achieved a remarkable popularity for a short period during the depression '30's. It was one of a number of "get rich quick" schemes that appeared when there was plenty of thinking time and little spending money. The recipient, whom we call Doe, of such a chain letter found an explanation of its purpose, a solemn plea not to break the chain, and the following directions:

i) a dime was to be sent to the person whose name headed a list of six names and addresses.

ii) five copies of the letter were to be prepared with the second name on top.

iii) Each of the five remaining names were to be moved up one position.

iv) a different new name and address was to be placed at the bottom of list on each new copy of the letter.

v) each new letter was to be sent to the person whose name was at the bottom of the list.

The participant patiently waited for the dimes to roll in.

Schematically the process is as follows:

1. Black
2. Green
3. Gray
4. White
5. Blue
6. Doe

Figure 29 Stage 0.

1. Green	1. Green	1. Green	1. Green	1. Green
2. Gray	2. Gray	2. Gray	2. Gray	2. Gray
3. White	3. White	3. White	3. White	3. White
4. Blue	4. Blue	4. Blue	4. Blue	4. Blue
5. Doe	5. Doe	5. Doe	5. Doe	5. Doe
6. Aarons	6. Abel	6. Abrams	6. Adams	6. Allen

Figure 30   Stage 1, five examples.

1. Gray	1. White	1. Blue	1. Doe
2. White	2. Blue	2. Doe	2. Aarons
3. Blue	3. Doe	3. Aarons	. 3. Baer
4. Doe	4. Aarons	4. Baer	4. Cox
5. Aarons	5. Baer	5. Cox	5. Duke
6. Baer	6. Cox	6. Duke	6. Evans
Stage 2 – 5^2	Stage 3 – 5^3	Stage 4 – 5^4	Stage 5 – 5^5

Figure 31

If the chain is not broken, the progression continues with Doe's name moving up one step each time. At the fifth stage, lucky Doe receives $5^5 = 3125$ dimes which is not bad for a 22¢ investment (in those good old days of the 2¢ postage rate). For every lucky Doe, there was an unlucky postman. At the beginning of the craze, there were sufficient lucky Does so that a number of small post offices could not handle their business and so that many automatic cancelling machines became jammed from the dimes in the letters. The state of affairs became so serious that the chain letter was made illegal. However, by the time the law existed to be enforced, the excitement was essentially over.

Suppose that Gray originated the idea in the city of population 10^5 of Doe's residence and by careful management made certain that the names down to Doe, i.e., position 6 on 675 letters were reliable. That would have used up 675 persons out of the 100,000 and it would still leave 99,325 not yet approached However, by the time Doe reaches position 3, the total number of letters (again assuming that the chain is not broken) mailed would be 97,500 which practically exhausts the residents of Doe's town. By the time he reaches position 1 the number of letters circulated would have reached 2,441,250, provided that the chain had not been broken. This would mean that if the letters were circulated internally in Doe's town with only a few going out of town, each person would on the average have been contacted about 20 times. Most people would have tired of the game long before that— they might have mailed a dime or two, but certainly not 10 or 20 without receiving any returns. So, while poor Doe was on the original list, it is still unlikely that he would have derived any benefits.

What have we learned? First that anything that can be transferred from one person to five or six, after 8 iterations can, in principle, if the motivation exists, encompass an enormous population quickly. On the other hand, if the motivation factor, i.e., the multiplication factor, is small, the process soon burns itself out. Controlled nuclear fission is a good example of an exponentiation process which is sensitive to a multiplication factor. If the factor is too large, one has a nuclear explosion; if it is just right, one has a controlled reactor; if it is too small, nothing happens. One of the first investigations of this type of exponentiation process was made by Galton who wondered why many of the famous old English family names seemed to have disappeared by the late 1800's. Here is a case in which the multiplication factor was too small, going from one generation to another.

We now examine the possibility of applying the mathematical mechanism discussed above to the treatment of social problems whose solution requires a rapid training program.

As an example, suppose that we were asked to make recommendations on how one might develop a population control program in India. We will

D

assume the program involves the production and effective utilization of some kind of birth control device. Let us first list some of the difficulties involved in attempting to solve this most intractable problem. First of all, numerous people would have to be given the medical knowledge necessary to implement the program. The production and distribution of millions of small objects poses major problems. The great variations in local customs and dozens of different dialects create communication and acceptance barriers to any large scale program. People are naturally suspicious of anyone trying to sell something, especially a new idea, if he is not "one of them". Most important of all, the average Indian must *want* change, in this case population control, if the

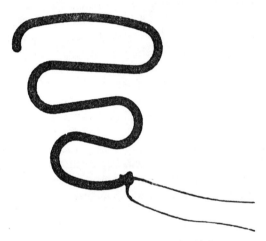

Figure 32   Schematic of an IUD.

program is to be successful. At the family and village level, the arguments for birth control center on a better life for those already alive. Given fixed household income, fewer family members means more food per mouth. However, Indian parents have a number of counterarguments. In Indian society, children have traditionally taken care of their parents in their old age. As there is no such thing as social security in India, and the life expectancy of any new-born child is very low, parents bet their lives in their later years on the reproduction lottery which determines their family size. They want to be assured that someone will be around to take care of them in their old age. Any large scale program of birth control must therefore stress a higher standard of living and include a social security program if it is to be successful. Furthermore, the practice of child marriage would have to be prohibited.

Assuming we are able to make progress at this most fundamental motivational level, let us then examine the more technical aspects of the problem as contained in the other four points listed above. Let us assume that our program will use an IUD, an interuterinary device. The best known of these is the Lippes Loop (see Figure 32).

The cost of producing an IUD is now below 1¢ if the appropriate mass production techniques are employed. Where in India could one find the plant and personnel to make millions of small identical objects per year? The mint is certainly a possibility. They can just as easily stamp out small plastic objects as metallic ones. Distribution of these loops might be performed by the Post Office although it is true the Indian postal system is a bit slow. However, a letter or small parcel can be sent from any part of India to any other in less than a month and this rate of service should suffice for distributing IUD's.

Our largest remaining problem is the training of sufficient personnel to implement the program. Usually IUD's are inserted by nurses but they really have a great deal more training than is necessary to insert a loop. Only a fairly short period of time should be required to train someone in the specific techniques of inserting the loop. In fact, we would claim that anyone of reasonable intelligence can be trained to do a clearly specified manual job in two weeks or less. India now has large numbers of girls that have received high school educations and as such have become a little too well educated for their villages. In fact, they presently present a problem because no one really knows how to make full use of their potential. Many of these girls might be trained to insert loops. One would start with a class of perhaps twenty in some city such as Madras, which already has many medically trained people. Ten of the graduates of the first class would become practitioners and ten would become teachers. There would be a sufficient number of nurses and physicians available at this stage to check up on the quality of instruction given by the new instructors. Furthermore, it is proposed that these new graduates teach in groups of two so that each new teacher would have someone against whom he could check himself. Each group of two new instructors would teach a new class of twenty which would, in turn, divide itself into ten practitioners and five groups of two teachers each upon graduation. This process could then be carried forth until such time as there were sufficient practitioners to carry out the proposed program. The first two stages of the process are represented diagrammatically in Figure 33.

Now suppose each practitioner can insert ten loops per day. The ten practitioners from the first stage have the capacity to insert $10(10) = 100$ loops per day. At the second stage there are 50 more practitoners who can then perform $50(10) = 500$ more insertions per day. At the next stage we find

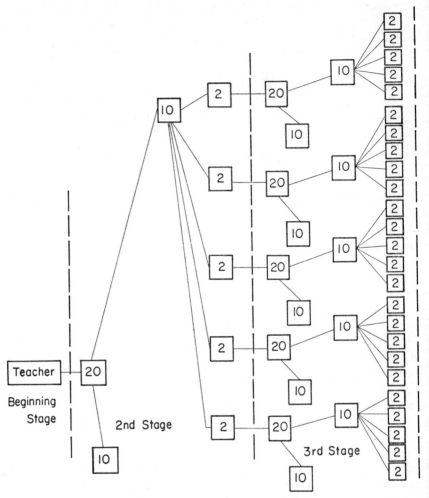

Figure 33   Teaching by exponentiation.

there are 250 additional practitioners and, in general, each stage gives us a factor of 5 *more* practitioners. For example, the seventh stage trains the personnel to insert 1,562,500 additional loops per day. An immediate question arises—can the techniques be transmitted without distortion through seven generations of teachers? We would like to think that the technique is simple enough and can be standardized sufficiently so that "quality control" will be maintained.

This still leaves the problem of differing dialects and customs. We propose that people from a given region be used to teach those in surrounding regions where the languages and customs differ minimally from their own. Knowledge of the techniques of loop insertion would diffuse outward from Madras much as a drop of ink diffuses outward when placed in a bottle of water.

Midwives now assist at almost all births in India. They would be ideally suited for the task for which our training program would be developed. However, a conflict of interest might develop. As our program would develop, so would a considerable intimidation factor which might encourage midwives to join the program as students. Vested interests will always resist social change and a positive approach to them may prove crucial in minimizing transitional strife.

We recently had the opportunity to discuss the above ideas with the Indian pediatrician Dr. C. Prakash. He showed considerable interest in the exponentiation mechanism and agreed that the training period was not unreasonable. However, he felt that the IUD is probably not the solution of India's population problem for two reasons which never would have occurred to us.

First, the sanitary napkin is essentially unknown in the Indian village and too expensive for most in the teeming cities. The oldest rags are used during menstrual periods, and vaginal infections are common. They become even more common and sometimes very serious when an IUD is worn. Second, the resting position of women in rural India is a squatting one, a posture which frequently causes the expulsion of an IUD. While a government subsidy and an appropriate educational program might popularize the sanitary napkin (whose price for a box of 24 in India is ∼ 3 rupees while the daily salary of an unskilled worker is ∼ 3 rupees at 1 rupee = 20¢ U.S.), we have no positive ideas on how to stop village women from squatting. Incidentally, parliamentary debates on whether or not the sanitary napkin should be subsidized would, no doubt, lead to interesting newspaper stories.

After explaining these difficulties, Dr. Prakash went on to state that our proposed educational program seemed at first glance to be excellent for other public health measures such as water purification, sterilization techniques, treatment of certain common diseases, etc., and that upon returning to India he would present it to various government officials.

At first we were happy with this response to our proposal; as we thought further we wondered whether we had performed a service or a disservice. Suppose that some interest is shown in the scheme and that new public health measures are developed. Then life expectancy would increase which would be fine but, if population control measures would not be dealt with effectively, our original proposals would have had just the opposite effect from that which was intended. These points indicate the delicate coupling of social improvement program and the importance of instituting them in the correct order.

The concept of each one teaching ten is more neglected than it is original with us. An important and interesting example can be found in Sir John Fielding's description of life in London. Among other things he notes that poor, foreign-looking Jews were very unpopular in London (as were many others of foreign extraction whose appearance might be somewhat bizarre); Jew-baiting became a sport . . .

I have seen many Jews hooted, hunted, cuffed, pulled by the beard, spit upon . . . without any protection from passers-by or by the police . . . One circumstance among others put an end to the ill-usage of the Jews.—About the year 1787, Daniel Mendoza, a Jew, became a celebrated boxer and set up a school to teach the art of boxing as a science. The art spread among the young Jews and they became generally expert at it. The consequence was, in a very few years, seen and felt, too. It was no longer safe to insult a Jew unless he was an old man and alone. . . . Moreover, Jewish proficiency in the ring gained the sympathies of the mob and much of their unpopularity disappeared.[1]

In conclusion we also wish to emphasize a need for examining educational programs for developing countries or for groups of people who are seeking new professional horizons. Traditional programs involve long periods in school during which the emphasis is on theory and basic principles. Those being educated are separated from the points at which the action is needed and, frequently, after graduation, the real work to be done is considered beneath the dignity and interest of the graduate. When area development is of great urgency, our exponentiation scheme should be given some consideration for employment in such a manner that in a period of two years, each student has learned, applied and taught three or four crucial skills. The more adaptable and skillful students might then be given two or three years of concentrated and systematic education. After their two years of practical experience, they should be better motivated toward goals which are creative for development rather than becoming candidates for a class of dissatisfied and unemployable intellectuals.

The appearance of the exponentiation process in the spreading of news and rumors has been discussed in Reference 2.

REFERENCES

1. M. Dorothy George, *London Life in the Eighteenth Century* (Reprint Edition, Capricorn Books, New York, 1965).
2. D. J. Bartholomew, *Stochastic Models for Social Processes*, Chapter 7 (New York, 1967).

CHAPTER III

Probability Distributions and their Underlying Mechanisms

1 Gaussian and Poisson Distributions

FEW OF THE attributes by which one would characterize an individual or, for that matter, any part of our society, are exactly the same for all persons or units. Sometimes the number or fraction of individuals with a given level of the characteristic (e.g., height, weight, or head circumference), seems to be beyond our control, while the magnitude of other variables (e.g., the number and size of industrial enterprises, political party affiliation by districts, or the distribution of personal incomes) seem to evolve in a manner which is related to the way our society functions. Our interest in the frequencies of various maxima and minima in the daily temperatures during the cold months (see Figure 36) is mainly adaptive. Possessing this kind of information we can, for example, more efficiently plan fuel oil deliveries. The expected number of people having IQ's in various ranges seems to depend partly on genetic factors and partly on environmental factors. An example of IQ data is given in Figure 34. On the other hand, the extent and apportionment of social security benefits is strictly a function of how we choose to govern ourselves.

Data on the heights of adult males is given in Figure 35. Unexpected changes in this type of distribution can be an embarrassment or even lead to a serious national problem. The average height of Japanese children of high school age increased by the order of 4 or 5 inches during the period 1945 to 1965. Desks which were purchased during the period of rapid expansion of the high schools in the 1950's were still in good condition in the 1960's, but were much too small for the students. This situation became critical at a time when various modernization and enrichment programs were being considered. Hard decisions had to be made as to whether limited funds were to be used to improve the mind or one's physical comfort.

Bell-shaped curves such as those in Figures 34–36 are commonly associated with characteristics of people, weather, machine-made objects, and even the distribution of velocities of molecules in gases. An important mathematical

91

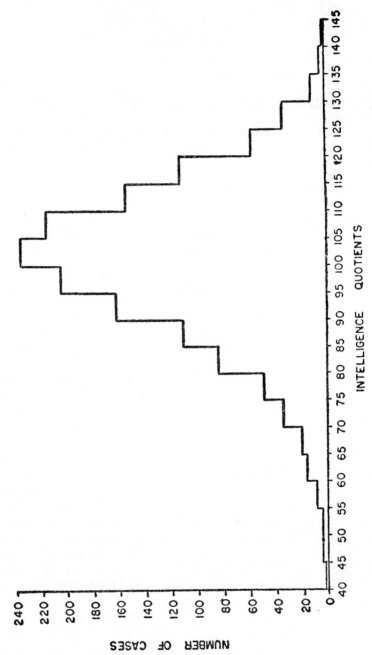

Figure 34 Distribution of Wechsler adult intelligence scale intelligence quotients. Ages 16–75 and over (2052 cases).[9]

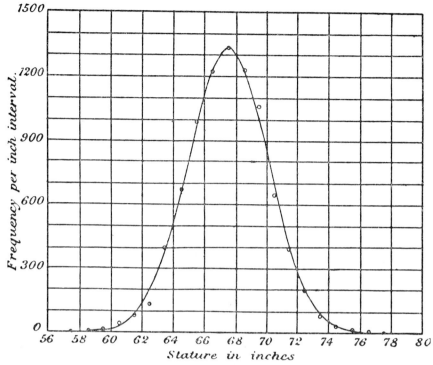

Figure 35 The distribution of stature for adult males in the British Isles.[10]

function whose graph is also bell shaped is the Gaussian or normal distribution function which is defined by the equation

$$g(x) = [(2\pi)^{-\frac{1}{2}}/\sigma] \exp [-(x-\bar{x})^2/2\sigma^2] \qquad (1)$$

The significance of the parameters σ and $\bar{x}$ will be discussed below.

The function $g(x)$ is "normalized" so that its integral from $-\infty$ to ∞ is unity:

$$\int_{-\infty}^{\infty} g(x)\, dx = [(2\pi)^{-\frac{1}{2}}/\sigma] \int_{-\infty}^{\infty} \exp [-(x-\bar{x})^2/2\sigma^2]\, dx$$

$$= \pi^{-\frac{1}{2}} \int_{-\infty}^{\infty} \exp (-y^2)\, dy = 1 \qquad (2)$$

Mathematicians and statisticians call a function $f(x)$ a probability density function of a random variable X if the probability that X lies between x and $x+dx$ is $f(x)\, dx$. Physicists generally call $f(x)$ a distribution function. The physicists *cumulative distribution* function

$$F(x) = \text{Prob}\,(X < x) = \int_{-\infty}^{x} f(x)\, dx \qquad (3)$$

is called the distribution function of X by mathematicians and statisticians.

D*

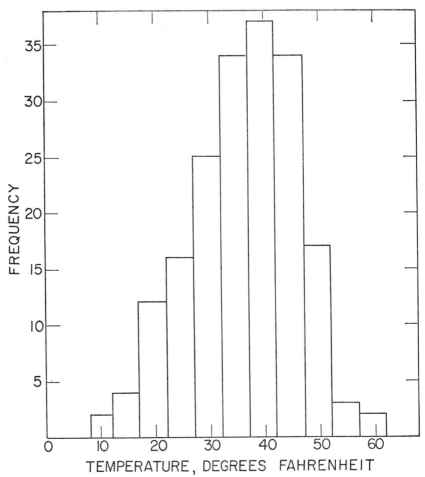

Figure 36   The distribution of daily maximum temperatures in New York City during the month of January for the period 1919–1923.

From force of habit, we adopt the physicists language. Notice that

$$dF(x)/dx = f(x) \tag{4}$$

Various averages over the distribution function $f(x)$ are important. We use the notation

$$\langle u(x) \rangle = \int_{-\infty}^{\infty} u(x)f(x)\, dx \tag{5}$$

for the average value of a function $u(x)$ of x when the probability distribution function of the variable X is $f(x)$. Averages of powers of x are called moments of the distribution function $f(x)$ so that the nth moment is

$$\langle x^n \rangle = \int_{-\infty}^{\infty} x^n f(x)\, dx = \mu_n \tag{6}$$

The average value of the variable x itself is the first moment

$$\bar{x} \equiv \int_{-\infty}^{\infty} x f(x)\, dx \tag{7}$$

The *standard deviation* is defined by

$$\sigma^2 = \int_{-\infty}^{\infty} (x - \bar{x})^2 f(x)\, dx \tag{8}$$

We now show that the parameters $\bar{x}$ and σ which appeared in the definition of the Gaussian distribution are indeed the same quantities that are defined in (7) and (8). From (1) we see that

$$\int_{-\infty}^{\infty} x g(x)\, dx = \int_{-\infty}^{\infty} (x - \bar{x}) g(x)\, dx + \bar{x} \int_{-\infty}^{\infty} g(x)\, dx \tag{9}$$

However, since $g(x)$ is an even function of $(x - \bar{x})$, the first integral on the right hand side of this equation vanishes. From (2) the second integral is just $\bar{x}$. Hence $\bar{x}$ satisfies the definition (7) of a first moment. Now note that

$$\int_{-\infty}^{\infty} (x - \bar{x})^2 g(x)\, dx$$
$$= -[(2\pi)^{-\frac{1}{2}}/\sigma][d/d(1/2\sigma^2)] \int_{-\infty}^{\infty} \exp\{-(x - \bar{x})^2/2\sigma^2\}\, dx \tag{10}$$

However, from (2) the integral to the right is $\sigma(2\pi)^{\frac{1}{2}}$ so that

$$[d/d(1/2\sigma^2)]\sigma = -\sigma^3(d/d\sigma)\sigma = -\sigma^3 \tag{11}$$

and, as required,

$$\int_{-\infty}^{\infty} (x - \bar{x})^2 g(x)\, dx = \sigma^2. \tag{12}$$

The normal or Gaussian distribution is plotted in Figure 37.

Let us now consider a sequence of similar events and their starting time so that t_1, t_2, t_3, ... represent respectively the starting time of the first, second, etc., events. An example of such a sequence is the list of precise times during the day when one receives a telephone call; another is the sequence of times when a room reaches a certain prescribed temperature so that the thermostat turns on an automatic heater. A third example of a more political nature is the sequence of times when a war somewhere in the world begins. In any of these cases, one can count the number of starting times which have occurred in a very long time, T, that is much greater than any of the intervals between starting times, $\Delta_j = t_j - t_{j-1}$. Suppose that this average number of starting times is λ per unit time so that in a time interval t the expected number of starting times is λt.

Now suppose that the events considered occur in a random manner, independently of each other, so that the probability of an event starting in any

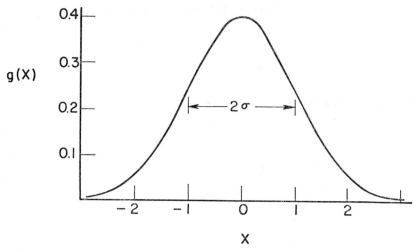

Figure 37 Gaussian or normal distribution function.

time interval is proportional to the duration of the interval. On this basis we can find the probability distribution function $w(t)$ of the intervals Δ between the starting time of events. If an event occurred at time $t = 0$, the probability that another occurs within the interval $(0, t)$ is

$$\int_0^t w(t)\, dt$$

so the probability that none has occurred in this interval is

$$\{1 - \int_0^t w(t)\, dt\}$$

Then the probability that the duration of the interval Δ between the start of two events is between t and $(t+dt)$ is

$$w(t)\, dt = \{\text{probability that no event started in interval } (0, t)\} \times$$
$$\{\text{probability that event occurs in time interval } (t,\ t+dt)\}$$

$$= \{1 - \int_0^t w(t)\, dt\}\lambda\, dt \tag{13}$$

where λ is the average number of starts of events per unit time. If we cancel out the dt's on both sides of this equation and differentiate with respect to time, we find

$$dw/dt = -\lambda w \tag{14}$$

so that

$$w(t) = Ce^{-\lambda t} \tag{15a}$$

where the constant of integration C is to be determined from the fact that

$w(t)$ must be normalized to unity,

$$1 = \int_0^\infty w(t)\, dt = C\int_0^\infty e^{-\lambda t}\, dt = C/\lambda. \tag{15b}$$

Hence $w(t)$ is the exponential distribution

$$w(t) = \lambda e^{-\lambda t} \tag{16}$$

These results lead naturally to another important distribution function, the Poisson distribution, which arises in response to the following question. Given a long time interval T and divide it into n smaller intervals $t = T/n$. What is the probability that $0, 1, 2, 3, 4, ...$ events start in a time interval t? We shall show that

$$\text{prob}\,(N_t = r) = [(\lambda t)^r/r!]\exp(-\lambda t), \tag{17}$$

which is called the Poisson distribution.

The scheme of the calculation will be clear by considering successively the cases $r = 0$, and 1, and then proceeding to general positive integer r. If $r = 0$, the probability that no event has started in the interval t is (see eq. (13)),

$$\text{prob}\,(N_t = 0) = 1 - \lambda\int_0^t e^{-\lambda t}\, dt = \exp(-\lambda t) \tag{18}$$

If there is to be exactly one event starting in time t, it must start at some time τ which has equal probability of being any time in the interval $(0, t)$. Hence

$$\text{prob}\,(N_t = 1) = \int_0^t \lambda e^{-\lambda \tau}\, \text{prob}\,\{N_{t-\tau} = 0\}\, d\tau \tag{19a}$$

since no new event can start in the interval (τ, t). Then, from (18),

$$\text{prob}\,(N_t = 1) = \int_0^t \lambda e^{-\lambda t}\, d\tau = (\lambda t)e^{-\lambda t} \tag{19b}$$

Generally, if r events are to start in the interval $(0, t)$, the first must occur sometime τ in that interval and exactly $(r-1)$ must occur in the remaining time $(t-\tau)$. Hence,

$$\text{prob}\,(N_t = r) = \int_0^t \lambda e^{-\lambda \tau}\, \text{prob}\,(N_{t-\tau} = r-1)\, d\tau \tag{20}$$

This recurrence formula can be used to derive (17) by induction. We see from (18) and (19a) that (17) is correct when $r = 0, 1$. Now assume that it is correct for $(r-1)$. Then it can be substituted into (20) to yield

$$\text{prob}\,(N_t = r) = \lambda^r e^{-\lambda t}\int_0^t (t-\tau)^{r-1}\,d\tau/(r-1)! = \{(\lambda t)^r/r!\}\exp(-\lambda t)$$

as required.

There are many known situations to which the Poisson distribution applies. We introduce two here as examples, the first being related to automobile traffic, and the second to frequency of the occurrence of wars.

When the traffic density on a multilane highway is so low that passing occurs with no difficulty and no platoons of cars develop, the Poisson distribution gives excellent agreement with the observed frequency with which r cars pass a preassigned point on a road in a fixed time interval.[2,3] Observations were made on a single lane of a six-lane divided highway facility, counting the frequency with which 1, 2, 3, ... cars passed a marker during 30-second intervals. The exponential gap distribution was verified and the parameter λ found to have the value 4.93. Table VI, below, summarizes the data.[3] The agreement is very good, especially in the region in which the

TABLE VI Poisson distribution of number of automobiles passing a marker on a highway in 30-second intervals.[3]

N_{30}	Measured Frequency	Measured Probability	Poisson Probability	Poisson Frequency
0	1	0.0061	0.0072	1.2
1	7	0.0424	0.0356	5.9
2	14	0.0848	0.0878	14.5
3	25	0.1515	0.1443	23.8
4	31	0.1879	0.1779	29.3
5	26	0.1576	0.1754	28.9
6	27	0.1636	0.1441	23.8
7	14	0.0849	0.1015	16.7
8	8	0.0485	0.0625	10.3
9	3	0.0182	0.0343	5.7
10	4	0.0242	0.0169	2.8
11	3	0.0182	0.0076	1.2
12	1	0.0061	0.0031	0.5
13	0	0.0	0.0012	0.2
14	1	0.0061	0.0004	0.1
> 15	0	0.0	0.0001	0.0

measured frequency is high, the most important region. As the traffic density increases, one eventually reaches a regime in which the cars are very close to each other so that they are no longer mutually independent. Then the number of cars passing a marker forms a very narrow Gaussian distribution about some mean value which is determined by the speed and density.

An excellent agreement between observations and the Poisson distribution was also noticed by Richardson in his studies of the frequency of wars. We think of wars as being the result of irreconcilable conflicts between nations or various factions within nations. At first glance it would seem that to determine the number of wars starting in a given time interval, one would have to examine the political situation as it develops in that period. However, we shall see from the statistics presented below that if we do not ask about where wars occur but merely count them, the starting and stopping of wars has important random features. If, for example, there was some office in the United Nations which had to deal with and attempt peace negotiations for any war which started, the statistics given below would help the office decide on the kind of staff it would need.

Quincy Wright[4] published a collection of "Wars of Modern Civilization Extending from 1482 to 1940" and recorded almost three hundred of them, listing their dates of declaration and peace settlement. Wright's selection was "intended to include all hostilities involving members of the family of nations, whether international, civil, colonial, or imperial, which were recognized as states of war in the legal sense or which involved over 50,000 troops. Some other incidents are included in which hostilities of considerable but lesser magnitude, not recognized at the time as legal states of war, led to important legal results such as the creation or extinction of states, territorial transfers, or changes of government".

L. F. Richardson[5] prepared another type of list of "deadly quarrels", paying no attention to their legality or results. Riots, insurrections, and undeclared wars would qualify to this characterization, as well as major wars. These were classified by "magnitude" in the same manner that astronomers classify the brightness of a star through the logarithm of the ratio of its intensity to that of a standard star. A jth magnitude conflict would lead to the death of 10^j persons and the magnitude of a quarrel which involved N casualties is $\log_{10}N$. The magnitude 3.5 corresponds to between 3162 snd 3163 deaths, and magnitude 4.5 between 31,622 and 31,623 deaths.

The Poisson distribution became apparent to Richardson through the listing (from Q. Wright's data) of the number of wars which began in each year from 1500 to 1931, inclusive. Then he counted the number of years in which no war began, one war began, etc. The data is recorded below. The value of λ, the mean number of outbreaks per year is $\lambda = 0.692$/year.

Number x, of outbreaks/year	0	1	2	3	4	>4	Total
Frequency y of years with outbreak x	223	142	48	15	4	0	432
Frequency from Poisson distribution	216	149.7	51.8	12.0	2.1	.3	432.1

Similar results were obtained from the Richardson data on the beginnings and the ends of deadly quarrels in the magnitude range 3.5 to 4.5 for the period 1820–1929

x outbreaks in a year	0	1	2	3	4	>4	Total
y for war	65	35	6	4	0	0	110
Poisson	64.3	34.5	9.3	1.7	0.2	0.0	110.0
y for peace	63	35	11	1	0	0	110
Poisson	63.8	34.8	9.5	1.7	0.2	0.0	110.0

When the interval 1500–1931 is divided into two equal parts, it was observed that 143 wars started in the first half and 156 in the second. Upon further subdivision into eight consecutive units of 54 years each, the extremes were 54 outbreaks in the interval 1824–1877 and 16 from 1716–1769.

Richardson also noticed that in characterizing and counting deadly conflicts, the larger, the fewer. Thus the number in various magnitude ranges in the period 1820–1929 are

magnitude range	$7 \pm \frac{1}{2}$	$6 \pm \frac{1}{2}$	$5 \pm \frac{1}{2}$	$4 \pm \frac{1}{2}$
number	1	3	16	62

In the limiting case of murder, the one-person deadly conflict estimate is 5×10^6 in the above period. To give an idea of some extreme situations, the murder rate per million of population per year in Chile in 1932 was 610, while in Denmark in the period 1911–20 it was 0.3 per year per million.

W. J. Horvath has examined labor strikes in the same manner that Richardson considered the duration of wars. Table VII contains data on strikes which can be fitted very well to a Poisson distribution. The cumulative duration of strikes and wars as plotted by Horvath as shown in Figure 38. The resemblance is very striking.

We showed that the exponential distribution function is the appropriate distribution for time intervals between successive starts of random events. Corresponding distribution functions exist for nearest neighbor random points on a line, a plane or in three dimensional space. Consider a plane which has been dotted with random points of density n per unit area. Every point has a nearest neighbor point. We shall be concerned with the determination of the probability that if one starts with a given point, its nearest neighbor point lies at a distance between r and $r+dr$ from it.

This question can be discussed in 1, 2, and 3 dimensions simultaneously. Generally we let n be the number of points per unit length, area, or volume, depending on the number of dimensions. We let dA_j be the infinitesimal region which represents the volume element associated with the region whose distance is between r and $r+dr$ from a chosen random point. Thus

$$dA_1 = 2dr; \quad dA_2 = 2\pi r \, dr; \quad dA_3 = 4\pi r^2 \, dr \tag{21}$$

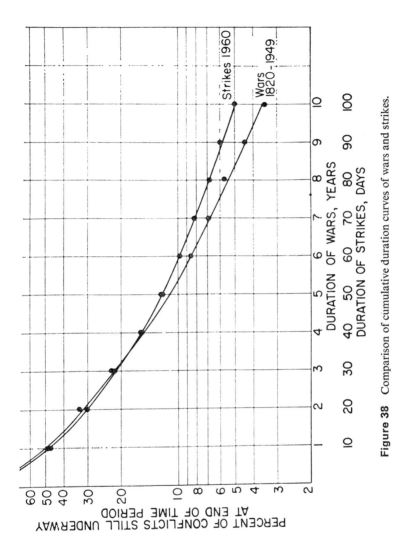

Figure 38 Comparison of cumulative duration curves of wars and strikes.

TABLE VII Duration of strikes settled in calendar year 1961*

Time, x Days	Number Lasting Exactly x Days	Time, x Days	Number Lasting Exactly x Days	Time, x Days	Number Lasting Exactly x Days	Time, x Days	Number Lasting Exactly x Days
1	388	44	15	87	4	130	2
2	317	45	14	88	3	131	0
3	241	46	10	89	2	132	2
4	159	47	14	90	5	133	5
5	175	48	14	91	10	134	3
6	117	49	14	92	5	135	1
7	130	50	9	93	2	136	3
8	112	51	14	94	2	137	4
9	78	52	12	95	3	138	1
10	72	53	6	96	2	139	1
11	56	54	10	97	4	140	2
12	63	55	12	98	5	141	1
13	76	56	10	99	4	142	1
14	55	57	11	100	2	143	0
15	72	58	5	101	5	144	0
16	55	59	5	102	3	145	2
17	57	60	3	103	1	146	0
18	32	61	7	104	2	147	1
19	32	62	9	105	2	148	1
20	34	63	6	106	3	149	1
21	38	64	8	107	3	150	0
22	34	65	8	108	0		
23	27	66	6	109	3		Strikes
24	27	67	4	110	2	Interval	Settled
25	26	68	8	111	1	Days	in
26	18	69	5	112	2		Interval
27	28	70	11	113	2		
28	24	71	8	114	2	151–160	6
29	22	72	7	115	5	161–170	7
30	20	73	3	116	2	171–180	2
31	19	74	2	117	2	181–190	6
32	15	75	4	118	2	191–200	7
33	31	76	3	119	1	201–220	8
34	21	77	1	120	2	221–240	5
35	15	78	3	121	1	241–260	3
36	23	79	3	122	1	261–280	3
37	13	80	3	123	0	281–300	1
38	13	81	5	124	1	301–400	7
39	12	82	6	125	2	401–500	2
40	20	83	5	126	0	501–600	2
41	14	84	4	127	1		—
42	13	85	5	128	2		3317
43	11	86	2	129	2		

*U.S. Bureau of Labor Statistics.

and

$$dA_j = \alpha_j \, dr^j \quad \text{with} \quad \alpha_1 = 2; \alpha_2 = \pi, \quad \text{and,} \quad \alpha_3 = \frac{4}{3}\pi \qquad (22)$$

Notice that in the 1-D case, the factor two appears because a nearest neighbor can be to the left or right of the point of interest. The probability of finding a point in the infinitesimal region dA_j is ndA_j. Hence, if $\rho_j(r)$ is the j dimensional nearest neighbor distribution function, the probability that the nearest neighbor to a given point lies between r and $r+dr$ is

$\rho_j(r)dr = $ (probability that no point is nearer than r) $\times$

(probability one point is between r and $r+dr$)

$$= \{1 - \int_0^r \rho_j(r) \, dr\} n \, dA_j \qquad (23)$$

If we divide by dA_j and take the derivative with respect to r, we find

$$\frac{d}{dr} \{\rho_j/r^{j-1}\} = -jn\alpha_j\rho_j \qquad (24)$$

or

$$d\log{(\rho_j/r^{j-1})}/dr = -jn\alpha_j r^{j-1}$$
$$\rho_j/r^{j-1} = c_j \exp{(-n\alpha_j r^j)} \qquad (25)$$

where the integration constant c_j is to be determined so that $\rho_j(r)$ is normalized with

$$1 = \int_0^\infty \rho_j(r) \, dr = c_j/jn\alpha_j$$

so that with the α_j defined by (22),

$$\rho_j(r) = jn\alpha_j r^{j-1} \exp{(-n\alpha_j r^j)} \qquad (26)$$

This formula was first derived by Paul Hertz.[7,8]

This distribution function is useful in estimating critical concentrations when two random points being too close to each other leads to a crisis condition. As an example, consider a number of boats in a lake when a fog suddenly developes. Let A be the effective area of a boat and suppose that when centers of two boats are within a distance $2\sqrt{A}$ from each other, they collide. If one decides that when the probability of a collision is 1/100, then the boat concentration is too high, the critical density, n, can be determined when ρ_2 in (26) is set equal to 1/100 and r is set equal to $2\sqrt{A}$. A rough order of magnitude of dangerous aircraft densities might also be determined by setting $\rho_3 = 10^{-6}$ in (26) and choosing r to be a distance such that if two pilots do not notice each other until that distance is reached, it is slightly too late to be certain that they will avoid each other. Since aircraft are not random points, the result of this calculation would not be too accurate, but it would give an indication as to whether or not the situation at a given time warrants a more detailed and accurate investigation.

REFERENCES

1. E. B. Mode, *The Elements of Statistics*, (Prentice Hall, 1947).
2. W. F. Adams, *J. Inst. Civ. Eng.*, **4**: 121(1936).
3. R. Rothery, Car Following—A Deterministic Model for Single Lane Traffic, Ph.D. Thesis, Brussels (1968).
4. Q. Wright, *A Study of War*, (Chicago, 1942).
5. L. F. Richardson, Statistics of Deadly Quarrels, (Reprinted in Vol. II, *World of Mathematics*, by James Newman, p. 1254).
6. W. J. Horvath, *Behavioral Science* **13**: 18(1968).
7. P. Hertz, *Math. Ann.*, **67**: 387(1909).
8. S. Chadrasekhar, *Rev. Mod. Phys.*, **15**: 1(1943).
9. D. Wechsler, *The Measurement and Appraisal of Adult Intelligence*, 4th Ed., p. 107 (Williams and Wilkins Co., Baltimore, 1958).
10. Yule and Kendall, *Introduction to the Theory of Statistics*, (14th Ed., 1950) Chas. Griffin and Co., London.

2 Characteristic Functions and The Central Limit Theorem

A construct which has proven to be useful in deriving theorems about distribution functions is the characteristic function $\phi(\alpha)$, which, for a distribution function $f(x)$ (see eq. (1.3)) is defined to be

$$\phi(\alpha) \equiv \langle e^{i\alpha x} \rangle \equiv \int_{-\infty}^{\infty} e^{i\alpha x} f(x)\, dx \tag{1}$$

This Fourier transform can be inverted to yield the distribution function in terms of the characteristic function

$$g(x) = \frac{1}{2\pi} \int_{-\infty}^{\infty} e^{-i\alpha x} f(\alpha)\, d\alpha \tag{2}$$

As an example, the characteristic function of a Gaussian distribution is (if we let $y = (x - \bar{x})/\sigma 2^{\frac{1}{2}}$)

$$\phi(\alpha) = \frac{1}{\sigma\sqrt{2\pi}} \int_{-\infty}^{\infty} e^{-i\alpha x} \exp\{-(x-\bar{x})^2/2\sigma^2\} dx$$

$$= \pi^{-\frac{1}{2}} \exp(-i\alpha\bar{x}) \int_{-\infty}^{\infty} \exp\{-y^2 - i\alpha\sigma y 2^{\frac{1}{2}}\}\, dy$$

$$= \exp\{-i\alpha\bar{x} - \tfrac{1}{2}\alpha^2\sigma^2\} \tag{3}$$

An important feature of a Gaussian distribution is that if it is very broad, its characteristic function is very narrow and vice versa (i.e., if $\sigma \to 0$, $\phi(\alpha)$ becomes broad).

In the limit as a Gaussian distribution becomes narrower and narrower, (i.e., $\sigma \to 0$), one has a very sharp distribution called a *delta function* $\delta(x - \bar{x})$. The most important characteristics of this function are[2]

$$\delta(x - \bar{x}) = 0 \quad \text{if} \quad x \neq \bar{x} \tag{4a}$$

$$\int_{-\infty}^{\infty} \delta(x - \bar{x})\,dx = \int_{\bar{x}-\varepsilon}^{\bar{x}+\varepsilon} \delta(x - \bar{x})\,dx = 1 \quad \text{if} \quad \varepsilon > 0 \tag{4b}$$

and for a wide class of functions $u(x)$

$$\int_{-\infty}^{\infty} u(x)\delta(x - \bar{x})\,dx = u(\bar{x}) \tag{4c}$$

A useful explicit formula for a delta function is its Fourier representation. The general Fourier integral inversion formula states that for a wide class of functions $u(x)$, if

$$w(\alpha) = \frac{1}{\sqrt{2\pi}} \int_{-\infty}^{\infty} u(x)e^{i\alpha x}\,dx \tag{5a}$$

then

$$u(x) = \frac{1}{\sqrt{2\pi}} \int_{-\infty}^{\infty} w(\alpha)e^{-i\alpha x}\,dx. \tag{5b}$$

If we introduce $\delta(x)$ into (5a) as $u(x)$, then

$$w(\alpha) = \frac{1}{\sqrt{2\pi}} \int_{-\infty}^{\infty} \delta(x)e^{i\alpha x}\,dx = 1/(2\pi)^{\frac{1}{2}}.$$

Then, from the inversion formula (5b),

$$\delta(x) = \frac{1}{2\pi} \int_{-\infty}^{\infty} e^{-i\alpha x}\,d\alpha \equiv \frac{1}{2\pi} \int_{-\infty}^{\infty} e^{i\alpha x}\,dx \tag{6}$$

Certain important discrete distribution functions can be expressed in terms of delta functions. One such example is the Bernoulli distribution which is that of a random variable which has two possible values, one with a probability p and the other with a probability $q = 1 - p$. A situation in which this distribution arises is the random walk problem. Let us suppose that the steps taken by a random walker can be identified by intervals on a line. If the walker is originally at the origin and he has a probability p of taking a step of one unit to the right and $q = 1 - p$ of taking a step to the left, the probability distribution function $f(x)$ (see eq. (3)) for his taking a step of length between x and $x + dx$ is

$$f(x) = p\delta(x - 1) + (1 - p)\delta(x + 1) \tag{7}$$

Clearly, from (4b) this function is normalized to unity as required. The average step distance and standard deviation are obtained from (1.7), (1.8), and (7):

$$\bar{x} = \int_{-\infty}^{\infty} \{xp\delta(x-1)+x(1-p)\delta(x+1)\}dx = p-(1-p) = 2p-1 \qquad (8a)$$

$$\sigma^2 = \int_{-\infty}^{\infty} (x-\bar{x})^2 f(x)\, dx = \int_{-\infty}^{\infty} (x^2-\bar{x}^2)f(x)\, dx = 1-\bar{x}^2$$

$$= 1-(2p-1)^2 = 4p(1-p) \qquad (8b)$$

since $x^2 = 1$ if $x = \pm 1$. The characteristic function of the Bernouilli distribution is

$$\phi(\alpha) = p \exp i\alpha + (1-p) \exp -i\alpha \qquad (8c)$$

One frequently encounters situations in which several random variables achieve certain values simultaneously. In the case of two variables, X_1 and X_2, we define $f(x_1, x_2)$ to be the joint distribution function of X_1 and X_2 if the joint probability that X_1 lies between x_1 and (x_1+dx_1) and X_2 lies between x_2 and (x_2+dx_2) is

$$f(x_1, x_2)\, dx_1\, dx_2$$

The variables X_1 and X_2 are said to be independent of each other if each achieves a specific value with no influence from the other; i.e.,

$$f(x_1, x_2) = f_1(x_1)f_2(x_2)$$

where $f_j(x)$ is the distribution function of the jth variable. Generally, the joint distribution function of n random *independent* variables is

$$f(x_1, x_2, \ldots x_n) = f_1(x_1)f_2(x_2) \ldots f_n(x_n). \qquad (9)$$

A very important topic in the theory of probability is statistical properties of sums of random independent variables. Under rather broad conditions it can be shown that the probability distribution of the sum

$$S_n = X_1+X_2+ \ldots +X_n \qquad (10)$$

of n random independent variables is Gaussian as $n\to\infty$. This is called the central limit theorem. It is the basis for so many observed distributions being Gaussian.

Let us suppose that the distribution function of X_j is $f_j(x)$. Then its characteristic function is

$$\phi(\alpha) = \langle \exp i\alpha X \rangle = \int_{-\infty}^{\infty} e^{+i\alpha x}f_j(x)\, dx \qquad (11)$$

The characteristic function of S_n is

$$\Phi_n(\alpha) = \langle \exp i\alpha[X_1 + X_2 + \ldots + X_n] \rangle$$

$$= \int_{-\infty}^{\infty} \ldots \int f(x_1, x_2, \ldots, x_n) \exp [i\alpha(x_1 + x_2 + \ldots + x_n)] dx_1 \ldots dx_n$$

$$= \int_{-\infty}^{\infty} \ldots \int \{f_1(x_1)e^{i\alpha x_1}dx_1\}\{f_2(x_2)e^{i\alpha x_2}dx_2\} \ldots \{f_n(x_n)e^{i\alpha x_n}dx_n\}$$

$$= \prod_{j=1}^{n} \phi_j(\alpha). \tag{12}$$

Then if we employ the inversion formula (5) which relates a distribution function to a characteristic function, we find that the distribution function $F_n(x)$ of S_n is

$$F_n(x) = \frac{1}{2\pi} \int_{-\infty}^{\infty} d\alpha \left\{ \prod_{j=1}^{n} \phi_j(\alpha) \right\} e^{-i\alpha x} \tag{13}$$

As a first example suppose that all $f_j(x)$ are Gaussian and that the first moment of $f_j(x)$ is $\mu_1^{(j)}$ while the standard deviation is σ_j. Then

$$\prod_{j=1}^{n} \varphi_j(\alpha) = \exp \{i\alpha n M_n - \tfrac{1}{2} n \alpha^2 \Sigma_n^2\} \tag{14a}$$

where

$$M_n = (\mu_1 + \ldots + u_n)/n \tag{14b}$$

$$\Sigma_n^2 = (\sigma_1^2 + \sigma_2^2 + \ldots + \sigma_n^2)/n \tag{14c}$$

Then, since the fourier transform of a Gaussian is still a Gaussian

$$\exp(-y^2/2p^2) = \frac{p}{\sqrt{2\pi}} \int_{-\infty}^{\infty} e^{-i\alpha y} e^{-p^2\alpha^2/2} d\alpha \tag{15}$$

eq. (13) becomes

$$f_n(x) = \left\{ \left(2\pi n \Sigma_n^2 \right)^{\frac{1}{2}} \right\}^{-1} \exp \left\{ -(x - nM_n)^2/2n \Sigma_n^2 \right\} \tag{16}$$

This shows that the distribution function of a sum of random variables, each with a Gaussian distribution, is Gaussian with the indicated mean and standard deviation given in terms of (14b) and (14c).

We now indicate how a similar result follows as $n \to \infty$ when each X_n has a distribution function all of whose moments are finite. In this case there are two equivalent forms for the characteristic function $\varphi(x)$. By expanding the exponential in (1), one finds that

$$\varphi(\alpha) = 1 + (i\alpha)\mu_1 + (i\alpha)^2\mu_2/2! + (i\alpha)^3\mu_3/3! + \ldots \tag{17}$$

μ_j being the jth moment defined by (1.b). The alternative expression is obtained by writing $\varphi(\alpha)$ in an exponential form

$$\varphi(\alpha) = \exp\{(i\alpha)\lambda_1 + (i\alpha)^2\lambda_2/2! + (i\alpha)^3\lambda_3/3! + \ldots\} \tag{18}$$

If the exponential expression is differentiated with respect to $i\alpha$ and the result is set equal to the derivative of (17) the resulting equations are

$$\varphi(\alpha)\{\lambda_1 + (i\alpha)\lambda_2 + (i\alpha)^2\lambda_3/2! + (i\alpha)^3\lambda_4/3! + \ldots\}$$
$$= \{1 + (i\alpha)\mu_1 + (i\alpha)^2\mu_2/2! + (i\alpha)^3\mu_3/3! + \ldots\}$$
$$\times \{\lambda_1 + (i\alpha)\lambda_2 + (i\alpha)^2\lambda_3/2! + (i\alpha)^3\lambda_4/3! + \ldots\}$$
$$= \mu_1 + (i\alpha)\mu_2 + (i\alpha)^2\mu_3/2! + (i\alpha)^3\mu_4/3! + \ldots$$

Then if one equates coefficients of various powers of $(i\alpha)$ of both sides of the equation he obtains

$$\mu_1 = \lambda_1 \tag{19a}$$

$$\mu_2 = \lambda_1\mu_1 + \lambda_2 \tag{19b}$$

$$\mu_3 = \lambda_1\mu_2 + 2\lambda_2\mu_1 + \lambda_3 \tag{19c}$$

$$\mu_4 = \lambda_1\mu_3 + 3\lambda_2\mu_2 + 3\lambda_3\mu_1 + \lambda_4 \quad \text{etc.} \tag{19d}$$

These recurrence formulae for λ_n can be solved to yield

$$\lambda_1 = \mu_1 \tag{20a}$$

$$\lambda_2 = \mu_2 - \lambda_1\mu_1 = \mu_2 - \mu_1^2 \equiv \sigma^2 \tag{20b}$$

$$\lambda_3 = \mu_3 - 3\mu_2\mu_1 + 2\mu_1^3 \tag{20c}$$

$$\lambda_4 = \mu_4 - 4\mu_3\mu_1 - 3\mu_2^2 + 12\mu_2\mu_1^2 - 6\mu_1^4 \quad \text{etc.} \tag{20d}$$

The λ_j's are called Thiele semi-invarients after their originator. In the case of the Gaussian distribution $\lambda_3 = \lambda_4 = \lambda_5 = \ldots = 0$.

It should be noted that moments do not exist for all distributions. The Cauchy (or to physicists the Lorentz) distribution

$$f(x) = a/[\pi(x^2 + a^2)] \quad -\infty < x < \infty \tag{21}$$

does not even have a finite second moment since

$$\mu_2 = \frac{a}{\pi}\int_{-\infty}^{\infty} \frac{x^2 dx}{x^2 + a^2} = \frac{a}{\pi}\int_{-\infty}^{\infty} \frac{[(x^2 + a^2) - a^2]dx}{x^2 + a^2}$$

$$= -a^2 + \frac{a}{\pi}\int_{-\infty}^{\infty} dx = \infty$$

We now return to the estimation of the probability distribution of the sum

S_n (eq. 10) of n random variables when n is large. Let us assume that each has finite moments and that the characteristic function of each has the form (18) where the m-th Thiele semi-invarient of the j-th variable X, is $\lambda_m^{(j)}$. Then

$$\prod_{j=1}^{n} \varphi_j(\alpha) = \exp\{i\alpha n\Lambda_1^{(n)} + (i\alpha)^2 n\Lambda_2^{(n)}/2! + (i\alpha)^3 n\Lambda_3^{(n)}/3! + \ldots\} \tag{22a}$$

where

$$n\Lambda_j^{(n)} = \lambda_j^{(1)} + \lambda_j^{(2)} + \ldots + \lambda_j^{(n)} \tag{22b}$$

We shall assume that each $\Lambda_j^{(n)}$ approaches a finite limit as $n\to\infty$. In this case, after making the transformation $\alpha n^{\frac{1}{2}} = \beta$ we find from (13) and (22) that

$$f_n(x) = \frac{1}{2\pi n^{\frac{1}{2}}} \int_{-\infty}^{\infty} \exp\{-i\beta(x - n\Lambda_1^{(n)}) - \tfrac{1}{2}\beta^2\Lambda_2^{(n)} + i\beta^3 n^{-\frac{1}{2}}\Lambda_3^{(n)} + \beta^4 n^{-1}\Lambda_4^{(n)} + \ldots\}d\beta$$

When n becomes very large we neglect those terms in the exponential which are of order $n^{-\frac{1}{2}}, n^{-1}, n^{-\frac{3}{2}}, \ldots$ and find that after application of (15)

$$f_n(x) \sim \{\Lambda_2^{(n)}\sqrt{2\pi n}\}^{-1} \exp\{-(x - n\Lambda_1^{(n)})^2/2n\Lambda_2^{(n)}\}, \tag{23}$$

which, in view of (20b) is equivalent to (16) as $n\to\infty$.

This Gaussian form for the distribution function of the sum of n random variables as $n\to\infty$ is known as the Central Limit Theorem of the theory of probability. It was first mentioned by De Moivre and appears in Laplace's famous book on The Theory of Probability which was published in 1812. Our condition that all moments be finite for the distribution function of each X_j in (2.10) is stronger than is needed to make a rigorous proof of (23). For example it is sufficient that the $(2 + \delta)$ moment with $\delta > 0$ be finite for each X_j. The necessary and sufficient condition for the validity of (23) was first determined by the mathematician Y. W. Lindberg. An important branch of the theory of probability is concerned with this theorem.

The name Gauss is associated with the distribution (1.1) because of a paper which he published in 1809. This paper was thought by many to contain the first application of that function in the context of probability. It was actually discussed independently of de Moivre by the American primitive, Robert Adrain, in the first issue (1808, before publication of the work of Gauss and Laplace), of a long defunct journal "The Analyst or Mathematical Museum", published in Philadelphia. He was apparently motivated by an investigation of firing errors in rifle and artillery fire. He derived the normal distribution function by essentially the same method that Maxwell used some 45 years later in his derivation of the Maxwell distribution function for the momentum of particles in a gas. Incidentally, Adrain also develops the method of least squares in the same remarkable paper. This method is usually attributed to Gauss who published it after Adrain. The applications of least squares made in the paper were to the corrections of dead reckoning at sea by an observation of a latitude and to the correction of a land survey.

Adrain was a professor at what is now Rutgers University when this work was done. He later moved to Columbia University after having some personal difficulties with the Rutgers students.

The "explanation" of the Gaussian distribution of variables such as shoe sizes is based on the Central Limit Theorem in the following way. The bones in the foot are made up of many cells. Each cell varies in some manner from person to person and the total length of the foot is the sum of the lengths of the individual cells. Hence whatever the distribution of cell sizes, (as long as they satisfy the requirement for the derivation of the central limit theorem), their sum has a normal distribution.

REFERENCES

1. J. V. Uspensky, *Introduction to The Theory of Probability*, McGraw-Hill, (New York, 1937).
2. P. A. M. Dirac, *The Principles of Quantum Theory* (Oxford 1947); for a slightly more rigorous discussion, cf. B. Friedman, *Principles and Techniques of Applied Mathematics*.
3. P. Laplace, *Theorie Analytique de Probabilities* (Paris, 1812).
4. A. Fisher, *Math. Theor. of Probability* (McMillan, p. 190, 1926).
5. B. V. Gnedenko and A. N. Kolmogorow, Addison Wesley (1954).
6. K. F. Gauss, *Collected Works*.
7. R. Adrain, *The Analyst or Mathematical Museum*, I, 93 (1808).
8. Y. W. Lindberg, *Math. Z.* **15**: 211(1922).

3 Distributions with Long Tails, Pareto and Log Normal

All intellectuals have a few friends who brag of having IQ's of the order of 150 (half again the mean value) but we practically never hear of any one with twice the mean score. We all have a few tall friends, the tallest friend of one of us being $6'7\frac{1}{2}''$, but no one is twice $5'\ 9''$, the approximate average height of the American adult male. On the other hand, if one investigates the distribution of annual incomes of individuals in a large country, he finds a significant number with 10 times that of the average person and some with 100 times that of the average. Such distributions with long tails were first studied by the

Italian social economist, Pareto, who collected statistics on income and wealth of individuals in many countries at various times in history.

The Pareto distribution has the form

$$1 - p(x) = ax^{-v} \tag{1}$$

so that

$$\log [1 - p(x)] = \log a - v \log x$$

and if the number of persons with income x or greater is plotted as a function of x on log-log paper, the resulting curve is a straight line with slope $-v$.

Pareto's analysis of his data convinced him that[1,2]

In all places and at all times the distribution of income in a stable economy, when the origin of measurement is at a sufficiently high income level, will be given approximately by the empirical formula $y = ax^{-v}$ where y is the number of people having income x or greater and v is approximately 1.5.

The existence of such a pervasive empirical fact is rather surprising. As Pareto stated,

These results are very remarkable . . . The form of this curve seems to depend only tenuously upon different economic conditions of the countries considered, since the effects are very nearly the same for the countries whose economic conditions are as different as those of England, of Ireland, of Germany, of the Italian cities, and even of Peru.

Figure 39 gives the income distribution for the United States in 1918 according to the Pareto formulation.

The distribution curve abruptly stops in the range of about $600. This is called the "wolf point", the income below which the wolf is at the door; i.e. it is the minimum annual value of goods and services necessary for maintenance of life with a modicum of dignity. That income was $600/year in 1918. At that point the curve bends over and the number of individuals drop exceedingly rapidly as a function of income. A number of other income distributions are plotted in Figure 40.

H. T. Davis collected and analyzed data on the number of persons with several other strange skills besides making money. We have plotted his observations on a number of people who wrote various numbers of mathematical papers, and of the number of persons who made various billiard scores in 50 inning. Note that the data can be fitted very well with a Pareto distribution. Lotka,[3] who was apparently the first to discuss scientific productivity statistically, suggested a Pareto exponent of $v = 2$ for the distribution of authors with x published papers. De Sola Price[4] extended Lotka's work and produced the graph in Figure 42.

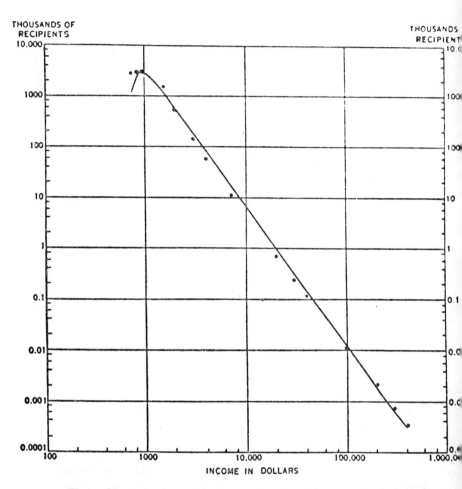

Figure 39 Frequency distribution of incomes in the United States, 1918. Data taken from ref. 2. The value 1.5 for the Pareto parameter is not as universal as Pareto thought. In fact tables now exist for the time variation of the parameter in different countries.

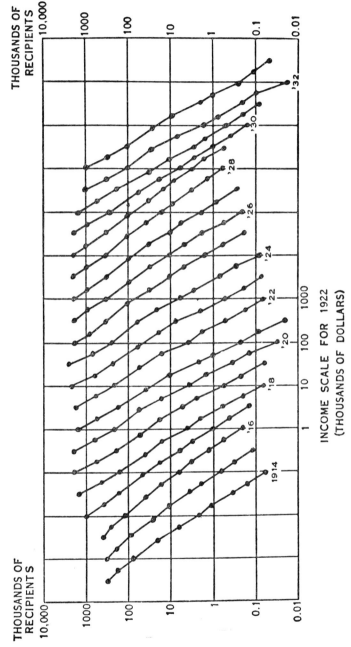

Figure 40 Comparison of income distribution[2] in the United States, 1914–1933.

Cumulated frequencies, both scales logarithmic. The vertical lines are one cycle apart, as are the horizontal ones, the scale shifting one-half cycle to the right for each successive year. The point nearest the date in each case measures the number of incomes in excess of $1,000,000 in that year.

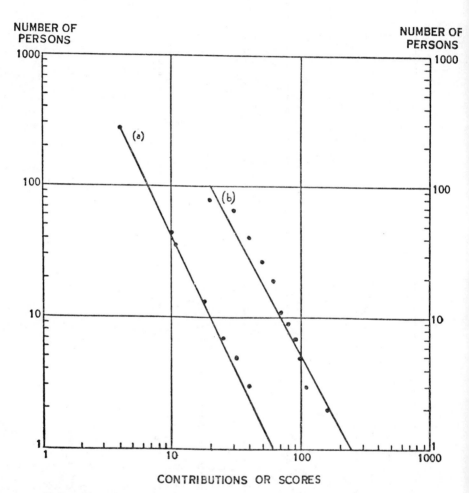

Figure 41   Cumulative frequency distributions of mathematical contributions (a)
and of billiard scores (b). Data taken from ref. 2.

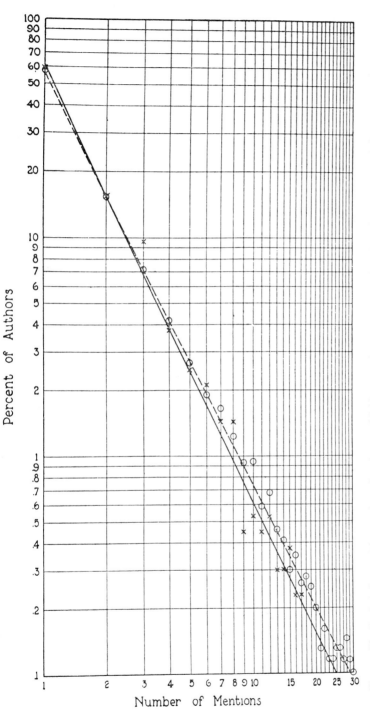

Figure 42 Lotka's Law.—The number of authors publishing exactly *n* papers, as a function of *n*. The open circles represent data taken from the first index volume of the abridged *Philosophical Transactions of the Royal Society of London* (17th and early 18th centuries), the filled circles those from the 1907–16 decennial index of *Chemical Abstracts*. The straight line shows the exact inverse-square law of Lotka. All data are reduced to a basis of exactly 100 authors publishing but a single paper.

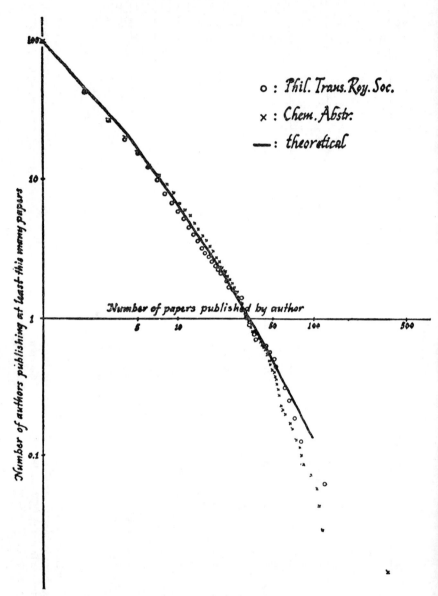

Figure 43   Number of authors publishing at least *n* papers as a function of n, curve taken from de Sola Price, *Little Science, Big Science.*[4]

Note the curvature at the high end. The curve is normalized so that all data is expressed relative to 100 authors who produce one paper.

B. Mandelbrot has investigated mechanisms which lead to the Pareto distribution. We review these later in this chapter but now consider another distribution, the log normal distribution which is also frequently associated with distributions with long tails.

The log normal distribution is defined by

$$p(x) = x^{-1}(2\pi\sigma^2)^{-\frac{1}{2}} \exp\{-(\log x - \langle\log x\rangle)^2/2\sigma^2\} \qquad (2)$$

$\langle\log x\rangle$ being the average value of $\log x$.

Note that

$$\log p(x) = -\tfrac{1}{2}\log(2\pi\sigma^2) - (\log x - \langle\log x\rangle)^2/2\sigma^2 - \log x \qquad (3)$$

so that on a log-log graph the curve would be parabolic, as seems to be the trend of the data in Figure 43.

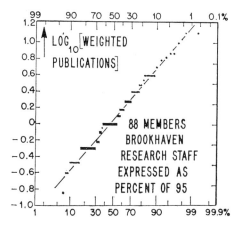

Figure 44 Cumulative distribution of logarithm of "weighted" rate of publication at Brookhaven National Lab. plotted on probability paper.[5]

It is often difficult to make a clear distinction between curve fitting of our two long tailed laws. U.S. Treasury reports of annual income have often been plotted on the log normal basis. Wm. Shockley has given good evidence for the log normal fit to the production of journal articles and patents of members of several laboratories, Brookhaven, U.S. National Bureau of Standards, Columbia University and "a large industrial laboratory". Two examples of his data are plotted in Figures 44 and 45.

E

Shockley proposed the following mechanism to explain why long tails exist in the distribution of achievements which require the successful conclusion of a number of separate tasks, the failure of any one of which would lead to the failure of the project. He uses the publication of a technical paper as an example. A list of those abilities which are important are 1) ability to think up a good problem, 2) ability to work on it, 3) ability to recognize a worthwhile result, 4) ability to make a decision as to when to stop and write up the results, 5) ability to write adequately, 6) ability to profit constructively from

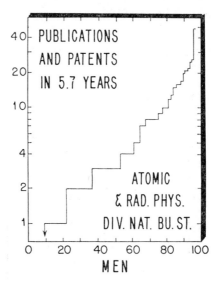

Figure 45   Cumulative distribution on logarithmic scale for publications and patents for Atomic and Radiation Physics Div., National Bureau of Standards, for a period of 5.7 years.[5]

criticism, 7) determination to submit the paper to a journal, 8) willingness to withstand referee's objections. Then he states that to some approximation the probability that a worker will produce a paper in a given time will be the product of a set of probabilities that he can successfully deal with each of the items listed above

$$P = p_1 p_2 \cdots p_8 \qquad (4)$$

If one man's probability in each item exceeds another by 50% his productivity will be the larger by a factor of 25.

The log normal aspect becomes apparent by taking logarithms of (4). Then

$$\log P = \log p_1 + \log p_2 + \cdots + \log p_8 \qquad (5)$$

Since $\log P$ is the sum of a set of individual variables, each with a distribution function of its own, the central limit theorem might be applicable so that the distribution function of $\log P$ would be Gaussian.

It is highly likely that our readers who are over 26 and who live in the University publish or perish atmosphere will have had no difficulty following the Shockley argument. But to our younger friends, under 26, publishing is not important but having meaningful relationships with members of the opposite sex is. So lets put the above ideas into this context, and incidently interpret some of the data in The Kinsey Report on the sexual behavior of the human male.

We ask the question: what fraction of male undergraduates have sexual relations during their collegiate life with a given number of girls. In complete analogy with the publication records of the professors, many have relations with one girl (often his future wife), many with two, perhaps less with three, and not an insignificant number with ten. But like that small number of highly prolific publishers, one finds one or two Don Juans per hundred students who play the game at all, who have seduced 20 or 50, or even 100, times as many girls as the average undergraduate (if one is to believe dormitory gossip and Kinsey staff interviews).

A not-unreasonable list of required abilities are, 1) ability to select a girl who seems to be worth approaching, 2) ability to make the first date, 3) ability to activate a continuing dating sequence, 4) ability to recognize the moment when petting should be the natural next step, 5) ability through petting and otherwise to win the girl's affection and stimulate her emotions to the point where the proposal of the crucial stage of the affair is inevitable, 6) a willingness to persist even if rebuffed, until consent is obtained, 7) determination to find the appropriate quarters where the seduction can be completed, 8) ability to physically perform. This completes the analogy and we need say no more. Being men we are not competent to comment on the statistics in Kinsey, Vol. II. Incidentally, our analysis does not apply to one who traffics with prostitutes anymore than Shockley's analysis applies to the publication record of the prominent public official who publishes the speeches written by his ghost writer.

Several points are immediately apparent from the discussion above. Suppose that the items listed in either or both of our examples were ill chosen and that others more relevant were left out. Would our results have been different? The answer is no. The crucial point in the argument is that a large number of individual acts must be successfully performed before publication or coition is complete. The chain may be cut in many places. A Gaussian distribution of each $\{\log p_j\}$ is not necessary in order to obtain a distribution with a long tail. It is clear from (4) that a small difference in all the p_j's for two individuals is enough to make the performance of one individual much better or much worse than another.

Now suppose we have a situation which is analogous to the one described above (many small successes being required before the goal is achieved) and suppose we demand that the goal be achieved. What strategies are available? Either redundancy can be introduced into the system so that there are many possible ways of being successful, or the probability of each step being successful is, by some means, brought to within an ε of unity. NASA's space program is an excellent example of such a situation. The astronauts were to be placed on the moon with probability 1. The enormous cost of the project reflects the tremendous redundancy of the system and quality control of the components.

REFERENCES

1. V. Pareto, Cours d'Economie Politique (Lausanne and Paris 1897).
2. H. T. Davis, *The Theory of Econometrics* (Bloomington Ind. 1941).
3. A. J. Lotka, *J. Wash. Acad. of Sci.* **16**, 317 (1926).
4. D. de Sola Price, *Little Science, Big Science* (New York, 1967).
5. W. Shockley, *Proc. of IRE*, **45**, 279 (1957).
6. A. C. Kinsey, W. B. Pomeroy and C. E. Martin, *Sexual Behavior in the Human Male* (Saunders, Phil. 1948).

4   Probability Graph Paper

We have already seen that log graph paper and log-log paper are useful for dealing with exponentiating processes (see Figure 20) and with the Pareto distribution (see Figure 39). Several other types of graph paper are also available; for example, those which respectively represent cumulative Gaussian, Cauchy, and logistic distributions as straight lines.

Special purpose graph papers are constructed in the following manner.[1] Let $\Phi(x, \alpha, \beta)$ be the cumulative distribution function of a variable x which might assume any real value between $-\infty$ and $+\infty$. Also suppose that a reduced variable

$$y = \alpha(x-\beta)$$

exists such that the cumulative distribution function

$$F(y) \equiv \Phi(\beta+y/\alpha, \alpha, \beta)$$

is independent of α and β. To construct paper such that data sampled from

Φ lies on a straight line; the variable x is plotted as ordinate and y as abscissa, both on linear scales. On a second linear scale we mark off values of $F(y)$ associated with the value of y. The values $F(y) = 0$ and $F(y) = 1$ do not appear on the paper.

To show the effectiveness of probability papers we compare the symmetrical Laplace function with mean zero and standard deviation one[1]

$$F(x) = \tfrac{1}{2}\exp(2^{\frac{1}{2}}x) \text{ if } x \leq 0 \quad \text{and} \quad F(x) = 1 - \tfrac{1}{2}\exp(2^{\frac{1}{2}}x) \text{ if } x \geq 0$$

with the normal distribution. The two cumulative distributions are plotted in Figure 41. Their separate characters could hardly be noted in that figure. On the other hand when plotted on normal distribution paper as is done in Figure 40 their differences are amplified tremendously.

The quantity listed as return period at the top of Figure 40 is

$$T(x) = 1/[1 - F(x)]$$

Since

$$F(x) = \text{Prob}\,(X \leq x)$$

$$1 - F(x) = \text{Prob}\,(X > x)$$

and $T(x)$ is the average number of trials of the events with cumulative distribution $F(x)$ required before a value of $X > x$ is observed. This is an example of the general notion that if the probability of an event is p, the number of independent trials required on the average for its occurrence is $1/p$.

We close this section with a discussion of the detailed manner in which sampled data from a distribution is to be plotted on special probability paper. The basic problem in the analysis of statistical data through special graph paper is to plot the data and fit a best straight line to it. The first step is to list the observations x_m (with $m = 1, 2, \ldots, n$) in order of increasing magnitude. The next problem is to decide on the value of $F(x)$ to associate with each value of x. Since the smallest observation is x_1, $F(x) = 0$ until $x = x_1$ at which point the cumulative distribution achieves the value $1/n$. The curve is flat until $x = x_2$ at which point the cumulative distribution achieves the value $2/n$. This process continues so that at x_m the measured cumulative distribution function takes on the value m/n. On this basis the value x_n would not appear on the $F(x)$ step graph because $F(x) = 1$ never appears on the graph paper: Hence one observed point would never be used. Actually if our basic process is such that we know that x may be arbitrarily large even though $F(x)$ may become very close to 1, we would be in error in setting $F(x) = 1$ when $x = x_m$.

Gumbel has analyzed this plotting question in great detail. For reasons which he develops in reference 1 he recommends that the frequency $m/(n+1)$

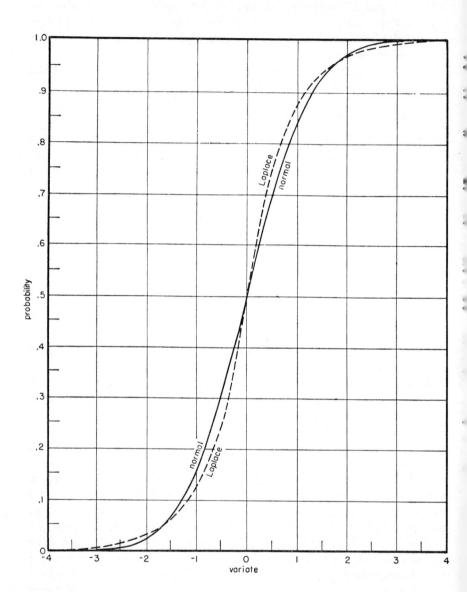

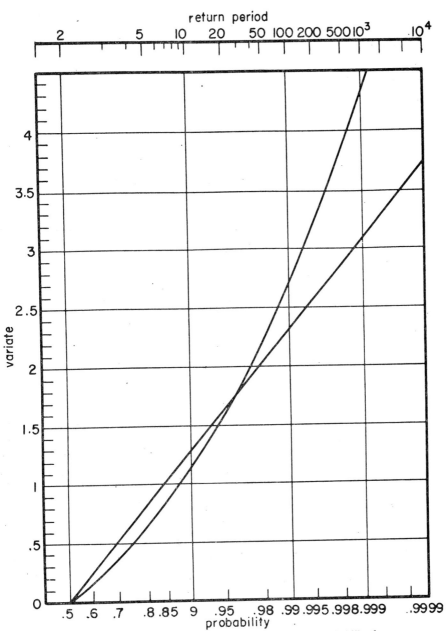

Figure 47 The First Laplacean and the Normal Probability.[1]

be assigned to plotting position associated with x_m. In this way all data is used and he shows that the choice is appropriate to a wide class of basic distribution functions.

REFERENCE

1. E. J. Gumbel, *Statistics of Extremes*, Columbia University Press 1958.

5   Stable Distributions and Random Walks

We have already noted that if each term in a sum of independent random variables is normally distributed (see eq. 2.10–2.16) then the sum is also normally distributed. For example, let $n = 2$ in (2.10)

$$S = X_1 + X_2 \tag{1}$$

Also let X_1 and X_2 be normally distributed random variables with means and standard deviations μ_1, μ_2 and σ_1, σ_2. Then S is also normally distributed with mean

$$\mu = \mu_1 + \mu_2 \tag{2a}$$

while its standard deviation σ is related to σ_1 and σ_2 by

$$\sigma^2 = \sigma_1^2 + \sigma_2^2 \tag{2b}$$

One has an analogous result for the Cauchy distribution. Let us now suppose that X_1 and X_2 each have Cauchy distributions instead of normal ones so that

$$\text{Prob}\,\{X_j < x\} = \tfrac{1}{2} - \frac{1}{\pi}\tan^{-1}\{(x-\mu_j)/a_j\} \tag{3}$$

Then the characteristic function of X_j is

$$\varphi_j(\alpha) = \frac{a_j}{\pi}\int_{-\infty}^{\infty}\frac{\exp(i\alpha x)\,dx}{a_j^2 + (x-\mu_j)^2} \tag{4}$$

$$= \pi^{-1}\exp(i\alpha\mu_j)\int_{-\infty}^{\infty}\frac{\exp(i\alpha z_j a)\,dz}{1+z^2}$$

$$= \exp\{i\alpha\mu_j - a_j|\alpha|\} \tag{5}$$

and from 2.12 that of the $S = X_1 + X_2$ is

$$\Phi(\alpha) = \exp\{i\alpha\mu - a\,|\alpha|\} \tag{6a}$$

with

$$\mu = \mu_1 + \mu_2 \text{ and } a = a_1 + a_2 \tag{6b}$$

By inverting the characteristic function (6a) we see that S also has a Cauchy distribution function and that its characterizing parameters are given by (6b).

The normal and Cauchy distributions are examples of *stable distributions*. If two independent random variables have the same form of distribution function and this form belongs to the class of stable distributions then the sum of the two random variables has the same form of distribution as they have individually.

The most general form for a stable distribution function has been derived by P. Lévy[1-3] when the variables X_1 and X_2 are continuous and have the range $(-\infty, \infty)$. Its characteristic function is

$$\varphi(\alpha) = \exp\{i\delta\alpha - \gamma|\alpha|^\nu[1 - i\beta(\alpha/|\alpha|)\tan v\pi/2]\} \tag{7}$$

When $v = 2$ this corresponds to the Gaussian distribution and when $v = 1$ and $\beta = 0$ it corresponds to the Cauchy distribution. Generally the distribution function can only be expressed as a fourier integral of $\varphi(\alpha)$. Only in the Gaussian, Cauchy, and $(v = \frac{1}{2}, \beta = 1, \delta = 0, \gamma = 1)$ cases can the fourier inversion be performed to give an explicit form for the distribution function. In the latter case the probability distribution is (as has been shown by N. V. Smirnov)

$$f(x) = \begin{cases} 0 & \text{if } x < 0 \\ \dfrac{1}{\sqrt{2\pi}} x^{-\frac{3}{2}} \exp(-1/2x) & x > 0 \end{cases} \tag{8}$$

Lévy has shown that the tails of all non Gaussian stable laws follow the asymptotic form of the law of Pareto in the sense that there exist two constants $C' = (\sigma')^2$ and $C'' = (\sigma'')^2$ related to β by

$$\beta = (C' - C'')/(C' + C'') \tag{9}$$

such that as $x \to \infty$

$$x^\nu \Pr(X > x) \to C' = (\sigma')^\nu \tag{10a}$$

$$x^\nu \Pr(X < -x) \to C'' = (\sigma'')^\nu \tag{10b}$$

Hence both tails are Paretein if $|\beta| \neq 1$. In the Cauchy case $\beta = 0$ so that

E*

$C' = C''$. As a verification of the general theorem we note that in this case

$$\Pr(X < -x) = \Pr(X > x) = \tfrac{1}{2} - \frac{1}{\pi}\tan^{-1}(x/a) \sim a/(\pi x)$$

if $x > 0$, as required.

The theory of stable distribution functions is closely related to the theory of continuous random walks on a line. Let us suppose that any point on the line is available to the walker and that the probability of a displacement of length x in time t,

$$\Pr(\text{step } x \text{ in time } t) = P(x, t), \tag{11}$$

depends only on x and not on the starting point. Let

$$x = x_1 + x_2 \tag{12}$$

Then, since $P(x, t)$ has the same mathematical form for all x and t

$$P(x, t) = \int_{-\infty}^{\infty} P(x_1, t_1) P(x - x_1, t - t_1)\, dx_1 \tag{13}$$

Now let $\varphi(\alpha, Ut)$ be the characteristic function of $P(x, t)$. The parameter U determines the time scale for the process. Then

$$P(z, t) = \frac{1}{2\pi}\int_{-\infty}^{\infty} \varphi(\alpha, Ut)e^{-i\alpha z}\, d\alpha \tag{14}$$

and

$$
\begin{aligned}
P(x, t) &= \frac{1}{(2\pi)^2}\int_{-\infty}^{\infty}\int d\alpha_1 d\alpha_2 \int_{-\infty}^{\infty} \varphi(\alpha_1, Ut_1)e^{-i\alpha_1 x_1} \\
&\qquad\qquad \times\, \varphi(\alpha_2, U[t-t_1])e^{-i\alpha_2(x-x_1)}\, dx_1 \\
&= \frac{1}{2\pi}\int_{-\infty}^{\infty}\int d\alpha_1 d\alpha_2 \varphi(\alpha_1, Ut_1)\varphi(\alpha_2, U[t-t_1])\,\delta(\alpha_1 - \alpha_2)\, e^{-i\alpha_2 x} \\
&= \frac{1}{2\pi}\int_{-\infty}^{\infty} \varphi(\alpha, Ut_1)\, \varphi(\alpha, U[t-t_1])\, e^{-i\alpha x} \tag{15}
\end{aligned}
$$

By comparing this expression with (14) we see that

$$\varphi(\alpha, Ut) = \varphi(\alpha, Ut_1)\, \varphi(\alpha, U[t-t_1])$$

This chain condition and therefore (13) can be satisfied when $P(x, t)$ is a stable distribution function, i.e. when $\varphi(\alpha, Ut)$ is given by (7) with the special identification $\delta = 0$ (since we choose $\langle x \rangle = 0$ at every step), $\beta = $ constant and

$$\gamma = Ut$$

An acceptable form for $P(x, t)$ is then the Lévy form

$$P(x, t) = \frac{1}{2\pi} \int_{-\infty}^{\infty} \exp \left\{ -i\alpha x - Ut|\alpha|^{\nu}[1 + i\beta(\alpha/|\alpha|) \tan (\nu\pi/2)] \right\} d\alpha \qquad (17)$$

Now let $w = \alpha t^{1/\nu}$. Then,

$$P(x, t) = t^{-1/\nu} Q(xt^{-1/\nu}) \qquad (18)$$

where

$$Q(y) = \frac{1}{2\pi} \int_{-\infty}^{\infty} \exp \left\{ -iwy - U|w|^{\nu}[1 + i\beta(w/|w|) \tan (\nu\pi/2)] \right\} dw \qquad (19)$$

When $\nu = 2$, (19) reduces to the usual Gaussian distribution which appears in the standard theory of random walks and Brownian mation. The wider choice of possible values of ν has been emphasized in recent years in the theory of speculative prices[4,5].

REFERENCES

1. P. Lévy, *Calcul des Probabilities* (Paris, 1925).
2. P. Lévy, *Theorie de l'addition des variables aleatoires* (Paris, 1934).
3. P. Lévy, *Processus stochastiques et mouvement Brownien* (Paris, 1948).
4. B. Mandelbrot, *International Economic Review* I, 79 (1960).
5. B. Mandelbrot, *J. of Business of the Univ. of Chicago*, 36, 394 (1963).

6 The Fokker-Planck Equation[1]

Let us consider a random process for which the so-called Smoluchowsky equation is satisfied

$$P(y_2|y_1, t) = \int P(y_2|y, t_1) P(y|y_1, t-t_1) \, dy \qquad (1)$$

where $P(y_2|y_1, t)$ is the probability that the variable y suffers a transition from y_1 to y_2 in time t. This relation is satisfied for so-called Markoff processes. In the special case in which $P(y_2|y_1, t)$ depends only on (y_2-y_1), Eq. (1) is equivalent to (4.13) as can be seen by letting $y_2-y_1 = x$ and $y-y_1 = x_1$.

When the moments of $P(y_2|y_1, t)$

$$a_n(z, \Delta t) = \int (z-y)^n P(z|y, \Delta t) \, dy \qquad (2)$$

have the property that only a_1 and a_2 are proportional to Δt as $\Delta t \to 0$ and that all higher moments vanish more rapidly than Δt in this limit, then it is possible to derive a differential equation for $P(x|y, t)$ in terms of

$$A(z) = \lim (\Delta t)^{-1} a_1(z, \Delta t) \tag{3a}$$

$$B(z) = \lim (\Delta t)^{-1} a_2(z, \Delta t). \tag{3b}$$

This differential equation is known as the Fokker-Planck equation.

We follow Wang and Uhlenbeck[1] and consider the integral

$$I = \int R(y_2)\{\partial P(y_2|y_1, t)/\partial t\}\, dy_2$$

where $R(y)$ is an arbitrary function which vanishes sufficiently rapidly as $y \to \pm\infty$. Then from (1)

$$I = \int R(y_2)\{\partial P(y_2|y_1, t)/\partial t\}\, dy_2$$

$$= \lim_{\Delta t \to 0} (\Delta t)^{-1} \int R(y_2)\{P(y_2|y_1, t+\Delta t) - P(y_2|y_1, t)\}\, dy_2$$

$$= \lim_{\Delta t \to 0} (\Delta t)^{-1}\{\int\int R(y_2)P(y_2|y, \Delta t)P(y|y_1, t)\, dy\, dy_2$$

$$- \int R(y_2)P(y_2|y_1, t)\, dy_2\} \tag{4}$$

Now

$$R(y_2) = R(y + [y_2 - y])$$

$$= R(y) + (y_2 - y)R'(y) + (y_2 - y)^2 R''(y)/2! + \dots \tag{5}$$

Hence, as $\Delta t \to 0$

$$(\Delta t)^{-1} \int R(y_2)P(y_2|y, \Delta t)\, dy_2 = R(y) + R'(y)A(y) + R''(y)B(y)/2! \tag{6}$$

When this expression is substituted into (4) and integration by parts is carried out to reduce R' and R'' to R, the resulting expression is

$$\int R(y_2)\left\{\frac{\partial P}{\partial t} + \frac{\partial}{\partial y_2}[A(y_2)P] - \tfrac{1}{2}\frac{\partial^2}{\partial y_2^2}[B(y_2)P\right\} = 0 \tag{7}$$

Since this integral vanishes for an arbitrary function $R(y_2)$, the quantity in the bracket must vanish. If we replace y_2 by y and y_1 by y_0, the value of y when $t = 0$, we obtain the Fokker-Planck equation

$$\frac{\partial P}{\partial t} = -\frac{\partial}{\partial y}[PA(y_2)] + \tfrac{1}{2}\frac{\partial^2}{\partial y^2}[PB(y)] \tag{8}$$

The function $P(y|y_0, t)$ has the property

$$\text{as } t \to 0, \quad P(y|y_0, t) \to \delta(y - y_0).$$

REFERENCE

1. M. C. Wang and G. E. Uhlenbeck, *Rev. Mod. Phys.* **17**, 323 (1945).

7 Population Variation Under Random Influences

We have already alluded to the deviations of the U.S. population curve from
the logistic in Figure 5. In various experiments on animal populations it is
noted that as the population in a limited volume with limited resources
approaches saturation, some random oscillations about the saturation level
are observed. The sheep population in Tasmania, as exhibited in Figure 48,
shows such a variation also. These fluctuations reflect changes in the birth and
death rates. The number of sheep grown depends on the economy, as does the
number of people born. The U.S. birth and death rates since 1900 are plotted
in Figure 7. Note the drop in birth rate during the depression and the rise in
the optimistic post-war boom of the 1950's. Epidemics, especially those of
The Black Plague, contributed to the population fluctuations of the Middle
Ages.

Some influences on the birth rate might be changes in the economy which
stimulate or oppose interest in marrying early and having children, changes in
average size of dwellings, changes in public attitudes (for example, in one year
it is stated to be essential that high IQ people should have more children, in
another year the zero population growth movement is popular; during one
year birth control pills are reputed to be safe, the next year they are dangerous,
etc.), variation in government tax regulation and social security policies, etc.
As was mentioned in Chapter I, Section 2, if the U.S. birth rate curves
continue to drop as they have for the past ten years, the death and birth rate
levels will be about the same in the middle 1980's, a state which some of the
countries in the Soviet Bloc have almost achieved.

In view of these fluctuating population driving forces, it would seem that a
more appropriate model for population variation would be one characterized
by the equation[1,2]

$$dN/dt = kNG(N/\theta) + NF(t) \qquad (1)$$

where $F(t)$ is considered to be a random function of time which reflects
changes in the economy and attitudes as described above. Since it is very hard
to predict changes in attitude in detail, one of the few mathematical
approaches left open to us is to incorporate them all in the random function

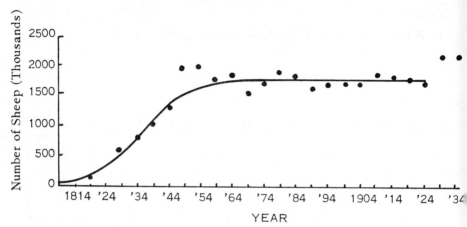

Figure 48   Variation of sheep population in Tasmania (from J. Davidson, *Transactions of the Royal Society of South Australia* **62**, 342 (1938)).

$F(t)$. The form of $G(x)$ which was discussed in Section 2 of Chapter I was

$$G(x) = (1-x^{\alpha})/\alpha, \tag{2}$$

$\alpha = 0$ being the Gompertz case and $\alpha = 1$ the Verhulst case.

Several postulates will be made about the statistical properties of $F(t)$ and their consequences will be examined. We assume first that $F(t)$ is generated by a Gaussian random process. Then we assume that the average value of $F(t)$, $\langle F(t) \rangle$, vanishes

$$\langle F(t) \rangle = 0 \tag{3}$$

while the average value of the correlation of $F(t_1)$ and $F(t_2)$ is proportional to a delta function as usually postulated in the theory of Brownian Motion, as discussed in the last Section,

$$\langle F(t_1)F(t_2) \rangle = \sigma^2 \delta(t_1 - t_2) \tag{4}$$

The random variable $F(t)$ is then characterized by a single parameter σ.

If $\langle F(t) \rangle \neq 0$, then in most interesting cases, either the saturation level or the rate constant can be changed so that the average value of the random component vanishes. Let us suppose that

$$F(t) = a + \delta F \quad \text{and} \quad \langle \delta F \rangle = 0 \tag{5}$$

Then for the form (2) of $G(x)$,

$$dN/dt = kN[1 - (N/\theta)^{\alpha}]/\alpha + aN + N\delta F$$
$$= k'N[1 - (N/\theta')^{\alpha}]/\alpha + N\delta F \tag{6}$$

where

$$k' = (k + \alpha a) \tag{7a}$$

$$\theta' = \theta\{1 + (\alpha a/k)\}^{1/\alpha} \tag{7b}$$

$$\text{as } \alpha \to 0, \; \theta' = \theta \exp(a/k)$$

The postulate (4) is appropriate when the random forcing function $F(t)$ has a memory which is very short compared with the life expectancy of an individual or with the period between generations. This is generally the case when economic and popular responses of the type mentioned earlier in this section are the basis of the driving force. W. L. Thorp and W. C. Mitchell[3] have analyzed the economic conditions of fifteen countries during the period 1790–1925. The duration of a business cycle was defined as the time interval between one peak in the prosperity of a country and the next one, a relative recession occurring between two successive peaks. Thorp and Mitchell then found the frequency distribution of duration of business cycles to be a log normal distribution which peaked for cycles between 3 and $3\frac{1}{2}$ years (see Figure 60 of Section IV), a time short compared with the life expectancy of an individual. Various fads and popularist movements generally seem to last a similar length of time.

If we again let

$$v = \log N/\theta, \tag{8}$$

Eq. (1) becomes

$$dv/dt = G(e^v) + F(t). \tag{9}$$

This equation and the various postulates made above are just those required to derive a Fokker-Planck equation[4] for the probability $P(v, t)$ that the log N/θ has a value v at time t. It has been shown in the last section that the Fokker-Planck equation has the form[1,2]

$$\frac{\partial P}{\partial t} = -k\frac{\partial}{\partial v}\{PG(e^v)\} + \tfrac{1}{2}\sigma^2 \frac{\partial^2 P}{\partial v^2}. \tag{10}$$

This equation for the Verhulst case was first derived by Leigh[5].

The equilibrium distribution function can be obtained by setting $\partial P/\partial t = 0$. Then it must satisfy

$$-k\frac{\partial}{\partial v}\{PG(e^v) - (\sigma^2/2k)\partial P/\partial v\} = 0$$

That is, with the normalization constant P_0,

$$P(v, \infty) = P_0\{\exp(2k/\sigma^2) \int_0^v G(e^v) \, dv\}. \tag{11}$$

In particular when

$$G(e^v) = (1 - e^{\alpha v})/\alpha, \tag{12a}$$

$$P(v, \infty) = P_0 \exp\{(2k/\alpha^2\sigma^2)(1 + \alpha v - e^{\alpha v})\}. \tag{12b}$$

The easiest case to deal with is the Gompertz form of $G(e^v)$, that with $\alpha = 0$, for then $P(v, \infty)$ becomes Gaussian. The normalized equilibrium population distribution in terms of N is then

Gompertz case:

$$P(N, \infty) = (k/2\pi\sigma^2)^{\frac{1}{2}} N^{-1} \exp\{-k[\log(N/\theta)]^2/2\sigma^2\}. \tag{13}$$

For general α:

$$P(N, \infty) = \frac{\alpha}{\theta} \left\{ \frac{2k}{\alpha^2\sigma^2} \left(\frac{N}{\theta}\right)^\alpha \right\}^{2k/\alpha^2\sigma^2}$$

$$\times \frac{(2k/\alpha^2\sigma^2)^{1/\alpha}}{\Gamma(\alpha^{-1} + [2k/\alpha^2\sigma^2])} \exp\left\{ -\frac{2k}{\alpha^2\sigma^2} \left(\frac{N}{\theta}\right)^\alpha \right\} \tag{14}$$

The equilibrium distribution function (12b) has the interesting property that if v is small (i.e., if deviations from the population saturation level are small) then $P(v, \infty)$ is independent of α and has the Gaussian form

$$P(v, \infty) = P_0 \exp\{-kv^2/\sigma^2\} \tag{15}$$

An alternative form of the Fokker-Planck equation of our process is obtained by letting[1,2]

$$P(v, t) = \Psi(v, t) \exp\left\{ k\sigma^{-2} \int_0^v G(e^v) \, dv \right\} \tag{16}$$

then

$$(2/k)\Psi_t = \sigma^2 k^{-1} \Psi_{vv} - \left\{ \frac{\partial G(e^v)}{\partial v} + k\sigma^{-2}[G(e^v)]^2 \right\} \Psi \tag{17}$$

This is to be compared with the Schrödinger equation

$$\hbar i \Psi_t = (\hbar^2/2m)\Psi_{xx} - U(x)\Psi \tag{18}$$

and the Bloch equation in which $-it/\hbar$ is replaced by $\beta = 1/kT$ (which is used in statistical mechanics)

$$\Psi_\beta = (\hbar^2/2m)\Psi_{xx} - U(x)\Psi \tag{19}$$

Notice that if, in the Bloch equation we choose the mass to be 1/2 and then identify

$$\beta \text{ with } \tfrac{1}{2}kt, \quad \hbar^2 \text{ with } \sigma^2/k \quad \text{and}$$

$$U(x) \text{ with } W(v) \equiv k\sigma^{-2}[G(e^v)]^2 + \partial G(e^v)/\partial v \tag{20}$$

it has the same form as our basic equation (17). Of course, there is no connection between the physical significance of the two equations; however, there is a mathematical convenience in their similarity because the literature on the Schrödinger and Bloch equations is immediately available to us.

Let us again choose the special form of $G(e^v)$, (2.12a). Then

$$W_\alpha(v) \equiv k(\alpha\sigma)^{-2}(1-e^{\alpha v})^2 - e^{\alpha v} \tag{21}$$

In the Gompertz $\alpha = 0$ case,

$$W_0(v) = (k/\sigma^2)v^2 - 1 \tag{22}$$

which is the harmonic oscillator potential in quantum theory. Generally

$$W_\alpha(v) = A(e^{2x\alpha} - 2e^{x\alpha}) + k(\alpha\sigma)^{-2} \tag{23a}$$

where

$$x \equiv (v - v^*), \quad \exp(\alpha v^*) = 1 + [(\alpha\sigma)^2/2k] \tag{23b}$$

$$A \equiv [k/(\alpha\sigma)^2]\{1 + [(\alpha\sigma)^2/2k]\}^2. \tag{23c}$$

If we introduce a new function Φ by

$$\Psi = \Phi \exp\{-\tfrac{1}{2}k[E + k(\alpha\sigma)^{-1}]t\} \tag{24}$$

then Φ satisfies the differential equation

$$(\sigma^2/k)\Phi_{xx} + \{E - A(e^{2\alpha x} - 2e^{\alpha x})\}\Phi = 0 \tag{25}$$

which is just the Schrödinger equation for a diatomic molecule with a Morse[6] potential when the reduced mass is taken to be $1/2$ and $\hbar^2$ is identified with σ^2/k. Generally, our x is replaced by $-x$ in studying diatomic molecules. Mathematically this difference is of no importance. We seek solutions of (25) which vanish at $x = \pm\infty$.

Discussions of the Schrödinger equation for the harmonic oscillator and the Morse potential are available in the quantum mechanics literature. The relevant results were translated into the language required for our equations in reference 1. We merely state some of the results here. The Gompertz $\alpha = 0$ case which corresponds to a harmonic oscillator is easiest to analyze. One finds that if at time $t = 0$, the population is $n(0) = n_0$ so that

$$v_0 = \log(N_0/\theta), \tag{26}$$

then the probability of a transition from v_0 to v in time t (i.e., of a population transition from $N(0) = \theta \exp v_0$ to $N(t) = \theta \exp v$) is

$$P(v, v_0; t) = \left\{\frac{k}{\pi\sigma^2(1 - e^{-2kt})}\right\}^{\frac{1}{2}} \exp\{-(v - v_0 e^{-kt})^2 k/\sigma^2(1 - e^{-2kt})\} \tag{27}$$

The variation of various moments of the population can be determined as a function of time from the above equation[1]:

$$\langle N/\theta \rangle = (N_0/\theta)^{\exp(-kt)} \exp \left[(\sigma^2/4k)(1-e^{-2kt}) \right] \tag{28a}$$

while

$$\langle (N-\bar{N})^2 \rangle / (\bar{N})^2 = -1 + \exp \left\{ (\sigma^2/2k)(1-e^{-2kt}) \right\} \tag{28b}$$

Generally

$$\langle (N/\theta)^{2\lambda} \rangle = (N_0/\theta)^{2\lambda \, \exp(-kt)} \exp \left\{ (\lambda\sigma^2/k)(1-e^{-2kt}) \right\} \tag{28c}$$

An arbitrary initial distribution develops according to

$$P(v, t) = \int_{-\infty}^{\infty} P(v, v_0; t) P(v_0, 0) \, dv_0 \tag{29}$$

We will not discuss the general saturation inducing function $G(e^v)$ in detail, but we will note its consequences in two important regimes. The first is the regime far from saturation. Let us assume that as $\theta \to \infty$,

$$G(N/\theta) \to 1/\alpha < \infty \quad \text{and} \quad k' = k/\alpha. \tag{30}$$

Then the Fokker-Planck equation (2.10) becomes

$$\frac{\partial P}{\partial t} = -k' \frac{\partial P}{\partial v} + \sigma^2 \frac{\partial^2 P}{\partial v^2} \tag{31}$$

whose solution is[1]

$$P(v, t) = (2t\pi\sigma^2)^{-\frac{1}{2}} \int_{-\infty}^{\infty} P(v', 0) \exp \left\{ -(v-v'-k't)^2/2t\sigma^2 \right\} dv' \tag{32}$$

In the case that the population is precisely N_0 at time $t = 0$,

$$P(v', 0) = \delta(v'-v_0) \tag{33a}$$

where

$$v'-v_0 = \log N'/N_0 \quad \text{or} \quad N'/N_0 = \exp(v'-v_0) \tag{33b}$$

Then the probability that v lies between v and $v+dv$ is

$$P(v, t) \, dv = (2t\pi\sigma^2)^{-\frac{1}{2}} \exp \left\{ -(v-v_0-k't)^2/2t\sigma^2 \right\} dv \quad -\infty < v < \infty \tag{34}$$

so that, as $\sigma \to 0$, v follows the Malthusian exponential trajectory

$$v-v_0 = tk' \quad \text{or} \quad N/N_0 = \exp tk' \tag{35}$$

The probability that N lies between N and $N+dN$ at time t is

$$P(N, t) \, dN = \frac{dN \exp \left\{ -(\log [N/N_0] e^{-tk'})^2/2t\sigma^2 \right\}}{N(2t\pi\sigma^2)^{\frac{1}{2}}} \quad 0 < N < \infty \tag{36}$$

The first two moments of this distribution are

$$\bar{N} = N_0 \exp{(k' + \tfrac{1}{2}\sigma^2)t} \tag{37a}$$

$$\langle(N - \bar{N})^2\rangle / \bar{N}^2 = -1 + \exp{t\sigma^2} \tag{37b}$$

The next important regime is that in which v is small. This means the system is making small fluctuations about saturation. That is exactly the equilibrium distribution (2.11). When v is small, (since $G(1) = 0$),

$$G(e^v) = vG'(1) + \dots \tag{38a}$$

so that

$$P(v, \infty) \simeq P_0\{\exp{[(v^2/\sigma^2)G'(1) + 0(v^3)]}\} \tag{38b}$$

Generally $G'(1) < 0$. For example, when (2.12a) is chosen for $G(e^v)$,

$$G'(1) = -1. \tag{38c}$$

The intermediate regime in which the finiteness of θ becomes apparent, but before saturation occurs, depends on the detailed form of $G(x)$. Some of these details are given in reference 1 for the form (12a).

In conclusion we summarize our findings for the form (12a) as follows: In the first, (the $\theta \to \infty$ regime), the population grows freely with no interference. This is analogous to a free particle which accelerates in a field. In the second regime, the population has grown to the point that it is affected by other influences such as other species (and, in the case of human population growth, by fluctuations in the economy, by changes in personal attitudes, by agricultural successes and failures, etc.). In our Morse-type equation, this is analogous to the system falling into the highest energy bound state of the Morse potential, then dropping into lower energy states until it reaches the ground state. In the ground state the population fluctuates around its average value with statistics characterized by the equilibrium distribution (38b). These fluctuations are the analogues of the zero point fluctuations of a Morse oscillator.

REFERENCES

1. N. S. Goel, S. C. Maitra and E. W. Montroll, *Rev. Mod. Phys.* **43**, 231 (1971).
2. E. W. Montroll, Some Math Problems in Biology, 4, Am. Math. Soc., 100, 1972.
3. W. L. Thorp and W. C. Mitchell, Business Annuals, Nat. Bur. of Econ. Res., Inc. (N.Y., 1926).
4. M. C. Wang and G. E. Uhlenbech, *Rev. of Mod. Phys.* **17**, 323 (1945).
5. E. G. Leigh, Some Math Problems in Biology, 1; Am. Math. Soc., (1969).
6. P. M. Morse, *Phys. Rev.* **34**, 57 (1929).

8   Statistics of Extreme Events

Many questions which arise in our society are naturally posed in terms of extreme values of some variable. While in the United States flood control is not considered to be one of the major problems today, it did have that distinction in the 1920's and early 1930's. The Mississippi and other rivers frequently overflowed their banks leaving thousands of people homeless, washing away all their possessions and ruining their crops. This is still the case in many parts of the world. Since the Netherlands has so much of its area below sea level, storms which cause the North Sea to flow over the dikes can render farm land unusable for years and, indeed, if severe enough can cause hundreds or even thousands of human casualties (as did the great storm of 1 February 1953, which flooded 150,000 hectares of land and took 1,800 lives). The sufferers in the recent Pakistan catastrophe numbered over a million.

Designers of aircraft must have some estimate of the magnitude of extreme wind gusts which an airplane might encounter in its lifetime. Architects and construction firms in earthquake areas must make judgments concerning the magnitude of future earthquakes.

It is clear that a planner who must prepare for extreme events is faced with the dilemma which is clear from Figure 49. While the probability of an extreme event diminishes rapidly as a function of its magnitude, the destruction it might bring generally rises rapidly with the magnitude as does the cost for protection against it. The planner is confronted with the need to spend more and more money to prepare for an event which becomes less and less likely. There are several old "rules of thumb" for coping with the problem. One is to trace the records of the past for the largest observed magnitude of the event in question. Then prepare for double that magnitude. This policy is generally an extremely expensive one and usually prepares for an event which might not occur for thousands of years, if ever. Another approach is to assume that an event more than three standard deviations, 3σ, from the mean will never occur. The fallacy of this argument is that, if the basic variable is not limited in a natural way, its distribution has a tail which also extends without limit and that, if the sample size is increased, one can expect that the largest value observed will also increase. Hence the basic question is, how does the largest value observed depend on the number of observations? The 3σ condition may be far too strong when the sample size is small and too weak when the sample size is too large.

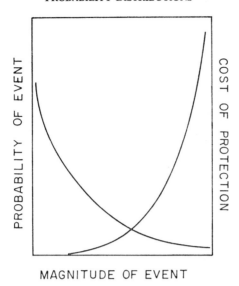

Figure 49 The Planner's Dilemma.

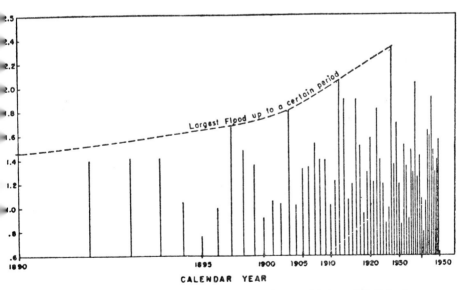

Figure 50 Annual floods of the Mississippi River at Vicksburg, Mississippi, 1890–1949.

We have plotted the variation of the highest annual flood level of the Mississippi River as a function of time. Observations at a given point were made daily and the highest observed daily flood level of the year[3] is plotted in Figure 50 for the period 1890–1949. Notice that while the annual highest level varies in a rather wild way, the curve formed by connecting the levels of the largest flood up to a certain period is a rather smooth function. This gives some hope that something may be said about it. Incidentally, the frequency of very low river levels is also very important in these days of concern about water pollution. When the river level is low, the water pollution level is high. There is also less water available for irrigation and human consumption.

An approach sometimes used for examining the basic data of the past for decision making utilises the exceedence frequencies, i.e., the probability that a given variable will exceed a certain level in a given time. In Figure 51 we have plotted (following references 1 and 2) exceedence frequencies for sea level heights at high tide at the Hoek van Holland for sixty winters 1888–1939 and 1945–1954. The exceedence frequency $n(h)/n$ ($n(h)$ being the number of years in which the height exceeded h and n the total number of years of observation) is plotted in Figure 51 on logarithmic graph paper. It is essentially a straight line function of h. Even the disastrous flood level of 1953 is not completely out of line with previous points. The unfortunate feature of that flood was not the ignorance of the statistics, but rather the lack of time and money to respond to the demands of the statistics. ". . . In 1939 the government appointed a committee to investigate the question, which measures had to be taken in order to increase the security offered by our dike system. Had not the German invasion and its aftermath, the reconstruction period needed after the war, prevented to carry out the measures it proposed, the 1953 flood would have caused no disaster. It struck us unprepared because it came too soon after the war."[2] Figure 51 states that the exceedence probability $\{1 - F(h)\}$ is an exponential, $\exp(-\alpha h)$.

The exponential distribution is an empirical result which has not been based on any fundamental theory. One direction taken by the more systematic work in the prediction of rare events is that of deriving distribution functions from first principles and then finding the best values for the parameters of the theoretical formulae empirically. This is the program followed by Gumbel[3] and discussed below. The basic assumption is that the stochastic process which determines the magnitude of our variable is stationary, i.e., that at all times the determining factors for the level are the same. We further assume that successive measurements of our random variable are independent. Generally, we are interested in a variable which represents the highest value some variable such as a river height achieves in a year. Some short range dependence does not change the results derived below.

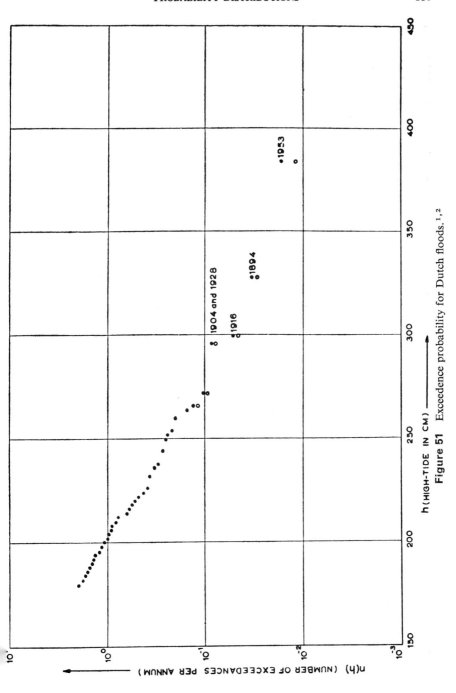

Figure 51 Exceedence probability for Dutch floods.[1,2]

While we have been motivated by Gumbel's exposition, the pioneering work on this subject is due to Fréchet,[5] Fisher and Tippett[6] and von Mises.[7]

The function which characterizes the stochastic process is its cumulative distribution function $F(x)$ defined by Eq. 1.3. If X is our variable of interest, then

$$F(x) = \text{Prob}\,(X < x) \tag{1a}$$

$$1 - F(x) = \text{Prob}\,(X > x) \tag{1b}$$

If we are concerned with river levels, $F(x)$ is the probability that in a given day the level does not exceed x. A very useful quantity which depends on $F(x)$ is $T(x)$, the return time of the variable x:

$$T(x) = 1/[1 - F(x)] \tag{2}$$

On the average, $T(x)$ will be the time (or number of observations, if one is made per unit time) required before one observation is made such that x equals or exceeds x. We clarify this remark through an example. Consider a fair (unloaded) die. When tossed, the probability that any specified face will come up is 1/6. The average number of throws required for that face to turn up is $1/[1/6] = 6$. Generally the average number of trials required for an event to occur is the reciprocal of the probability for the event to occur on a single trial.

We now define two quantities which will later be seen to be the parameters which differentiate one "extremal" distribution from another. All major American rivers seem to behave according to the same "extremal" distribution (to be derived), but each has its own characteristic pair of parameters. The first is u_n defined by the relation

$$F(u_n) = 1 - \frac{1}{n} \tag{3}$$

where n is the number of observations or, more generally, the statistical sample size. It should be noted that u_n is the value of x for which the return time is n. This can easily be seen by solving equation (3) for n and comparing the result with (2). Perhaps the most fundamental way to look at u_n is to rewrite (3) as

$$n[1 - F(u_n)] = 1 \tag{4}$$

Here the left side of the equation gives the expected number of values equal to or exceeding u_n out of n trials. Since the product is unity, u_n is termed the *expected largest value*. While u_n is not the same thing as the mean or average extreme value, it has the same central importance for the asymptotic "extremal" distribution as the mean $\bar{x}$ had for the normal distribution. We show later that, as the sample size n gets very large, the most probable extreme value becomes u_n for a large class of initial distributions.

The second parameter to be defined is α_n, (with $f \equiv dF/dx$)

$$\alpha_n = nf(u_n) \tag{5}$$

We eliminate n between (5) and (4) to obtain

$$\alpha_n[1 - F(u_n)] = f(u_n) \tag{6}$$

The parameter α_n bears the same relation to the "extremal" distribution as the standard deviation σ did to the normal distribution. Both say something about the width or dispersion of their respective distributions. The parameter α_n is of most immediate interest because it tells us how rapidly u_n changes as a function of sample size n.

Let us differentiate (3) with respect to n to obtain

$$f(u_n) \, du_n/dn = 1/n^2$$

Then, from (5),

$$\frac{du_n}{d \log n} = \frac{1}{\alpha_n} \tag{7}$$

so that $1/\alpha_n$ gives us a measure of the variation in u_n associated with a given variation in the logarithm of the sample size. If α_n increases (decreases) with n, then the expected largest value increases more slowly (more rapidly) than $\log n$. A linear increase of u_n with $\log n$ thus gives us a standard of comparison. If we let the number of years for which we have records of floods be the sample size (instead of choosing n equal to the number of days per year) and let u_n be the largest flood observed in n years, we see the motivation for plotting the largest flood as a function of $\log n$ in Figure 49.

We now derive a distribution function for extreme values observed over fixed times. Let us make n observations of the variable X. If we are observing flood levels, we suppose that we make an observation every day so that $n = 365$. Then, if the observations are independent of each other, the probability that the largest value of X observed over the year is less than x is

$$\Phi_n(x) = [F(x)]^n \tag{8}$$

since for $X < x$ to be true throughout the year, it must be true every day. We might expect that the level on succeeding days would be correlated. However if the correlation memory does not extend over many days, one obtains the same result which we find by postulating independence. Hence we use the simpler model.

The distribution function $\varphi_n(x)$ can be obtained from the cumulative distribution function (8) by differentiation

$$\varphi_n(x) = nF^{n-1}(x)\, dF/dx = nF^{n-1}(x)f(x) \tag{9}$$

if $f(x)$ is the distribution function which corresponds to $F(x)$. We now seek an asymptotic form for $\Phi_n(x)$ when n is large. In the case of daily records $n = 365$ and $\varphi_n(x)$ would be the distribution function of greatest annual levels.

We start our search for the distribution of extreme values by considering the special case of initial distribution

$$F(x) = 1 - e^{-\alpha x} \tag{10a}$$

so that

$$f(x) = dF/dx = \alpha e^{-\alpha x} \tag{10b}$$

The quantities α_n and u_n defined by (3) and (5) are then given by

$$n \exp(-\alpha u_n) = 1 \text{ and } \alpha_n = n\alpha \exp(-\alpha u_n) \tag{11a}$$

Hence

$$\alpha_n = \alpha \text{ and } u_n = (1/\alpha)\log n \tag{11b}$$

and

$$F(x) = 1 - \exp\{-\alpha[(x-u_n)+u_n]\}$$

$$= 1 - \frac{1}{n}e^{-y} \tag{12a}$$

where

$$y \equiv \alpha_n(x-u_n) = \alpha(x-u_n). \tag{12b}$$

The distribution function for the largest value of x in a sequence of n observations is then

$$\Phi_n(x) = F^n(x) = \left(1 - \frac{1}{n}e^{-y}\right)^n$$

$$\sim e^{-\exp-y} \qquad \text{as } n \to \infty \tag{13}$$

The probability density function is

$$\varphi_n(x) = d\Phi_n/dx = nF^{n-1}(x)f(x).$$

$$\sim \alpha \exp -\{y+e^{-y}\} \tag{14}$$

The density function $\varphi_n(x)$ has a maximum value which corresponds to the most likely largest value of x after n observations.

It is easily shown for our special initial distribution (10a) that u_n is indeed the most probable value for the largest value of X in n observations as we anticipated while u_n was being defined. We see from (9) that $\varphi_n(x)$ has a peak or a maximum value, since as $x \to -\infty$, $F(x) \to 0$ and as $x \to \infty$, $f(x) \to 0$. To find the value of x at which $\varphi_n(x)$ has a maximum, we set $d\varphi_n(x)/dx = 0$. This yields

$$nF^{n-2}(x)f(x)\{(n-1)f(x)+F(x)d\log f(x)/dx\} = 0 \tag{15}$$

Then substituting (10a) and (10b) into this equation we find

$$(n-1)\alpha e^{-\alpha x}-(1-e^{-\alpha x})\alpha = 0$$

or $n \exp(-\alpha x) = 1$, which from (11) is the defining relation for $x = u_n$ as required.

Incidentally the expected time required for y to achieve a preassigned value is, from (2) and (13)

$$T(y) = 1/\{1-e^{-\exp-y}\} \tag{16}$$

$$\sim \exp y, \text{ if } y \text{ is large}$$

That is,

$$y \sim \log T(y)$$

with

$$y = \alpha(x-u_n), u_n = \log n.$$

While the equations derived above are limit results for large n, in applications the value of n is fixed but large. For example, in discussing annual flood records, $n = 365$. The distribution function (13) would be that appropriate to the results of an ensemble of many sets of 365-day measurements.

The above results are also valid for a wide class of initial distribution functions for which, as $x \to \infty$

$$\frac{f'(x)}{f(x)} \sim \frac{f''(x)}{f'(x)} \sim \frac{f'''(x)}{f''(x)} \sim \cdots \tag{17}$$

Such distributions are called exponential type. Clearly our example

$$F(x) = 1-e^{-\alpha x} \quad \text{with} \quad f(x) = \alpha e^{-\alpha x}$$

is of this type with $f'(x)/f(x) \sim -\alpha$ as $x \to \infty$. The Gaussian (1.1) also has this property with

$$-2(x-\mu)/\sigma^2 \sim \frac{f'(x)}{f(x)} \sim \frac{f''(x)}{f'(x)} \sim \cdots \tag{18}$$

We will again need the equations

$$n[1-F(u_n)] \equiv 1, \quad \alpha_n \equiv nf(u_n) \tag{19a}$$

$$-\alpha_n \equiv \frac{-f(u_n)}{1-F(u_n)} \sim f'(u_n)/f(u_n) \tag{19b}$$

where we have applied L'Hopital's rule. Our postulate (17) implies that all the ratios given in the chain are $\sim -\alpha_n$ when $x = u_n$. In the case of the Gaussian

$$\alpha_n = 2(u_n-\mu)/\sigma^2 \tag{20}$$

The derivation of (13) follows from the identity

$$\log \{n[1-F(x)]\} = \log \{n[1-F(u_n)+F(u_n)-F(u_n+[x-u_n])]\} \tag{21}$$
$$= \log \{1-n[F(u_n+y/\alpha_n)-F(u_n)]\}$$
$$= \log \left\{1-n\left[(y/\alpha_n)f(u_n)+\tfrac{1}{2}(y/\alpha_n)^2 f'(u_n) \right.\right.$$
$$\left.\left. + \frac{1}{3!} (y/\alpha_n)^3 f''(u_n)+... \right]\right\}$$

However, from (19a)

$$(n/\alpha_n)f(u_n) = 1$$
$$(n/\alpha_n^2)f'(u_n) = [f'(u_n)/f(u_n)]/\alpha_n \sim -1$$
$$(n/\alpha_n^3)f''(u_n) = [f''(u_n)/f(u_n)]/\alpha_n^2$$
$$= [f''(u_n)/f'(u_n)][f'(u_n)/f(u_n)]/\alpha_n^2 \sim 1, \quad \text{etc.}$$

as $n \to \infty$ and $u_n \to \infty$ upon application of (17), (19a), and (19b). Hence, under these conditions,

$$\log n[1-F(x)] \sim \log \left\{1-y+\tfrac{1}{2}y^2 -\frac{1}{3!}y^3+...\right\} = -y \tag{21a}$$

so that, as required,

$$F(x) \sim 1-\frac{1}{n}e^{-y} \tag{22}$$

and

$$\Phi_n(x) = F^n(x) \sim \left(1-\frac{1}{n}e^{-y}\right)^n \sim e^{-\exp-y} \tag{23}$$

Equations (14)–(16) are then applicable to our wider class of initial distributions.

It is to be noted that (17) is not satisfied by all distributions. For example, in the case of the Pareto distribution, one has for large x, $f(x) \sim ax^{-\lambda}$. Hence, as $x \to \infty$

$$f'(x)/f(x) \sim -\lambda/x$$
$$f''(x)/f'(x) \sim -(\lambda+1)/x$$
$$f'''(x)/f''(x) \sim -(\lambda+2)/x, \quad \text{etc.}$$

which is contrary to (17). These exceptional cases will be discussed at the end of this section.

The application of (23) and (16) is best accomplished through the employment of Gumbel's extreme value probability paper. If a random variable x has a cumulative distribution function $\Phi(x)$ of form (23), then the plot of x against $\Phi(x)$ on this graph paper is a straight line. The return period for a given value of x is given at the top of the paper according to the point on the curve associated with that value of x. We have reproduced a number of such graphs from Gumbel's article, listed as Reference 3.

The first example involves the extreme duration of human life. The data represents the oldest age at death in Switzerland in the 55-year period, 1879–1933. In each of these 55 years, the age of the oldest person who died in the given year was recorded. As is evident from Table V, there was one year in which the oldest person dying was 97, three years in which the oldest dying was 98, etc. The cumulative distribution function (which is a step function since the ages were given in years only) is easily constructed as shown in the table. The plotting scheme used is that outlined at the end of Section 3 and can be deduced in detail by comparing Table VIII with Figure 52. The oldest observed age at death over a 55-year-time span was 106, while the extremal theory predicts 106.4.

Our next examples are derived from flood control studies. Figure 53 shows straight line fits to annual flood data for two particular rivers.

Data for three more rivers in the Columbia River Basin is included in order to convince you that rivers really do seem to follow the "extremal" distribution.

There are a number of good climatological applications of the "extremal" distribution. Figure 56 presents some information about the largest daily snowfalls in Boston, while Figure 57 gives some data on earthquakes.

Extrema on the low side can be as dangerous as those on the high side. Unexpected very low temperatures in temperate regions which are not prepared for them can be disastrous. We can easily derive an asymptotic law for the distribution of minima in a manner analogous to (23) in the case in which the initial variate is unlimited to the left and is of exponential type as $x \to -\infty$; i.e., as $x \to -\infty$

$$\frac{f'(x)}{f(x)} \sim \frac{f''(x)}{f(x)} \sim \frac{f'''(x)}{f''(x)} \sim \cdots \tag{24}$$

This can easily be verified for a Gaussian distribution.

Let us define n_1 as the value of x such that

$$nF(u_1) = 1 \tag{25}$$

and α_1 by

$$\alpha_1 \equiv nf(u_1) = f(u_1)/F(u_1). \tag{26}$$

TABLE VIII　Oldest ages in Switzerland, 1879–1933, both sexes.

Oldest age	Number of individuals	Cumulative number, m	Plotting positions, $m/(N+1)$
97	1	1	0.018
98	3	2 to 4	0.036 to 0.071
99	6	5 to 10	.089 to .178
100	14	11 to 24	.196 to .428
101	12	25 to 36	.446 to .643
102	7	37 to 43	.660 to .768
103	7	44 to 50	.786 to .893
104	3	51 to 53	.911 to .946
105	1	54	0.9643
106	1	55	.9821
	N = 55		

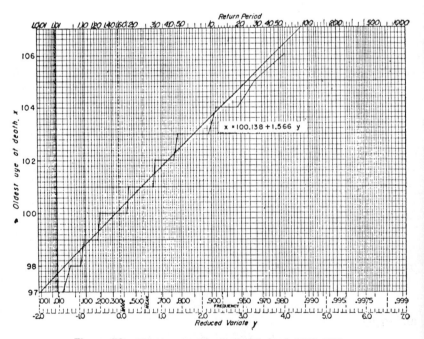

Figure 52　Oldest ages at death, Switzerland, 1879–1933

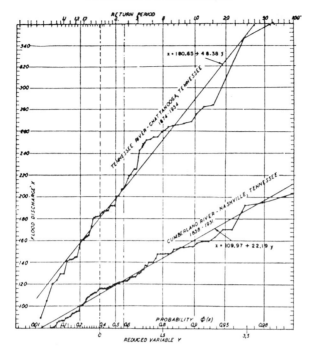

Figure 53 Annual floods of Tennessee and Cumberland Rivers, 1874–1934 and 1838–1931.
(Discharge in 1,000 ft³/sec).

Since both $f(x)$ and $F(x)$ vanish as $x \to \infty$ and as $n \to \infty$, $u_1 \to -\infty$, we see from L'Hopital's rule that

$$\alpha_1 \sim \frac{f'(u_1)}{f(u_1)} \tag{27}$$

Hence all the ratios in (24) approach α_1 if $x = u_1 \to -\infty$.

The probability that $X > x$ is $1 - F(x)$. Hence the probability that each of n independent measurement of X is $> x$ is $[1 - F(x)]^n$. Hence the probability that the smallest of n measurements of X is $< x$ is

$$_1\Phi_n(x) = 1 - [1 - F(x)]^n \tag{28}$$

Let

$$y_1 = \alpha_1(x - u_1) \tag{29}$$

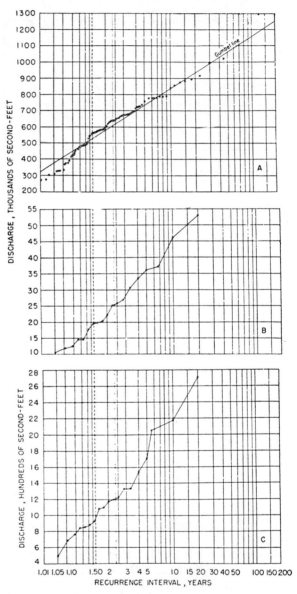

Figure 54 Magnitude and frequency of annual floods in three rivers of the Columbia River Basin.[3]

A. Columbia River near The Dalles, Oregon, 1858–1948. B. Clark Fork below Missoula, Mont., 1930–1948. C. Boulder Creek near Leonia, Idaho, 1929–1933, 1935–1948.

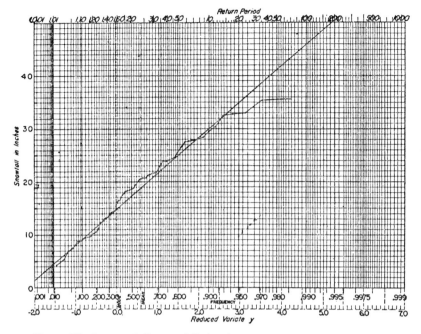

Figure 55 Largest daily snowfalls in winter, Boston, Mass., 1871–1872 to 1939–1940.[3]

and consider the identity

$$\log nF(x) = \log n[F(u_1) + F(u_1 + [x - u_1]) - F(u_1)] \qquad (30)$$

$$= \log 1\{+n[F(u_1 + y_1/\alpha_1) - F(u_1)]\}$$

$$= \log \{1 + n[f(u_1)y_1/\alpha_1 + \tfrac{1}{2}f'(u_1)y^2/\alpha_1^2 + ...]\}$$

$$= \log \{1 + y_1 + \tfrac{1}{2}y_1^2 + ...\} = y_1 \qquad (31)$$

where we employed (26) and (24) and proceeded in the same manner as was done in the derivation of (21a). Then for large n,

$$F(x) \sim \frac{e^{y_1}}{n} \qquad (32)$$

and

$$_1\Phi_n(x) \sim 1 - \exp - e^{y_1} \quad \text{with} \quad y_1 = \alpha_1(x - u_1) \qquad (33)$$

As an example of an application of these ideas, we have plotted the lowest temperatures recorded each year in Alabama in the period 1884–1942.

F

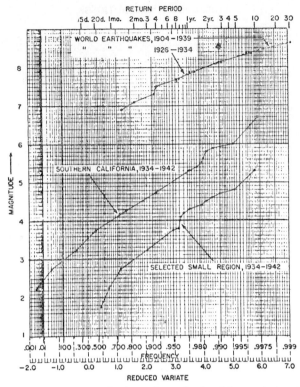

Figure 56 Observed distributions of magnitudes of the greatest earthquakes.[3]

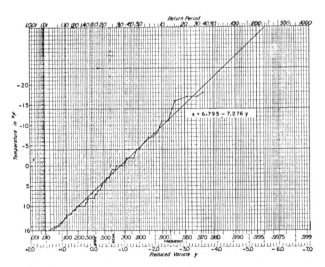

Figure 57 Lowest temperatures, Alabama, 1884–1942.[3]

Many other examples of distributions of extrema, maxima and minima are given in Reference 3.

There are two interesting classes of events in which one does not expect straight line plots on Gumbel paper. The first would correspond to initial distributions which are not of an exponential type. Then a systematic curve would appear but it will not be a straight line. That case will be discussed below. The second class would correspond to situations in which the basic variable would be generated by one stochastic process up to a certain time t after which a new basic stochastic process might take over. The observer might become aware of this shift by noticing that observed extrema would go completely off the scale. In a set of observations over 50 years, an extreme point whose return period might be 1000 years, might appear. While this is possible, it is so unlikely that an astute observer would investigate the possibility that the basic processes have changed. We will discuss just such a situation when we analyze certain aspects of the stock market.

Consider the basic distribution function of "Cauchy type"

$$F(z) = 1 - Az^{-k}$$

which is not of exponential type. If the expected largest value in n measurement v_n is introduced through the definition (3), then

$$F(z) = 1 - \frac{1}{n}(v_n/z)^k$$

Then the distribution function for maxima is, from (8), as $n \to \infty$

$$\Pi(z) = \Phi_n(z) = \exp -(v_n/z)^k \quad 0 < z < \infty$$

where v_n depends on n but k is a constant. This result can be linked to our previous one (13) by defining a new variable x such that

$$(v_n/z)^k = \exp\{-\alpha_n(x-u_n)\}$$

and, as before defining,

$$y = \alpha_n(x-u_n).$$

Conversely, the asymptotic distribution of the Cauchy type is obtained from the asymptotic distribution of the exponential type by a logarithmic transformation. Gumbel paper can then be used for estimating return periods for Cauchy type initial distributions if $\log x$ instead of x is plotted as an ordinate.

REFERENCES

1. P. J. Wemelsfelder, De Ingenieur 9, Bouw-en Waterbouwkunde 3, 1–5 (1939).
2. D. van Dantzig, Proc. Int. Congress of Math, Series II, 7th Congress Amsterdam I, 218(1959).

3. E. J. Gumbel, Statistical Theory of Extreme Values and Some Practical Applications, No. 33, National Bureau of Standards App. Math. Series, 1954.
4. E. J. Gumbel, *Statistics of Extremes*, Columbia Univ. Press, 1958.
5. M. Fréchet, Ann. de la Soc. polonaise de Math. (Cracow), 6, 93, 1927.
6. R. A. Fisher and L. H. C. Tippett, *Proc. Camb. Phil. Soc.* **24**, 180 (1928).
7. R. von Mises, *Review math. de l'Union Interbalkanique* (Athens) **1**, 1, 1936.

9   The Entropy Strategy for Attacking Problems Characterized by a Limited Amount of Macroscopic Knowledge

A common attitude concerning situations which are described statistically by several variables is that the variables tend to become as randomly distributed as possible under macroscopic constraints which might exist. A more precise mathematical formulation of this statement is generally made in terms of the *entropy function*, a function first defined by L. Boltzmann[1] in his work on the kinetic theory of gases.

Let us consider a discrete variable x which can achieve any one of a set of states $a_1, a_2, ..., a_n$. We identify these states by the integers 1, 2, ..., n and define the probability that x be in the state i to be p_i so that

$$\text{prob}\,(x = a_i) = p_i \tag{1}$$

The entropy of the process which generates the variable x is defined to be

$$H = -\sum_{i=1}^{n} p_i \log_e p_i \tag{2}$$

This definition generalizes immediately for the case in which x is a continuous variable with a range $-\infty$ to $+\infty$. Let $p(x)$ be the probability density of x so that

$$\text{Prob}\,(x < X) = \int_{-\infty}^{X} p(x)\, dx. \tag{3}$$

Then the entropy of the process which generates x is

$$H = -\int_{-\infty}^{\infty} p(x) \log p(x)\, dx. \tag{4}$$

There are several ways of indicating that the entropy is large for processes in which the values achieved by x in successive trials are "random" and small for processes in which the value achieved by x is always the same. Suppose first that x is discrete and that it has the same probability $p_i = 1/n$ (for $i = 1, 2, ..., n$) of achieving any of its n possible values. As n increases we would say that the process becomes more and more random and, if the entropy has the property stated above, it should increase with n. From (1)

$$H = -n(1/n) \log (1/n) = \log n \qquad (5)$$

as required. Indeed, if $n = 1$ so that x has a single possible value, then $H = 0$. If any state becomes more probable, we would say that the process becomes less random so that if H has the properties we attributed to it, it should decrease under this condition. Let us suppose that

$$p_i = n^{-1}(1+\delta_i) \qquad (6)$$

Then, since the probabilities are normalized,

$$1 = \sum_{i=1}^{n} p_i = \sum_{i=1}^{n} n^{-1}(1+\delta_i)$$

$$= 1 + n^{-1} \sum \delta_i$$

or

$$\sum_{i=1}^{n} \delta_i = 0 \qquad (7)$$

The entropy associated with the probabilities (6) is

$$H(\delta_1 \ldots \delta_n) = -\sum_i n^{-1}(1+\delta_i) \log \{n^{-1}(1+\delta_i)\}$$

$$= \log n - n^{-1} \sum (1+\delta_i) \log (1+\delta_i)$$

$$= \log n - (1/2n) \sum_{i=1}^{n} \delta_i^2 + O(\delta^3) \qquad (8)$$

Hence any small tendency to give one of the states a larger probability than the others decreases the entropy.

Now let us consider a continuous variable x of range $(-\infty, \infty)$, with the distribution function $p(x)$, with mean value 0 and with dispersion σ^2. Then

$$1 = \int_{-\infty}^{\infty} p(x)\, dx \quad \text{and} \quad \sigma^2 = \int_{-\infty}^{\infty} x^2 p(x)\, dx \qquad (10)$$

An interesting question is to ask what distribution function $p(x)$ corresponds to the largest entropy under the two auxilliary conditions. By employing the method of Lagrangian multipliers, we are required to maximize the functional

$$F[p] = -\int_{-\infty}^{\infty} \{p(x) \log p(x) + \lambda p(x) + \mu x^2 p(x)\}\, dx \qquad (11)$$

We require that, for all variations δp in p,

$$\delta F[p] = -\int_{-\infty}^{\infty} \{\log p(x) + 1 + \lambda + \mu x^2\} \delta p\, dx = 0 \qquad (12)$$

This is so when

$$p(x) = \exp -(1+\lambda+\mu x^2) \tag{13}$$

The appropriate values of λ and μ are obtained by substituting (13) into (10). Then we find that $p(x)$ is the Gaussian distribution[5]

$$p(x) = (2\pi\sigma^2)^{-\frac{1}{2}} \exp(-x^2/2\sigma^2) \tag{14}$$

When this expression is substituted into (4), the result is

$$H = - \int_{-\infty}^{\infty} p(x)\{-\tfrac{1}{2}\log 2\pi\sigma^2 - (x^2/2\sigma^2)\} \, dx$$
$$= \log (2\pi\sigma^2)^{\frac{1}{2}} + \tfrac{1}{2} = \tfrac{1}{2}\log (2\pi e\sigma^2). \tag{15}$$

As the dispersion σ increases, the variable x becomes more random and the entropy increases as we might expect. It is easy to show in a similar manner that the normalized distribution function in the range $0 < x < \infty$ with fixed first moment c is the exponential distribution

$$p(x) = c^{-1} \exp(-x/c) \quad \text{for} \quad x > 0. \tag{16}$$

Equation (4) can be generalized to apply to a situation which is described by m variables $x_1, x_2, ..., x_m$ whose joint distribution function is

$$p(x_1, x_2, ..., x_m) \tag{17a}$$

Then

$$H = - \int_{-\infty}^{\infty} \int p(x_1, ..., x_m) \log p(x_1, ..., x_m) \, dx_1 ... dx_m \tag{17b}$$

In general we say that

$$H = - \langle \log p(x_1, ..., x_m) \rangle, \tag{17c}$$

the brackets $\langle F \rangle$ represent the average value of a function F weighted by the appropriate distribution function of the variables required to characterize F. When the x_j's are independent of each other, (17a) has the form

$$p(x_1, ..., x_m) = \prod_{1}^{m} p_j(x_j) \tag{18}$$

with $p_j(x_j)$ being the distribution of the jth variable. Since each $p_i(x)$ is normalized to unity

$$H = - \sum_{j=1}^{m} \int p_j(x_j) \log p_j(x_j) \, dx_j \tag{19}$$

If all functions $p_j(x)$ are the same and equal to $p(x)$, then the entropy per variable is

$$H/m = - \int p(x) \log p(x) \, dx. \tag{20}$$

Now let us return to the general case of m variables and suppose that there are a number of constraints on a process, say that

$$\int_{-\infty}^{\infty} \dots \int F_i(x)p(x) \, d^m x = c_i \quad \text{with} \quad i = 1, \dots, l \qquad (21)$$

where

$$x \equiv (x_1, x_2, \dots, x_m) \quad \text{and} \quad d^m x \equiv dx_1 \, dx_2 \dots dx_m.$$

From the requirement that probabilities are normalized, one of the F's, say F_1, must be 1 and the associated $c_1 = 1$. How would we determine $p(x)$ such that the process would be as random as possible subject to the constraints (21)? We would again resort to the Lagrange multiplier technique and maximize

$$F[p] = -\int_{-\infty}^{\infty} \dots \int p(x)[\log p(x) + \lambda_1 + \lambda_2 F_2(x) + \dots + \lambda_l F_l(x)] \, d^m x \qquad (22)$$

Then we require that for all variations δp of p,

$$\delta F[p] = -\int_{-\infty}^{\infty} \dots \int [\log p(x) + 1 + \lambda_1 + \lambda_2 F_2 + \dots + \lambda_l F_l]\delta p \, d^m x = 0 \qquad (23)$$

This is the case when

$$p(x_1, \dots x_m) = \exp -(1 + \lambda_1 + \lambda_2 F_2 + \dots + \lambda_l F_l)$$

where the value of λ_1 is to be chosen so that

$$1 = \int \dots \int p(x) \, d^m x = [\exp -(1 + \lambda_1)] \int \dots \int \exp -(\lambda_2 F_2 + \dots + \lambda_l F_l) \, d^m x$$

Hence if we define the partition function Z as the sum over all values of the $\{x_j\}$

$$Z = \int_{-\infty}^{\infty} \dots \int \exp \left(- \sum_{j=2}^{l} \lambda_j F_j\right) d^m x \qquad (24)$$

Then

$$p(x_1, \dots, x_m) = Z^{-1} \exp \{\lambda_2 F_2(x_1, \dots, x_m) + \dots + \lambda_l F_l(x_1, \dots, x_m)\} \qquad (25a)$$

where each λ is to be chosen so that

$$\partial \log Z / \partial \lambda_j = -c_j \quad \text{with} \quad j = 2, \dots, l \qquad (25b)$$

Notice that the concept of a rate process has not entered into the entropy discussion. This is because the various distribution functions correspond to stationary, unchanging, or equilibrium distribution functions. If at some time the distribution function is not of the equilibrium type, the system is presumed to relax in such a way that equilibrium is established and the entropy becomes a maximum.

We introduce the method of application of the entropy strategy by reviewing Boltzmann's ideas. Consider first a gas composed of N independent (non-interacting molecules) whose x, y, and z velocity components are u_i, v_i, and w_i, the subscript i representing the ith molecule. Then the kinetic energy associated with a given component (say the x component) of the ith molecule is

$$\varepsilon_i(x) = \tfrac{1}{2}m\,u_i^2 \qquad (26)$$

We also let ε_i be the total kinetic energy of the ith molecule

$$\varepsilon_i(x)+\varepsilon_i(y)+\varepsilon_i(z) = \varepsilon_i \qquad (27)$$

During each collision between molecules, energy is exchanged so that the velocity of one molecule might increase while the other decreases. However, in the law of the conservation of energy, the total energy of the pair of colliding molecules is conserved, i.e., remains unchanged or invariant. Indeed, the total energy

$$E = \varepsilon_1+\varepsilon_2+\ldots+\varepsilon_N = \tfrac{1}{2}m\sum_{i=1}^{N}(u_i^2+v_i^2+w_i^2) \qquad (28)$$

of all our molecules remains invariant as the molecules collide with each other. Through various arguments which we do not repeat here, the temperature T of a gas is proportional to the mean kinetic energy per gas molecule, i.e.,

$$\tfrac{1}{2}m\langle V^2\rangle = m\langle u^2+v^2+w^2\rangle$$
$$= \tfrac{3}{2}m\langle u^2\rangle = \tfrac{3}{2}m\langle v^2\rangle = \tfrac{3}{2}m\langle w^2\rangle$$
$$= \tfrac{3}{2}kT \qquad (29)$$

k being "Boltzmann's constant". Since all directions in space should be equivalent (in the absence of any external field), the mean kinetic energy associated with velocities in the x, y, and z directions should be the same.

If we believe that the molecules of a gas tend to have as random a set of velocities as is possible, consistent with the energy conservation constraint, we quantify this idea by saying that the entropy should have the maximum value consistent with the constraint. The dispersion σ of the velocity distribution function for each component of the velocity is

$$\sigma^2 = \langle u^2\rangle = kT/m \qquad (30)$$

and any component of the velocity, say u, has the Gaussian (or Maxwellian) velocity distribution (see Eq. (14)) such that the probability of it having a value between u and $u+du$ is

$$p(u)du = (2\pi kT/m)^{-\frac{1}{2}}\exp-(\tfrac{1}{2}mu^2/kT)\,du \qquad (31)$$

which has been observed experimentally. The entropy per degree of freedom would then be

$$H/3N = \tfrac{1}{2} \log (2\pi e \sigma^2) = \log (\pi e kT/m)^{\frac{1}{2}} \tag{32}$$

If we let the energy per degree of freedom be ε, then

$$\varepsilon = \tfrac{1}{2}mu^2 \tag{33}$$

and the probability that ε has a value between ε and $\varepsilon + d\varepsilon$ is

$$(2m/\pi kT)^{\frac{1}{2}}\{\exp -\varepsilon/kT\}(du/d\varepsilon)\, d\varepsilon = (\pi kT)^{-\frac{1}{2}}\{\exp -\varepsilon/kT\}\varepsilon^{-\frac{1}{2}}\, d\varepsilon \tag{34}$$

Now suppose that the order of the experimental discovery of the law of the conservation of energy and of the Maxwell distribution function was inverted. What speculations might have been made? If one decided that the entropy maximumization principle was valid and that particles in a gas were independent, then the observation of the Maxwell distribution would imply that for each degree of freedom, (31) was valid. The mean value of the total kinetic energy would be

$$\langle \tfrac{1}{2}m\{u_1^2 + v_1^2 + \ldots + u_N^2 + v_N^2 + w_N^2\}\rangle = 3Nm\sigma^2/2 = (3N/2)kT = \langle E\rangle \tag{35}$$

From this one could, to within experimental error, deduce that the energy is conserved through collisions. This would be done through an application of Tchebyshev's inequality[2].

The statement of Tchebyshev's inequality is: Let X be a random variable with mean value $\mu = \langle X\rangle$ and dispersion $\Sigma^2 = \langle(X-\mu)^2\rangle$. Then for any $t > 0$,

$$\text{Prob}\,\{|X-\mu| > t\} < \Sigma^2/t^2. \tag{36}$$

Now let X be $(2E/m)$. Then $\mu = 3NkT/m$ and

$$\begin{aligned}
\Sigma^2 &= \langle\{(u_1^2 + \ldots + w_N^2) - 3N\sigma^2\}^2\rangle \\
&= 3N\langle u^4\rangle + 3N(3N-1)\sigma^4 - 9N^2\sigma^4 \\
&= 3N\{\langle u^4\rangle - \sigma^4\} = 6N\sigma^4
\end{aligned} \tag{37}$$

Hence, for any $t > 0$,

$$\text{Prob}\{|(2E/m) - 3N\sigma^2| > t\} < 6N\sigma^4/t^2 \tag{38}$$

Now let us choose $t = \sigma^2 N^{\frac{1}{2}+\eta}$. Then

$$\text{Prob}\,\{|(2E/m) - 3N\sigma^2| > \sigma^2 N^{\frac{1}{2}+\eta}\} < 6N^{-2\eta} \tag{39}$$

In the gas problem $N = O(10^{24})$ so that if one chooses $\eta = 1/8$, this inequality states that $(2E/m)$ varies from its average value of $O(10^{24})$ by an amount bigger than $10^{15}\sigma^2$ with a probability $< 6 \times 10^{-6}$. It would require an

F*

exceedingly accurate measurement to note that the conservation of energy might be ever so slightly violated. Hence, for all practical purposes, a measurement of the Maxwell distribution would imply conservation of kinetic energy in a gas without intermolecular interactions.

We now indicate how the entropy strategy might be used to investigate distribution functions of quantities of social importance. The equations of motion for individuals are not understood in the manner that those equations for molecules are understood. Hence, whatever deductions are to be made must be made from an examination of macroscopic statistical data. The example which we consider is that of the distribution of income, a topic which has already been alluded to in Section 3.

Through various transactions, money is transferred from individual to individual in a manner analogous to that in which energy is transferred from gas molecule to gas molecule by collisions. Through transfer of goods or services (or welfare), every family has someone with an annual income. One might argue that through many transactions money tends to get randomly distributed but, through some unclear constraints which are due to training, motivation, risk-taking, inheritance, intimidation, etc., some people obtain larger annual incomes than others. We will still apply our entropy principle, but at first without any clear understanding of the constraints. We will try to suggest a constraint in the same manner that we showed that the Maxwell distribution suggests the conservation of energy.

Let us suppose that the distribution of annual incomes is log normal, as was suggested as a possibility in Section 3. Then the probability that one's annual income is between x and $x+dx$ is

$$(2\pi\sigma^2)^{-\frac{1}{2}} \exp\{-(\log[x/\bar{x}])^2/2\sigma^2\}\, dx/x = p(x)\, dx \qquad (40)$$

The factor dx/x is exactly the variation of the Bernoulli utility function $U(x)$ defined so that

$$dU = dx/x \qquad (41)$$

The classical significance to this form is that a process which involves a transfer of money dx has a different meaning to persons of different levels of income. Two transactions made by two persons of different income levels might be more equivalent if they both involved the same fraction of the income of the participants. Hence, according to Bernoulli, the basic function which determines one's course of action is the utility function

$$U(x) = \log(x/x_0), \qquad (42)$$

$\log x_0$ being the constant of integration of (41). It would then seem reasonable that the quantity which would become as randomly distributed as possible during the many decision-making steps which determines one annual income would be related to the utility function. In every situation in which income is made, two or more persons make an arrangement in which each is attempting to do the best he can. An alternative form for (40) is

$$(2\pi\sigma^2)^{-\frac{1}{2}} \exp\{-[U(x)]^2/2\sigma^2\}(dU/dx)\, dx = p(x)\, dx. \tag{43}$$

The (dU/dx) is analogous to the density of states in a statistical mechanics problem.

If we followed the reasoning that was employed above to surmise the conservation of energy from the Maxwell distribution, we would find that the sums of the squares of the utility functions of the population would be conserved in economic transaction

$$\sum_j \{U_j(x_j)\}^2 = \text{constant} \tag{44}$$

or, rather, almost constant. The variation would be more than that estimated for gas molecules. For the U.S., $N = 0(10^8)$. Hence, an application of the Tchebyshev inequality would say that the probability of the variation of the constant from its mean value of $0(10^8)$ by an amount of $0(10^5)$ i.e., by a tenth of a percent) is of $0(10^{-2})$ or less.

The U.S. Commerce Department has produced detailed plots of annual incomes such as that given in Figure 58. Since the graph is plotted on log normal paper, the distribution would be a straight line if it were truly log normal. Notice a deviation in the very high and very low income ranges. A good $U(x)$ fit to this curve requires two parameters c and δ and one finds that

$$U(x) = c^{-1}\left[\exp\left\{-\frac{c}{\delta}\left[\left(\frac{\bar{x}}{x}\right)^\delta - 1\right]\right\} - 1\right] \tag{45}$$

As $c \to 0$, this becomes

$$U(x) = -\frac{1}{\delta}\left[\left(\frac{\bar{x}}{x}\right)^\delta - 1\right]$$

$$\to \log(x/\bar{x}) \quad \text{as} \quad \delta \to 0 \tag{46}$$

It is not surprising that $U = \log(x/\bar{x})$ is not appropriate over the entire range since the motivations and opportunities are quite different in various income levels. An excellent discussion of the general properties of the utility function has been given by Friedman and Savage.[4]

Our above discussion should be viewed as an example of how a strategy might be developed rather than as a definitive analysis of the wealth distri-

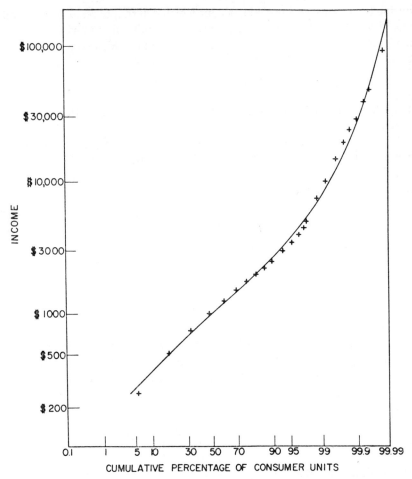

Figure 58 Distribution of families and single individuals by income levels 1935–36 (data from reference 3). The values of the parameters of Eq. (45) on which the curve is based are $\delta = 0.580$, $c = 0.561$, $\sigma = 0.750$ and $\bar{x} = 1009$.

bution. A more critical interpretation of the application is being prepared for publication elsewhere.

The entropy ideas have, of course, been applied with great success by Shannon[5] to the theory of transmission of information. A. G. Wilson has written extensively on the use of entropy in social modeling.[6,7] The specific case which he has emphasized is that of trip frequencies in travel between various points. His general philosophy leans heavily on Jaynes'[8] work on the relationship between statistical mechanics and information theory.

REFERENCES

1. L. Boltzmann, *Wissenschaftliche Abhandlungen*, Leipzig (1905); reprinted by Chelsea Press, 1968.
2. W. Feller, *An Introduction to Probability Theory and Its Applications* Vol. 1, Wiley, 1950.
3. U.S. National Resources Committee, Consumer Incomes in the U.S., 1935–36, (Govt. Printing Office, 1939).
4. M. Friedman and L. J. Savage, *Jour. of Political Economy* **56**: 279(1948).
5. G. E. Shannon, *Bell Systems Tech. J.* **27**: 379, 623(1948).
6. A. G. Wilson, Regional Science Association: Papers XXII, Budapest Conference (1968), p. 159.
7. A. G. Wilson, *Operational Research Quarterly* **21**: 247(1970).
8. E. T. Jaynes, *Phys. Rev.* **106**: 620(1957).

CHAPTER IV

Some Aspects of Speculation and The Stock Market

Some Historical Remarks on Speculation, The Tulip Mania, The Bubbles, and The Crash

a INTRODUCTION

TRADE FLOURISHED in Italy during the Renaissance with cargo afloat between important Italian ports such as Venice, Naples and Genoa, and between these Italian ports and more distant places such as Spain, the Levant and North Africa. Italian ships also sailed occasionally on the Atlantic, to and from the western European ports. Some uncertainty in the outcome of these voyages motivated a number of traders to band together in sponsoring a ship, each being assigned his due share of the proceeds of the sale of the exports and imports. The long duration of the voyages often stimulated some tension in the investors, especially when rumors of severe storms at sea, abnormally high activity of pirates, and soft foreign markets were rampant, and when profits from previous arrivals in port were disappointing. These events sometimes tempted investors to sell their shares at less than the originally expected later returns. In contrast, if it seemed that an item would arrive in large quantities which at the time was scarce in the port, speculators in that item might offer more than the originally expected returns for a share of the cargo.

As ships docked, the cargo was distributed through nearby markets or was sometimes auctioned upon arrival so that the impatient creditors and shareholders could be paid off quickly. This practice frequently led to disappointments when certain goods were temporarily in oversupply and, on occasion, to jubilation in times of scarcity.

As trade moved north, Antwerp and Bruges became great centers where burghers imported Scottish wool, arranged for its weaving at other locations in the Netherlands, and contracted for the sale of the cloth in Bohemia, France, and in the Hanseatic towns. The art of investment and speculation developed rapidly in this milieu. As the weaving industry expanded, money had to be lent to those organizing the weavers, who expected their wages before

162

the cloth was sold. The Scottish sheep herders had to be taken care of before the wool could be given to the weavers. Wool and finished cloth was sold short; and shares in these items rose and fell, depending on political and economic events throughout Europe. The great Bourse was established in Antwerp to provide a center where negotiations on all these matters could be executed.

Through the busy port and The Bourse, Antwerp became[1] the copper and spice mart of Europe, a depot of the English Adventurers, the Hanseatic traders, the South German and Italian bankers. Loans were floated here for the governments of England, Germany, Portugal, The Netherlands, and, under cover, France. Here were traded the laces of Mechlin and Valenciennes: tapestries of Brussels made after Italian designs; jewels, glass and clocks; Flemish sculpture produced *en gros* for Spain or Greenland; leatherware, pewter, iron of Namur and munitions of Liége; Spanish cochineal and paints for the palettes of the 'colorist' schools. England stood in relation to Antwerp as old Rome had stood to Alexandria; she sent coarse products like canvas, tin, lead, sheep and rabbit skins, to exchange for manufactured and refined articles—cloth of gold, sugar and spices, furniture and mirrors, armor and breviaries.

The traffic of Antwerp surpassed all previous notions. Every week 1,000 freight-wagons with wares from France and Germany entered the gates; more than 10,000 peasant carts brought provisions from the countryside; and every day came and went 500 pleasure vehicles and 200 passenger wagons. Postal messengers hurried to and fro, in a service paid for and organized by merchants, so that the most distant royal wedding or war might react as soon as possible upon the money market.

Over the door of the Antwerp exchange was written in 1531 "for the service of merchants of all nations and languages". The excitement now so prevalent in the New York, London, Paris and other great stock exchanges had its root in the Antwerp exchange. At its peak, its annual turnover was reckoned at about 40,000,000 ducats, a ducat containing about $5 worth of gold. It was in this period that the Spanish control of the Netherlands (through marriage, not conquest) developed. As a result of financial mismanagement, the Spanish monarchy led by Chas. V who abdicated (in the face of economic disaster) to his son Phillip II, went bankrupt in 1557. With it, the Spanish Netherlands with Antwerp its financial center also went bankrupt (as did France and Portugal).

The United Provences of the Northern Netherlands managed to free themselves from the Spaniards and Amsterdam picked up the leadership in world trade which had been held by Antwerp. While the sophistication of the Amsterdam Exchange was not so highly developed as that of the Antwerp Bourse, a new dimension was added to trading practice through the Dutch mastery of the art of shipbuilding. By the middle of the 17th Century, the Dutch (with a population of only slightly over a million persons) owned four-fifths of the larger sea-going ships in Europe[2]; of the 20,000 of respectable size, 16,000 were Dutch. The French fleet numbered about 500.

It was these ships that carried most of the goods around the world and which made the Northern Netherlands tremendously wealthy for such a small country. To quote Daniel Defoe,

The Dutch must be understood to be as they really are, the *Carryers of the World*, the middle Persons in Trade, the Factors and Brokers of Europe: That, as is said above, they *buy* to *sell* again, *take* in to *send* out; and the greatest Part of their vast Commerce consists in being supply'd from all Parts of the World, that they may supply all the World again: Thus they supply some Nations with Corn, others with Ships, or Naval Stores for Ships; others with Arms and Ammunition of all kinds; such as Powder, Shot, Shells, Lead, Iron, Copper, Cannon, Mortars, etc. others with Fish, other with woolen Manufactures. *and the like.*

During the early part of the 17th century, hardly anything could be moved without a Dutchman's help.

The Dutch dominance in trade required more than ships.[3] It evolved from the development of a most ingenious but simple system based on a delicate interplay of three activities: shipping, warehousing, and banking. Instead of disposing of his cargo at the Amsterdam dock on arrival, the Dutch captain stored it in warehouses. These old 17th century structures are still visible along the canals near the port of Amsterdam. It was understood by the traders that in any year a shortage of any given goods would develop in some part of Europe. On this basis, if they were in no hurry to sell, they could wait for a favorable market and with the excellent fleet available, ship the required merchandise at short notice to the point where it was most needed. The Dutch bankers were patient and willing to collect their interest until their debtors could dispose of their wares at a profitable price. In the long run, it meant that the traders would have more money to deposit in the banks so that the bankers could with profit aid other traders during the warehousing cycle of their operation.

The warehouses full of all kinds of goods, the ships sailing to and from all ports in the world, and the existence of a large number of affluent people with extra cash were natural stimulants of an active speculation market in Amsterdam. While there were booms and busts in the early days of the Antwerp and Paris exchanges, they did not reflect speculation fever in large masses of the people (as did the later 1928 stock market boom in the U.S.). They resulted from machinations of wealthy shrewd traders and financial mismanagement of governments. The first popular boom and bust was the Dutch Tulipomania.

b   TULIPOMANIA[4]

In springtime, travel agents describe the Netherlands as the land of the tulip.

Buses, trains, airplanes and private cars pour out hundreds of thousands of people every April to witness the glorious tulip displays at Keukenhof and Linnaeushof, and to drive or tramp along the tulip fields which furnish bulbs for the gardens of the rest of the world. The tulip was not originally native to the Netherlands, but was imported from Turkey in 1559. Within the next ten years, tulips were much sought by the wealthy of Holland and Germany. Rich Amsterdamers obtained theirs directly from Constantinople, paying extravagant prices. By 1630, the rage of possessing tulips had caught the middle class of society, and merchants and farmers of even moderate means began to vie with each other for the possession of rare varieties.

It is said that there are few plants which acquire through accident, weakness, or disease, so many variegations as the tulip. In 1634 the urge among the Dutch to possess these fragile blossoms was so great that ordinary industry of the country became neglected and the population, generally, embarked in the tulip trade. A bulb planted in the sandy Dutch soil produces five or six new bulbs by the next year so that at the early stages of the mania, the amplification factor motivated many to obtain a rare variety for propagation. At the later stages, bulbs were bought to be sold within a few weeks with the bulbs themselves resting in some tulip mart. Everyone imagined that the passion for tulips would last forever and that the whole world would order tulips from Holland and pay whatever price was asked. The first two hypotheses are still valid, but the third, alas, was true for but a short time.

The demand for rare species increased so that by 1636 regular marts were established on the Amsterdam stock exchange, in Rotterdam, Haarlem, Leyden, and other towns. Symptoms of gambling now became apparent for the first time. As with all gambling mania, when confidence was at its height, prices continued to rise, and everybody gained. A bulb of species "Admiral Liefkin" commanded 4400 florins, a "Viceroy", 3000 florins, and a "Semper Augustus" was considered cheap at 5500 florins. Three old silver florins weighed about the same as a standard U.S. silver dollar. Eventually the more prudent began to doubt that the folly could continue forever and sold large quantities of bulbs. Prices dropped. Persons who agreed several weeks earlier to pay thousands of florins for bulbs delivered at a certain date reneged at the moment of delivery when the prices had fallen somewhat.

Defaulters were announced day after day in all the towns of Holland. Hundreds who, a few months previously, had begun to doubt that there was such a thing as poverty in the land suddenly found themselves the possessors of a few bulbs, which nobody would buy, even though they offered them at one quarter of the sums they had paid for them. The cry of distress resounded everywhere, and each man accused his neighbour. The few who had contrived to enrich themselves hid their wealth from the knowledge of their fellow-citizens, and invested it in the English or other funds. Many who, for a brief season, had emerged from the humbler walks of life, were cast back into their original obscurity. Substantial merchants were reduced almost to beggary, and many a representative of a noble line saw the fortunes of his house ruined beyond redemption.[4]

The government attempted to restore public credit and it was agreed that all contracts made in the height of the mania or prior to November, 1636 should be considered null and void and that later contracts could be satisfied by payment of ten percent of the agreed prices. This satisfied few creditors and actions for breach of contract were threatened through the courts, but the latter refused to recognize "gambling" transactions.

As with all booms, there was a good reason for it starting. Tulips were in demand; they are today, representing one of the most important of Dutch exports. Indeed, traffic in bulbs is sufficiently rewarding so that the Japanese and Californians are attempting to break the Dutch monopoly in the field. New species occasionally attract public attention. In 1835 a bulb of the species "Miss Fanny Kemble" sold at auction in London for seventy-five pounds. Prices fluctuate with variation in supply and demand, as is the case with all commodities; but it is no longer an item which inspires those who wish to make a fortune overnight effortlessly.

The next great popular speculative orgy occurred in France in the period 1716–20 in the form of the Mississippi scheme. This and the South Sea Bubble, which followed it only by a year or two were based on less substance and more rumor and romance than the Tulipomania.

c   THE MISSISSIPPI SCHEME[4,5,6]

Of the many speculative bubbles since the tulipomania, the Mississippi Scheme deserves special attention because its conception is close to the basis of modern money management and it showed how, in a crisis environment, a complete outsider with an idea and a strong personality could become a key figure in a major country almost overnight. It also was a scheme which first saved a scandalously mismanaged country from bankruptcy and then, through the greed of its prominent citizens, caused a later bankruptcy.

John Law, the author of the scheme, was born in Edinburgh in 1671, son of a wealthy Scottish goldsmith and banker. He entered his father's counting house at fourteen, showed exceptional mathematical aptitude (especially in estimating probabilities, a talent which was a boon to his later gambling career), and soon acquired a mature insight into the banking practice of his day. As he grew older, his attire became more extravagant and his presence was found to be attractive to the ladies[4] . . . "to the young, the rich, the witty and the obliging". As a young adult he became a dedicated gambler and a careless suitor, an affliction which led him to a duel (1694) with an aging dandy, Beau Wilson, over the attention of a Miss Elizabeth Villiers, later Countess of Orkney. It was his misfortune "to shoot his antagonist dead upon the spot" (according to one account[4] and "in a single pass . . . put his blade an inch or two into the breastbone of the ancient coxcomb . . ." according to another[5]). Law was tried in Old Bailey, found guilty of murder, but escaped to Amsterdam.

While Law was a fugitive in Amsterdam, the Bank of Amsterdam issued its first paper bank notes. The East India Company exerted strong political pressure, forcing the Bank to make a large loan under conditions which violated its charter. Instead of issuing bullion or credit at the bank, the Bank gave the company banknotes which it agreed to honor with bullion when presented to the Bank. It was one of the earliest acts of converting a loan to an individual into currency, "bank money" in modern terminology. At that time payments in Amsterdam were normally made in mixed gold and silver of many realms. Each country had its own gold-silver ratio and it was a rare regent who did not tamper with the ratio or devalue his coins (France experienced 294 changes in the previous four centuries while coins from all these changes continued to circulate). Amidst this monetary chaos, the Bank of Amsterdam discovered that its paper notes were considered to be so convenient that they passed at a 10% premium over coins.

Law perceived that the bank was creating money. He also recognized that, by creation of money in this manner, the problem of money shortage which traditionally plagued nations might be solved. Commerce was generally restricted by the amount of money available. The great trade expansion of the 16th and 17th centuries was based on the enormous output of Latin-American silver and gold mines. In 1705 Law developed his ideas for growth of trade in countries short of bullion in a pamphlet entitled "Money and Trade Considered, With a Proposal for Supplying a Nation with Money".

For a brief period, he attempted to sell his paper money program to the Scottish parliament but without success. He returned to the continent where, for fourteen years, he profited from his great skill at the gaming tables of Flanders, Holland, Germany, Hungary, Italy, and France. He became intimately acquainted with the trade practises of these countries, as well as with their prominent citizens, many of whom were frequenters of the gambling dens.

The year of the death of the "Sun King" Louis XIV, 1715, was a depressing one for France. His extravagant construction projects, pretentious displays, corrupt servants, and profitless wars and explorations had impoverished the country. The palace at Versailles alone cost 116 million livres. While tourist admission receipts for many years has made the palace a successful long-range investment, creditors demanded payment in the short range. The total national debt at the time of Louis' death was three billion livres. The total annual tax income was 145 million livres, while total annual expenditures were 142 million livres. This left three million livre for interest payments on the enormous debt, only about 4% of what was required.

French foreign colonies and trade of this preindustrial period did not show the profitable returns realized by English, Dutch and Spanish traders and adventurers. Taxes from the already squeezed artisans and modest farmers were the main sources of income for the French government, and two-thirds of these taxes went into the pockets of the wealthiest and most despised members of French society, the tax farmers. The executors of Louis XIV saw no way of paying the interest on the national debt, let alone the principal, and considered national bankruptcy as the only possible solution. When the Regent, Duc d'Orleans, of the boy king Louis XV rejected this policy, another extreme measure was adopted by the Comptroller General. He ordered every person who had made any profit out of state offices or contracts in the previous twenty-seven years, to make an exact accounting of profits made and taxes paid. Rewards were offered to informers. The richest and most powerful men of the kingdom were dragged through the courts. Yet, after all these proceedings, a relatively small amount of the required income was raised.

It was into this atmosphere that John Law had returned to France. He had in earlier years befriended the Duc d'Orleans at the gaming tables and the Duc was impressed with Law's lectures on economics, as well as his gambling ability. Law asked for a permit to open a private bank with the condition that he would finance it himself.

It was to receive deposits and discount bills and notes; it could make loans and issue its own notes ... The company issued 1700 shares of 5000 livres each. The subscribers were to pay for the shares in four installments—one-fourth in cash and three-fourths in billet d'etat—government securities which were valued at no more than twenty or thirty livres on the hundred.

Since these were accepted at face value, it was easy to find subscribers. Law's notes had the same success as those of the Bank of Amsterdam and many merchants brought their bullion to the Bank in exchange for notes. The bank was successful; the stock rose in value. The notes were guaranteed at a time when there was a great fear that government money would be devalued.

The subject of this section, The Mississippi Bubble, started in 1717. Law planned and proposed to the Regent a scheme for the development of the Louisiana Territory through a Mississippi company which would colonize the area. While little was known of the resources of the territory, the speculative mood of the French people at that time would, if supported, encourage such a program. The proposal was accepted and the company was capitalized at 10,000,000 livres but

... Law, either against his better judgment or carried away by his enthusiasm, agreed that subscriptions could be made in state obligations, billet d'etat, instead of coin. Thus the capital of the company, intead of being represented by ships, stores, forts and warehouses, was invested in obligations of a government whose credit was exceedingly poor. . . .[4]

Law then obtained the tobacco monopoly of France, as well as absorbing the French East India and China trade companies into his company. His prospectuses were exciting. He advertised plans to make New Orleans, a tiny settlement on the mud banks of the Mississippi, a metropolis equal to any in Europe. Rumors circulated that diamonds had been found in Arkansas, and gold and silver in Louisiana.[4]

Departing emigrants were feted and paraded. Finding it difficult to get emigrants, young men were taken from the jails and girls from the streets and marched off garlanded to the strains of music as if they were honest citizens.

A trick which was also used later by new holding companies during the boom of the late 1920's was invented by Law. At the first general meeting of his company on July 26th, 1719, before there had been any earnings, he proposed and carried a dividend declaration of 12% on the par value of the shares.

Within the forty days June 20th to July 27th, the value of the stock doubled, going from 500 livre to 1000. By September, shares sold at 5000. New issues were sold in October so that 1.5 billion livres of stock was outstanding. In order to provide money to purchasers of the stock, Law printed paper money to loan to the potential speculators.

In the midst of government disasters, Law's bank and its stock, were doing very well. Through his paper

... business relations abroad were renewed, interest rates on good paper dropped from 30% to 6% and then to 4%. Bewildered money lenders closed their shops. Law's management seems to have been judicious and conservative. In October 1716, tax collectors were ordered to make their remittances payable in Paris by notes of the bank . . . in effect making the bank notes legal tender.[4]

The bank was so successful that the Regent offered Law new powers. In 1718 his Banque General was converted into a state bank. In those days there were no brokers offices in Paris. The narrow Rue Quincampoix on which Law's bank was located was jammed with traders, which included princes, shopkeepers, valets and coachmen. Speculators from all of Europe congregated there. It was estimated that 30,000 fortune seekers descended on Paris in the winter of 1719. By November the shares were quoted at 10,000 and the market peaked in January, 1720, at 18,000 livres.

"All France, all Europe, was deceived by this sudden vision of untold riches. The overburdened country of Louis XIV was transformed into a fairyland."[4] During this excitement, Law advanced the state 1,500,000,000 livres at 3% interest to pay off the national debt. Just as the Federal Reserve Bank prints paper money when it lends money to banks, Law printed paper money to cover the debts of the state. He felt that with the new prosperity and development of industry, more taxes would be collected and the state could pay off the debt. While the concept was not completely foolish, he misjudged the temperament of the times. He had expected that his new money would initiate a frenzy of commerce and production. He had hoped that uncultivated lands would be tilled, fisheries developed, canals dug, ships built, distribution streamlined, and that France would take the world lead in commerce. It had not occurred to him that when it was discovered that money could be made more easily through speculation than through commerce and agriculture, those arts would be neglected.

In the period of optimism, one only had to make a 10% down payment on the stock. Hence most speculators bought ten times as much as they could afford, driving prices still higher. Even before the January peak, large blocks of stock started to appear for sale. Some of the more prudent investors were quietly converting their stock and banknotes into bullion and foreign securities. Land was equally in demand with the result that land prices doubled and tripled in a short time. The especially cautious were shipping bullion, plate, art treasures and other movable items abroad. By February 1720, Law became concerned about removal of specie. Hoarding of gold and silver was then prohibited.

Vermalet, a jobber, who sniffed a coming storm, procured gold and silver coin to the amount of nearly a million livres which he packed in a farmer's cart and covered over with hay and cow dung. He then disguised himself in a dirty smock-frock of a peasant and drove his precious load into Belgium. From thence he soon found means to transport it to Amsterdam.[4]

Events seemed to be getting further out of control and on March 11th, Law instituted an edict prohibiting the use of gold or silver for making payments. These responses aroused suspicion and encouraged more sale of stock and attempted conversion of currency with a catastrophic drop in value of both. On March 20th, shares were officially stabilized at 9000 livres (half the January peak value). The bank agreed to purchase stock at this price (in bank notes). Chaos developed when it was clear that the paper money was becoming further inflated. It became illegal to possess more than 500 livres in coin while no one in his right mind would accept paper money for payment. More paper money was printed, but by May 1720 the system collapsed. The cost of living had more than doubled in the previous year while wages had hardly changed. The weak and cowardly Regent threw all the blame on Law who was relieved of his post in May. He was soon recalled when it was clear that there was no one else available to untangle the mess.

Law tried to reorganize the system in many ways over the next six months, but without success. He resigned his posts December 10th and with the ". . . mob howling for his head"; he left France with a diamond, 800 livres in gold, and the coach of Madame de Prie, mistress of Duc de Bourbon who had become fabulously rich through Law's adventure. France was bankrupted; the new national debt was over three billion livres as compared with the 1715 one of one-and-a-half billion. At least 511,000 persons made claims that the government could not honor. Law himself traveled through Europe; he was plagued by lack of money and returned to England waiting for an invitation to proceed to France to attempt to apply his system again but with a better understanding of required controls. This possibility disappeared with the death of Duc d'Orleans in 1723. Law died in Venice in 1729, almost poverty stricken. Many of the ideas of modern money management developed from his experiment. In the United States, the debacle of 1929 led to the strict government controls that are now depended upon to keep speculation from getting out of hand.

d THE SOUTH SEA BUBBLE[4,7]

France was not alone in the enjoyment of the speculative orgies of the period 1715–1720. In England the South Sea Bubble and the numerous other bubbles which it inspired had many characteristics of the Mississippi Bubble. Fortunes were made and lost, but a fortunate combination of common sense, luck, political pressure and, perhaps, even bribery in the British Parliament saved the government from paralleling the French disaster.

The South Sea Company was originated by Harley, Earl of Oxford in 1711, with a view of restoring public credit which had suffered by the dismissal of the Whig ministry, and of providing for the discharge of Army and Navy debentures, and other parts of the floating debt, amounting to nearly £10,000,000. A company of merchants took this debt upon themselves and the government agreed to secure them for a certain period at the interest of 6%. To provide for this interest, the duties upon wines, vinegar, India goods, wrought silks, tobacco, whale-fins, and some other articles were rendered permanent. The monopoly of trade in the South Seas was granted . . . .[4]

The concept of a private company managing part of the public debt was not unusual at that time. The Bank of England, which now plays the same role in England as the Federal Reserve Bank in the U.S., started through just such an operation. To aid in the financing of the war with France in the 1690's, William Peterson (as spokesman for a syndicate) proposed to lend the British government £1,000,000 for which the government would accord to him and his associates $6\frac{1}{2}\%$ interest, costs of management and authority to issue bills which should be legal tender. While many Lords were suspicious, the pressures of the time forced Parliament to accept the proposal. It was not long before the Bank did a considerable amount of simple routine financial management for the government simply because the Bank personnel were much more competent than the civil servants in these matters. By now the Bank is essentially part of the government.

Shortly after the incorporation of the South Sea Company, its management tried to make an arrangement with Philip V of Spain, who then controlled the gold and silver mines of Peru and Mexico, for trading privileges in Latin America. He did make some concessions allowing one ship to trade per year under the condition that the King of Spain should enjoy one-fourth of the profits and apply a tax of 5% to the remainder. The first annual ship was sent in 1717 and in the following year a rupture with Spain occurred which supressed trade completely. During the negotiation period, optimistic rumors spread and the company stock slowly increased in value. The 1717 ship was well advertised and a further increase in the value of the stock occurred as it sailed.

During Parliamentary sessions of 1717, George I discussed the state of public credit and recommended that proper measures should be taken to reduce the national debt (has there ever been a politician who has not made this suggestion?). Both the Bank of England and the S.S. Co. made proposals to lend the government money in return for certain advantages, and appropriate arrangements were made. This show of strength of the company was useful in keeping up public interest in the company.

These events occurred at the time when signals of Law's successes in his Mississippi scheme echoed loud and clear from France. The British did not want to miss the fun. The S.S. Co. then laid before Parliament its famous plan, à la Law, for paying off the national debt. Rumors started to circulate to the effect that treaties between England and Spain were being considered whereby the latter was to grant free trade in all her colonies.

For cotton and woolen goods which England could supply in abundance, the dwellers in Mexico were to empty their silver mines. The company of merchants trading in the South Seas would be the richest the world ever saw . . . .[4]

The S.S. Co. stock went to 400. It was further rumored that Earl Stanhope had received overtures in France from the Spanish government to exchange Gilbralter and Port Mahon for some places on the coast of Peru for the security and enlargement of trade in the South Seas. The King of Spain was said to be considering removal of all restrictions on the number of trading ships and was ready to remove his claim for 25% of the profits. The stock increased even faster in price. A million pounds worth of new stock was issued and sold immediately. 10% dividends were declared and another new issue of a million pounds was absorbed by the public.

Speculation was in full swing. New entrepreneurs quickly appeared to accommodate the public with numerous investment schemes. Companies who wished to issue stock required official permission. On 12 July 1720, no less than eighteen petitions were presented. Stock was issued for enterprises with standard aims such as production of muslin, production of iron and steel, for insuring horses, for importing walnut trees from Virginia, for paving streets in London, for furnishing funerals to any part of Great Britain. Some more speculative issues were concerned with the development of a perpetual motion wheel, for the erection of salt works in the Holy Land, for transmutation of quicksilver into malleable fine metal. Puckles Machine Company was incorporated to develop cannon using cubical cannonballs. Shares were gobbled up indiscriminately and quickly. Between 9 a.m. and 3 p.m. on one day, one thousand shares of £100 each, with only an initial deposit of £2 required, were taken in "a company for carrying on an undertaking of great advantage, but nobody to know what it is".[4]

Through this excitement, the value of the S.S. Co. was advancing steadily, being at 550 on 28 May 1720 and in four days taking its greatest leap to 890. It was then that many thought it would rise no higher. Considerable dumping occurred, especially by members of the Court who were planning to soon leave for Hanover with George I on his annual summer tour in his other kingdom. On 3 June, the stock dropped to 640 but, through various buying schemes by the directors of the company, rose again to 750. It peaked again in August at 1000 and on September 2nd a big drop to 700 was recorded. This created a panic; the next day, going to 640, a day later to 540, and thence to 400 by 13 September.

At this point the wrath of the multitude was aimed upon the directors of the South Sea Company for allowing the catastrophe to occur. Mr. Broderick, M.P., states that

... they have stretched credit so far beyond what it would bear that specie proved insufficient to support it. Their most considerable men have drawn out, securing themselves by the losses of the deluded, thoughtless numbers whose understandings have been overruled by avarice and the hope of making mountains out of molehills. Thousands of families will be reduced to beggary. The consternation is inexpressible, the rage beyond description, and the case so desperate that I do not see any plan or scheme so much as thought of for averting the blow . . . .[4]

During the progress of this famous bubble, England presented a singular spectacle. The public mind was in a state of unwholesome fermentation. Men were no longer satisfied with the slow but sure profits of cautious industry. The hope of boundless wealth for the morrow made them heedless and extravagant for today. A luxury, till then unheard of, was introduced, bringing in its train a corresponding laxity of morals. . . .

The Bank of England was urgently requested to aid the S.S. Co. at the time when other banks closed their doors from having lent out so much money with S.S. Co. stock as security. The situation was essentially the same as during the crash of 1929. People used their borrowed money to make down payments (usually 10%) on stock. As prices fell, they could not pay back their notes and the bank failed. While the Bank of England did furnish some aid, it soon became clear to them that it was ridiculous to throw good money out in an attempt to save the bad. They realized they would be swept away also if they tried to bolster the S.S. Co. stock.[8]

At the time (29 September 1720) when so many smaller banks were failing, there was a run on the Bank of England by its frightened depositors. Even though its position was fundamentally sound, they would not have been able to survive without the employment of an ingenious device which we believe to be the first public application of the basic ideas of queuing theory.[2] They engaged men to stand in line at the bank windows, then to withdraw small amounts of specie only to quietly go to another window to redeposit the withdrawal. Rough estimates were made of the length of time each would stand in line, how many persons would be needed to slow down the line of serious withdrawers so that by closing time, the bank would not run out of specie. There was a danger that if too many were employed in this dodge, the news would get out to the public, while, if there were too few, the scheme would not work. By good fortune, a Bank Holiday (Festival of Michaelmas) was due the next day. Specie was obtained from all possible sources and large depositors were urged to remain calm. Public alarm subsided somewhat after the holiday and the Bank survived. A similar crisis developed in 1745 and was met successfully in the same manner.

While many personal disasters followed the bursting of the bubble, the British government did not suffer the fate of the French. Against the advice of Prime Minister Walpole (who worked closely with the Bank of England), Parliament did allow a significant portion of the National Debt to be converted to S.S. Co. stock. However, the Bank of England continued with its previous responsibilities in similar matters and remained strong during the crisis. It managed to avoid lending significant sums on stock. Because of its conservative policies, its own stock fluctuated only between 200 and 265 so that it suffered neither a great inflation of its value nor a sudden collapse. After the plunge of the S.S. Co. stock, Walpole released the company from some of its government obligations, thus keeping it solvent and giving some stability to the low stock price.

The directors of the S.S. Co. personally suffered much more than the company. After the collapse

... public meetings were held in every considerable town of the empire, at which petitions were adopted, praying vengeance of the legislature upon the South Sea directors who, by their fraudulent practices, had brought the nation to the brink of ruin. Nobody seemed to imagine that the nation itself was as culpable as the South Sea Company. Nobody blamed the credulity and avarice of the people—the degrading lust of gain, which had swallowed up every nobler quality in the national character, or the infatuation which had made the multitude run their heads with such frantic eagerness into the net held out for them by scheming projectors. These things were never mentioned. The people were a simple, honest, hardworking people, ruined by a gang of robbers, who were to be hanged, drawn and quartered without mercy.[4]

The story of the Parliamentary inquiry makes as interesting reading as the development of the Bubble. At its conclusion, the case of every director of the S.S. Co. was analyzed. A sum of £2,014,000 was confiscated from the directors' estates to be used to repair the damage that had been done. The proportion left to each to begin life anew depended on the character of his involvement. Sir John Blunt was allowed £5,000 of a fortune of £183,000; Sir John Fellows, £10,000 out of £243,000; Mr. Edward Gibbon (grandfather of Edward Gibbon of Decline and Fall of Roman Empire fame), £10,000 out of £106,000. These are representative but the most extreme penalty left one director with £31 out of a fortune of £400,031. It is seldom that such prominent members of the Establishment are dealt with so severely. Considerable criticism of the trial is given by the Decline and Fall Gibbon in his autobiography.[9]

By now the reader is probably tiring of these accounts of men's weakness under temptation. When the story of one of these episodes is told, that of all of them have been told. As MacKay said in 1841:

In times of great commercial prosperity, there has been a tendency for overspeculation. The success of one project generally produces others of a similar kind. Popular imitativeness will always, in a trading nation, seize hold of such successes, and drag the community too anxious for profits into an abyss from which extraction is difficult. Bubble companies of a kind similar to those engendered by the South Sea Project lived their little day in the famous year of the panic, 1825.

The panic of 1825 developed at the time when the industrial revolution was expanding rapidly. New industries were rising and speculation increased. It was not long before some discovered that it was easier to make money in speculation than in planning industrial production. The romance of the South Seas and Latin America again hypnotized the British. As the newly-formed states in South America won their freedom from Spain, British investment money to the extent of £150,000,000 was sunk in government loans and corporate investments in Mexico and South America. At that time, private banks in England (as well as in the U.S.) of a wide variety, could issue their own notes which circulated as coin of the realm. Apparently many country banks were exceedingly liberal in making loans for speculation, issuing bank notes on the loans. The panic came in 1825 as a result of the overinflation of the stock issues as in the South Sea Bubble. The South American governments were badly mismanaged and often could not pay off their bonds; new industries were often started with more enthusiasm than understanding. During the 1824–25 bubble, stocks for a company which planned to drain the Red Sea with the hope of recovering gold lost by the Egyptians when pursuing the Israelites, sold at least as well as those for Iron Foundries in the Midlands.

The memory of the Panic of 1825 had not long faded before the railroad network started to spread through England. The reader can guess how the Great Railway Mania developed and how the panic of 1845 resulted.

e THE PANIC OF 1837[10]

No new ideas will be presented in the remainder of this section. The reader in a hurry may proceed to the next section while those interested in Americana will see that the American speculation pattern is no different from the European.

Andrew Jackson, in his messages to Congress in 1831 and 1832, pointed to "the rare example of a great nation abounding in all the means of happiness and security". Domestic manufacturing was rapidly increasing, internal improvements for trade and transportation were developing and providing new markets for farmers. There has seldom been a more optimistic and forward-looking country than the U.S. of the early 1830's.

Each of the three regions of the country, the East, the South, and the West had set its own pattern for expansion and development. Industrial growth characterized the East. In 1830 there were 202 iron furnaces producing 150,000 tons of iron per year. In 1840, 804 furnaces were producing 286,000 tons annually. In Lowell, Massachusetts, there were 22 cotton mills producing 36,000,000 yards of cloth annually. By 1836, 2,500,000 pairs of shoes were being manufactured in Lynn, Massachusetts. The wealth of the South was based on its cotton crop. The factories of both old and New England were hungry for raw cotton, using a home consumption of 100,000,000 pounds per annum and stimulating annual exports amounting to 385,000,000 pounds. The foreign market for cotton was the main contributor to the U.S. balance of payments of that period. The availability of land in the West (or rather the Midwest), attracted many easterners and foreigners. Large new farms were created as well as industrial towns. Both agriculture and trade flourished with land values soaring accordingly.

The Erie Canal had been completed and was considered such a great success that other canals were dug in New York State. Other states followed and, soon, canal fever had spread throughout the country. By 1835 Pennsylvania had 1,000 miles of canals and 620 miles of railroad lines. With the appearance of the railroad, much of the canal construction was obsolete before the networks were completed, causing considerable money to be wasted.

Funds and more funds were required to support the universal craze for internal improvements, as well as for the expansion of industry. In 1833, South Carolina had expended nearly $2,000,000 in the construction of roads which hardly yielded income sufficient to pay current expenses. Kentucky planned for $6,000,000 worth of improvements. Indiana's plans in 1835 called for 840 miles of canals, 90 miles of railroads, and 325 miles of turnpike at a cost of $20,000,000. Michigan with an impoverished settler population of less than 200,000 was committed to the expenditure of $8,000,000 and making plans for employing another $6,000,000. Southern farmers required more and more money to provide for expanded crops. Traditionally farmers were frequently deeply in debt. One of the reasons for Southern enthusiasm for the Revolutionary War was to be able to forget debts to English banks.

Money and banking in the U.S. were in a chaotic state in the 1830's. Since very little gold and silver had been coined since the Revolution, the hard money circulating (other than pennies) was a mixture of Spanish, Mexican, Dutch and English coin, combined with a small amount of native specie. Banks could be organized under state charters and a charter included the right to issue bank notes. Hence most business was conducted with a mélange of private bank notes of uncertain origin and value. Each bank president acted like a small John Law, but with less understanding of economics and under less government restrictions and responsibility. In some states, if one could borrow $50,000 to show the existence of capital, and develop (or buy) the friendship of a member of a state legislature, he could obtain a bank charter, print some paper money, start making loans, pay off his own loan and proceed to higher realms of finance. Stocks and bonds for canal companies, railroads and state turnpikes were issued. Money would be loaned to speculators in this paper.

Merchants were tempted and indeed invited to borrow money from these new banks. With so much expansion of all sorts, land became a favorite item for speculation.

Men of limited resources in their mad haste to be rich, bought land, city lots and stocks. A restless spirit of adventure and daring enterprise swept the nation. Overtrading, speculation, and investments in unproductive undertakings became the dominant note in American society.[10]

The sales of public lands outstripped the wildest expectations; and as our nation paid off its debt, and began to pile up a surplus in the treasury, largely as a result of the sales of the public domain, our credit was expanded to maintain the overaction in trading. When such credit could not be secured here, the Americans were confident it could be obtained abroad. Thus a large foreign indebtedness was incurred at a time when our imports were exceeding our exports.

This state of unnatural and artificial prosperity did not last very long. On July 11th, 1836, in order to curb speculation on government land sales, the Specie Circular was issued by which public lands would be exchanged only for gold or silver. This caused a considerable fraction of the small amount of specie in the U.S. to be transferred from the trade centers in the Atlantic States into the rural West.

In order for eastern banks to have some specie available for demands of depositors and foreign creditors, they put pressure on their customers to make part payment, at least, on their notes in specie. This made the public aware of the scarcity of specie and frightened people into being careful about accepting uncertain paper money,

At the same time there were crop failures due to the effect of the Hessian fly. Farmers were unable to pay their notes. Governor Moray observed a falling off of $275,000 in canal tolls in N.Y. State in consequence of the scanty crops of 1836. The great fire of December, 1835 which destroyed twenty million dollars worth of business property—apparently the greatest business disaster of a single day in the world to that time—made it impossible for some of New York's most prominent businessmen to pay their debts. Banks failed and business houses failed; public canal and road construction was severely curtailed and, in some states, essentially stopped.

The inability of planters to dispose of their crops and the failure of banks in Virginia forced the state to abandon its improvement projects. The greatest pressure was felt in the deep South. In Alabama, property almost entirely changed hands—in Mobile, there was not a single significant solvent business firm. Slaves formerly worth $1200 to $1500 each could be bought for $250 to $500. Lands in Mississippi which sold for $20 to $50 per acre could be purchased for $3 to $5 while some fetched only 50c. per acre at sheriff sales. The cotton market had no buyers; on some days, not a bale was shipped from Niles, normally a bustling cotton trade center.

In the long run, the poor man and the laborer were the greatest sufferers. Six thousand masons and builders were discharged in New York City in 1837 when building construction stopped; nine-tenths of the factories on the east coast closed. One-third to one-half of the clerks and salesmen in larger Philadelphia stores were without work by June 1837. The situation was similar to that after the stock market crash in 1929. The important difference, however, appeared in the government programs WPA, CCC, Relief, etc., of the 1930's and the absence of such after the Panic of 1837. In 1837–42, mothers begged on the streets of New York. Almshouses could not accommodate the cold and starving.

Some died of starvation, some were frozen to death. Many, through exposure and privation, contracted fatal diseases. Respectable mechanics were known to offer their services as waiters in eating houses for their food.[10]

At the beginning professional and salaried classes did better, but with the collapse of banks and all forms of industrial enterprise, and with the increased cost of living and reduction of wages, their lot became as strenuous as their fellow workers. It was not until the middle 1840's that some recovery started.

f DURATION OF BUSINESS CYCLES

One could continue with many similar stories.[13] For example, there was the time when J. Gould tried to corner the U.S. gold market, forcing gold prices up until Black Friday, September, 1869. When the gold market collapsed, numerous banks failed but no general depression resulted.

Jay Cooke, a Philadelphia banker, was the first of the great advertisers and salesmen in this country. As the organizer of the government's war bond sales drive during the Civil War, he was one of the first to use full-page ads in many newspapers. He went on a country-wide campaign from city to city with brass bands, flowery speakers, and commission salesmen indoctrinated by his pep talk to make non-buyers look like traitors. He sold over a billion dollars worth of war bonds. From his commissions he organized the largest and most important bank in the country. He devised railroad projects with the same enthusiasm, the largest being the transcontinental Northern Pacific Railroad (1869). He set forth to sell a hundred million dollars worth of these railroad bonds as John Law sold Mississippi stocks. The timber of the Pacific Northwest would sell at an enormous profit and be replaced by orange and banana groves, etc., etc. When the project collapsed, so also did thirty-seven banks and brokerage houses. Within forty-eight hours, railroad construction closed, not only on the Northern Pacific but throughout the country. The Panic of 1873 was on and lasted until 1878.

The stock market panic of 1907 did not bring the country down with it. On

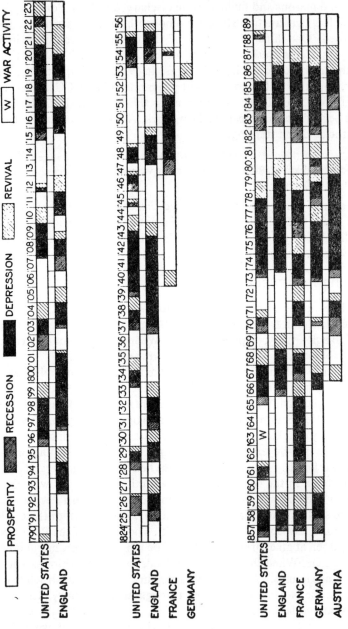

Figures 59a and 59b   Conspectus of business cycles in various countries 1790–1925.[11]

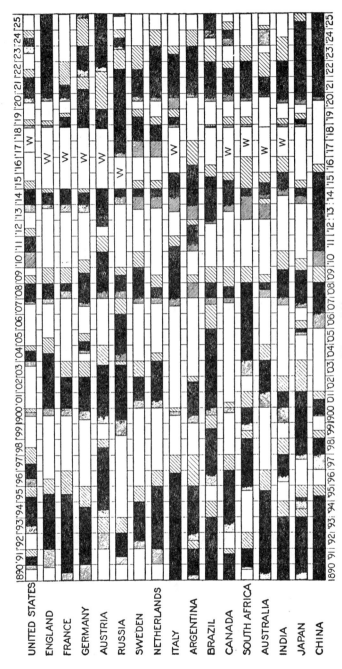

Figure 59b

a critical day as stocks were falling in October, J. P. Morgan raised $25,000,000 to be lent to the N.Y. Stock Exchange to stabilize it. When by November 2nd the panic seemed to renew its original force, Morgan intimidated a group of trust company heads to put another twenty-five million into weakening concerns. By mid-November the panic seems to have run its course and stability was achieved.

W. L. Thorp[11] has made detailed analysis of the business conditions in fifteen countries in the period 1790–1925 (in some countries over short and others over long periods in this range). He reviews business conditions and financial crises, as well as booms, each year in this period. A survey of his findings are given in Figure 59.

A business cycle might be defined as the sequence: depression, revival, prosperity and recession. The period from the beginning of one depression to that of another is called the duration of the cycle. Wesley C. Mitchell, a colleague of Thorp counted 166 cycles in Thorp's data and found the frequency of cycles of a given length to follow a log-normal distribution function as shown in Figure 60.

g   THE FLORIDA REAL ESTATE BOOM[12]

Everyone over 45 has some memory of the Great Depression. Even though it occurred 40 years ago it affected the U.S. and, indeed, the world so violently that when new fiscal policies are considered, some small thought is given in terms of lessons learned from that period. It is hard to drop a narrative on the annals of speculation without including the two predepression speculative orgies, the Florida Real Estate Boom and the Crash of 1929.

After World War I, the U.S. became a nation on wheels. The war veterans and the veterans of the war production plants were accustomed to and rather enjoyed traveling and visiting new places. The automobile had become cheaper and more reliable and the roads better. By 1922 the short post-war depression was over, new consumers' gadgets were being put on the market, construction and automobile production were booming. A period of optimism was setting in. By 1923 there was practically no unemployment and farm prices were higher (except for wheat). The new gadgets were easing the women's lot and shorter working hours gave more leisure time.

It is not surprising that Florida was beginning to attract winter visitors and that many people noted it was possible to make a living in the sunshine as easily as in the colder climates. The population of Miami rose from 30,000 in 1920 to 75,000 in 1925 with the number of winter visitors at least equalling the number of locals. Any time an area grows so rapidly, there is a boom in real estate. Homes, hotels, and apartments had to be built.

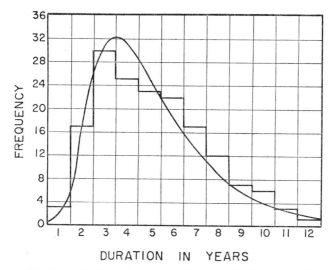

Figure 60 Logarithmic normal curve fitted by Davies' method to the frequency distribution of 166 observations upon the duration of business cycles.[11]

The rise in real estate prices attracted the attention of speculators and by 1924 a sensational boom was developing. To quote F. J. Allen,[12] the historian of the boom, "there were a number of causes—

1   First of all, of course, the climate—Florida's unanswerable argument.

2   The accessibility of the state to the populous cities of the North-east—an advantage which Southern California could not well deny.

3   The automobile, which was rapidly making America into a nation of nomads; teaching all manner of men and women to explore their country, and enabling even the small farmer, the summer-boarding-house keeper, and the garage man to pack their families into flivvers and tour southward from auto-camp to auto-camp for a winter of sunny leisure.

4   The abounding confidence engendered by Coolidge Prosperity, which persuaded the four-thousand-dollar-a-year salesman that in some magical way he too might tomorrow be able to buy a fine house and all the good things of the earth.

5   A paradoxical, widespread, but only half-acknowledged revolt against the very urbanization and industrialization of the country, the very concentration upon work, the very routine and smoke and congestion and twentieth-century standardization of living upon which Coolidge Prosperity was based. These things might bring the American businessman money, but to spend it he longed to escape from them.

6   The example of Southern California, which had advertised its climate at the top of its lungs and had prospered by so doing: why, argued the Floridians, couldn't Florida do likewise?

7   And finally, another result of Coolidge Prosperity: not only did John Jones expect that presently he might be able to afford a house at Boca Raton and a vacation-time of tarpon-fishing or polo, but he also was fed on stories of bold business enterprise and sudden wealth until he was ready to believe that the craziest real-estate development might be the gold mine which would work this miracle for him."

As the boom developed, the usual kind of rumors developed. The success stories were slightly amplified by each relator.[12] "A lot in the business center of Miami Beach had sold for $800.00 in the early days of the development and had resold for $150,000.00 in 1924—A poor woman who bought a piece of land near Miami in 1896 for $25.00 was able to sell it in 1925 for $150,000.00."

Unfortunately most of the profits, especially in the later stages of the boom were paper profits. Land was not really sold; usually only a binder was sold. When a new selection of lots was marketed and exhibited on a blueprint (which might appear in New York or Chicago as well as in Miami—blueprints seemed to be more inspiring than the lots themselves), one generally bought a binder for 10% of the lot price to reserve the lot for future purchase. Transactions could be quickly consummated this way without waiting for title searches and recording of deeds. Usually the purchaser did not want to develop the lot but merely to sell it again at a substantial profit before the first payment fell due in thirty days.

Prices continued to rise through 1925. New hotels, apartment houses, and subdivisions were planned and when construction materials were not short, construction boomed. One day in the summer of 1925, the Miami Daily News had an issue of 504 pages (mostly ads), a record for newspaper size. New Years Day 1926 was celebrated with "The Fiesta of the American Tropics". But by then, trouble was in the wind. Not as many buyers were around as had been in September and October. The number of winter visitors was below expectations. Some binder holders were having trouble making monthly payments on lots, something which they had not anticipated. By summer 1926, binder holders were defaulting in droves and the binding privilege was reverting to previous binder holders. Original property holders were suddenly in possession of their property again, burdened with taxes and sometimes a half-finished development.

Just as it began to be clear that a wholesale deflation was inevitable, two hurricanes showed what a Soothing Tropic Wind could do when it got a running start from the West Indies No malevolent Providence bent upon the teaching of humility could have struck with a more precise aim than the second and worse of these Florida hurricanes. It concentrated upon the exact region where the boom had been noisiest and most hysterical—the region about Miami—it left behind some four hundred dead, sixty-three hundred injured, and fifty thousand homeless—it had destroyed the remnants of the Florida boom—. By 192 dead subdivisions lined the highways—whole sections of outlying subdivisions were composed of unoccupied houses, past which one speeds on broad thoroughfares as if traversing a city in the grip of death—. In 1928 there were thirty-one bank failures and in 1929 fifty-seven—

at a time when the remainder of the country was prosperous.[12]

The blame for the catastrophe is not to be put on the people of Florida entirely. While they started a bit of the fun and had done most of the shouting, the hysteria became a national one with speculators from everywhere appearing on the scene to make their easy money.

The appearance of the outsider who takes over the market is characteristic of many of the speculative booms and busts. The situation is completely removed from the small group who discovered a good thing and were making some unexpected profits on it.

h THE GREAT CRASH OF 1929[12,14]

The collapse of the Florida real estate boom had little effect on the mood of optimism and economic expansion prevalent in the rest of the country. Coolidge's State of the Nation address of 4 December 1928 resembled those of Jackson in 1831 and 1832 which were referred to in our discussion of the Panic of 1837.

No Congress of the United States ever assembled, on surveying the state of the nation, has met with a more pleasing prospect than that which appears at the present time . . . . In the domestic field there is tranquility and contentment and the highest record of prosperity . . . .

The evidence of prosperity was everywhere. During the period from 1925 to 1929, the number of manufacturing establishments increased from 183,900 to 206,700. Auto production was 4,301,000 in 1926 and became 5,358,000 in 1929. Other production figures paralleled these. It was a period of tremendous suburban development and the construction boom was universal.

Consumer credit grew even more rapidly as installment buying became an accepted way of life. By the late 1920's, some 15% of all retail sales were on the installment plan with some six billion dollars of "easy payment" outstanding. The availability of credit, the general optimism, and the ingenuity which produced and advertised new products, stimulated the public demand for increased production. Production stimulated industrial growth and industrial growth with a promise of even more industrial growth stimulated rising stock prices.

The New York Times average of the prices of twenty-five industrial stocks (the so-called Times Industrials Index), rose from 106 in May 1924 to 134 by December, and by 31 December 1925 reached 181. A setback in March 1926 dropped the level to 143, but recovery was fairly prompt and the increase was steady in 1927. During this period of prosperity, more people with a little extra cash were attracted to the market.

The rising market also attracted English investors. In 1925 Winston Churchill, as Chancellor of the Exchequer, overvalued the pound sterling pegging it at the 1914 level of $4.86, an historic rather than an economically sound gesture. This made British goods expensive in the world market, causing a decline in foreign sales and a business crisis which was met by cutting prices and wages. Labor's response was the general strike of 1926. British capital flowed into the United States banks and investment houses seeking the higher returns. In the spring of 1927, in response to pleas from the Bank of England and other European central banks, the Federal Reserve Bank cut its interest rate from 4 to 3.5 percent to deter foreign gold flow. While it might have accomplished this to some degree, its most important effect was to make money cheaper for native borrowers who wished to expand their production or speculation activities.

All the events listed above contributed, at least to some small degree, to the inflation of a market that was already becoming bullish. Stocks were not yet going wild, but the news of the continuing rise of stock prices in 1927 was moved from the financial section to the front pages of the newspapers. A pronouncement by John J. Rascob, a director of General Motors, to the effect that GM stock should be selling at twelve times earnings, $225 per share rather than $187, was big news on 23 March 1928. On Saturday, 24 March, GM went up 5 points, followed by 9 more on Monday, 25 March. The surge in GM set off a burst of trading elsewhere. Optimistic predictions by the sages of Wall Street came more frequently, were more publicized, and stimulated more public response.

A good indicator of the growth of optimism of the 1920's was the increase in "call loans": broker loans of money for stock purchase. When stock is purchased on margin, it is left in the hands of the broker as collateral for the loan required to make up the difference between the first (margin) payment and the value of the stock. When stock prices are rising, the benefit accrues to the owner and outweighs the interest (which is generally high). Between 1920 and 1925, the totality of brokers' loans fluctuated between a billion and a billion-and-a-half dollars. In 1926 it rose to 2.5 billion, continued to grow to 3.5 billion in 1929. For a while, as call loans increased, the margin required went down with only 30 to 35 percent being needed in 1928. Brokers became more cautious by the summer of 1929 when customers had to furnish 45 to 50 percent in cash.

The interest rates on call loans increased with the demand, becoming 12% in 1928. The fact that the interest rate was so high indicates the magnitude of the demand for venture capital because the loans were well secured by the stock. Normally such safe loans would command only about 5% interest.[14]

In Montreal, London, Shanghai, and Hong Kong, there was talk of these rates. Everywhere men of means told themselves that 12 percent was 12 percent. A great river of gold began to converge on Wall Street, all of it to help Americans hold common stock on margin. Corporations also found these rates attractive. At 12 percent Wall Street might even provide a more profitable use for the working capital of a company than additional production. A few firms made this decision: instead of trying to produce goods with its manifold headaches and inconveniences, they confined themselves to financing speculation. Many more companies started lending their surplus funds on Wall Street.

There were still better ways of making money. In principle, New York banks could borrow money from the Federal Reserve Bank for 5 percent and re-lend it in the call market for 12. In practice they did. This was, possibly, the most profitable arbitrage operation of all time.

In 1929 even a company as substantial as the Standard Oil of New Jersey put a daily average of 69 million dollars into the call market. The situation was starting to resemble that of the South Sea and Mississippi Bubbles. 1929 was becoming one of those years during which money could be made easier through speculation than through production.

The number of shares traded regularly set new records in the spring of 1928; 3,879,510 shares being traded on March 27th; 5,052,790 shares changed hands on 12 June, a day which shook up quite a number of speculators because the market dropped significantly and the ticker fell two hours behind. There was some recovery in July and by August people forgot the shock of 12 June.

It was said so frequently and with such conviction during the presidential campaign of 1928 that if Hoover were elected, prosperity would achieve even greater heights; then on the day after his election, market leaders advanced 5 to 15 points. Sales volume reached 4,894,670 shares on November 5th and a new sales record was set on November 16th with 6,641,750 shares sold on a rising market with a net gain of $4\frac{1}{2}$ points in the Times Industrials.

As a whole, 1928 was a remarkable year. The Times Industrials increased 86 points from 245 to 331. Some growth stocks went wild with RCA advancing from 85 to 420, Dupont from 310 to 525, and Wright Aeronautics from 69 to 289. Margin buying was becoming more widely practiced. Women entered the Market as they never had before. The prices of steel, radios, and oil stocks were more discussed at ladies' gatherings than the price of meat and drapes. With wives as plungers, husbands could speculate without fear. The broker's office with the big board in the customers' room became a social center for the leisure class. It was easy to become hypnotized by watching the changing numbers at the daily seances. The working speculator lengthened his lunch hour, preferring the broker's office to a restaurant or a club as his noon-time haunt. During the spring and summer of 1929, the action was undoubtedly in the stock market.

At a time of demand for a special commodity, some improvisors always appear on the scene to satisfy the demand. During the South Sea Bubble, companies were organized overnight to produce and promote almost every conceivable item. Most of them bogged down after the production and sale of stock certificates, and collapsed completely before a legitimate operation could be established. By the 1920's, people were a bit more sophisticated. Furthermore, the stock exchanges were rather careful about the kinds of stock they traded. It took considerable time and organization to develop a company to the degree necessary for it to have some impact on the market. A clever innovation used to produce an instant company was the formation of an investment trust.

An investment trust was a company which held a certain amount of stock in other companies. It sold its own shares and provided expertise in stock selection for those speculators who lacked the time or courage to choose their own. The advertising of investment trusts claimed that with their ingenuity and understanding of the market, they could out-perform the novice in both the buying and selling of securities. The value of the stock of an investment trust was correlated to both the value of the stock holdings of the trust and the confidence of the potential buyer in the expertise of the staff of the trust. In a sense, the investor in trust stock bought stock in a company whose product could not be divulged. If its holdings were publicized, then anyone could buy the same stock in the same proportion without having to deal with the trust.

The investment trust was not a new idea. It existed in Europe for many years and even to some extent in the U.S. before the Bull market. It was a service to individuals and estates. For the small investor, it would spread the risk by holding investments in a number of companies. Traditionally its management was satisfied to be paid as money managers and did not attempt to use the trust as a device for stock manipulation and as an inflationary scheme. Those of us who use the Teachers' Insurance CREF plan acquire the traditional investment trust services. However, Teachers' Insurance does not promote its own stock and one can at any time obtain an account of its holdings.

The number of investment trusts grew from 160 in January 1927 to 486 in January 1929. During the early months in 1929, a new investment trust was registered almost every day.[14]

In 1927 the trusts sold to the public about $400,000,000 worth of securities; in 1929 they marketed an estimated 3 billion dollars worth. This was at least a third of all the new capital issues of that year; by autumn 1929, the total assets of the investment trusts were estimated to exceed eight billion dollars. They had increased approximately eleven fold since the beginning of 1927.

The popularity of the trust came from its amplification capability. If the value of the holdings of the trust appreciated by a significant percentage (by proper promotion and advertising) the sagacity of its staff could be lauded. On this basis one could imagine (as it indeed actually happened) that the value of the stock of the trust might increase by a larger percentage than the holdings themselves. Once the amplification principle (leverage, as it was called) is understood, then the next step is to form another holding company which specializes in holding stock in other investment trusts. The amplification factor would then be applied twice.

All sorts of networks of companies might then be invented and were. Trust B might have stock in Trust A which might own stock in RCA (a bona fide company producing radios) while Trust C has stock of B. An increase in RCA stock value would be amplified three times in determining the value of C. The situation could be made even more interesting by A holding some shares in C. Then the circle would be closed so that the increase in value of the stock of A would, through the feedback mechanism, lead to another increase in its value, etc. Hence the small pulse introduced by a rise in RCA stock would, in principle, be amplified indefinitely by recycling through the loop. Paper fortunes could rise remarkably as long as occasional buyers appear so that some real sales can be made. Since neither the speculator, the broker, nor the economics professor (who was the frequent consultant of the investment trusts) were burdened with the second law of thermodynamics, they were convinced they had an economic perpetual motion machine. To make life even more interesting, careful examination of the structure of companies A, B and C often revealed that they were owned and managed by the same people.

Now, what were some of the tricks in getting the operation started? A proper investment house had to be convinced to make the public sales. During the late 1920's, such houses were constantly searching for stock to sell since the demand was great. Brokers accepted new issues in a less questioning manner than they had in the past. A certain number of shares were first sold at a reduced price to the brokers before the public sales started. Shares were sometimes given or sold at low prices to persons "in the know" whose tips were sought and acted upon. Following John Law's practice, dividends of as high as 10% to 12% were declared shortly after the stock appeared on the market. Such dividends were higher than those offered by companies which had to produce something. Money might be borrowed in order to pay the dividends, with full confidence that the stock price would rise and that profits

F*

made on later sales could be used to pay back the loan. The leverage ideas outlined above were explained (in somewhat different language than we have used) to potential customers who were excited by the idea. University professors of economics with good reputations were employed as consultants. Their optimistic statements appeared in news releases and in company reports. The companies made attractive arrangements with buyers, offering to trade investment trust stock for shares of more mundane industrial stocks.

As anyone familiar with electronic devices knows, an amplifier which amplifies positive signals generally amplifies negative ones unless special precautions are taken. In a dropping market, one is hardly excited about paying geniuses a premium for selecting stocks which are losing their value; anyone can do that. Hence one would expect the investment trusts to be the most unstable items in a falling market. No special controls existed to prevent an amplification of negative inputs.

The 1928 boom continued into the early weeks of 1929. In January the Times Industrials gained 30 points. The first significant pause in the boom followed some statements of concern by the Federal Reserve Bank about the boom getting out of hand and the news that the Bank of England was raising the bank interest rate from $4\frac{1}{2}$ to $5\frac{1}{2}$ percent in an attempt to keep British pounds from escaping to Wall Street. The Federal Reserve Bank instructed its member banks to be cautious in making loans to commercial banks when there was evidence that the loans would be used in stock speculation. The Times Industrials responded on February 7th by dropping 11 points. There was an "Inaugural Market" surge following Hoover's inauguration on March 4th. However, toward the end of March, the Federal Reserve board was meeting daily without issuing any statements. There was even an unprecedented Saturday meeting on March 23rd. The uncertainty became unbearable. The cautious (or nervous) began to sell. On Monday, March 24th, the Times Industrial average dropped $9\frac{1}{2}$ points and, on the 25th, 15 more points, with a record of 8,246,740 shares traded. The interest rate on the call market went to 14% on the 24th and to 20% on the 26th. It could have been the end. As the prices fell, those who had bought stock on margin were notified by their brokers to pay more margin because the value of the stock held as security had diminished. If money remained tight, as it could have if the Federal Reserve Bank wished it to be, those who had to borrow to make margin payments would have been in trouble and their stock sold to the first possible buyer by the broker who held it as collateral. Each fall in prices would force more margin sales which, in turn, would induce another drop.

In the absence of any Fed policy, Charles E. Mitchell, a director of the prestigious National City Bank of New York (as well as of the New York Branch of the Federal Reserve Bank), prevented the catastrophe. He announced that the National City Bank would loan money as required to prevent liquidation. It would also borrow from the Federal Reserve Bank if necessary. The National City Bank then stated that it would put 25 million into the call market, 5 at 16% and 5 million at each additional percentage point. Since the Fed remained silent and Mitchell was a director of the New York Branch, his move was interpreted to be policy. The National City Bank in its monthly letter justified its position and stated very clearly the dilemma which faced the Fed:[14]

The National City Bank fully recognizes the danger of overspeculation and endorses the desire of the Federal Reserve authorities to restrain excessive credit expansion for this purpose. At the same time the bank, business generally and, it may be assumed, the Federal Reserve Banks . . . wish to avoid a general collapse of the securities markets such as would have a disastrous effect on business.

Nothing was heard from the Fed until the Crash, with the exception of a weak response in August 1929 when the rediscount rate was raised to 6%, at which time the market weakened for a day and then went gloriously on.

Those in the government who understood what was happening (and apparently Herbert Hoover was one; since 1926 when he was Secretary of Commerce he made quiet but not public warnings about the instability of the market) were in a delicate position. If firm policies on margin requirements and on call loans were made, the market would have crashed; if nothing was done, the Bull market would continue and eventually crash, as the high level would finally price stocks out of the market, so no new buyers could be found. If the first policy were followed, the villains who stopped prosperity would be clearly identified. No one had the courage to be forceful; policy meetings were held, nothing was done, and there was a vague hope that some high level would be reached in prices, that the public would slowly lose interest and that everything would be all right.

There were some prophets of doom. During the March crisis Paul W. Warburg of the International Acceptance Bank

. . . called for a stronger Federal Reserve policy and argued that if the present orgy of unrestrained speculation were not brought promptly to a halt there would ultimately be a disastrous collapse . . . It would bring about a general depression involving the entire country.

The most charitable on Wall Street called Warburg obsolete;[14] most considered him to be jeopardizing American prosperity. As the market continued to rise, his warnings were treated with contempt. It is interesting to note that John Galbraith, the author of the classic, *The Great Crash* which is our main reference source for this section, is the Warburg professor at Harvard.

During the summer of 1929, the rising market was part of American culture.

It was the main item of discussion. Even transatlantic ships had brokers offices so that travelers could keep in touch. Optimistic and exciting articles describing how everyone could be rich appeared in all the important magazines.

While critics were few, Warburg had a vocal companion in Roger Babson. He was a well-known educator, philosopher, statistician, forecaster, and generally a jack-of-all-intellectual trades, who had his system of graphs and charts and a certain amount of common sense which he used in making market predictions. During 1929 they were gloomy.

On September 5th, speaking before his National Business Conference, Babson[14] observed

sooner or later a crash is coming and it may be terrific . . . what happened in Florida would now happen on Wall Street . . . factories will be shut down . . . men will be thrown out of work . . . and the result will be a serious business depression.

Incidentally, Babson is well known to physicists through his Gravity Institute, one of his hobbies which he can well afford since he practiced what he preached and sold his extensive holdings before the crash. A number of one of the author's friends have benefited from this as winners of Babson's prizes for essays and original research on gravity.

The market unexpectedly responded to Babson's September 5th speech by a break which sent the Times Industrials down 10 points and with 5,565,280 shares being unloaded. Babson was promptly denounced by Wall Street. Barron's said that he should not be taken seriously as anyone familiar with his notorious inaccuracy would know. The market rallied the next day and people seemed to lose their fear.

The academic booster of the boom was Irving Fisher, Professor of Economics at Yale and probably the most original academic economist in America at that time. His was the voice of authority; his credentials were without question. In frequent interviews and speeches, he expounded his reasons why prosperity would continue and he was a well-advertised consultant for several investment trusts. Fisher's response to Babson was that everything was fine;

dividends were rising, that the suspicion of common stocks was receding, and that investment trusts now offered the investor wide and well-managed diversification—there may be a recession of stock prices but not anything in the nature of a crash.

As a professor, Fisher made important contributions to the theory of index numbers, to monitary theory, and to other aspects of economics that have become classical. He was the only experimental Ph.D. student of Josiah Willard Gibbs, America's greatest mathematical physicist. His thesis was concerned with a hydraulic model of the economy. He arranged tanks of water to represent various segments of the economy; industries, rails, agriculture, etc. These tanks were connected by pipes and valves so that, by opening and closing appropriate valves, one could determine the effect of different segments of the economy on each other.

Fisher apparently acquired his passion for the stock market from Gibbs who played it quite seriously. In his years as a professor at Yale, Gibbs' total salary was no more than $20,000. He was offered a salary only after he was a professor for ten years, Yale's generosity being coupled with Johns Hopkins University's attempt to recruit him. Gibbs' father left him another $10,000. However, Gibbs' estate was the order of $110,000, much of which was derived from his astute investments in the market. Gibbs frequently gave tips to the townspeople in New Haven with whom he dealt—the butcher, the barber, the green grocer, etc.—but his suggestions seem to have been dismissed as the ravings of an absent-minded professor.

Business was declining in the fall of 1929. By October the Federal Reserve index of industrial production was 117 as compared with the June level of 126. Steel production and home building also declined over the summer months and in October the freight car loadings were also diminishing. Some cautious people reasoned that high stock prices were a measure of expected industrial prosperity. With the economic decline they decided to sell, causing the market to drift slowly downward.

The Times Industrials dropped 7 points on Friday, October 18th. During Saturday half-day trading on the 19th, 3,488,100 shares were traded and the Times Industrials slid another 12 points, with some speculative shares going down as much as 40 points. There was a tense Sunday pause. The Sunday papers carried[14]

... three comments which were to become familiar in the days that followed. After Saturday's trading, quite a few margin calls were out—the speculator was being asked for more cash. The other two observations were more reassuring—the worst was over. And it was predicted that on the following day the market would begin to receive organized support. Some thought of the bankers ... Charles Mitchell had acted once before, he would again. Some had in mind the investment trusts; if stocks did become cheap, the investment trusts would be in the market picking up bargains.

Monday, October 21st, was ominous—sales 6,091,870, the ticker was 100 minutes behind at closing time but a late rally made the drop less than Saturday's. However, people were shaky. Professor Fisher said that the decline of the previous week represented a shaking out of the lunatic fringe, while Babson said sell stock and buy gold. On Tuesday there was a slight gain. Charles Mitchell said the decline had gone too far. Wednesday opened quietly, then toward mid-morning motor accessory stocks were sold heavily, and slowly the sales volume built up until a great crescendo of the last hour of trading when 2,600,000 shares were traded. The Times Industrial average dropped from 415 to 384, the level at the end of June.

That afternoon and evening thousands of speculators decided to get out while—as they mistakingly supposed—the getting out was good. Others were told they had no choice but to get out unless they posted more collateral for, as the day's business came to an end, an unprecedented volume of margin calls went out. Thursday, October 24th, is the first of those days which history identifies with the Panic of 1929. That day 12,894,640 shares changed hands, many of them at prices which shattered the dreams and hopes of those who owned them. Of all the mysteries of the stock market there is none so impenetrable as why there should be a buyer for everyone who wishes to sell. October 24th, 1929, showed that what is mysterious is not inevitable. Often there were no buyers, and only after wide vertical declines could anyone be induced to bid.[14]

The remarkable thing about October 24th was that the panic was stopped by noon when organized support appeared. As in the Panic of 1907, a meeting of important bankers was held in the office of J. P. Morgan and Company (J. P., Senior, was dead and his son in Europe but, for historical reasons, it was a good place to have the meeting). The host of the meeting, T. H. Lamont, the senior partner at Morgans, met with reporters after the meeting and told them that there was some distress selling due to technical conditions, but that the bankers had decided to better things. The word spread like magic. At 1:30 Richard Whitney, representing the group that met, went to the post on the exchange where steel stocks were traded, bid 205 per share for 10,000 shares and continued on his way, placing orders for another fifteen or twenty kinds of stocks. At closing on Black Thursday the Times Industrials were off only 12 points from the day before. The ticker, however, was hours behind so that margin accounts were being closed by selling stock held as security on loans even though a rally was taking place on the floor.

The small speculators who invested all their possessions in the market as many did were wiped out on Black Thursday, so that it was small consolation to them that the market rebounded. They had put all their money into margin payments. If in the rising market earlier in the year they had made some profits, they were used in making margin payments to purchase new stock. In the excitement of getting rich overnight, homes were mortgaged to get more money to make down payments on more stock. While the market was falling, every possible source of money had to be exploited to pay more margin since the devalued stock was no longer sufficient security for the original loan. The drop was so great during Thursday morning that most small but over-extended speculators could not raise the required funds at short notice. The banks and the wealthier crowd then picked up bargains in the morning which increased in value during the afternoon rally.

Heavy trading continued on Friday and Saturday, with prices varying but little. The weekend newspapers effectively congratulated the country for its strength in avoiding, thanks to the bankers and the basic power of business with its good prospects, what started as a disaster. It was agreed that stocks, being again cheap, would sell well into the next week.

The real disaster, however, started on Monday and continued on for several years.[14]

The singular feature of the great crash of 1929 was that the worst continued to worsen. What looked one day like the end proved the next day to have been only the beginning. Nothing could have been more ingeniously designed to maximize the suffering, and also to insure that as few as possible escaped from the common misfortune. The fortunate speculator who had funds to avoid the first margin call presently would get another—and still another. In the end, all the money he had was extracted from him and lost. The man—who was safely out of the market—naturally went back to pick up bargains. The bargains then suffered a ruinous fall. Even the man who waited out all of October and all of November who then bought common stocks would see their value drop to a third or a fourth of the purchase price in the next twenty-four months.

Monday, October 28th, was a terrible day—volume over 9 million shares and Times Industrials down 49 points. On this day there was no recovery. The bankers met, but their concern was that no "air holes" would appear in any stock. If prices would fall, it would be in an orderly way. On the evening of the 28th, there was no feeling of security that the powerful banks would be available to stop a panic.

Tuesday, October 29th, was the most catastrophic day in the history of the New York Stock Market and, possibly the worst day in the history of speculation. Great blocks of stock were offered as soon as the market opened. The trading rate for the first half-hour was 33 million shares per day, the recorded sales for the day 16,410,030. Some sales went unrecorded because of the feverish activity. Other markets showed similar activity. "Air holes" were so common that they could not be filled. The Times Industrials were down 43 points (Monday and Tuesday had drops totaling 92 points), canceling the gains of the previous exciting year. Losses would have been worst had not a last minute rally developed. The magnitude of the fluctuations were unusual. American Can opened at 130, went down 20 points and then up 10, for example. The investment trusts were very severely hit. Blue Ridge which early in September sold at 24 was down to 12, October 12th; opened at 10 on October 29th and dropped to 3. Goldman Sachs was 104 during the summer of 1929 and 1-3/4 in 1932. Corporations and out-of-town bankers called back two billion dollars worth of call loans between October 23rd and October 30th. New York banks came to the rescue by lending about a billion dollars, preventing an even worse catastrophe.

On Wednesday, October 30th, there was some recovery with Times Industrials rising 31 points and another 21 on Thursday, October 31st. Margin was then at 25% and the Federal discount rate down to 5%. The next week showed a reversal again with Times Industrials down 22 points on Monday. On

Wednesday, down another 37. On November 11th, 12th and 13th, a total drop of 50 points so that by the 13th the level was 224 as compared with 452 on September 3rd, down to less than half. Then for a while, for the rest of November and on until March, there seemed to be a small but steady revival. It was assumed that the decline had run its course.

Another serious drop then occurred in June. From that time on, for several years, the drop was continuous until by July 8th, 1932, the Times Industrials were down to 58, not much larger than the daily rise or fall during the period of excitement. The number of shares traded on that July day were 730,278. Pig iron production was only 12% of capacity and the lowest since 1896. The Great Depression was well under way.

We close this historical review of speculational orgies with a brief summary of the mechanism behind practically all these events. We use the words of the stock exchange, but the basic ideas are general and, in fact, can be translated into other examples of public hysteria quite easily. There are eight important steps:

(I) Increasing industrial production and sales (or demand for some commodity such as land) in a period in which there is general optimism causes a rise in price of stock (or of the commodity).

(II) If at the same time private savings and uncommitted cash is increasing, the rise attracts new investors and enlarges the depth of involvement of those already in the market.

(III) This induces larger rises in market prices and attracts less sophisticated people who pay attention only to changes in market prices, essentially ignoring the activity of the companies whose stock they purchase.

(IV) The small down payment (margin, in stocks, binders in Florida real estate, etc.) becomes widely used so that the demand for stock increases more rapidly than the rate at which real money is put into the market. Furthermore, the behavior of the market becomes practically uncoupled from industrial production, or the actual value of the use of the object being invested in. The investor is buying only to sell soon after profits are made.

(V) Success and demand for stock breed enterprises which have nothing to do with production; for example, investment trusts or, in the case of real estate booms, swamp land, etc.

(VI) As values skyrocket, the number of new people entering the speculative orgy decreases. Those already committed become more sensitive. They know they want to get out while they are ahead, but they also become a little greedy so that they stay in as long as there is some rise.

(VII) A small, more-knowledgable, group observes that the original reason for the excitement, industrial production and its future prospects has not kept up with the inflated values of the stock. They start to sell out.

(VIII) Since new buyers are few, prices go down somewhat as these sales are made. The sensitive people react. As the continuous drop occurs, the installment (or margin) buyers are in trouble. The stock held as security is sold in a market of few buyers and the panic is on.

This, of course, is a simplified model but still it contains most of the main ideas. It should not be difficult to make a mathematical formulation of this mechanism. We hope to discuss such a scheme elsewhere. We now develop some quantitative aspects of speculation, Dow Jones variation in the stock market and variation in number of speculators in coins in the 1960's.

REFERENCES

1. Miriam Beard, *A History of Business*, Vol. 1, (Univ. of Mich. Press, 1963).
2. Elgin Groseclose, *Money and Man*, (Univ. of Oklahoma Press, 1934; reprinted Ungar, 1961).
3. Violet Barbour, *Capitalism in Amsterdam in the 17th Century*, (Univ. of Mich. Press, 1963).
4. Charles MacKay, *Extraordinary Popular Delusions and The Madness of Crowds*, (London 1841; reprint Noonday Press 1932).
5. John T. Flynn, *Men of Wealth*, (Simon and Schuster, 1941).
6. George Ondard, *The Amazing Life of John Law*, (New York, 1928).
7. Viscount Erleigh, *The South Sea Bubble*, (New York, 1933).
8. John Clapham, *The Bank of England, Vol. I*, (Cambridge, 1958).
9. Edward Gibbon, *Autobiography*, (London, 1794, Reprint Meridian Press, 1961).
10. Reginald C. McGrane, *The Panic of 1837*, (Univ. of Chicago, 1924; reprint edition, 1965).
11. Willard L. Thorp, *Business Annals*, (National Bureau of Economic Research, 1926).
12. Frederick L. Allen, *Only Yesterday*, (Harper, 1931; Reprint Bantam, 1946).
13. Stewart H. Holbrook, *The Age of the Moguls*, (Doubleday, 1953).
14. John K. Galbraith, *The Great Crash*, (Houghton Mifflin, 1954).

2   An Indicator for Booms and Another for Busts

Suppose one wishes to determine whether investors are entering into the wild speculative behavior mode or whether market reports merely reflect the normal fluctuations stimulated by variations in product interest, international affairs, interest rates, tax structure, supply and demand, etc. One scheme for making this decision is to analyze the extreme value statistics of a variable which measures the state of the market.[1] The Dow-Jones industrial average is such a measure of the state of the U.S. stock market.

The prices of some thirty stocks are weighted together to give the "Dow-Jones average". Other weightings are made by the New York Times finance department, as well as by other organizations. Any of these would be satisfactory for analysis. Standard and Poor's "Basic Statistics" gives the daily highs and lows of the Dow-Jones average going back to 1897. The daily average is a measure of both the stochastic character of the market (which will be discussed in detail in the next section) and of longer range trends. The theory of extreme events as presented in Section III.8 is applicable only to stochastic processes. Hence, if it is to be applied to boom watching, the trend component must be subtracted from the data.

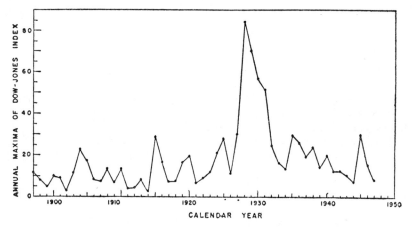

Figure 61   Annual maxima, Dow-Jones Index, 1897–1947.

The Dow-Jones central value characterizes the trend component. It is defined as the arithmetic mean of the median of the daily highs and the median of the daily lows over a calendar year. An annual maxima can be defined as the difference between the largest daily high and the annual central value. A plot of these annual maxima for the years 1897–1947 is given in Figure 61. This represents the extreme values of the stochastic part of the Dow-Jones averages. Without even trying to apply our extreme value theory, we can see that the stochastic process was quite extraordinary in the period 1927–1933. Figure 62 arranges the annual maxima in order of increasing size and plots them on "extremal" paper. These graphs are taken from Gumbel.[1]

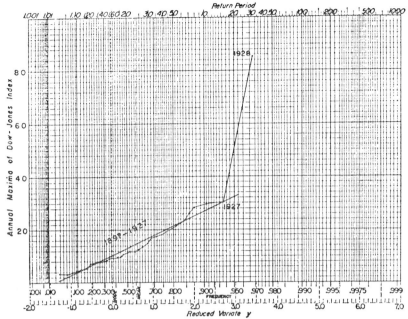

Figure 62 Dow-Jones maxima plotted on probability paper, 1897–1928.

The fit over the period 1897–1927 is very good, while the point representing 1928 is almost out of the picture, with its return period being over 2000 years. From this one can conclude that something changed in the basic mechanism.

With our great expertise in hindsight, we can list some of these changes. As was mentioned in the last section there was

(i) A tremendous increase in popular participation in stock speculation. Instead of it being a game of a few professionals, traders and well-to-do people, it became an obsession of an enormous number of modest folk.

(ii) A drastic change in buying on margin. By 1929, all that was required for the purchase of stock was a 25% down payment. This allowed a speculator to buy four times as much stock as he could afford with his available capital. The amount of real money (and not promises to pay) in the market was probably less than 35% of the listed market value.

(iii) The growing popularity of the investment company. Such a company bought a certain amount of stock from a number of other companies. Then it would issue its own stock on the basis of its holdings. Because of its reputed expertise in stock selection, people were willing to buy its stock at a level far higher than justified by the then present and potential worth of the companies' holdings.

All of these changes inflated stock values and gave fuel to sustain the mania. The stochastic process which governed stock fluctuation had changed tremendously so that the 2000 year point of 1928 in Fig. 62 had a right to be off the Gumbel line.

It might seem surprising to the reader that we use the stochastic component of Dow-Jones variations and not the trend component as an indicator of a speculator's orgy. We do this because a rapid rise in stock prices may reflect inflation, expectations of peace or war, or other important international events. On the other hand, a drastic change in the stochastic component is a measure of the change of the basic mechanism which generates fluctuations in stock prices.

Now suppose that the economy is in a wild speculative mode. Can one find an indicator to give warning of the impending bust? Of course the general knowledge of such an indicator or even a general belief that that indicator was sound (whether it was or not) would invite catastrophe as its dial approached the bust position. Variations of market prices depend on the changing attitudes of investors and speculators. The number of investors and speculators also depends on these attitudes. During a speculative orgy, people buy stocks (or whatever the speculative item might be) only to sell them soon and reap profits. Interest in owning the object per se diminishes. It would then seem that a counter of the number of interested people would be an excellent indicator of expected drastic variations in the market. It would show a rapid rise as the speculative mode developed. Each new person in the market is a customer for shareholders. When the number of interested people levels off, no new customers appear. The high level of the market could be sustained for but a short time with shareowners merely buying from and selling to each other.

Perhaps a properly organized poll could act as a counter. We feel that it is better to find a counting scheme which represents the response of individuals to their own emotions rather than to questions posed by interviewers. If possible, it should register a commitment which shows that the individual is serious about playing the game.

In these days of almost universal literacy, one or several journals or newspapers become the chief sources of information and gossip concerning a speculative boom. They radiate enthsuiasm as the mania develops and make solemn pleas for confidence and optimism when prices level or drop slightly. After the bust, they analyze what went wrong, and they try to identify the culprits (by name or class) who were responsible for the disaster. Finally, they propose regulations and a new ethic to prevent busts while they insist that nothing has basically changed if people would only lose their fears.

The act of subscribing to the significant market journal represents a small commitment by the subscriber. It is a more considered act than making a purchase at a news stand. The Wall Street Journal has probably been the most important newspaper in the securities field for many years. However, it has for many years achieved recognition as a national newspaper so that it is read for general information as well as for investment news. A more appropriate journal would be one of the private investment tip sheets. We have been unable to find subscription records of any of 1920–30 vintage. However, we have investigated sale variations of the "Coin World" during the period 1959–1970, which includes the years 1962–1965 when speculation in rolls of uncirculated U.S. coins went wild.

Coin collecting is an ancient hobby having been practiced by princes and newsboys alike. Mayer Rothschild's numismatic trade and his attractive catalogues of old coins and medals brought him in contact with the local nobility of Frankfurt. This paved the road from which the family influence expanded from Juden Gasse in that city to the exchanges and parliaments of the important capitals of Europe.

Until 1950 the prices of old and rare coins rose slowly. There were occasionally periods when the extraordinary popularity of some type of coin created a flourish in the market. For example in the years 1935–37, US commemorative half dollars were sought by so many that their values rose by factors of five or more within a period of a year, only to drop drastically again. Such occasions were rare and few speculators entered the market when they did occur.

New types of coin albums appeared in the 1950's, coin clubs became common in large cities, better catalogues were published, and the hobby achieved a broad popularity. Numerous children tried to fill penny boards with specimens of Lincoln cents of all dates and mint mark, and many parents were drawn into the act by their children. This upsurge in interest stimulated more rapid price rises and higher price levels than had been traditional.

It was noted that while circulated specimens of some dates and mint marks (the mint mark being a mark on a coin which indicates the city of its origin; for example, on a U.S. penny, a letter D or S appears under the date if the coin was minted in Denver or San Francisco) were fairly common; uncirculated ones were extremely rare and commanded large premiums. Collectors started to put away several uncirculated rolls (of 20, 40 or 50 coins, depending on denomination) from each mint each year. Optimistic parents did this for their young children, reasoning that if the annual price rise would continue at the same rate until the children entered university, the hoard would pay for their education.

The news that rolls of uncirculated coins had risen steadily in value during the 1950's while other markets had their fluctuations came to the attention of a few speculators who were generally not serious coin collectors. They bought rolls in considerable quantity, forcing the prices higher and attracting more speculators. Not only rolls, but soon bags of freshly minted coins were hoarded. By 1964 hoarding for speculation reached such proportions that the U.S. Treasury Department warned against it and pleaded that the practice was creating a coin shortage (although the tremendous increase in the number of coin vending machines and parking meters was probably a more serious contributing factor). As a defense against hoarding, the mint mark for the first time in its 126-year history was omitted from coins minted at the branch mints. During the early 1960's, a roll of fifty 1960 Denver-minted pennies of the small date variety which sold for $1.50 in 1961, fetched twenty-six dollars in 1964. A roll of 1955 half dollars advanced from $15 to $200 in that period. Price rises by factors of 5 to 10 in three years were not unusual.

The primary journal of the coin boom was the Coin World which has appeared weekly since 1959. It features a column called Trends which lists the current values, estimated from ads and auction prices, at least once a month for all denominations of U.S. coins, and once a week for Lincoln pennies of all dates and mint marks. This weekly quotation of prices is analogous to the daily New York Stock Exchange quotations. Before the boom period, cataloguers found annual price lists to be sufficient to meet the demand. Coin World also lists on its front pages the number of paid copies distributed of that issue (either paid for in advance by subscriber or coin dealers who distribute the copies).

We have plotted the number of prepaid copies of the Coin World distributed each week since 1959 in Figure 63. Prices of some of the speculative items are plotted in Figure 64. We feel that the number of prepaid copies gives a good measure of both the collector and speculator interest in U.S. coins. It varies more smoothly with time than do prices and, as discussed in the analysis below, it gives an indicator of the softening and collapse of the speculative market.

The price history of rolls of three coins is plotted in Figures 64. The first in Fig. 64a corresponds to the 1960D small date penny which was a great speculative item. At first it was thought to be somewhat rare, but by the end of 1960 anyone could see that enough of them were around to keep collectors satisfied for the next fifty years. However, speculators who were interested in resale within a few months were not concerned with the long range point of view. Since the coin market is more informal than the stock exchange, there is no official daily listing of coin prices determined by the last registered sale (except perhaps of rarities which are sold at auctions). Value estimates are made by examining the range of prices which are found in advertisements. We have used bars in Figure 64a to indicate the range of prices. Most sales were transacted at a price near or perhaps a little below the middle of the range. The ranges reflecting ads in Coin World in the period January 1964– May 1965 varied very little with the exception of that recorded for the week of January 1, 1965 (which probably corresponded to after-Christmas sales).

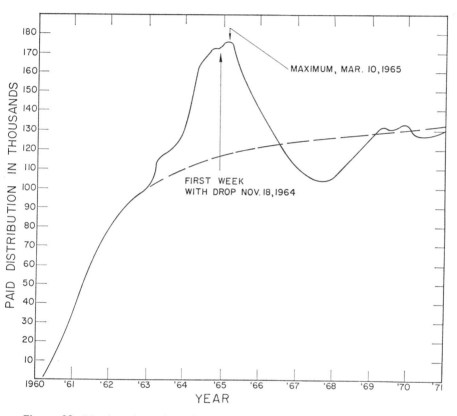

Figure 63 Number of prepaid copies of Coin World distributed each week since 1960.

The big break came during the summer of 1965 when, as is clear from the July 1 range, a number of bargains were available. The break lagged the March 10 peak of Figure 63 by a few months. A prudent follower of subscription statistics would have concluded that the big excitement of a rising market was over by December 1964.

The fall in prices in the summer and autumn of 1965 was not quite as

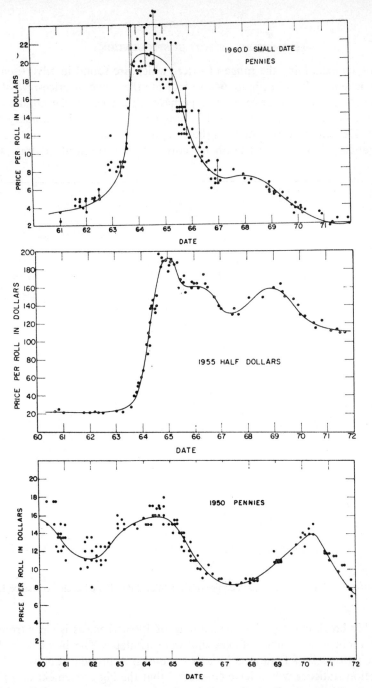

Figures 64a, b, c The price history of some typical rolls of US uncirculated coins. It is a decade which overlapped the great coin boom of the middle 60's. The 1900 D small date penny was a highly speculative item which was not rare. The 1955 half dollar was speculative and rather rare, while the 1950 penny was neither rare nor speculative.[3]

dramatic as the Black Thursday collapse of the Stock Market. This was because bank borrowing by dealers and speculators was not the same as margin buying of stock. Most borrowing was done through 90-day notes so that coins were not dumped on the market by creditors when a prespecified low level was reached. However, when purchasers became rare and notes had to be met, advertised prices of mail order dealers were reduced. Speculators who were concerned started to sell and other dealers had to reduce prices, also. The market steadily dropped until the spring of '66 when it hardened a bit, but as can be seen from Figure 64a, the price decline of the 1960D small date penny continued in a manner similar to the decline of the stock market into the early 1930's. The price of a roll of these coins during the summer of 1971 was $1.95.

The 1955 half dollar was a favorite of speculators because of its low mintage, 2,876,381 as compared with some other dates such as 1952D with 25 million, 1942 with 47 million, 1943 with 53 million, etc. Of over a billion half dollars which circulated in the early 1960's, very few were dated 1955. A collector who watched for scarce dates of coins in his pocket change had little likelihood of finding a 1955 half in circulation and frequently had to buy one from a dealer if he wanted it for his collection. Its price history, as exhibited in Fig. 64b, is similar to that of the 1960D small date penny except that its relative rarity has caused it to level off at a fairly high value of about $110 a roll, as compared with the peak speculative value of $200.

The 1950 penny is fairly common in worn or circulated form. Even twenty years after its minting, it can still be found occasionally in one's pocket change. It never became a speculative item. It is slightly scarce in uncirculated condition since it was minted before rolls of uncirculated coins were hoarded in great quantity. Its price history in Figure 64c shows that its value did rise somewhat, but never went wild. Its price today is about half the peak value.

Coin World subscriptions for the past two years fluctuated between 125,000 and 130,000. This is correlated with the number of serious collectors of U.S. coins and dealers. The '67–'68 dip in Figure 65 is probably a reflection of disappointment of serious collectors as well as speculators after the coin market crash. The collecting disease was apparently more severe than the disappointment of serious collectors so that they eventually again became interested in their collections and reinstituted their subscriptions.

If there ever is another U.S. coin boom, we conjecture that one of the early indicators will be a rapid rise in the number of Coin World subscribers and, perhaps, of the founding of a new competing journal. Incidentally, England and Switzerland experienced great coin booms several years ago, the Netherlands is in the throes of one now, and the interest in coins in Japan is becoming quite strong.

REFERENCES

1. E. J. Gumbel, Statistical Theory of Extreme Values and Some Practical Applications, No. 33, NBS App. Math. Series, 1954.
2. *Coin World*, 1960–1971.

3　More Dow-Jones Fluctuations

Most trading in securities is conducted in periods without heroic booms or busts. The price of the item being traded goes up or down in some more or less random way. Some traders search for tips, and inside advice about companies and certain classes of industries. They may try to become experts in the development of the electronics industry or in gold mining.

There are those speculators who search for indicators and patterns of the movement of the market as a whole, wishing to follow the old adage—buy when stocks are low and sell when they are high without being too concerned with the specific stock being bought. It is not difficult to get fooled. When the market seems low it may remain there for a long time or even go lower. A speculator's money that is tied up in stock that is going no where could have been more productive by drawing interest in a dull but steady manner in a bank. Hence there is considerable interest in "technical analysis", the search for patterns which indicate when a low price level is temporary and when a rapid rise will stop.

An example particularly rich in structure is the "three peaks and the domed house" pattern discovered by George Lindsay.[1] Figure 65a gives a generalized model of the pattern or trend, and Figure 65b sketches its confirmation during the period 1946–1948.

The advice of the analyst favoring this pattern would be clear. Watch for three successive peaks with an interval of about eight months between the first and last, relax for five months until the bottom is reached, mortgage your home, buy furiously, and sell at a great profit in about seven months. Implied in reliance on patterns is the conviction that the market is governed by a complicated mechanism as yet not understood. The mechanism contains a certain inertia or long term memory such that when an appropriate pattern begins, it is inevitable that a special sequence of events will be generated; i.e. the system gets locked into a mode which will persist for a year or two.

One can of course take the opposite point of view and assert that the motion of the market is a purely random process being driven by external events, international and national related to war and peace, economic successes and failures, crop failures, fits of optimism and pessimism about where the country is going, population shifts, interest rates, etc. Even though there might be laws relating all of these events—the network which relates them is so complex that few individuals, if any, understand it. Hence the response

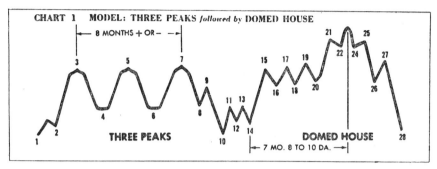

Figure 65a An example of patterns in the stock market used by technical analysts.[1]

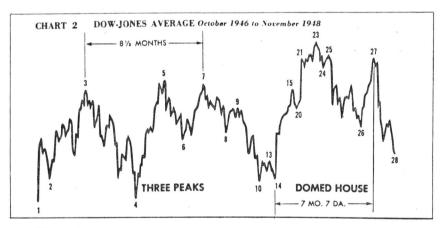

Figure 65b An example of patterns in the stock market used by technical analysts.[1]

of the individuals who buy and sell securities varies from time to time so that the market seems to be responding to a random force and behaves in a manner not unlike a molecule in a fluid which is buffeted about by many other molecules. While there are specific equations of motion, the enormous number of impulses experienced by a molecule makes it seem as though a purely random force is applied.

One of the most systematic investigations of economic time series has been made by the statistician M. G. Kendall[2] who examined 22 price series ranging from 486 terms of weekly intervals to 2387 terms of weekly intervals. This was for industrial share prices on as varied a set of markets as investment trusts, cotton, oil, shipping, coal, wheat, stores and catering, all classes of industrials combined, etc. He examines various correlation coefficients such as

$$r_k = \{(n-k\}^{-1} \sum_{j=1}^{n-k} u_i u_{i+k}\}/n^{-1} \sum_{i=1}^{n} u_i^2$$

where u_1, u_2, u_3—is a sequence of weekly quotations. If a pattern has a strong correlation between an i-th and $i+k$-th quotation, r_k is much larger than it would be if the various u_i's are statistically independent of each other. Kendall concludes that the correlation coefficients that should be expected are random sequences. In his own words:[2]

Broadly speaking the results are these:

(a) In series of prices which are observed at fairly close intervals, the random changes from one term to the next are so large as to swamp any systematic effect which may be present. The data behave almost like wandering series.

(b) It is therefore difficult to distinguish by statistical methods between a genuine wandering series and one wherein the systemic element is weak.

(c) Until some way has been found of circumventing this difficulty, trend fitting, and perhaps the fitting of any model, is a highly hazardous undertaking. It may be possible for an econometrician to test whether the data agree with a hypothesis suggested by prior analysis, but it may be impossible to discriminate between quite different hypotheses which all fit the data.

(d) There is experimental evidence and theoretical support for the belief that aggregative index numbers behave more systematically than their components. This might be due to the reduction of the random elements by averaging and the consequent emergence of systematic constituents; but it could equally well be due to chance. If it is, there will appear spurious time-correlations in aggregative series and the use of index-numbers in econometric work needs extensive reconsideration.

(e) An analysis of stock-exchange movements revealed little serial correlation within series and little lag correlation between series. Unless individual stocks behave differently from the average of similar stocks, there is no hope of being able to predict movements on the exchange for a week ahead without extraneous information.

H. V. Roberts has presented the case for the random mechanism in more graphical but less systematic terms. He constructed a chance model in which

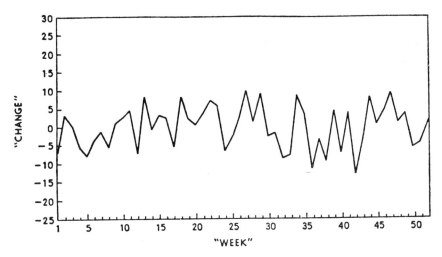

Figure 66 Simulated market changes for 52 weeks.[4]

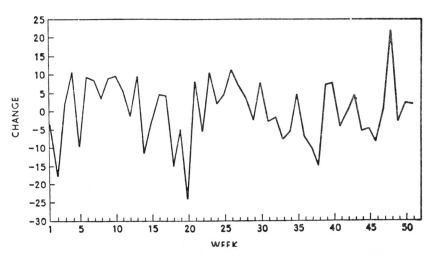

Figure 67 Changes from Friday to Friday (closing) January 6, 1956—December 28, 1956. Dow-Jones Industrial Index.[4]

the weekly change in the Dow-Jones index was determined choosing numbers from a table of random numbers with the special restriction that the mean of those to be chosen was 0.5 and standard deviation 5.0. The positive mean was chosen to correspond to the average inflation of prices that has taken place in the comodity market over the years.

Roberts' simulated market changes for 52 weeks are plotted in Figure 66 and are to be compared with a one-year record of the Dow-Jones changes. If several other Dow-Jones changes were also included it would be clear that

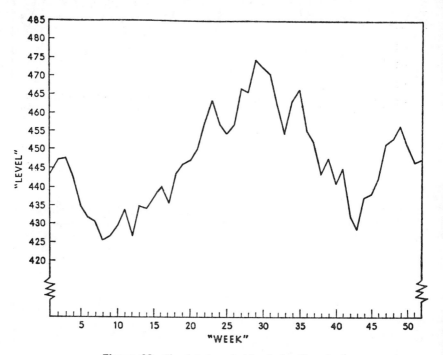

Figure 68   Simulated market levels for 52 weeks.[4]

the difference between any two of them would not be significantly less than the simulated market from any of them. (See Figure 67.)

The simulated level itself is plotted in Figure 68 and is to be compared with the Dow-Jones records of 1956. The same remarks can be made about the levels as about the changes. The simulated level would not differ significantly more from most annual records than they would from each other. In records as short as those plotted a detailed similarity between one simulated record

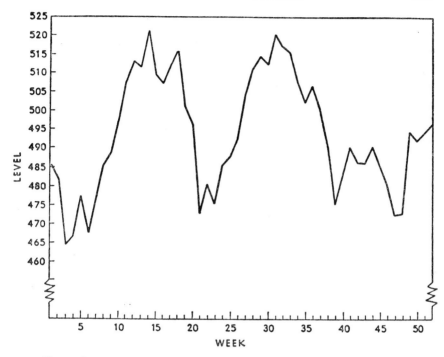

Figure 69   Friday closing levels, December 30, 1955—December 28, 1956.
Dow Jones Industrial Index.[4]

and one annual record would not be great nor would that between two successive annual records.

Roberts has also discussed the applicability of another test for randomness
in a sequence. It has to do with runs of weekly changes of the same sign. A
positive change over a week is represented by a "+" and a negative by a "−".
Figure 67 contains the following sequence of +'s and −'s

− − + + − + + + + + + − + − − + + − − − − + − + +

+ + + + − + − − − − − + − − − − + + − − + − − − + +

− + +

A run is a consecutive sequence of the same symbol. One sees that the first
four runs are − −, + +, −, + + + + + +. The number of runs in the
sequence is 24. This is very close to the expected number 26.41 in a random
sequence of the above length.

REFERENCES

1. Yale Hirsh, Inc. (For Hayden Stone, Inc.) *The Trader's Almanac and Record*, 1969.
2. M. G. Kendall, *T. of Roy. Stat. Soc.* **96**, 11 (1953) (Reprinted in reference 3).
3. P. Cootner (Editor). *The Random Character of Stock Market Prices* (MIT Press 1964).
4. H. V. Roberts, *J. of Finance* **14**, 1 (1956) (Also reprinted in reference 3).

4   Brownian Motion in The Stock Market

It was mentioned at the beginning of Section 2 that the stock market or any speculative activity has a trend component and a random component. In our discussion of the extreme value theory of the random component, we did not say anything about the stochastic process itself. Also, our extreme value theory was concerned with the market as a whole as reflected in Dow-Jones and other such indices. In this section we discuss the statistical variations among individual stocks. The results of this section are not applicable to making money in the market.

We choose the theory of stock market price fluctuations as a prototype of general situations in which a slowly varying amount of money gets distributed among a number of items. The total amount of money invested in the market changes only slowly over a period of time which is short compared with that required for large changes in the economy or the market itself, but long compared with that required for an enormous number of stock transactions to occur. Individual stocks compete with each other for a share of this money. Those which seem to be rising in value or which the public thinks will rise in value will be in greater demand than those whose future seems dim. If an investor sells shares of the latter class to purchase those of the former class, he will have to offer a bargain in order to dispose of the undesirable stock and offer a premium to purchase the desirable stock. Hence the desirable stock will rise and the undesirable one will fall in market value. The situation is rather analogous to that of a collection of molecules whose total energy is fixed and which, through intermolecular collisions, can suffer momentum exchange between molecules. When the momentum of one increases through collision, that of the other decreases. An ensemble of stocks is always close to equilibrium since no stock is sold unless a buyer is available to complete the sale. The instantaneous value of the stock at the time of the sale is established by the sale.

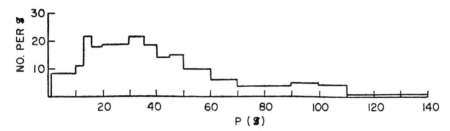

Figure 70 Distribution function of closing prices for July 31st, 1956 (all items, NYSE). [1]

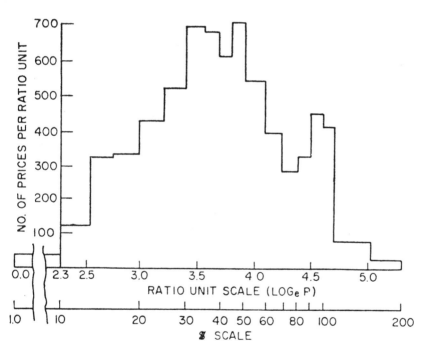

Figure 71 Distribution function for $\log_e P$ on July 31st, 1956 (all items NYSE). [1]

H

The first statistical investigation of this mechanism was made by Bachelier in 1900 in a remarkable Ph.D. thesis that was ignored for many years. It contained many of the ideas used later by Einstein in his theory of Brownian Motion and by other authors in the theory of stochastic processes. The economic ideas were later developed independently and extended by M. F. M. Osborne who was led to his formulation of the theory by a detailed examination of market data. Incidentally, the initials M. F. M. are those of Osborne's illustrious great-grandfather, Mathew Fontain Maury, one-time director of the U.S. Naval Observatory and father of the science of oceanography. At the declaration of the Civil War, Maury, as a good Southerner, took the lenses out of the telescopes of the Naval Observatory and carried them across the Long Bridge from Washington, D.C., into Virginia, thus decomissioning the Observatory.

The English translation of the Bachelier thesis, Osborne's papers and those of a number of other authors have recently been reprinted in reference 3. Bachelier's thesis advisor was Poincaré.

Osborne started his investigation by considering the distribution of closing prices on all items listed on the New York Stock Exchange. We have plotted his observed distribution function for July 31st, 1956, in Figure 70. The number of stocks in a given price range is plotted as a function of the price.

The long tail in the curve suggested that the distribution function be plotted on a logarithmic scale as had been done in Figure 71. The two peaks indicated that the New York Stock Exchange quotations were for two different types of stock and, indeed, when separate plots were made for common and preferred stock, Figures 72a and 72b were obtained. Notice that the distributions, as constructed from the histograms, have the appearance of normal distributions; i.e., the logarithm of the stock price seemed to be distributed normally.

As was discussed in Section III.3 a good test for log-normal distribution is to plot the cumulative distribution function on a logarithmic scale. If the CDF is a straight line, then the data has a log-normal distribution function. This type of plot has been made in Figure 73. Notice the good fit of the data to a straight line.

It is interesting to search for the basis of log-normal nature of the distribution function. The stimulus to which a speculator responds is the change in stock prices. This change has a different meaning for low price and high price stocks. An increase of five dollars in the value of a $200 stock is uninteresting while the same change in a three-dollar stock is exciting. Clearly, the relative change in price $dP/P = d \log P$ is the important stimulus. That is, the fundamental variable is the logarithm of the price. It is this quantity which is normally distributed among stocks. It is this quantity which has the "Maxwell distribution".

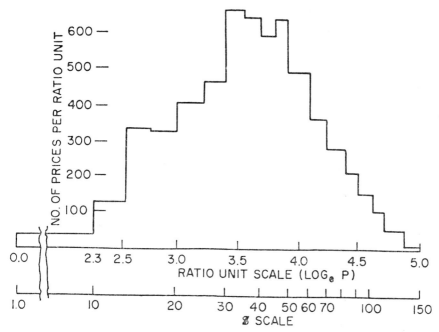

Figure 72a Distribution function of $\log_e P$ for common stocks (NYSE, July 31st, 1956).[1]

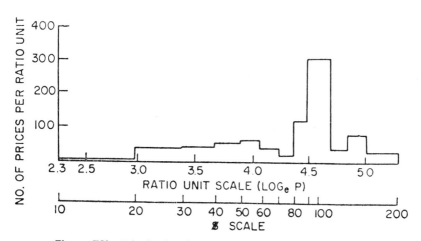

Figure 72b Distribution function of $\log_e P$ for preferred stocks (NYSE, July 31st, 1956).[1]

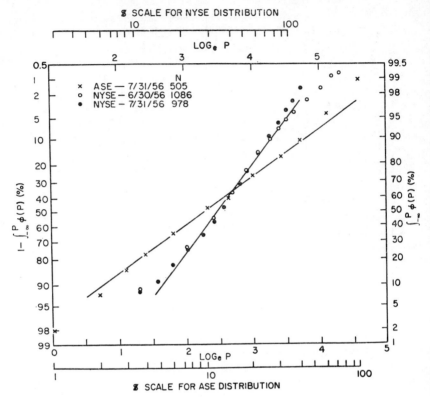

Figure 73   Cumulated distributions of $\log_e P$ for NYSE and ASE
(common stocks).[1]

We now consider, following Osborne,[2] some statistical aspects of the time
variation of stock prices. We choose as our basic variable for stock i

$$F_i(\tau) = \log [P_i(t+\tau)/P_i(t)], \tag{1}$$

$P_i(t)$ being the price of a share of the ith stock at time t. The cumulative distribution function of $F_i(\tau)$ with $\tau = 1$ year is plotted in Fig. 74. The distribution
of $F_i(\tau)$ over many i is also Gaussian.

At time $\tau = 0$, each $F_i(\tau)$ is zero and the average over a large number, N,
of stocks

$$F(0) = N^{-1} \sum_{1}^{N} F_i(0) \tag{2}$$

is also zero. As τ increases, the mean value $F(\tau)$ fluctuates, increasing or

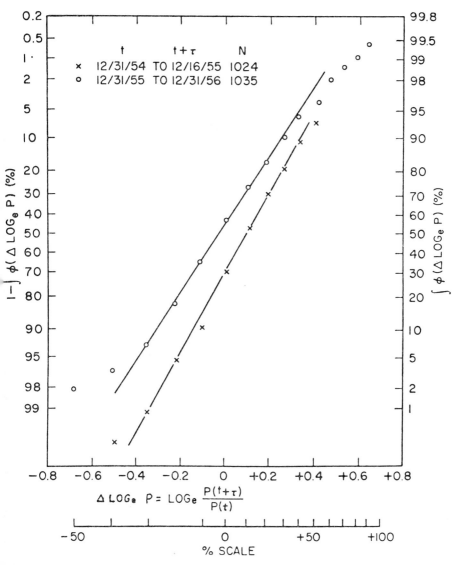

Figure 74 Cumulated distributions of $\Delta \log_e P = \log_e[P(t+\tau)/P(t)]$ for $\tau = 1$ year (NYSE common stocks). Data from NYSE Year Book, 1956, and *The Exchange* (February, 1957).[1]

decreasing. It is, of course, a measure of the trend in the market. The dispersion from the mean,

$$\sigma^2 = \langle (F_i(\tau) - F(\tau))^2 \rangle = \frac{1}{N} \sum_1^N [F_i(\tau) - F(\tau)]^2 \tag{3}$$

reflects the random character of the market. As an alternative to plotting σ as a function of time, Osborne plotted the semi-interquartile range of $F(\tau)$ as a function of time (see Figure 75). Both of these quantities have essentially the same dependence on time. Notice that if $\sigma = \alpha t^{\frac{1}{2}}$ (α being a constant), then

$$\log \sigma = \tfrac{1}{2} \log t + \log \alpha \tag{4}$$

and a plot of $\log \sigma$ vs $\log t$ is a straight line with slope $\tfrac{1}{2}$. This is indeed the character of Figure 75. Another quantity which has the same significance as σ is the mean absolute value of index changes (see reference 2 for a detailed

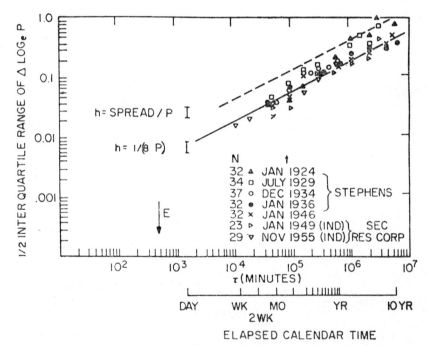

Figure 75a Semi-interquartile range of $\Delta \log_e P = \log_e[P(t+\tau)/P(t)]$ for τ as a Calendar time interval (NYSE common stocks). N = number of stocks in sample. This data may be regarded as 0.6745 $\sigma_{S(\tau)}$ for an assumed normal distribution.[1]

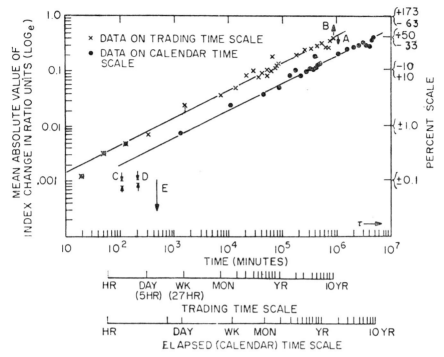

Figure 75b   Mean absolute value of index changes according to Cowles, in ratio units, as a function of time interval. The arrows *A–D* denote approximate corrections to convert the data to s.q.r. = 0.6745 $\sigma_{M(t)}$ of a normal distribution.[1]

discussion of this quantity). On a log-log plot it also has a slope $\frac{1}{2}$. The fit is best when the time is given on a trading scale rather than on a calendar scale. Weekends and holidays are omitted in the trading time scale.

Osborne interpreted the observation that $\sigma = \alpha t^{\frac{1}{2}}$ to indicate that changes in log $P_i(t)$ for a given stock can be interpreted as having been generated by a random walk (or "Brownian Motion") type process. The value of log $P_i(t)$ at a given time would be the result of a large number of transitions so that the central limit theorem could be applied to give it a Gaussian character. If we refer back to equation (19) in Section (III.5), we see that the probability $P(X, t)$ of a displacement X in time t in a Gaussian random walk ($v = 2$ in eq. (18)) is

$$P(X, t) = t^{-\frac{1}{2}}Q(Xt^{-\frac{1}{2}}) \tag{5a}$$

where Q is a Gaussian function of $Xt^{-\frac{1}{2}}$. The dispersion, σ, (since the mean was chosen to be zero in that case) is given by

$$\sigma^2 = \int_{-\infty}^{\infty} X^2 t^{-\frac{1}{2}} Q(Xt^{-\frac{1}{2}}) \, dX \tag{5b}$$

$$= t \int_{-\infty}^{\infty} y^2 Q(y) \, dy \qquad \text{if} \quad y = Xt^{-\frac{1}{2}} \tag{6}$$

so that

$$\sigma = \alpha t^{\frac{1}{2}},$$

α being the square root of the integral which is independent of t. This is just the relation observed by Osborne.[2]

The dependence of the dispersion on the time has an alternative form in a one-dimensional random walk process. Let a walker move with equal likelihood to the right or left with a step of length h. Then, if T is the number of steps taken

$$\sigma = hT^{\frac{1}{2}} \tag{7}$$

As T becomes large the process becomes Gaussian with this dispersion. The interior semiquartile range is 0.6745σ. Hence, if log P can be modeled by a random walk process

$$\text{s.q.r. of } \Delta \log P = 0.6745hT^{\frac{1}{2}} \tag{8}$$

An appropriate choice of h and T which would check with Osborne's data would give another test of the theory.

The number of steps in the random walk model must be related in some way to the number of transactions since stock quotations are merely records of transactions which have been completed. Some transactions involve many shares and others only a few while the theory is concerned with the dispersion in the logarithm of the price of a single share. Hence T should be related to the number of shares in each transaction as well.

The smallest price variation recorded is $(1/8)$. Since the basic variable is log P the variation in log P is $\Delta P/P$. Since the smallest increment in P is $(1/8)$, that in log P is $h = 1/(8P)$. On a typical trading day at the time of Osborne's investigation the total number of shares traded was about 2×10^6 or 2×10^4 round lots of 100 shares each. For a thousand issues traded this would correspond to about 20 round lots per issue, or between 10 and 20 transactions per issue if each transaction averages between 1 and 2 round lots. If a typical share price is $40 one finds

$$\text{s.q.r.} = 0.6745 \, (1/320) \, (15 \pm 5)^{\frac{1}{2}} = (7.95 \pm 1.35) \times 10^{-3}$$

The observed semiquartile range is generally in this range so that there is an order of magnitude agreement between observations and a rough random walk model.

The order of magnitude relation between number of transactions and volume can be made more precise. In Figure 76 the number of transactions is plotted as a function of volume (in round lots per day) for 14 stocks. It is interesting to note that $V = 1.5T$ fits the data very well as was suggested above.

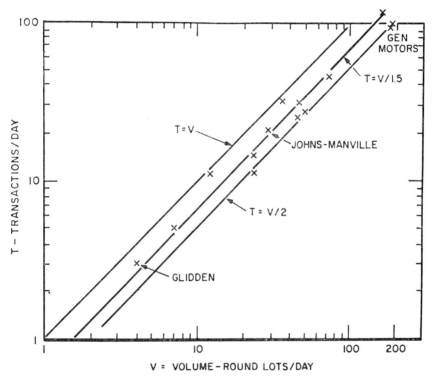

Figure 76 Transactions per day vs. round lot volume per day, for October 30, 1959. Data from Fitch's "A Daily Market Quotation Publication," 138 Pearl St., New York 5, N.Y.[2]

If the theory of the dispersion is correct, it should be valid for a group of high priced stocks, say \$80–\$120 per share, as well as for a group of low priced ones, say \$20–\$30 per share. Since

$$\sigma \simeq hT^{\frac{1}{2}}/\bar{P} = h(2V/3)^{\frac{1}{2}}/P_{\text{initial}}$$

this would imply that the dispersion of our low priced stocks should be four times that of the high priced ones. In analyzing the data for a number of stocks

* H

in each range, Osborne found that the dispersion for low priced stock is only 1.5 times that of the high priced issues rather than 4 times. Hence this random walk aspect of the theory is not as good as was hoped.

It is interesting to see if anything new can be learned by studying the statistics of the volume of stock sold instead of the price. Let us consider the volume, $V_j(\tau)$, of stock of the jth kind sold in time τ. Two statistical hypotheses that might be examined are: (i) that the probability of any transaction occurring in an interval τ is independent of any other one occurring, and (ii) that the probability of an occurrence of a transaction is proportional to τ. Certain consequences would follow from these hypotheses.

The number of transactions $T_j = 2V_j/3$ per time τ, say per day, should have a Poisson distribution. If T is large (say >10), the Poisson distribution approaches a Gaussian one with dispersion $\sigma_T = T^{\frac{1}{2}}$ or for the volume $\sigma_v = (3V/2)^{\frac{1}{2}}$.

As the mean volume of stock under consideration increases, one expects in the case of a Poisson or Gaussian distribution about the mean

$$S^2 = \langle [(V - \overline{V})/\overline{V}]^2 \rangle = k/\overline{V}$$

where k is a proportionality constant. The mean $\overline{V}$ can be increased by increasing the number of stock issues considered while leaving the time interval fixed. It can also be increased by keeping the number of issues fixed while the time interval τ is increased. In this case $S(\tau) \sim \tau^{-\frac{1}{2}}$.

The cumulative sequential frequency distribution of individual stocks, as well as of the entire market, are plotted in Figure 77. Generally speaking, the distributions favor the Log Normal Law rather than the Normal one, contrary to the prediction made above; i.e., the points in (b) can better be fitted to a straight line than (a). For the largest daily volumes, the choice of Normal and Log Normal fit the data almost equally well. This is always the case when the dispension is small compared to the mean.

Osborn has shown that the various predictions concerning the variation of S of the equation with the inverse half powers of $\overline{V}$ or τ seem to fail. From the manner in which they fail, he concludes that hypotheses (i) and (ii) are invalid and that a tendency exists for stock to be traded in concentrated bursts. This is consistent with one of the major operational problems facing the New York Stock Exchange, to prevent concentrated bursts of orders from completely disrupting the exchange.

The duration of bursts and gaps, i.e., of accumulated interest and indifference, seems to be of the order of a month or more. In periods of bursts the distribution function of the daily volume of stock traded seems to be log normal. The fundamental variable is then log V so that the decision to buy is proportional to the relative change in volume traded; i.e., if the volume

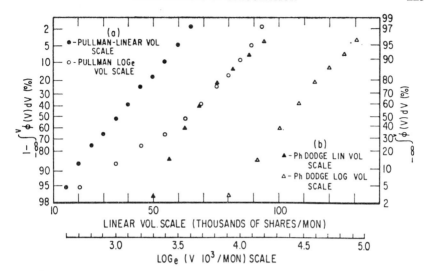

Figure 77 Cumulated sequential distribution of monthly volume, tested for normal (filled data points) vs. log normal (open points) distribution. (a) Pullman, data from June 1945 to June 1957, $N = 144$; (b) Phelps Dodge, data from June 1952 to June 1961, $N = 108$. Data taken graphically from charts of Securities Research Corporation. No splits occurred in the span of data.[2]

traded measures the interest or attention to a stock, the increment of interest is proportional to interest already present. This tendency of people is already well known to professional manipulators who attempt to generate real interest by producing a semblance of interest by spurious trading. If the presence of a large volume of trading induces bigger volume fluctuations, then hypothesis (i) of independence of trades is not valid and therefore Poisson distribution of volumes of trade cannot be expected to be valid.

REFERENCES

1. M. F. M. Osborn, *Operations Research* **7**, 145 (1959).
2. M. F. M. Osborn, *Operations Research* **10**, 345 (1962).
3. L. Bachelier, Ph.D. Thesis (Paris 1900); English translation available in P. Cootners, *The Random Character of Stock Market Prices* (MIT Press, 1964) which also reprints many other important papers in this field.

CHAPTER V

Vehicular Traffic

1 Historical Remarks

PEOPLE have always been "on the go". When they walked, they got blisters and tired. When they rode horses, the horse got wild, tired, ill, and expensive. Now that they drive motor vehicles, the damn things don't start in winter and, when they perform well mechanically, the vehicles which precede them in traffic go so slowly that the simple trip from A to B becomes a major frustration. Perhaps the ultimate solution of the traffic problem will be to stay home while attending to one's business with the aid of closed circuit 3-D TV networks, phototelephones and facsimile facilities with feel and smell consoles for those whose activities depend on these senses.

Traditionally the public has sought a transportation system which could carry one to his destination as rapidly, safely, cheaply and comfortably as possible. A "new" requirement is that the system be pollutionless, as well. It is said by some that by the year 2000 our vehicular pollution will suffocate us.

Since traffic pollution has become such a public issue, we note in passing the following self-explanatory table:[1]

Horse weight	Avg. 944 lbs.	Range 845–1043
Excrement, solid	Avg. 35 lbs/day	Range 26–44
Excrement, liquid	Avg. 16.5 lbs/day	Range 13–20

This is very recent data. It confirms older figures of Mayhew[2] except that Mayhew's urine figures seem too low (see table IX).

"Assuming a speed of 3 mph and roughly an eight-hour-day, the distance covered is about 25 miles/day. On this basis the emissions on a grams/mile basis are:[3]

635 grams/mile, solid   300 grams/mile, liquid

For comparison, the 1980 piston engine standards are:

Hydrocarbons	0.25 grams/mile
CO	4.7 grams/mile
NO_x	0.4 grams/mile."

Clearly, getting a horse is no solution.

The canonical manner in which traffic pollution was dealt with in London during the 18th and 19th centuries is vividly described in Mayhew's "London". One of the commonly practiced occupations in London was crossing sweeping. Crossing sweepers were strategically situated at every important corner in London. A path was swept before anyone crossed the street so that the effect of traffic pollution could be minimized. The usual tip was a farthing or a halfpenny. If one was served frequently near his home by the same sweeper, the tip at Christmas time was a shilling or even a half-crown by the very appreciative or wealthy. The total number of sweepers was in the thousands. They had an especially hard time when cattle and pigs were driven to market through the city streets.

TABLE IX   Food consumed by and excretions of a horse in twenty-four hours [2]

	FOOD			EXCRETIONS	
	Weight in a fresh state in grammes	Weight in a fresh state in pounds		Weight in a fresh state in grammes	Weight in a fresh state in pounds
		lb. oz.			lb. oz.
Hay ...	7,500	20 0	Excre-		
			ments	14,250	38 2
Oats ...	2,270	6 1	Urine	1,330	3 7
	9,770	26.1			
Water ...	16,000	42.10			
Total ...	25,770	68.11	Total ...	15,580	41.9

One of the earliest records of an attempt to control the flow of traffic appears in the Corpus Inscriptionum Latinarum[4]

... let no one after the Kalends of January drive or conduct a wagon between the time of sunrise and the tenth hour of the day along those streets which lead or will lead into the city of Rome in the regions where there is populous habitation, unless it be necessary that material be carried or transported for the sake of building sacred temples of the immortal gods, or for the sake of public works, or unless it be necessary that materials that have been publicly contracted for demolition be carried out from the city or from these regions, on the condition that permission shall have been granted through this law to specific men in specific cases to drive or conduct wagons for this purpose.

We referred in Chapter 1 to John Graunt's statement ". . . that old streets are unfit for the present frequency of coaches . . .". The issue which concerned him was the fact that most of the streets in London were so narrow that two coaches proceeding in opposite directions could not, upon meeting, pass around each other. When coaches were rare, this created no problem; but, by Graunt's time one could not proceed very far without encountering this crisis. While the London coach drivers swore and tried to intimidate those they encountered, after a short ritual some patience would be demonstrated

Figure 78   Traffic at Dearborn and Randolph Streets, Chicago, 1910 (from W. Owen, The Metropolitan Transportation Problem, Brookings Institution Press).

and the driver who proceeded on his course helped the one who had to execute the difficult maneuver of pushing the carriage in reverse through the muddy streets. In Paris the coachmen were generally more high-strung than their English counterparts. Some streets would remain impassable for hours while each driver refused to retreat. Toughs were sometimes added to the coach staff to protect one's right of way and many bloody fisticuffs started from the meeting of two coaches on a narrow street.

As the density of traffic increased and as fires burnt out sections of cities (a common catastrophe), broader streets and boulevards appeared; but, as today, the magnitude of the traffic grew more rapidly than the corrective measures. In Figures 78, 79 and 80, we exhibit a number of typical traffic jams of the premotorcar period. We especially like those which were drawn and not photographed. Clearly the artists must have had plenty of time to render the records of the events. Figure 81 contains a photograph of smoothly flowing traffic to show that it did exist sometimes. Notice that traffic pollution developed even on the relatively quiet street of this figure.

Figure 79 Philadelphia before the automobile, (from W. Owen, The Metropolitan Transportation Problem Brookings Inst. Press).

REFERENCES

1. P. V. Fonnesbeck, *J. of Animal Science* **27**, 1350 (1968).
2. H. Mayhew, *London Labour and the London Poor* 1851 (Reprint Edition Entitled Mayhew's London, p. 21, 381 (Spring Books, London).
3. F. J. Winchell, private communication.
4. R. Herman, *Proc. of 3rd Conf. of the Australian Road Res. Board* **3**, 25 (1966).

Figure 80 Traffic at Ludgate Circus, London 1870.   Print taken from Gustave Doré, *Impressions of London*, published by Blanchard Jerrold, London, 1872.

Figure 81 Smoothly flowing traffic in Paris. From a print in Jardin des Arts, November 1965.

2 Some Random Statistical Observations on Traffic

This section contains a collection of assorted quantitative information on traffic in various cities and countries. The Inaugural Address[1] of Professor R. J. Smeed as Professor of Traffic Studies at University College, London, has been especially useful in its preparation.

One of our problems is that when a certain level of prosperity is achieved in a country, the number of motor vehicles increases according to the

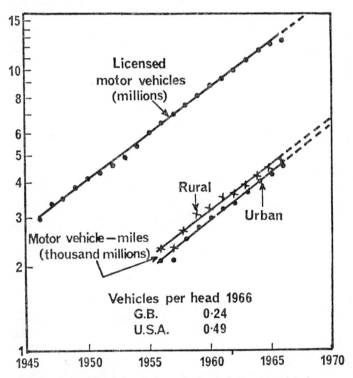

Figure 82 Trends in Traffic and Licensed Motor Vehicles[1].

Malthusian exponential mode. We have plotted the exponential trend in number of licensed vehicles and miles traveled per year in Figure 82 as found in Great Britain. Similar graphs could be constructed for other countries. The U.S. has passed the exponential growth stage and a growth curve more reminiscent of that of Verhulst seems to be developing.

With the increase of affluence, more people drive their own cars and less use public transportation, thus reducing the income of public carriers and leading to a deterioration of service. The number of passengers per private car also decreases with affluence, leading to even greater traffic congestion. An interesting correlation of car occupancies with income of driver is given in Table X:

It is apparent that car pools are more common among the lower income classes. The asymptotic level of car occupancy associated with very high incomes depends on the mores of the time; for example, fifty years ago it went up to 2 when every wealthy motorist had a chauffeur. Today it levels off close to 1, with many wealthy motorists soloing to work in a sports car.

TABLE X Car occupancies during work trips in St. Louis, Missouri, 1957[1]

Average income (thousands of dollars)	Car occupancy
Less than 2	1.67
2–3	1.40
3–4	1.38
4–5	1.32
5–6	1.30
6–7	1.18
7–9	1.17
Greater than 9	1.13

A question frequently discussed is the average distance people drive to work (one way). Surveys and questionnaires on this subject have been analyzed in many cities. One way of investigating the "theoretical basis" for the observations would be to consider why people live in certain sections of a city, how long they are willing to travel to work, etc. A more primitive way would be to say that if a *universal* law existed for all cities, then it might be sought by dimensional analysis. Since we wish to investigate a length, we search for a length which characterizes a city. The square root of its area is just such a length. Hence we might expect the dimensionless ratio $l/A^{\frac{1}{2}}$ to vary only slightly from city to city. This has indeed been observed. It seems that, generally,

$$l/A^{\frac{1}{2}} \simeq 0.85$$

For example, in London 1960, the ratio was 0.87.

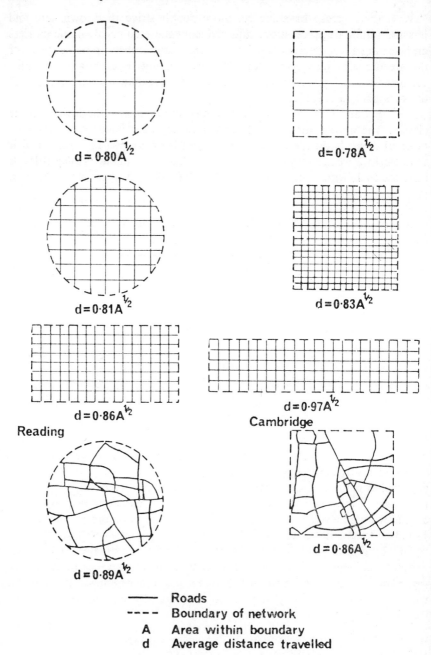

Figure 83   Average distance traveled on some imaginary and real road networks.[1]

R. J. Smeed[1] has considered various models to see why the ratio is of the order of 0.85. One model which he analyzed is a circular city with an internal grid of streets. He postulated workplaces to be uniformly distributed along the grid and residences to be uniformly distributed along the outer circle. Then he assumed that anyone who lived on the circle had an equal probability of working at any point on the grid and found the numbers given in figure 83. He also made similar hypotheses about square and rectangular cities, as well as of a model of Reading and Cambridge.

Another topic concerning volume of travel is the estimation of the number of trips between two cities or generally between two residential regions of a large metropolitan area or between two sections of a country. Let i and j represent two populous zones and P_i and P_j the populations of those zones. It has been proposed by J. G. Wardrop[2] that the number of trips per unit time between those zones, N_{ij}, is given by

$$N_{ij} = P_i P_j f(z_{ij})$$

where $f(z_{ij})$ is called a deterence function. It must depend on journey time, between i and j, cost of the trip, and perhaps some other quantity. Various forms of $f(z)$ such as $f(z) = z^{-p}$ or $f(z) = z^{-1} \exp(-\lambda z)$ have been proposed.

After considerable analysis of travel costs and some travel statistics, J. C. Tanner[3] has proposed the form (α being a constant)

$$f(z) = \alpha z^{-1} e^{-\lambda z}$$

where z is the cost of the round trip. As the length of the trip increases, z is roughly proportional to twice that length. λ^{-1} has the dimensions of cost. In England in 1951 λ^{-1} was estimated to be 3.75 shillings. If j is a work zone, rather than a resident zone, P_j was to be replaced by a quantity b_j which was determined by the character of the work zone.

REFERENCES

1. R. J. Smeed, *J. of Transport Economics and Policy II*, 1 (1968).
2. J. G. Wardrop, *Theory of Traffic Flow*, (Editor R. Herman), p. 57, (Elsevier 1961).
3. J. C. Tanner, Factors Affecting the Amount of Travel. Dept. Sci. Ind. Research, *Road Research Tech. Paper No.* 51, H.M. Stationery Office, London 1961.

3 Acceleration Noise

While driving a car on an open road in the absence of traffic, the driver generally attempts, consciously or unconsciously, to maintain a rather uniform velocity, but never quite succeeds. His acceleration pattern has a random appearance. The acceleration distribution function associated with this pattern is essentially Gaussian. The random component of the acceleration pattern is called acceleration noise.

A measure of the smoothness—or jerkiness—of the driving is then given by the dispersion σ of the acceleration noise. The mathematical definition of this quantity is

$$\sigma^2 = \frac{1}{T} \int_0^T a(t)^2 \, dt \qquad (1)$$

where $a(t)$ is the acceleration (positive or negative) at time t and T is the total running time. Alternatively, if one considers that the acceleration is sampled at successive time intervals Δt, then he can define

$$\sigma^2 = (1/T) \, \Sigma \, a(t)^2 \, \Delta t. \qquad (2)$$

The dispersion σ is simply the root-mean-square of the acceleration, and it has the dimensions of acceleration. Its values are usually quoted in ft. sec.$^{-2}$ or as a fraction or multiple of $g = 32$ ft. sec.$^{-2}$.

Acceleration distribution functions of experienced drivers driving in the range 20–60 mph on an excellent road have dispersions of the order of 0.01 g or 0.32 ft/sec^2. One finds that σ increases at extreme speeds >60 mph or <20 mph.

The acceleration noise of a given driver will vary considerably as he drives on different roads or under different physiological or psychological conditions. The dispersion of the acceleration noise observed in a run in the Holland Tunnel of the New York Port Authority (with no traffic interference in the lane in which the run was made) was 0.73 ft. sec.$^{-2}$. Although the roadbed of the Holland Tunnel is quite good, its narrow lanes, artificial lighting and confined conditions induce a tension in a driver which is reflected in the doubling of his acceleration noise dispersion from its perfect road value. The acceleration noise associated with runs on poorly surfaced, winding country roads may have a dispersion as large as 1.5 to 2 ft. sec.$^{-2}$. The acceleration noise is very large on winding roads and in the pattern of drivers who change lanes frequently while driving in heavy traffic. It is also large in the case of intoxicated or fatigued drivers or in situations in which the attention of the driver is shared between the road and his traveling companions. Further systematic measurements should be made in these various situations.

The dispersion of the acceleration noise of a vehicle was first measured by Herman et al.[1] by using an accelerometer to record on photographic film the car's acceleration as a function of time. From an analysis of the curve, the value of the dispersion was then determined. Although preliminary results were obtained by this method, the reduction of the data was rather tedious. Apparatus for automatically recording the acceleration in a form which can be converted to digital data suitable for computer input has now been developed by Herman and his group.

An inexpensive and simple method of estimating the dispersion employs the "Kienzle" TCO8F model tachograph* with a speed recording range of 0–45 mph. The speed is recorded by stylus on a circular chart which revolves once in 24 minutes. A typical record is illustrated in Figure 84. On the chart the concentric circles give a speed scale in m.p.h. and the scale on the outer circumference is in minutes. The inner trace is formed by an additional stylus which can vibrate in any of three modes of vibration. The choice of the mode is decided by the position of a tachograph key which can be operated by the driver; it enables him to indicate when he passes selected points on the highway. A stylus for recording distance traveled was not used, as the mileometer on the tachograph was more suitable and accurate.

The acceleration distribution function is plotted in Figure 85a for a car moving with a traffic stream at 35 mph. No passing was possible. The distribution function plotted in Figure 85b corresponds to a driver who, in a situation where passing is occasionally possible, tries to drive 5 to 10 mph faster than the stream when the stream is traveling about 35 mph. The road on which the experiments were done (Woodward Avenue, Detroit) was a good road on which the dispersion was about 0.32 ft/sec^2. Notice that in traffic the dispersion becomes multiplied by a factor of 3 to give a value 0.96 ft/sec^2. This is due to the fact that a given driver not only has his natural acceleration noise, but he also responds to that of his predecessor who responds to his predecessor, etc. Experiments have been done by Herman and Rothery to determine how far the influence of the random acceleration pattern of a given vehicle propagates. The results are shown in Figure 86 where the dispersion for various cars in a platoon is plotted as a function of the position in the platoon. The lead car is numbered 1. Since the dispersion becomes independent of the platoon position from car 5 on, it would seem that the influence of a given car extends about 5 cars down the line.

The difference between Figures 85a and b suggests at least one application. A locked tachograph could be put in the car of any driver whose record was such that the wisdom of letting him keep his license was in doubt. It could then

*The Kienzle tachograph is distributed under the name ARGO in the U.S.A. Other tachographs are manufactured by VDO and Wagner. Various models are available; some have circular charts, others use paper wound on spools. Models with slow moving charts are used by trucking and bus companies; those with fast moving charts are ideal for many traffic engineering purposes.

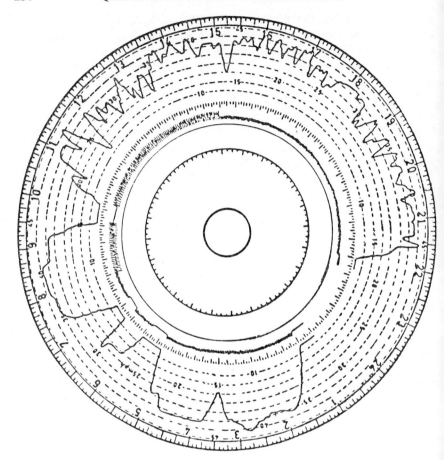

Figure 84   Typical tachograph tracing.

be determined whether or not he had mended his ways during a probationary period by looking at the speed (shown directly on the tachograph) and smoothness (as shown by the acceleration distribution) with which he drove. Quantitative tests of the effects of sleepiness, drunkenness, and other psychological or physiological states which we think impair driving performance could also be made via this method.

Now suppose we want to estimate how changing a particular aspect of a road system, such as disallowing parking on a particular street, might affect the flow of traffic. Usually this would be done by noting the average change in time it takes to drive through the street and/or by counting the difference

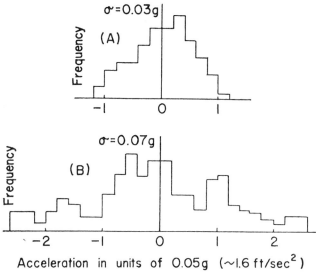

Acceleration in units of 0.05g ($\sim$1.6 ft/sec^2)

Figure 85 Histograms of acceleration distribution function. (a) represents a driver going with the traffic at about 35 mph. (b) corresponds to one who is trying to go 5 to 10 mph faster than the stream.

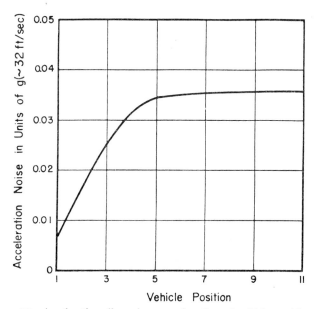

Vehicle Position

Figure 86 Acceleration dispersion as a function of vehicle position in a platoon.

in the number of cars passing through the bottleneck per unit time. However, these methods are usually expensive and time consuming. In order to get a quick estimate, one might simply drive a car equipped with a tachograph along the route in question. If the mean speed has increased and the acceleration dispersion decreased, the change would have been a good one.

As a final example, one might make use of acceleration dispersion measurements when attempting to set speed limits. Suppose test drivers are sent on a particular road with instructions to make successive runs at 40, 50,

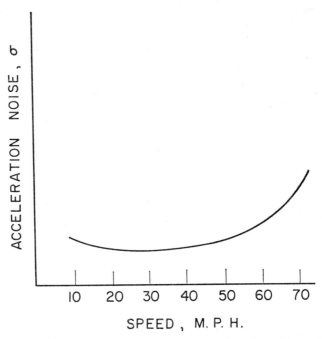

Figure 87 Schematic variation of acceleration dispersion with speed for regulating speed limits.

60, 70, and 80 mph. If we then plotted their average acceleration dispersions as a function of speed, we might get something like Figure 87. We might then look for that speed at which σ first increase more rapidly with speed than a certain large value $d\sigma/dt = K$. The exact value of K would have to be determined by a certain amount of experience with this method of setting speed limits. We might then say that driving at speeds above this level will be unsafe and that the speed limit should be set at or slightly below this level. Measurements can also be carried out with various traffic densities, under various weather conditions, and at various times of the day. These can then be used as a basis for setting variable speed limits. This has been done in Australia.[5]

REFERENCES

1. R. Herman, E. W. Montroll, R. B. Potts and R. W. Rothery, *Oper. Research* **7**, 86 (1959).
2. E. W. Montroll and R. B. Potts, "Car Following and Acceleration Noise", Chapter II in *An Introduction to Traffic Flow Theory*, N. R. C. Highway Research Board Publication No. 1121, 1964.
3. Robert Herman and Keith Gardels, "Vehicular Traffic Flow", *Scientific American* **209**, No. 6 (December, 1963).
4. E. W. Montroll, "Theory and Observations of the Dynamics and Statistics of Traffic on the Open Road", *Proceedings of the First Symposium on Engineering Applications of Random Function Theory and Probability*, (New York, 1963).
5. T. R. Jones and R. B. Potts, "The Measurement of Acceleration Noise—a Traffic Parameter", *Operations Research* **10**, 745 (1962).

4 Car-Following Mechanism and Criteria for Stability of Traffic

Let us now consider the manner in which vehicles (and of course their drivers) interact with each other. One does not have to think very seriously about driving patterns in traffic to realize that they lie in the realm of behavioral rather than physical science. Since a driver responds to stimuli generated by drivers of other vehicles, equations which describe traffic interactions must relate these stimuli and responses.

In this section we limit ourselves to a regime of single lane traffic in which passing is impossible. This is the regime of high traffic density, that associates with the "traffic problem" which confronts most cities. It is commonly experienced in the expensive bottlenecks of traffic systems, the tunnels and bridges where high costs keep down the number of traffic lanes. Studies of this regime can be useful in a search for the most effective manner of managing bottleneck traffic. Incidently the interaction of drivers in a single lane is one of the most elementary problems of social psychology. Each driver interacts with only one other, namely the one in front of him and the response to a stimuli can be expressed in terms of a single variable, the acceleration. The graph of interacting individuals in most other social situations is not a simple chain graph and the response generally is made in more than one variable. We shall see however that even this simple example is very suggestive of effects which can be expected in more complicated situations.

We suppose that the driver of each vehicle is forced to drive slower than he would of his own volition. We also postulate the road to be so good and the drivers so alert that the acceleration pattern of each vehicle depends essentially on the behavior of his predecessor in the traffic platoon rather than on his own natural acceleration noise so that the latter can be neglected.

Several features of the law of following are self-evident. A moving line of traffic should not amplify small disturbances. If, for example, the platoon leader decelerates slightly and then accelerates, the resulting perturbation should not be amplified as it propagates down the platoon. On the other hand, the law of following must not be such that a strong perturbation such as a very sudden stop cannot result in a collision, since such events are quite common. Also responses are never instantaneous. A certain time Δ_1 is required for a driver to notice that his speed relative to his predecessor and his separation distance have changed; a time Δ_2 is required to decide on the proper response to a variation; and a time Δ_3 is required for the response to be effected. In practice $\Delta_1 + \Delta_2 + \Delta_3$ is about 1.5 sec.

We first exhibit some laws of vehicular interaction which satisfy our requirements and others which do not; then we discuss the connection between observational data and the reasonable laws. Calculations will often be made in a coordinate system which moves with the average traffic stream speed. A line of identical, uniformly spaced, constant speed vehicles is chosen as a norm and $x_n(t)$ is defined as the deviation of the position of the nth vehicle at time t from its norm position. The propagation of small deviations from this norm will be used to identify reasonable laws of interaction in the range of linear responses.

Perhaps the simplest law of following might have the jth driver accelerate at time t by an amount proportional to the deviation in the spacing from the normal value at that time:

$$\ddot{x}_j = \mu(x_{j-1} - x_j). \tag{1}$$

The stability of this model can be investigated by assuming that the lead car oscillates around the place where it should be according to

$$x_0 = f_0 \exp(i\omega t) \tag{2}$$

with frequency ω and with f_0 known. The reaction of jth vehicle to this driving force can be written as

$$x_j = f_j \exp(i\omega t) \tag{3}$$

If this expression is substituted into (1) it is found that

$$-\omega^2 f_j = \mu(f_{j-1}-f_j)$$

or

$$f_j = f_{j-1}/[1-(\omega^2/\mu)]$$

so that

$$f_j = [1-(\omega^2/\mu)]^{-j} f_0$$

Notice that there is a resonance at $\omega = \mu^{\frac{1}{2}}$ and fourier components of the motion of the lead car in the neighborhood of this resonance are amplified so that our required stability to small disturbances is violated. Hence (1) could not be a satisfactory law of following.

Another law which might be investigated is

$$a_j(t) = \dot{v}_j(t) = \lambda[v_{j-1}(t)-v_j(t)] \tag{4}$$

i.e. if the $(j-1)$-st car is moving faster than the jth, the jth driver accelerates to compensate and reduce velocity differences and vice versa when $v_{j-1}(t) < v_j(t)$, the parameter λ being positive.

We again choose the driving force to be the motion of the lead car as characterized by $v_0(t)$. The frequency component ω at the jth car is

$$v_j(t) = f_j \exp i\omega t \tag{5}$$

with f_0 and ω given. Then

$$i\omega f_j = \lambda(f_{j-1}-f_j) \tag{6}$$

and

$$f_j = \lambda f_{j-1}/(\lambda+i\omega) = f_0/(1+i\omega\lambda^{-1})^j \tag{7}$$

When (7) is substituted into (4) it is easy to show that

$$v_j(t) = f_0(1+\omega^2\lambda^{-2})^{-n/2} \exp i[\omega t - j\cos^{-1}(1+\omega^2\lambda^{-2})^{\frac{1}{2}}] \tag{8}$$

Hence

$$|v_j(t)/v_j(0)| = (1+\omega^2\lambda^{-2})^{-n/2} \to 0 \quad \text{as} \quad n \to \infty$$

for all $\omega > 0$. If law (4) is valid all disturbances are damped out as they progress down the line of traffic and therefore satisfy our requirement that the traffic stream does not amplify small disturbances.

The velocity of propagation of a disturbance of frequency ω can be obtained by setting the exponent in (8) equal to zero; or

$$\omega t = j\cos^{-1}(1+\omega^2\lambda^{-2})^{\frac{1}{2}}$$

Hence, if the units of ω are sec^{-1} we find

$$\text{velocity of disturbance} = \Delta j/\Delta t = \omega/[\cos^{-1}(1+\omega^2\lambda^{-2})^{\frac{1}{2}}] \tag{9}$$

in units of cars per second.

A remarkable feature of Eq. (4) is that if one neglects the influence of time lags and works in the regime of small deviations from equilibrium (linear regime), he is essentially forced to choose (4) as the law of the following. If one assumes that the acceleration is proportional to linear combinations of difference between the kth derivatives of the separation distance between two successive vehicles he finds resonances (and therefore instabilities) when any even derivatives are employed. Since it is doubtful that a driver could be sensitive to third derivatives one is left with only one law (4) as a possible one for further investigation.

Before Eq. (4) is compared with experimental data we must incorporate an important feature which has already been mentioned above, namely the time lag, Δ, between perception of and response to a fluctuation. A more realistic equation is then

$$a_j(t+\Delta) = \dot{v}_j(t+\Delta) = \lambda[v_{j-1}(t)-v_j(t)] \qquad (10)$$

Where the acceleration at $t+\Delta$ is related to the velocity difference at t. One might also choose

$$a_j(t) = \int_0^t [v_{j-1}(t-\tau)-v_j(t-\tau)]\, d\sigma(\tau) \qquad (11)$$

where $\sigma(\tau)$ weights various parts of the previous velocity history in different ways. Equation (10) corresponds to

$$\sigma(\tau) = \begin{cases} \lambda & \text{if } \tau > \Delta \\ 0 & \text{if } \tau < \Delta \end{cases}$$

The results quoted below are relatively insensitive to the exact form of $\sigma(t)$ as long as it is a monotone increasing function with its greatest variation occurring in the neighborhood of $\tau = \Delta$, after which it rapidly approaches an asymptotic value.

If we seek solutions of (10) in the form (5) we find that

$$v_j(t) = (1+\omega^2\lambda^{-2}-2\omega\lambda^{-1}\sin\Delta\omega)^{-j/2} \qquad (12)$$

$$\times \exp i\{\omega t - j\cos^{-1}(1+\omega^2\lambda^{-2}-2\omega\lambda^{-1}\sin\Delta\omega)\}.$$

The amplitude factor decreases with increasing j if

$$1+\omega^2\lambda^{-2}-2\omega\lambda^{-1}\sin\Delta\omega > 1,$$

or if

$$\omega/\lambda > 2\sin\Delta\omega. \qquad (13)$$

Low frequencies present the greatest limitation on the sensitivity λ. In this limit $\sin\Delta\omega \simeq \Delta\omega$ so that $|v_j(t)| < 1$ for all j if[1]

$$\lambda\Delta < \tfrac{1}{2} \qquad (14)$$

Qualitatively a stability condition like this is to be expected because if the time lag between an input fluctuation and a response is long and the response is very sharp, one may be responding too strongly to a situation which may have long since passed away so that the response may deteriorate the control rather than improve it.

The regime of applicability of (10) can be expanded by making an appropriate adjustment to allow one to go beyond the small vibration range. Let $y_j(t)$ be the location of the jth vehicle at time t. Then $\dot{y}_j = v_j$. At large separation distances the jth driver will not respond to stimuli from the fluctuations in the driving of the $(j-1)$-st driver in as strong a manner as he would when the two cars are close together. Indeed at enormous separation distances there would be no interaction, whatsoever. One possible revision of (10) is to postulate that the sensitivity λ should be inversely proportional to the car spacing so that

$$a_j(t+\Delta) = \ddot{y}_j(t+\Delta) = \lambda_0 \left\{ \frac{\dot{y}_{j-1}(t)-\dot{y}_j(t)}{y_{j-1}(t)-y_j(t)} \right\} \tag{15}$$

A number of car following experiments were performed on the General Motors test track as well as in the Holland and Lincoln Tunnels in New York.[1-4] Each of a number of drivers using an instrumented car was told to follow a lead car as he would in normal city driving. In each case a continuous record of the acceleration of the second car $a(t)$ as well as the relative velocities $V(t)$ and spacing $d(t)$ of the two cars were taken. For each driver a best value of λ and Δ was obtained in the equation

$$a(t+\Delta) = \lambda_0 V(t)/d(t) \tag{16}$$

(which is equivalent to (15)) so that

$$\sum_t [a(t+\Delta) - \lambda_0 V(t)/d(t)]^2 = \text{minimum.} \tag{17}$$

The results of the car following experiments are summarized in Table XI.

TABLE XI

Locality	Number of Drivers	λ_0 (m.p.h.)	Δ (sec.)
General Motors Test Track	8	27.4	1.5
Holland Tunnel	10	18.2	1.4
Lincoln Tunnel	16	20.3	1.2

The correlation coefficients for the best values of λ_0 and Δ were usually greater than 0.9 and for some drivers as high as 0.97. If Eq. (15) were exact and no experimental error existed on the data the correlation coefficients would be 1. Some deviation from 1 must be expected because we have omitted the acceleration noise contribution to $a(t)$. There is some variation in the values of λ_0 and Δ for different drivers. For example in the General Motors test track experiments Δ varied from 1.0 to 2.2 sec with half the drivers having Δ values between 1.4 and 1.7. It would be interesting to find these constants on a given road for a large number of drivers to enable one to obtain reliable statistics on personal variations between drivers. In applying (15) to a line of traffic we assume that all drivers have the same characteristics, namely the average ones.

The velocity of propagation of a signal of frequency ω was given in Eq. (9). One of the simplest velocity fluctuations involves a given car increasing its speed and soon returning to its initial speed. Such a pulse is a linear combination of periodic pulses of many frequencies. Its propagation down a line of traffic is easily investigated through Eq. (10). It broadens and the magnitude of the peak decreases as $n^{-\frac{1}{2}}$, n being the number of vehicles through which the pulse has propagated. The velocity of propagation is $\lambda = \lambda_0/d$, where d is the average space per vehicle in the line of traffic.

Although a line of traffic may be stable to small perturbations, it may be unstable to larger ones. Indeed, rear end collisions are frequently observed and are due to local instabilities in which one or more cars are unable to compensate rapidly for large disturbances ahead of them. It can be shown that the condition wherein no serious local instabilities occur is that $\lambda\Delta < 1/e$, an inequality rarely satisfied by drivers in follow-the-leader experiments.

We conclude this section with a discussion of the influence of adding a random (acceleration noise) term to Eq. (10). From this we should be able to understand the traffic broadening of the acceleration distribution function which was mentioned in the last section.

The broadening of the acceleration distribution by traffic depends on the parameters of the law of following. The acceleration of the nth car at time t is a superposition of its natural acceleration noise and its response to the motion of its predecessor. In smoothly moving traffic the separation distance varies only slightly from the equilibrium distance, d. Hence Eq. (12) can be linearized so that when the natural acceleration $\beta(t)$ is added one finds

$$\dot{v}_n(t+\Delta) = \lambda[v_{n-1}(t)-v_n(t)]+\beta(t) \tag{18}$$

where

$$\lambda = \lambda_0/d.$$

The $\beta(t)$ is a random function whose value at time t is not specified but which is determined by its distribution function $f(a)$ so that $f(a)\,da$ is the probability that $\beta(t)$ has a value between a and $a+da$ at time t. For simplicity we assume that $\beta(t)$ has the same distribution for all drivers on the road of interest. One can use the standard methods of the theory of Brownian motion to determine the statistical properties of $a_n(t) = \dot{v}_n(t)$ from those of $\beta(t)$ in terms of λ and Δ. If the acceleration noise is peaked in the low frequency range one finds that the dispersion σ of the distribution function of $a_n(t)$ (as $n \to \infty$; i.e. for cars far from the beginning of a platoon) is related to the dispersion σ_0 of $\beta(t)$ by

$$\sigma = \sigma_0/(1-2\lambda\Delta)^{\frac{1}{2}} \quad \text{if} \quad 2\lambda\Delta < 1. \tag{19}$$

The stability condition (14) again makes its appearance. The closer the traffic reaches the limit of stability ($2\lambda\Delta \to 1$) the larger the traffic broadening of the acceleration noise.

As was mentioned in Eq. (15), $\lambda = \lambda_0/d$. If we substitute this expression into (19) and solve for the average spacing we find

$$d = 2\lambda_0\Delta/[1-(\sigma_0/\sigma)^2]. \tag{20}$$

This equation was checked with the Holland Tunnel observations of Herman, Potts, and Rothery. The traffic broadening of the acceleration noise dispersions σ/σ_0, in the tunnel varied from about 1.5 to 1.75 depending on the density during the experiment. The value of λ_0 was determined from fitting Eq. (15) to the observed flow vs. density curve for the tunnel, and the average time lag of 1.5 sec which was observed in car following experiments was substituted into (20) as was the observed ratio σ/σ_0. The computed values of d were converted into appropriate densities ($d = 1/\rho$) which were compared with the observed densities made at the same time as the σ/σ_0 was determined. These calculated values generally did not deviate from the measured ones by more than 10 or 15%.

Several alternatives to Eq. (14) have been considered in the literature. The so-called $[l, m]$ form

$$\lambda = c\frac{[dy_n(t+\Delta)/dt]^l}{[y_{n-1}(t)-y_n(t)]^m}$$

where $l = 1$ and $m = 2$ has been considered by Edie and the general case has been discussed in Reference 11. An extensive investigation of several values of l and m was made, but no dramatic improvement was evident over the results of the [0, 1] case originally proposed.

J

REFERENCES

1. R. E. Chandler, R. Herman, and E. W. Montroll, *Oper. Res.* **6**, 165 (1958).
2. R. Herman, E. W. Montroll, R. B. Potts, and R. W. Rothery, *Oper. Res.* **7**, 86 (1959).
3. R. Herman and R. B. Potts, *Theory of Traffic Flow*, (R. Herman, Editor), Elsevier Publishing Co., 1961, p. 120.
4. D. C. Gazis, R. Herman, and R. B. Potts, *Oper. Res.* **6**, 499 (1959).
5. E. W. Montroll, Proc. of First Sympos. on Eng. Applic. of Random Function Theory and Prob. p. 231 (John Wiley, 1963).
6. E. W. Montroll and R. B. Potts, Chapter 2 in "An Introduction to Traffic Flow Theory" (Nat. Res. Council, 1964).
7. R. Herman, Proc. of 3rd Conf. of the Australian Road Res. Board 3, 25 (1966).
8. E. W. Montroll, *Theory of Traffic Flow*, (R. Herman, Editor), Elsevier Publishing Co., 1961, p. 147.
9. R. Herman and R. W. Rothery, *Jour. of Oper. Res. Soc. Japan* **5**, 74 (1962).
10. L. C. Edie, *Oper. Res.* **11**, 21 (1963).
11. D. C. Gazis, R. Herman, and R. W. Rothery, *Oper. Res.* **9**, 66 (1961).
12. D. C. Gazis, *Science* **157**, 273 (1967).

5 Equation of State of Traffic

Our basic rate Eq. (4.15) can be integrated to yield an equation of state of traffic: i.e. an equation which relates flow rate q (say in cars/hour passing a given point) to the traffic density, ρ (cars/mile). Clearly

$$q = v\rho, \tag{1}$$

v being the mean velocity of the stream (say in miles/hour). Our aim will be to use (15) to determine v as a function of ρ, and therefor q as a function of ρ. At zero density (no cars on the road) q vanishes as it also does when $\rho = \rho_c$, close packing density when cars are bumper to bumper. One hopes that q is greater than zero in the range $0 < \rho < \rho_c$. Indeed he might even ask if there is a density on a given road such that q is a maximum. If so, the most effective use could be made of the road by encouraging people to drive at the optimal density. Since the mean velocity is related to the density there would be an optimal velocity. When the velocity is greater than that optimal value the increased spacing required for safe driving would decrease the density, thus reducing q.

The first step in the determination of the local velocity of the jth car is to integrate (4.15). Then (since $v_j \equiv \dot{y}_j$)

$$v_j(t+\Delta) - v_j(t'+\Delta) = \lambda_0 \log\,[y_{j-1}(t) - y_j(t)] - \lambda_0 \log\,[y_{j-1}(t') - y_j(t')]$$

or

$$v_j(t+\Delta) - \lambda_0 \log d_j(t) = v_j(t'+\Delta) - \lambda_0 \log d_j(t') = \text{constant.} \qquad (2)$$

We define $d_j(t)$ to be the space per car in the neighborhood of the jth car at time t:

$$d_j(t) \equiv y_{j-1}(t) - y_j(t) = \text{number of feet per car} \qquad (3)$$

Now let us average (2) over a long line of smoothly flowing traffic and suppose that variations in the flow pattern occur only in times $\gg \Delta$ (i.e. $\gg 1.5$ sec). Then we can neglect the time lag in the velocity terms. Let us also define an average velocity $v(t)$ as the arithmetic mean of the velocity of N cars so that

$$v(t) = \frac{1}{N} \sum_{j=1}^{N} v_j(t) \qquad (4)$$

and an average spacing as the geometric mean of the spacings:

$$d(t) = [d_1(t)d_2(t) \ldots d_N(t)]^{1/N} \equiv 1/\rho(t). \qquad (5)$$

The average spacing is the reciprocal of an average density since the average spacing gives the average distance per car while the density is the average number of cars in a given distance. Also

$$\log \rho(t) = -\frac{1}{N} \sum_{j=1}^{N} \log d_j(t). \qquad (6)$$

By averaging (2) and employing these definitions and neglecting the short time lag Δ, we find

$$v(t) + \lambda_0 \log \rho(t) = \text{constant.} \qquad (7)$$

The value of the constant is obtained by referring back to a comment that was made at the beginning of this section. When the traffic is at close packing, i.e. bumper to bumper, it does not move. Hence if $\rho_c = $ close packing density $v = 0$ and the value of our constant is $\lambda_0 \log \rho_c$. Then at time $v(t)$, the stream velocity and density are connected by

$$v(t) = \lambda_0 \log (\rho_c/\rho) \qquad (8)$$

so that from (1) the flow rate q is

$$q = v\rho = \lambda_0 \rho \log (\rho_c/\rho). \qquad (9)$$

This relation between flow and density is plotted in Figure 88 along with data points observed by H. Greenberg in the Lincoln Tunnel in New York City. The density which yields an optimum flow rate is obtained by setting

$dq/d\rho = 0$. One finds this to be true at the density ρ_0 defined by

$$\log(\rho_c/\rho_0) = 1$$

i.e. $\rho_0 = \rho_c/e$. The optimal velocity is (from Eq. 8) $v_0 = \lambda_0$.

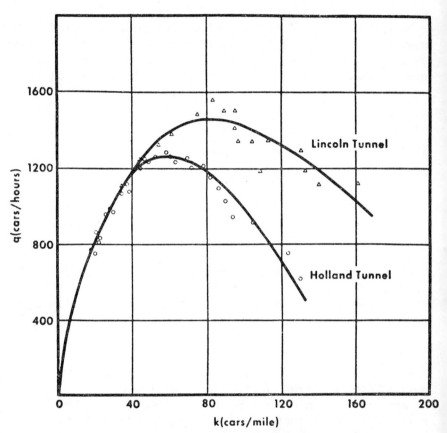

Figure 88 Flow (cars/mile) versus vehicle concentration (cars/mile) for the Lincoln and Holland Tunnels. The Lincoln Tunnel data are those of Greenberg (reference 3). The two solid curves correspond to "least squares" fits of the reciprocal-spacing model to the data.[1]

From a large sample of more than 24,000 vehicles in the Holland Tunnel, the best fit value of λ_0 was found to be 18.95 mph, which is to be compared with $\lambda_0 = 18.2$ mph obtained in car following experiments in the same tunnel (Table XI), providing a good check for the theory.

Notice that λ_0 is the velocity which gives a maximum flow rate. It has been observed that λ_0 is small under hazardous driving conditions—poor lighting, narrow roadway with two lanes in tunnels; while it is large on good roads— freeways with no turns. Since the expensive parts of a highway system such as bridges and tunnels are frequently its bottle necks the traffic engineer should examine means of making λ_0 as large as possible to increase maximum possible flow rate and to regulate traffic so that for a given λ_0 this maximum is achieved.

Notice that by inverting Eq. (8) one finds that the traffic density decays exponentially with increasing velocity

$$\rho = \rho_c \exp\left(-v/\lambda_0\right) \tag{10}$$

This is to be expected because if one is to drive safely at high speeds more space should be left between cars so that the density of traffic should diminish.

REFERENCES

1. D. C. Gazis, R. Herman, and R. B. Potts, *Oper. Res.* **7**, 499 (1959).
2. E. W. Montroll, Proc. of First Sympos. on Eng. Applic. of Random Function Theory and Prob. p. 231 (John Wiley, 1963).
3. H. Greenberg, *Oper. Res.* **7**, 79 (1959).
4. M. T. Lighthill and G. B. Whitham, *Proc. Roy. Soc.* A229, 319 (1955).
5. L. C. Edie, R. S. Foote, R. Herman, and R. W. Rothery, *Traffic Eng.* **33**, 21 (1963).

6 Other Approaches to Theory of Traffic Flow

Here we briefly describe two other approaches to the theory of traffic flow. Further details can be found in the papers of Lighthill and Whitham[1] who applied methods of continuum hydrodynamics of a compressible fluid to the problem, and to the book of Prigogine and Herman[2] which summarizes the application of a Boltzmann-like equation to traffic flow.

The continuity equation of a compressible fluid is (ρ bding the local density and v the local velocity)

$$\frac{\partial \rho}{\partial t} + \frac{\partial}{\partial x}(\rho v) = 0 \tag{1}$$

Since the throughput at a point x at time t is

$$q = \rho(x, t)v(x, t), \tag{2}$$

the continuity equation is equivalent to

$$\rho_t + q_x = 0 \tag{3}$$

Lighthill and Whitham postulated the existence of an equation of state $q = q(\rho)$ (which would be similar to that derived from our car-following model and exhibited in Fig. 88). We note that

$$q_x = q_\rho \rho_x = V\rho_x \quad \text{with} \quad V \equiv \partial q/\partial \rho \tag{4}$$

so that

$$\rho_t + V\rho_x = 0 \tag{5}$$

The significance of this equation is that it tells how a localized density perturbation propagates down a line of cars. Suppose that in the absence of the perturbation the traffic has a certain mean density ρ. V can be obtained at that density by calculating $V = \partial q/\partial \rho$ at that density from (4). The solution of (5) is then

$$\rho(x, t, V) = F(x - Vt) \tag{6}$$

where the form of F is determined at the time $t = 0$ when the perturbation is postulated to have developed. Clearly $F(x)$ is the density profile at that moment. V can be positive or negative, depending on whether the density is greater or less than that associated with the peak throughput in Fig. 88. An important missing component of the theory is that it does not allow for any special driver response to a fluctuation. It is useful for the discussion of waves created by bottlenecks and for the periodic disturbances caused by traffic signals.

Another interesting model is that due to Prigogine and his collaborators. It is motivated by the kinetic theory of gases and employs a kinetic equation similar to the Boltzmann equation. Let $f(x, t, V)$ be the distribution function of speeds v of various vehicles as a function of time t, and position on the road x. Even on an isolated road with low traffic density, f is not a sharp function of v because various drivers at a given time wish to drive at different speeds. The rate of variation df/dt of the distribution function depends on influences which stimulate the change. The first is that at a given moment certain drivers are going slower or faster than they wish so there is an "internal" force being applied to make a change in f. This is called a "relaxation" influence by Prigogine and collaborators. The second is due to the interaction between vehicles. Then we can write

$$df/dt = \partial f/\partial t + v\partial f/\partial x = (df/dt)_{\text{relaxation}} + (df/dt)_{\text{interaction}}. \tag{7a}$$

The form chosen for the relaxation term is

$$(df/dt)_{\text{re}} = (f - f^0)/\tau \tag{7b}$$

where f^0 is some desired speed distribution characterized by the drivers on the road and is a relaxation time for the return to that distribution from an arbitrary one. The form chosen for the interaction term is

$$(df/dt)_{in} = (1-p)\rho(\bar{v}-v)f \qquad (7c)$$

where p is the probability of a car passing another if he wishes to do so, $\bar{v}$ is the average speed of the traffic, and ρ the traffic density. When ρ is small and p close to 1, the interaction is small.

Various solutions have been obtained for (7) and have been discussed in reference 2. An interesting one corresponds to the low density regime for the homogeneous relaxation of a highway of cars with $\partial f/\partial t = 0$. Then

$$f(v, t) = f^0(v) + [f(v, o) - f^0(v)]e^{-t/\tau} \qquad (8)$$

An equation of state for traffic can be found from (7) by seeking solution for which $\partial f/\partial t$ and $\partial f/\partial x = 0$. At low densities one finds the flow rate to be

$$q = \bar{v}_0\rho$$

where $\bar{v}_0$ is the average desired speed of the drivers. As the density increases, q goes below this value because some drivers cannot go as fast as they wish. At high densities, practically no one can go as fast as he wishes and a collective mode of motion develops which depends on the traffic and especially the probability of passing. The theory yields

$$q = 1/\tau(1-p)$$

so that the general shape of the flow vs. concentration curve is that of Fig. 88. A basic problem involved in the determination of the curve is to express the probability of passing as a function of the density. Also, as we saw in the last section, even when no passing is possible, some elasticity exists in the traffic stream. For further details of this approach, the reader is referred to reference 2.

REFERENCES

1. M. J. Lighthill and G. B. Whitham, *Proc. Roy. Soc.* 279A, 317 (1955).
2. I. Prigogine in *Theory of Traffic Flow* (R. Herman, editor), p. 158, (Elsevier, 1961); R. Herman and I. Prigogine.
3. D. C. Gazis, IBM Research Report RC 3343, 1971.

7 On the Control of Traffic and Traffic Signals

The last few sections have been devoted to the characterization of freely moving traffic on open highways. The traffic problem of cities is generally that of alleviating congestion and of keeping the traffic moving by some kind of control mechanism.

In the pre-automobile and pre-electronic days, the only control device was the policeman. He was even sometimes appreciated for his efforts, as is evident from James McCabe's description[1] of traffic on Broadway in New York in the 1870's:

... Oftentimes the throngs became so dense that the streets are quickly "jammed". Carriages, wagons, carts, omnibuses and trucks are packed together in the most helpless confusion. At such times the police are quickly on hand and take possession of the street. The scene is thrilling. A stranger feels sure that this struggling mass of horses and vehicles can never be made to resume their course in good order without loss of life or limb to man or beast, or to both, and the shouts and oaths of the drivers fairly bewilder him. In a few minutes he sees a squad of gigantic policemen dash into the throng of vehicles. They are masters of the situation and woe to the driver who dares disobey their sharp and decisive commands. The shouts and curses cease, the vehicles move on one at a time in the routes assigned to them, and soon the street is clear again to be "blocked" afresh, perhaps in a similar manner in less than an hour. Upward of 20,000 vehicles daily traverse the great thoroughfare. It is always a difficult matter for a pedestrian to cross the lower part of Broadway in the busy season. Ladies, old persons, and children find it impossible to do so without the aid of the police whose duty is to make a passage for them through the crowd of vehicles ....

In some unsung city, someone had the idea of stationing a policeman at a busy corner to try to keep the traffic flowing, and to postpone and even prevent the jamming described above. Officers were probably first assigned to traffic duty in 1903 in New York City.[15] Finally in 1914 the first automatic traffic signal was installed, in Cleveland. The first progression signal appeared in 1918. An excellent old review of traffic control is given in reference 15.

Sophistication in signal control is guided by two basic principles:[2]

(a) Synchronization of a group of lights, in order to provide maximum opportunity to as many cars as possible to move through a sequence of intersections without stopping;

(b) Flexible operation of "traffic-activated" signals, in order to reduce the delay at some critical intersections.

The basic idea for the synchronization of signals is described in Fig. 89. Suppose that we require that each car moving 30 mph along a main street encounters a green light at each intersection and that a split of equal time for red and green (we assume that there is no yellow signal on the lights) is

arranged on the lights. The intersections are located at points $x_1, x_2, x_3, \ldots$
on the vertical space axis. The horizontal axis represents the time. The lines
1 and 2 represent the trajectories of cars which pass the intersection at x_1,
respectively, at the beginning and the end of the first green time interval under
consideration. The "gates" between the solid lines in the figure represent the
times in which traffic can pass through the intersections $x_1, x_2, x_3, \ldots$, etc.
Notice that while the gates are synchronized for the passage at constant speed
through the successive intersections at $x_1, x_2, x_3, \ldots$, they are not so syn-

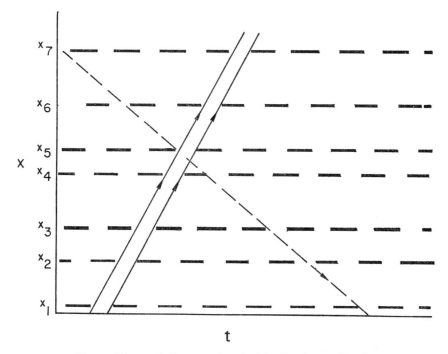

Figure 89   Traffic lights synchronized for flow in one direction.

chronized for traffic going in the opposite direction. There is a very narrow
band around the dotted line in the figure which allows noninterrupted flow
of a lower speed in this opposite direction.

One of the classical mathematical problems in the arrangement of light
cycles[2-4] is to allow "through bands" of the same duration for passage in
both directions through a sequence of intersections. An example of such an
arrangement is given in Figure 90. Only a fraction, here about 4/5, of the
green period is effectively used in each "through band". We shall not attempt

J*

to give an analysis of the problem here. The interested reader is referred to references 2–5 for details. There are a few obvious points that are worth mentioning, however. The cycle time and the speed cannot be independently assigned, as is evident from Figure 89. The appropriate way of starting an

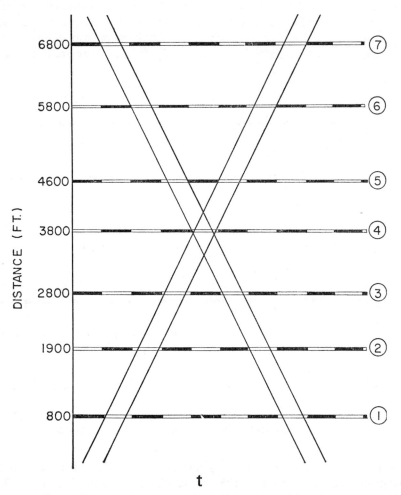

Figure 90   Traffic signals synchronized for flow in both directions.[2]

examination of the problem is to pick a range of reasonable speeds, say 30–35 mph, and a range of reasonable cycles, say 2–3 minutes. Then, through algorithms developed in references 2–5, to try to do the best one can in this range. If the speed found by the algorithm is 33.5 mph, which is hardly suitable as an instruction speed to give drivers, it could be converted to 30 mph or 35 mph by introducing a scaling factor at the expense of changing the cycle period. Suppose that a cycle period c is appropriate to a speed v. Then the speed λv has a cycle speed c/λ. The various algorithms are used to make the through bands as large a fraction of the green period as possible. If one wishes to make the through bands larger in one direction than in the opposite one, it can be done by sliding the offsets at some key intersections. A progression for unequal speeds in two directions can be obtained by shearing the diagram of Figure 90.

From symmetry, the offsets must be such that the middle of the green phase of any intersection must occur simultaneously with the middle of either the red or green phase of any other. Furthermore, it can be shown that if all the travel times between intersections are integral multiples of half cycles, then one can have the maximum possible throughput.

A basic difficulty in all through band designs is that their efficiency drops when the traffic density gets too high and when parked cars enter the streams. Every driver has observed that when a traffic signal changes from red to green, it requires some time for the first car to start, longer for the second, etc., so that a non-negligible fraction of the green part of the cycle is not used effectively. Almost any safe thing which can be done to minimize the "starting time problem" will be appreciated by drivers. Actually, a simple scheme devised in the 1950's by W. von Stein[6] for traffic in Dusseldorf, Germany, is quite effective. Its use has spread to other parts of that country but it does not seem to have been employed in the U.S. or in other parts of Europe. We will describe it here to stimulate readers to think about such techniques.

W. von Stein introduced a "systematic flying start" controlled by a pre-signal set about 100 feet ahead of the intersection. This pre-signal is a normal traffic light with the same total cycle time as the one at the intersection. However, its red phase is set shorter and it turns green about 5.5 seconds before the primary signal. This allows the first vehicles in the platoon to arrive at the intersection at almost full speed just as the signal turns green. In general, a four-to-six-second "starting time" loss is avoided down the line of traffic. Figure 91 schematically represents the normal situation (without a pre-signal), while Figure 92 represents the situation with a pre-signal. Note that as in Figure 90, the street is depicted on the right and distance measured vertically, while time is represented on the horizontal axis. The solid black lines which appear constricted in order to get through between red phases represent the positions of cars in two dimensions—space and time. The slope of such a line at any point instantaneously gives the car's speed. Our diagrams in Figures 90–93 are the traffic analogues of Feynman's diagrams in physics. Note, for example, that cars one through four start out (at the

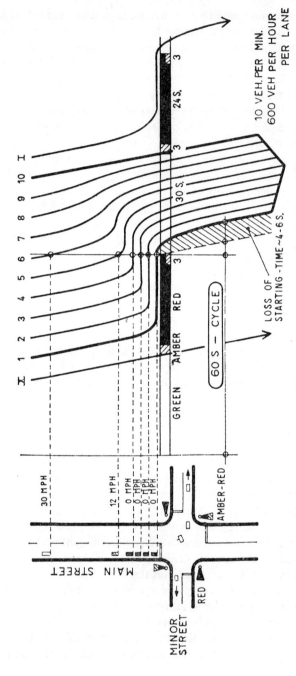

Figure 91   Time–space diagram of a normal crossing with start on the stop-line. [6]

top of Figure 92) going 30 mph and then have to stop at the pre-signal; note the horizontal segments of the curves representing these cars at that point. Compare the velocities of the first few cars in Figures 91 and 92 just as the primary signal becomes green. This is facilitated in each figure by small circles drawn along a vertical line which represent each car's position at that time. Without the pre-signal, the first four cars (or more, depending on how many have queued up) are at a complete stop, the next car back (the fifth) is rapidly braking to a stop, and the sixth is as yet unaffected. With the pre-signal, the first few cars in the line have already spread out as they accelerate to final speed

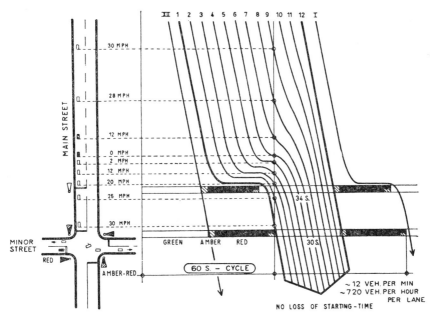

Figure 92 Time–space diagram of a crossing with pre-signal and flying start.[6]

and only the sixth car (or more, depending on how many are queued up) still remains stopped. Assuming a thirty-second green period during a one-minute cycle, the two diagrams show a 20% increase in the throughput; without a pre-signal 10 vehicles per minute proceed through the intersection, whereas with the pre-signal 12 vehicles can get through in the same time. One probably would not want to install pre-signals in tandem with every stoplight because of the cost, but they would be well worthwhile at "bottle-neck" intersections which frequently handle high density traffic. They have also proved their worth where there is an important source of traffic within

150 feet of an intersection. A pre-signal set up just ahead of the source allows cars to turn onto the main road where formerly a long queue of cars made this difficult or impossible. The pre-signal's red period also permits left-hand turns into parking lots or other facilities across what would otherwise have been the main stream of traffic. A criticism one might make to the installation of pre-signals is the possibility of side-swiping accidents if drivers are prone to running through amber lights. This has not proven to be a problem in Germany.

Von Stein's early technical experience was in vacuum tube design. He became an expert in electron bunching and control mechanisms. The vicissitudes of World War II interrupted his career in that field and, in canvassing post-war employment possibilities, he was happy to find a position in the traffic control department of the city of Dusseldorf where he originated the flying start scheme described above.

In the next stage in the development of his system, von Stein took a cue from his previous experience and conceived the possibility of bunching cars as they approach an intersection of perpendicular roads. The bunches from one road would appear at the intersection at a time when a gap appears between bunches on the other.[6] Of course, the limit case of such a coordinated interlacing would be the gamey practice of cars from one road alternating with those from the other at the intersection. While this maneuver is practised by circus motorcyclists, it would be a bit risky for most motorists. However, at the expense of a slight loss of efficiency, bunches of the order of twenty cars on each road might alternate with each other in passing through the intersection.

We now consider the technical manner in which the von Stein system accomplishes bunching. The numbers which we use at first are not necessarily the most efficient, but are chosen to merely indicate how a traffic "funnel" or buncher operates.

Assume that a traffic light at the intersection has a one-minute cycle duration with a 30-second red-amber phase. Also assume that the normal city speed limit is 30 mph and that the minimum speed drivers could safely be asked to maintain on a non-congested city street is 20 mph. One can then calculate how far behind an intersection a car must be in order that, starting from that point at the worst moment in the cycle, it will either arrive just at the end of one green phase if it is going 30 mph or at the beginning of the next green phase if it is going 20 mph. The arrival times in these two situations should differ by 30 seconds (the length of the red-amber phase) in the two cases. This distance is about 2800 feet, or a little over half a mile. The last 30 mph car would form the rear end of one bunch and the first 20 mph car would take the lead in the next bunch. A set of synchronized speed indicators

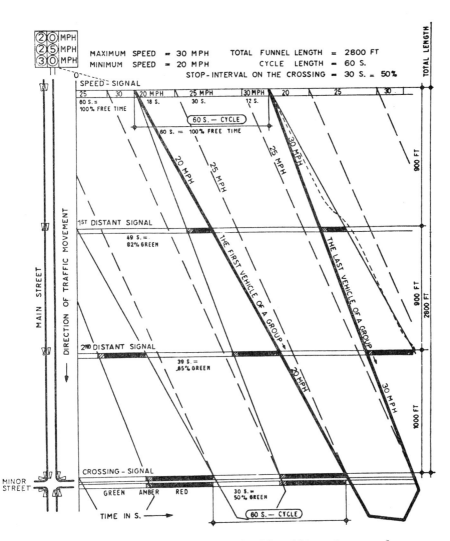

Figure 93 Time–space diagram of a signal funnel in an urban street.[6]

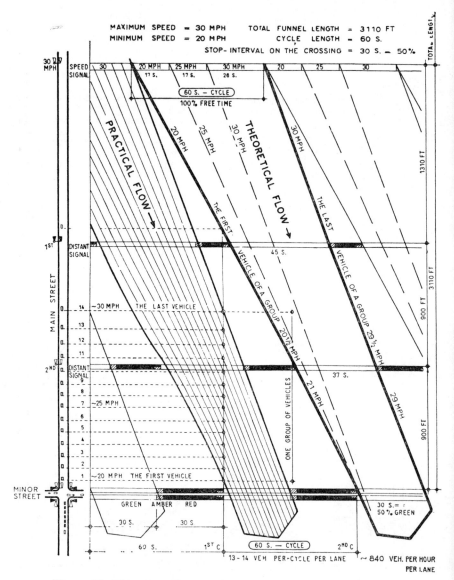

Figure 94 Time–space diagram of a staggered signal funnel in an urban street with speed signal and two pre-distant signals.[6]

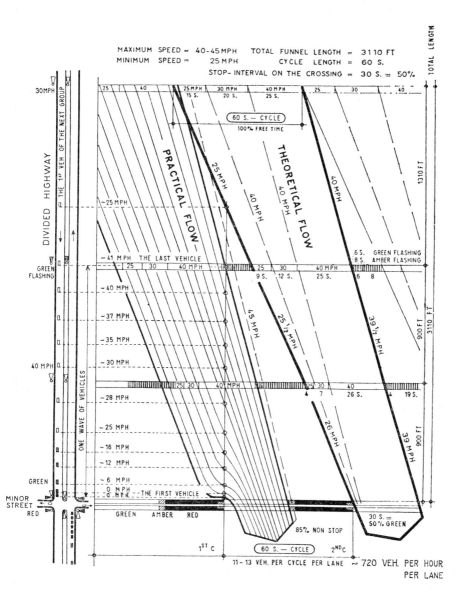

Figure 95   Time–space diagram of a signal funnel on a highway with speed signals only.[6]

would have to be arranged between the intersection and the point 2800 feet behind it where the separation into bunches would begin.

Von Stein's first version of pre-signals, or "traffic funnel", consisted of six movable signals of the type normally formed at an intersection. They had successively shorter red periods the farther they were from the intersection, the farthest away having only a six-second red period. A car reaching the first pre-signal just as it turned green would have to slow down and maintain a speed of about 20 mph in order to hit the next five pre-signals and, subsequently, the primary intersection signal, just as it turned green. A car reaching the first pre-signal just before it turned red would have to proceed at precisely the speed limit (30 mph) in order to just make all the other lights. It was found that this increased the efficiency of the intersection as a "traffic valve" to between 90% and 95% of what it would have been as a straight section of road. Only during rush hours was anyone ever forced to stop, whereas without the traffic funnel, only 45% of the cars had been able to pass through the intersection without stopping.

It was soon found, however, that drivers wanted a speed indicator to direct them through the traffic funnel without stopping. Standard traffic lights are, basically, on-off controls. Something a little more sophisticated was needed to urge drivers to go faster or slower. Von Stein's Mark II traffic funnel consisted of a speed signal placed in front of two pre-signals of standard variety. The speed signal showed 20 mph for 18 seconds, 25 mph for 30 seconds, 30 mph for 12 seconds, and then repeated itself. (See Figure 94). If a driver could keep his speed constant at the value on the speed indicator at his moment of arrival, he would reach the intersection on the green. The third and currently used version of the traffic funnel has suggested speed indicators on all signals. If one wishes to be an individualist and ignore the instructions, he arrives at one of the indicators or at the intersection on red and is detained while those behind him who follow the rules pass him as the signal becomes green since they have a flying start while he must start from rest as the signal changes. (See Figure 95).

The construction of a funnel which is to be adapted to several intersections with lights having different cycle durations requires a rather intricate timing and bunch splitting operation. This is exhibited in Figure 96 for two intersections, one with 50 seconds and the other with a 64-second cycle.

One of the authors (EWM) has driven a number of times through the Dusseldorf funnels with no difficulty and, indeed, with a certain amount of entertainment. The Von Stein traffic funnels are much cheaper than overpasses, underpasses, and cloverleaves.

Our discussions above described efforts to make traffic signals with fixed cycles as effective as possible. Still more efficient traffic control mechanisms

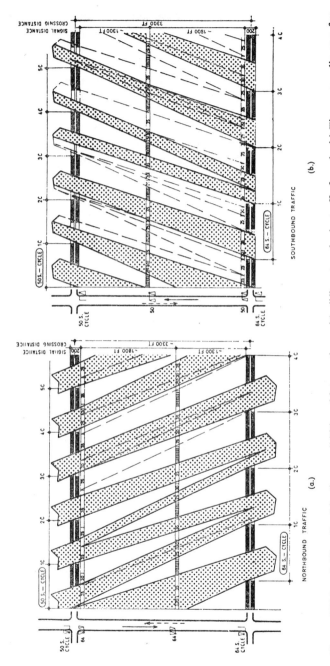

Figure 96(a) and (b). Combination possibilities of intersections with different cycles by traffic funnels. (a) Time–space diagram for the traffic movement from 50 second cycle intersection to 64 second cycle intersection. (b) Time–space diagram for the traffic movement from 64 second cycle intersection to 50 second cycle intersection.

take advantage of fluctuations in traffic density in unimportant side streets which cross main arteries, as well as in fluctuations in density along the main artery. A common arrangement is one in which the traffic signal is, in the absence of side street traffic, red for those approaching the intersection from the side street, the green being triggered by a car approaching the intersection or by a counter which counts a certain preassigned number of cars before triggering the green light. In the latter case, a timing circuit is sometimes set by the first car so that the green appears after a certain time if no other cars arrive to be counted. The theory of optimization of an isolated, unsaturated intersection has been discussed by Dunne and Potts[7] and by Grafton and Newell.[8]

The triggering or signals by car counting can be made more sophisticated through the use of control algorithms which process information on the intersection of interest as well as on the four neighboring ones. Analysis of such a system has been made by Ross et al.,[9] while Miller[10] has examined full network control. Since such a scheme involves many connected detection instruments, there has been reluctance to employ it.

Considerable interest exists in the computer control of traffic and, indeed, installations of varying complexity have existed for more than ten years. The first large scale system was built in Toronto. The most extensive testing of computer control methodologies was done in Glasgow. Overall delays in congested traffic seem to be reduced by about 10% by proper control. The interested readers can learn of the present state of the art from references.

Another promising method of control of traffic is through route control. This could be effected in several ways. When certain roads approach saturation while alternative routes have a lower traffic density, diversion of part of the traffic can be made, based on a computer analysis of flow over the entire network. The monitoring computer might work out the best routes available between a number of popular pairs of points. The information could be transmitted to drivers either by radio announcements or by appropriate electric signs distributed over the network. Various switching schemes for route control are discussed in References 13 and 14.

REFERENCES

1. J. D. McCabe, *"Light and Shadows of New York Life."* National Pub. Co., Phila. (1870); Reprint Ed. Farrar, Strauss and Giroux (1970).
2. D. C. Gazis, Proc. of IEEE, 59, 1090 (1971).
3. J. T. Morgan and J. D. C. Little, *Oper. Res.* **12**, 896 (1964).
4. J. D. C. Little, *Oper. Res.* **14**, 568 (1966).
5. W. D. Brooks, I.B.M. Report.
6. W. von Stein, *Theory of Traffic Flow* (R. Herman, Ed.), Elsevier, 1961, p. 68.
7. M. C. Dunne and R. B. Potts, *Oper. Res.* **12**, 870 (1964).

8. R. B. Grafton and G. F. Newell, Proc. 3rd International Symp. on The Theory of Traffic Flow, New York, Elsevier, 1967, p. 239.

9. D. W. Ross, R. C. Sandys, J. L. Schlaeffi and S. H. Hutchins, "Critical Subnetwork Control—A New Approach to Urban Traffic Control," *Final Report, Stanford Res. Inst.*, Menlow Park, Calif., Dec., 1968.

10. A. J. Miller, "A Computer Control System for Traffic Networks," *Proc. Second International Symp. on Traffic Theory*, Paris, 1965, p. 200.

11. J. Holroyd and J. A. Hillier, *Traff. Eng. and Control* 11, 220 (1969).

12. D. C. Gazis and R. S. Foote, *Transport Science* 3, 255 (1969).

13. D. C. Gazis and R. B. Potts, Proc. 3rd Conf. Australian Rd. Res. Bd., vol. 3, Part 1, 354 (1966).

14. D. C. Gazis, *Oper. Res.* 12, 815 (1964).

15. B. W. Marsh, *Annals of Am. Acad. of Pol. and Soc. Sci.* p. 90, Sept. 1927.

CHAPTER VI

Atmospheric Pollution in Cities

1 Some Historical Remarks and The Nature of Certain Pollutants

As was mentioned in the Introductory Historical Remarks at the beginning of this book, the smog menace was already evident in London in the year 1300.[1] As the city grew and coal was burned in ever-increasing amounts, the situation progressively worsened. The first scientific investigation of the matter was made in 1661 by John Evelyn who, as one of the founders of the Royal Society, submitted a paper on the subject to the Society. In his article entitled "Fumifugium, or the inconvenience of the Aer and Smoak of London", he noted that "London resembles the face rather of Mount Aetna, the Court of Vulcan, Stromboli or the suburbs of Hell than an assembly of rational creatures and the Imperial seat of our incomparable Monarch".

Until recently, most discussions of smog and pollution centered on the coal combustion problem and the evils of soot, dirt and SO_2. When one of the authors (EWM) was a boy in the Pittsburgh area, he was frequently exposed to these annoyances. There were many winter days when the city was dark and the street lights gave the only available illumination at noon. Optometrists and pharmacists did a flourishing business removing dirt from the eyes. As a steel center, and railroad center in the days of the steam locomotive, and with all residential heating done by locally mined soft coal, Pittsburgh was probably one of the greatest polluters on record. Most Pittsburghers' lungs were blackened by soot and the dutiful housewife changed curtains weekly. The situation became so severe that a tremendous clean-up campaign was instituted in the late 1940's and early 1950's. With the introduction of gas and oil heating, the employment of Diesel locomotives, and with conscientious factory pollution management, the character of the city was changed in a relatively short time. During the the same period, St. Louis also benefitted from an agressive antipollution campaign. There has been some recent regression, but to the old timers these cities are still much better than they were 35 years ago.

There are few days between the middle of November and the beginning of February when there is no fog over western Belgium and southeast England.

On foggy weekends, when there is practically no visibility on the roads, the number of automobile accidents reaches a fantastically high level per capita on U.S. standards. It is, of course, just the time of the year when domestic heating fuel consumption is at a maximum. While the Belgians have suffered the most from auto accidents, the Londoners suffered the most from the smog which results from inefficient heating practices and the occasional temperature inversions which occur over the city.

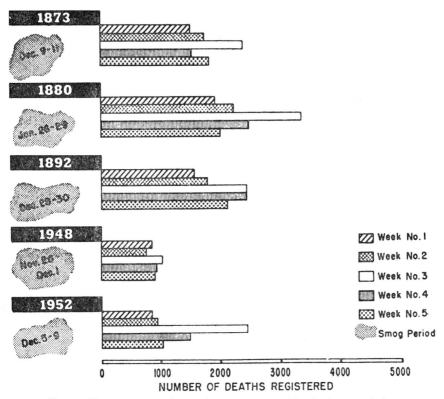

Figure 97 Death rates in London County. Weekly death rates during several winter-season smog periods are compared with the weekly rates preceding and following the week of the smog period.[2,5]

The great smog of 1952 is highlighted in all lectures and articles on air pollution. Several thousand deaths were attributed to it.[2] Visibility was so low that at certain times during the smog period, the London blind had to be recruited to conduct lost persons a block or two to their offices or flats, or to the nearest underground station if they wished to escape to the suburbs. As is evident from Figure 97, the 1952 smog was not the worst in London history. In 1880 the number of deaths during and immediately after the smog period was much larger in a city that was considerably smaller.[2] However, the 1952 situation was sufficiently severe and sufficiently frightening that rigid restrictions on coal usage were finally put into effect and the situation in London is considerably improved.

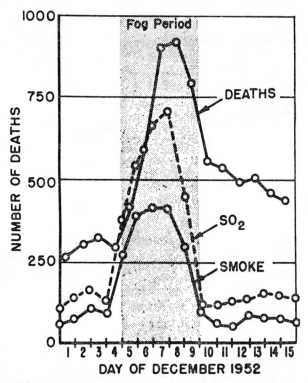

Figure 98 Deaths and air pollution in London County during December 1952. Daily mortality rates are compared with the concentrations of smoke and of sulphur dioxide (SO_2). Graph taken from reference 2.

Notice the high level of SO_2 during the peak of the smog period. One of the bad effects of SO_2 comes from the formation of sulphuric acid through the relations

$$2SO_2 + O_2 \rightarrow 2SO_3 \quad ; \quad SO_3 + H_2O \rightarrow H_2SO_4$$

We need not dwell on the character of sulphuric acid at this point. A first step in any antipollution campaign is to encourage the use of only low sulphur-

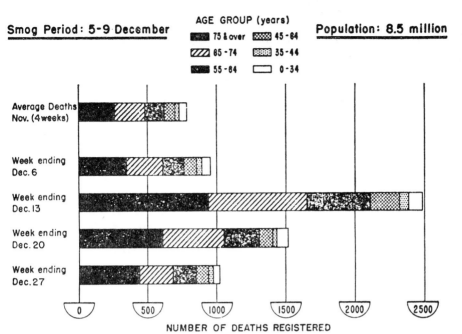

Figure 99a   Weekly death rates in London County in 1952 per age group.[2,5]

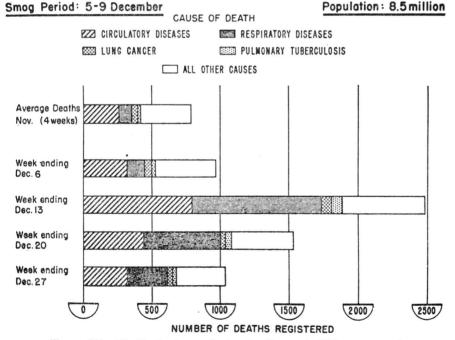

Figure 99b   Weekly death rates in London County in 1952 per cause of death.[2,5]

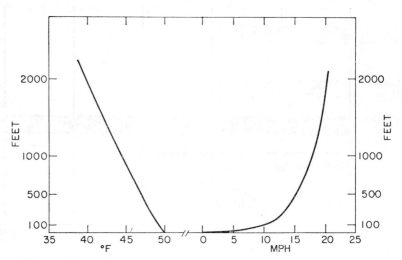

Figure 100   Typical temperature and wind structures over level ground during the day.[1]

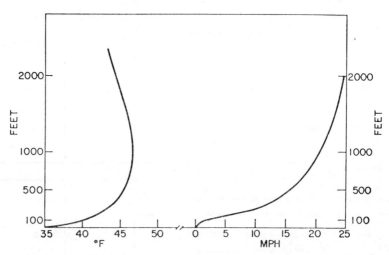

Figure 101   Typical temperature and wind structures over level ground on clear nights.[1]

content coal and fuel oils. Since these are less common varieties, the law of supply and demand has led to a considerable increase in their cost.

Some cities have, to some extent, controlled their air pollution; others are capable of doing so if they are willing to take appropriate measures. There are a few, however, in which the problem is severe and special local conditions are such that only the most heroic efforts can make even a small impact on it. Los Angeles is one of those unfortunate few. One could hardly have found a worse location for a city, considering modern pollution sources, and could hardly have developed a city in a more likely way to accentuate the difficulty.

We have plotted in Figures 100 and 101 typical day and night temperatures and wind profiles as a function of altitude. A bag of hot gas will rise if it is surrounded by cold gas. If one has a temperature profile as indicated in Figure 100, the gas would continue to rise even as it cools because at each altitude it is surrounded by colder gas. If the gas is not encased in a bag, it will still rise but the higher average wind velocities at higher altitudes will tend to disperse it and turbulent diffusion will carry it away as it is spread out over a large region. On the other hand, if the temperature is colder near the ground and the ground wind velocities are small, a pocket of warm gas will not disperse as rapidly. The photograph, taken from reference 1, shows the difference in oil fog dispersal under condition of Figures 102 and 103.

The typical temperature profile and wind direction of the Los Angeles area[5] is indicated in Figure 104. Notice the inversion layer where the temperature starts to increase with altitude. A parcel of hot gas would, at 1800 feet, be cooler than the warmer air at higher altitudes and would not penetrate efficiently into it. Since the winds are generally from the ocean blowing easterly, and since the mountains are to the east, the polluting gases get trapped, thus enveloping the L.A. residents with unpleasant and sometimes harmful fumes. Mexico City, being surrounded by mountains, has a similar problem, as do some of the Italian cities which face the sea with their backs to the mountains.

It is interesting to trace the development of concern with the L.A. situation and the development of a program to combat it.[6] In 1947 Raymond R. Tucker (who played an important role in the St. Louis clean-up campaign) wrote a report on the pollution situation in L.A. and emphasized the rate at which the character of the air over the city was deteriorating. The Los Angeles Times, with the aid of other civic groups, launched a vigorous antipollution campaign to make changes in factory and refinery operations before it was too late. In 1948, the state legislature responded by passing a public law which permitted the formation of air pollution control districts empowered to formulate rules for curbing smog and endowed with the necessary police power for the enforcement of new regulations. The L.A. County Control District was created in 1948.

Figure 102   Photograph showing an oil fog plume issuing from the Brookhaven Meteorology tower during daytime conditions. [1]

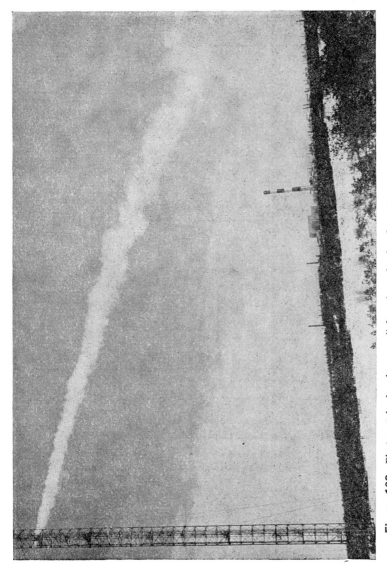

Figure 103 Photograph showing an oil fog plume issuing from the Brookhaven Meteorology tower during nighttime conditions.[1]

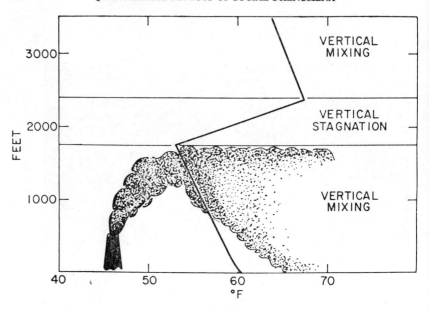

Figure 104   The typical temperature structure in the Los Angeles area, showing the inversion.[5]

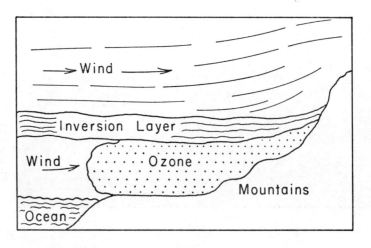

Figure 105   Inversion and pollution in Los Angeles basin.

The district administrators were responsive and aggressive. Ordinances were issued which legally limited dust and fume emission from steel mills and the oil refineries as well as from hundreds of smaller industries. The use of a million home incinerators was forbidden, as was certain burning practices in city dumps. The dustfall was reduced in some areas from 100 ton/sq. mile to 30 ton/sq. mile (the 1940 level for the city when it had half the population and half the industry of 1950). The legal enforcement was outstanding. Everything went well except that the smog, eye irritation and plant damage from pollution continued unabated as though no program existed. The type of campaign which was so successful in Pittsburgh and St. Louis had essentially no influence on Los Angeles.

Not knowing how to proceed further, the district supervisors instituted a research program to investigate the difficulty. The first surprising result was that a strongly polluted atmosphere in L.A. was oxidizing rather than reducing. In other areas, the compound associated with abnormally high pollution was SO_2, a reducing agent. The oxidant was found to be ozone with a lesser contribution from oxides of nitrogen and organic peroxides. During a heavy smog, the condition of the ozone concentration could be a factor of 10 to 20 over the normal concentration. It sometimes rose to 1/2 part per million, which is equivalent to 1000 tons in the Los Angeles basin. The daily variation of oxidant values at Pasadena during a smog period is plotted in Figure 106.

This observation created a dilemma. What was the source of the ozone? It was not a waste product of any Los Angeles industry. Electrical discharges in power lines and in other electrical equipment could not have been responsible for more than 1/1000th of that observed. Ozone is produced by photochemical reactions in the upper atmosphere. However, the reaction is induced by radiation of wavelength less than 2000 Å, which does not penetrate down to the lower atmosphere.

The mystery was solved by Haagen-Smit and his colleagues through a remarkable set of deductions and experiments. Sunlight was clearly important in the process since the oxidant and ozone levels were common during daylight hours and declined at night. After eliminating all possible industrial pollutants and the possibility of the occurrence of reactions common in the upper atmosphere, the only remaining source of a large quantity of gas was the millions of automobiles in the L.A. area. Traditionally the only gas of concern in automobile exhaust was the poisonous carbon monoxide. While it was the medium of a number of suicides and a few tragedies in unventilated tunnels, its concentration has never been serious under normal conditions. No special investigation previously had been made of the effect of other exhaust gases on the atmosphere until Haagen-Smit considered the question. After a number of experiments, it was deduced that the nitrogen dioxide

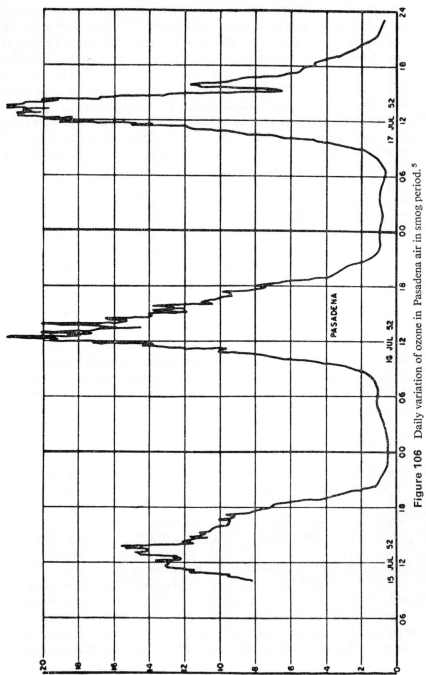

Figure 106 Daily variation of ozone in Pasadena air in smog period.[5]

common in automobile exhaust is converted by solar radiation to NO and atomic oxygen. Organic molecules of which there are many in the unburned hydrocarbons in auto exhaust combine with the atomic oxygen to form ozone and a variety of other oxidation products. Some of these, such as the peracyl-nitrates and formaldehyde are eye irritants, while the peracylnitrates and ozone can cause damage to plants. Finally, the oxidation reaction products are frequently accompanied by the formation of aerosols or hazes which amplify the influences of the individual smog components. The wonderful California sunshine which attracted so many sun worshippers to California also attracted their automobiles and the sun-hiding smog.

In summary, the primary photochemical reactions derived from automobile exhaust and the resulting secondary reactions are

$$NO_2 + h\nu \rightarrow NO + O$$

$$RCOH + h\nu \rightarrow R^\circ + HCO^\circ$$

$$O + O_2 + M \rightarrow O_3 + M$$

$$O_3 + NO \rightarrow O_2 + NO_2$$

$$O_3 + oliphin \rightarrow R, RO^\circ, RCO^\circ, ROOH, RCOOOH, Polymers$$

$$R^\circ + O_2 \rightarrow ROO^\circ$$

$$RCO^\circ + O_3 \rightarrow RCOOO^\circ$$

Here M is a third molecule which acts as a catalyst and R represents any of a variety of organic groups. This list does not include the reactions between the ozone and the atomic oxygen with industrial wastes such as halogens, styrene, etc., which through photochemical reaction lead to other irritants. Incidentally, the various oxidants also crack rubber and cause damage to other materials. In view of the Haagen-Smit observations, let us examine some characteristics of the internal combustion engine, as employed in the motor car.

REFERENCES

1. Maynard E. Smith, The Use and Misuse of the Atmosphere, Brookhaven Lecture Series 24, 1963.
2. Great Britain Ministry of Health, Reports on Public Health and Medical Subjects No. 98. Mortality and Morbidity during the London fog of Dec. 1952. H. M. Stationary Office, London, 1954.
3. Great Britain, Committee on air pollution, Interim Report, H. M. Stationary Office, 1965.
4. F. N. Frenkiel, *Advances in App. Mechanics* **3**, 61 (1953).
5. F. N. Frenkiel, *Ann. Reports of Smithsonian Institution* (Washington, 1956), p. 269.

K

6. A. J. Haagen–Smit, *Scientific American* **210**, 25 (1964).
7. A. J. Haagen–Smit, *Ind. Eng. Chem.* **44**, 1342 (1952).
8. A. J. Haagen–Smit, C. E. Bradley and M. M. Fox, *Ind. Eng. Chem.* **45**, 2086 (1953).
9. A. J. Haagen–Smit and M. M. Fox, *Ind. Eng. Chem.* **48**, 1484 (1956).
10. A. J. Haagen–Smit, *Advances in Geophysics* **6**, 1 (Acad. Press, 1969). This volume of Ad. in Geophys. contains the proceedings of an international symposium on atmospheric diffusion and pollution (editors F. N. Frenkiel and P. A. Shappard) and is an important reference on the influence of the aerodynamics of the atmosphere and transport of pollutants.
11. R. S. Scorer, *Air Pollution* (Pergamon Press, Oxford, 1968).

2 Effluent From The Internal Combustion Engine and Its Control

As we have seen in the last section, the gasoline fueled internal combustion engine has been identified as a prime generator of air pollution. To state the case more precisely, we list the 1967 sources of air pollution in the U.S. in millions of tons per year:[1]

Power generation	.. 20	Space heating	..	.. 8
Industry ..	 23	Refuse disposal ..		.. 5
Motor vehicles ..	.. 86.2			

The main components of the motor vehicle share (again in 10^6 tons per year) are:

Carbon monoxide	.. 66	Oxides of sulphur	..	1
Hydrocarbons ..	.. 12	Particular matter	..	1
NO_x ($NO + NO_2$)	.. 6	Lead compounds	..	0.2

One of the early references to the toxic nature of automobile exhaust gas is an article[2] in the Pittsburgh Sun, 30 November 1919. The nom de plume of the author was "Crucible". He stated "It is not uncommon to read about finding a man dead in his garage. When this happens, the account goes on to state that the engine was running and that the doors and windows were closed. The natural conclusion is that there must be a poisonous product generated by the engine and that this produce accumulated in the closed garage in sufficient quantity to cause death".

The chemical analysis of automobile exhaust had already been investigated by C. H. Chase[3] who experimented with 12 cars and three trucks. Carbon monoxide was a component present at a level of 6.8%. It is natural that the U.S. Bureau of Mines, with its broad experience in mine safety, mine catastrophies, and chemical analysis of gases found in normal and unsafe mines, should have been concerned with garage asphyxiations.[2] The Bureau was already well acquainted with the toxicity of carbon monoxide which, in mine accidents, was called black damp. As the reader no doubt knows, the CO attaches itself, preferentially in place of oxygen, to the hemoglobin molecules in red cells. One exposed to too much CO for too long a period suffers from oxygen deficiency. CO is more dangerous than other toxic gases such as H_2S because it is odorless and colorless so that the victim receives no warning of its presence. The great student of physiological effects of foul atmosphere in mines, pressure on underwater divers, etc., was J. S. Haldane,[4] the father of the more publicized biologist J. B. S. Haldane.

An important Bureau of Mines circular[5] on dangers of automobile exhaust, among other things, gave the following sound advice to a majority of motorists of those days, those who were do-it-yourself automechanics, ". . . it is not much pleasure to work over a car on a cold, winter day with the garage doors open . . . it is possible to fix a small arrangement . . . a short length of hose which is slipped over the exhaust pipe while the other end reaches the outdoors will do the trick". Gasoline vapor from flooded carburetors were also discovered to be toxic to mechanics working in confined, unventilated quarters.[2]

While carbon monoxide poisoning took its toll among auto buffs, the primary air pollution victims of the first quarter of the century were the very poor who couldn't even afford cars. The standard space heater in the urban tenement house was an old, corroded metal gas stove (in the better houses, it was the gas fireplace). Its unhooded combustion products were not unlike those of the automobile; the pipes and rubber connecting hose frequently leaked, the flame was often extinguished by a fluctuating gas pressure or by the draft of doors being opened or closed; unwatched children became the unwitting creators of their own destruction by playing with the stopcocks. After tuberculosis, pneumonia, influenza and diptheria, the gas heater was one of the most important killers in the crowded city.

The Bureau of Mines played an important role in furnishing specifications for tunnel ventilators.[3] The first two long automobile tunnels in the U.S. were the Liberty tubes through Mount Washington in Pittsburgh and the Holland Tunnel under the Hudson River in New York. One of the early memories of one of the authors (EWM) concerns the mass asphyxiation tragedy in the Liberty tubes shortly after their opening in 1924. The ventilating equipment had not yet been fully installed but, on the basis of some trials, the mile-long tunnel was considered to be safe for traffic while the installation was completed. It was a boon to the commuters from the developing suburbs and rural communities on the South Hills side of Mount Washington. The tunnel was indeed safe under normal conditions but, during the early morning rush hour on Saturday morning, May 10, 1924 a traffic jam developed on one of the roads near its Pittsburgh end, blocking the flow through the tunnel. Most of the drivers kept their motors running while waiting for the jam to clear until a critical safe concentration of carbon monoxide was exceeded, overcoming hundreds. The father of one of the authors (EWM) avoided the catastrophe through his habit (which has been inherited by his son) of arriving at work rather late in the morning, while a neighbor who normally was an early commuter was spared by a domestic argument which postponed his departure from home by some thirty or forty minutes.

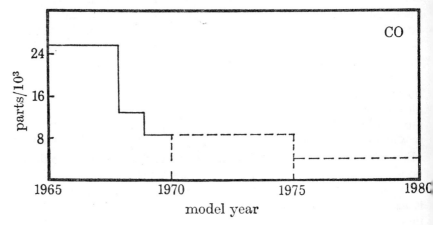

Figure 107   The California experience and the states' code for future restrictions on CO emissions.[1]

It is generally agreed that the dangers of CO are restricted to confined areas. A figure often given for the maximum allowed concentration for an eight-hour period is 50 parts per million. A large scale program[1] of gas analysis of the air was made on Fleet Street in London during 1962. Hourly samples were taken during the busy hours between 8 a.m. and 7 p.m. Typical on-hour averages were 17 ppm. An occasional high level was observed; the highest for an hour period was 55 ppm but such high levels never persisted for very long. Spot-checking over the past ten years has not indicated any significant change. The explanation for this is that traffic was already so saturated on Fleet Street in 1962 that no increase was possible in the ensuing years and there would be no reason to expect an increase in the CO level. Even though CO is generally not considered to be dangerous in unconfined areas, those responsible for the smog ordinances in California have opted to reduce the CO along with other more significant emissions. The history of CO levels achieved in California in the period 1965–1970 are represented by the solid line in Figure 107 while the legal restrictions for the period 1970–1980 are given by the dotted line in the figure.[1]

The smog and lacrimator producers were identified in the last section to be caused by NO_x and olefinic hydrocarbons in engine effluent. Three basic sources of engine pollutants are fuel tank and carburetor evaporation, crankcase blowby, and exhaust. An estimated 30% of the total emission (or 2% of supplied fuel) escapes through the engine from the seepage of gasoline vapor through the piston rings (even in a new car) into the crankcase. The evaporation into the atmosphere from the fuel tank and carburetor is especially great on hot days. Of the various undesirable emissions, 20% of the hydrocarbons (HC) come from fuel tank and carburetor evaporation, 20% from crankcase blowby, and 60% from the exhaust. All the CO and all the NO_x comes from the exhaust.

The simplest way of reducing vehicular pollution is to keep the engine tuned and properly maintained. While this reduces the emission by 25–50%, most car owners are no more diligent in maintenance than the slum dwellers were in caring for their gas heaters. Through proper engine sealing and the incorporation of blowby control devices, the evaporated gasoline can be carried back to the engine for combustion. This expedient has already been effectively used.

The controlled processing of engine exhaust requires more sophisticated engineering solution.[1,6] The obvious solution would be to operate the engine in such a manner that the unburned and partially burned exhaust components are at a minimum. However, as will be clear[1] from Figure 108 in which the effect of air fuel ratio on exhaust composition is plotted, we are faced with a dilemma in trying to achieve this state. The ideal gasoline-air ratio to obtain almost complete fuel combustion to H_2O and CO_2 is 15, a ratio which also yields almost the maximum level of NO_x, an undesirable component. Actually, an engine operating on a smaller ratio gives smoother operation and more power at the expense of less complete combustion. To reduce the formation of NO_x one should operate at a ratio of 18–20 but in that range, engine misfirings and stallings are common and there is an increase in hydrocarbon level. Another interesting trade-off is encountered in trying to maximize fuel economy and power output. A smaller ratio than 15 is more economical, but a larger-than-15 ratio yields a better power performance. Even if control can be maintained at a spark in a cylinder, the combustion flame at the colder

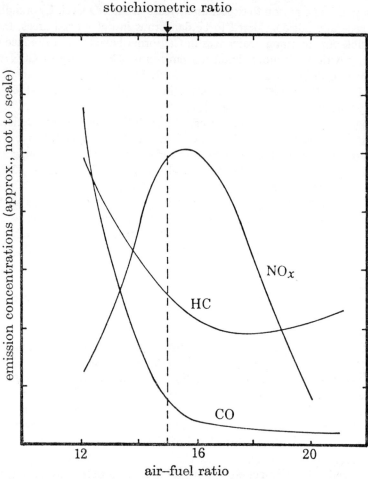

Figure 108   Emission concentrations of main pollutants in engine exhaust as a function of air fuel ratio in combustion.[1]

remote boundaries of the cylinder might be quenched yielding higher HC levels in the exhaust.

    There are still further complications in controlling exhaust composition. The relative amounts of various exhaust components depend on the driving mode[7] as exhibited in Figure 109. The idling, accelerating, decelerating, and cruising modes all yield different exhaust compositions. Some schemes for partial control of these differences have been incorporated into newer cars; they involve retarded spark timing, special engine and cooling systems, and automatic carburetor adjustments. All of these measures increase the cost of cars and of their maintenance. The motorist must keep his vehicle in good repair so that the effect of the delicate controls is not lost through negligence.

An alternative, less complicated, way of reducing vehicular pollution employs an afterburner which processes the exhaust. Two schemes have been proposed and applied.[6] In the first, the exhaust is burned in a flame ignited by a spark plug or through a small pilot light. The second is a catalytic

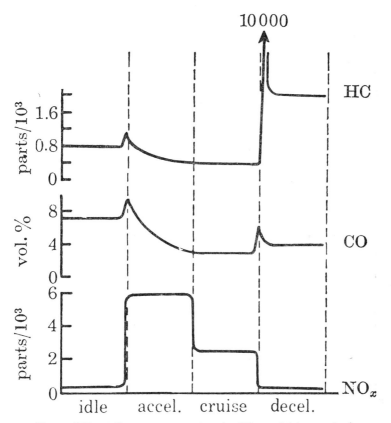

Figure 109 Pollutant concentrations in different driving modes.[1]

process in which the exhaust passes over a catalytic bed and burns at a lower temperature than is possible in the direct combustion. It was emphasized in Figure 109 that the composition of the exhaust gas varies considerably; the afterburner has to process the deceleration modes rich mixture which might, if not properly bypassed, burn at a temperature high enough to melt a ceramic casing as well as the catalyst; and a few moments later in another operating mode must treat such a poor mixture that the flame might die out. Ceramic casing and burning elements with good, high temperature, mechanical characteristics, are expensive and must be replaced fairly often if the afterburner is to remain effective.

These problems notwithstanding, automobiles produced today are less polluting than those of a decade ago. The automobile industry is being intimidated into providing an even better performance. The California experience

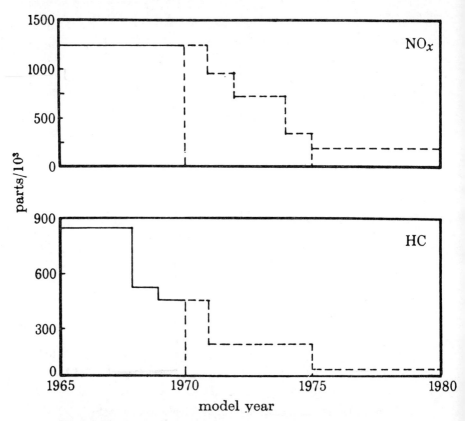

Figures 110, 111   The California experience and the states' codes for future restrictions on NOX and HC emissions.[1]

and the states' codes of future restrictions on NO_x and HC emission are given in Figures 110 and 111.

During the past year or two, another exhaust component has detracted attention from those already discussed. The toxicity of heavy metals such as mercury and lead has become widely publicized; with the mercury found in fish and lead in automobile exhaust heading the list. Since lead is an additive and not a native component of petroleum, we will discuss the reason for its inclusion. For background we first consider the nature of crude oil, the composition of gasoline, and the significance of various additives.

Crude oil is a mixture of many hydrocarbons and other organic molecules, the precise composition of a particular sample depending on its source. The refining process separates the crude oil into the components listed in Figure 112; those of low and high molecular weights appear respectively at the top and bottom of the column.

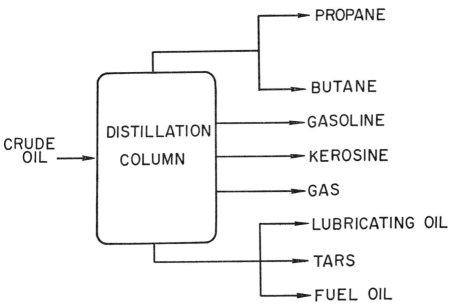

Figure 112   Schematic diagram of refinery.

Each fraction is in turn a mixture; gasoline contains over 200 compounds, the most common being[1]

butane	6.9%	toluene ⎫
isopentane	7.3	3,3-dimethylhexane ⎬ 12.5%
n-pentane	4.2	m-xylene ⎫
2,3,4-trimethylpentane ⎫	4.6	3,3,4-trimethylhexane ⎬ 4.6
tert-3-heptane ⎭		2,3-dimethylheptane ⎭
1,2,4-trimethylbenzene	2.4	

K*

The percentages vary somewhat from sample to sample. Those given above are typical. While the word octane appears frequently in the characterization of a gasoline, it does not appear in the component list. However, octanes are there. The formula for 2,3,4-trimethylpentane is C_8H_{18}.

Commercial gasoline generally contains a number of additives, some of which are listed in Table XII with their purpose.[1]

TABLE XII   Gasoline additives and their purpose

tetraethyl lead tetramethyl lead	anti-knock
ethylene dibromide ethylene dichloride	reduce lead deposits in engine
tritolyl phosphate cresyl diphenyl phosphate	modifies engine deposits, reduces spark plug fouling
2,4-dimethyl-6-tert-butyl phenol—anti-oxidant	
isopropyl alcohol hexylene glycol	prevents winter carburetor icing
alkyl amine phosphates—keeps carburetor and inlet valves clear	
1,4-di(isopropylamino)anthraquinine—coloring matter used as toxicity warning	

An appreciation of the role played by lead alkyls as an anti-knock agent can be obtained from a consideration of the mechanism of pressure generation in the cylinders through gasoline combustion. The desirable mode of force application to the piston would be one in which the pressure builds up slowly and smoothly until the peak is reached near the end of the expansion phase of the cycle at time T_C as shown in Figure 113a. Raw refinery gasoline generally has a pressure-time curve such as that in Figure 113b. The gasoline near the spark starts to burn, heating the rest in the cylinder which explodes at time T_C. The explosive mode of combustion is called knock. It is noisy, damages pistons, and leads to pressure oscillations which cause power losses. A small amount of lead alkyls such as tetraethyl and tetramethyl lead delays the explosion so that all the fuel can be consumed.

The knock property of a gasoline is characterized by its octane number; 91 octane is low with poor knock qualities, while 100 is high and good. The octane number is defined through an experiment which employs a well tuned ignition engine. The knock characteristics are studied in the "standard

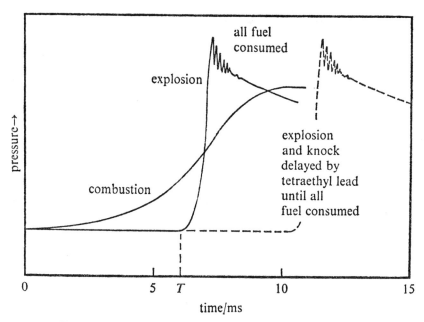

Figure 113   Pressure time curve for a cycle in a gasoline engine.[1]

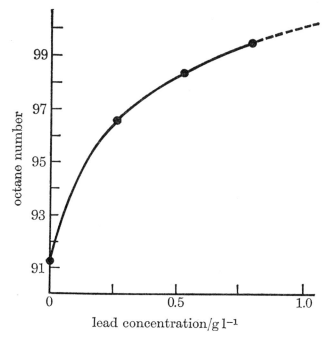

Figure 114   Variation of octane number with *Pb* concentration.[1]

engine" with various calibrating blends of 2,2,4-trimethyl pentane, C_8H_{18} and normal heptane C_7H_{16}. The knock phenomenon is observed as a function of octane concentration. If a gasoline being tested has the same knock characteristics as a calibrating mixture of x percent C_8H_{18}, it has an octane number x. One way of defining octane numbers greater than 100 is by the number of milliliters of tetraethyl lead required per gallon of iso-octane to give it the same knock performance as the sample being tested. The octane number of a typical gasoline is given in Figure 114 as a function of lead concentration.[1]

The cheapest and best method of making high octane gasoline is with the addition of lead alkyls. Under current pressures, alternatives are being sought. One promising substitute is n-methyl aniline which, though basically as toxic as lead alkyls, does undergo some change during the combustion process. Since it is very expensive, it adds a few cents per gallon to the cost of gasoline. Refinery processing may be changed to make the gasoline richer in iso-octane or triptone. This is a more expensive mode of operation and has the unfortunate feature that a higher concentration of olefins (which are smog producing) also appears in the gasoline refined in this mode. In areas of the country where smog is no problem this would not be serious, but in California it would be undesirable. Incidentally, in spite of all discussions about lead, there seems to be no direct evidence that the lead in exhaust emissions is contaminating the environment in any recognizable way. Even though the public has not responded favorably to the higher-priced leadless gasoline which is already on the market, it seems that the current trend is to eventually remove lead from gasoline.

Engines with high compression ratios need higher octane gas than those with lower because the tendency for gasoline to knock increases with the operating pressure. High compression ratios give more engine power and efficiency. The alternative manner of achieving equivalent power is to employ larger engines with greater cylinder capacity and lower compression ratios. Such engines burn much more gasoline per mile.

REFERENCES

1. Lord Rothschild, *Proc. Roy. Soc. Lond.* **A322,** 147 (1971).
2. Van H. Manning, *Sci. American Monthly* **1,** 64 (1920).
3. C. H. Chase, *The Automobile* **20,** 395, 422, 469 (1914).
4. J. S. Haldane, *Respiration* (Yale, 1922); 2nd Ed. Haldane and Priestly (Yale, 1935).
5. G. A. Burrell and A. W. Ganger, *Bureau of Mines Technical Paper* 215 (1919).
6. A. J. Haagen-Smit, Sci. American **210,** 25 (1964).
7. D. R. Fussell, *Petroleum Review* **24,** 192 (1970).

3   Mathematical Modeling of Diffusion of Pollutants

If a volume element of pollutant is injected into the atmosphere, it spreads and drifts. The drift is associated with the motion of the center of mass of the collection of molecules in the original volume element or "puff"; it is driven by the wind, temperature differences between the puff and the surrounding air, and temperature gradients in the atmosphere.

The spreading represents the random motion of the molecules of the original puff; i.e., its diffusion through the atmosphere. If a small drop of dye is placed in the center of a beaker of water, the diffusion of the dye is caused by collision with the water molecules until the dye is uniformly distributed through the beaker. This process is called molecular diffusion. G. I. Taylor[1] pointed out that diffusion in the atmosphere is driven by larger scale fluid motions which are generated by the winds, thermal convection currents, and motion of objects, natural such as raindrops and, at low altitudes, man-made such as various vehicles, through the atmosphere. The temperature-altitude profile is exceedingly important, especially when inversion layers exist. This type of diffusion is called turbulent diffusion.

Now let us consider the expansion of a puff containing $N(0)$ molecules concentrated at the origin of a coordinate system. The concentration as a function of position in classical diffusion theory as applied to a uniform isotropic system is

$$N(x, y, z, t) = N(0)\,(2\pi\sigma^2)^{-\frac{3}{2}} \exp\{-(x^2+y^2+z^2)/2\sigma^2\}$$

where (as was discussed in our section on Brownian Motion Theory)

$$\sigma^2 = \langle x^2\rangle = \langle y^2\rangle = \langle z^2\rangle = 2Dt,$$

D being the diffusion constant, t the time since the puff was placed. When a drift exists and the medium is anisotropic, one finds that

$$N(x, y, z; t) = N(0)\,[(2\pi)^{-3/2}/\sigma_x\sigma_y\sigma_z]$$
$$\times \exp\{-(x-f_x)^2\sigma_x^{-2}-(y-f_y)^2\sigma_y^{-2}-(z-f_z)^2\sigma_z^{-2}\}/2$$

where $f_x \equiv f_x(t)$ is the x component of the location of the center of mass at time t and $\sigma_x^2 = \langle x^2\rangle$. If the x component of the drift has constant value v_x, then at time t, $f_x(t) = tv_x$, etc. Also, in the basic Brownian Motion Theory,

$$\sigma_x^2 = 2tD_x$$

D_x being the diffusion constant in the x direction. In making atmospheric diffusion models one might leave $f_x(t)$ and σ_x^2 as empirical quantities which are determined from observations. One of the most controversial points in the modeling of atmospheric conditions is the manner in which forms of $f_x(t)$ and σ_x^2 are chosen.

Suppose one has a fixed continuous point source which emits Q fluid elements per unit time into a fluid medium which is moving in the x direction with a mean velocity U. Then it can be shown[3,6] that the average number of fluid elements which pass through an element of area $dydz$ of a plane perpendicular to the direction of flow during a unit of time is $S(x, y, z)Udydz$ where

$$S(x, y, z)U/Q = (2\pi)^{-3/2}(U/\sigma_x\sigma_y^2) \int_0^\infty \exp-\{(x-U\alpha)^2/2\sigma_x^2+(y^2+z^2)/2\sigma_y^2\}\, d\alpha$$

is the relative mean concentration flux distribution at (x, y, z) in the plane at x, if we assume that $\sigma_x^2 = \sigma_y^2$. Detailed discussions of this and other flow distributions of interest are derived in References 3 and 6.

We show diagrammatically the way such distribution functions would be associated with chimney sources in Figures 115 and 116. The smoke dispersal is caused by two principal factors, general air motion which carries it downstream and turbulent velocity fluctuations which disperses it in all directions. A variety of common smoke plumes from chimneys are shown in Figure 115, as well as an average plume which has been employed by Frenkiel. Iso-pollution concentration lines are marked off. The average curves are appropriate for a constant wind direction and are discussed in detail in References 3 to 6. As the wind velocity increases, the inner closed curves (or rather survaces) become elongated.

Once a reasonable model of diffusion is available, two other ingredients are required for the discussion of atmospheric pollution from a specified community. One must know the location and character of various sources of pollution and he must know the prevalent weather conditions of the area so that the drift path of puffs can be established. The collection and analysis of such data for a particular city was first made by Francois Frenkiel[4,5] for Los Angeles. We now outline his methods and summarize his findings.

A given city can be modeled as a number of pollution sources, some discrete and some continuous. Major industrial sources are interpreted as point sources of pollutants of a well specified composition. Secondary industrial sources and assemblies of residential sources (including the leaves of the autumn leaf-burning ceremonies as well as the summer weekend cookouts) are represented as a continuous distribution whose average outputs vary slowly over the season and sometimes more rapidly over the time of the day. The same is true of traffic sources. Frenkiel divided the Los Angeles area into a grid of squares, each of 16 square miles area. He obtained an estimate of the relative amount of traffic in each area at a given time of the day. In Figure 116 the relative density of traffic (and the ensuing pollution) is represented by

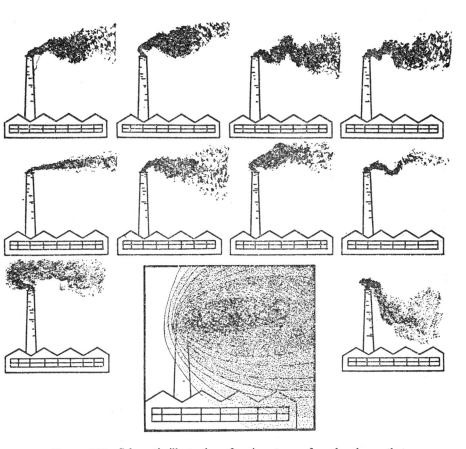

Figure 115 Schematic illustration of various types of smoke plumes that can occur under the same meteorological conditions. Mean concentration for an average smoke plume in the framed figure can be compared with theoretical results.[4]

a dark circle. Other distributed pollution sources can be treated in a similar manner.

There is considerable hourly traffic variation in any area. The relative hourly traffic variation at a single location is plotted in Figure 117 as a

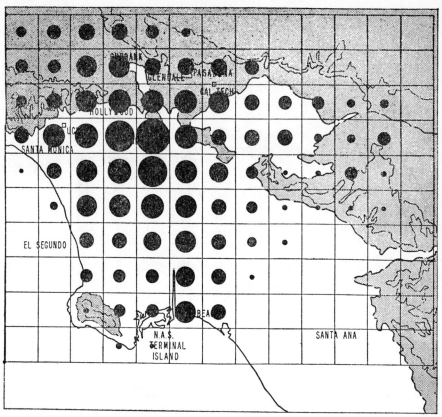

Figure 116 Geographical distribution of traffic in Los Angeles County.[4] Area of circles is proportional to the number of vehicles; each square represents 16 square miles (4 × 4 miles).

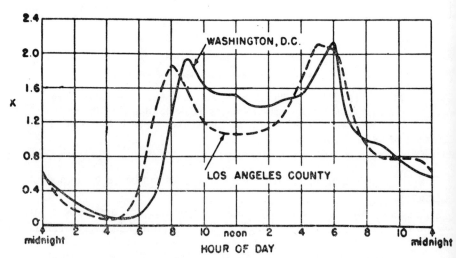

Figure 117 Example of hourly variation of traffic volume in Los Angeles.[4]

function of time. In the application of the model, it was assumed that the relative volume of traffic in each square varied in the same way with time as it did in the observed square. A detailed survey could, of course, be used to make corrections to this hypothesis.

When one has a model of pollution sources as a function of place and time in a large metropolitan area, he can then ask how the pollutant emanating from a given source disperses itself. For this purpose the micrometeorological characteristics of the area must be modeled. At a given time of the year, one can make a map of the average stream lines of the wind in the area. The motion of a puff of smoke from a given source would then be determined by combining the turbulent diffusion process of expansion of the puff with the stream lines which give it direction. Figure 118 indicates how, according to the model, two puffs of smoke would be dispersed on the average. The numbered points with successively expanded puffs represent hourly positions and pollutant distributions.

Now, the total pollution level at a given point in the city at a given time is the sum of pollutants which come from all sources at earlier times. That which arrives from nearby sources, of course, starts later than that which has arrived from more distant sources. In the calculation it was assumed that the ground and the temperature inversion layer act as reflecting barriers. Frenkiel estimated, according to the model described above, the hourly variation in pollution at a number of points in the Los Angeles area. His results for an average September day are plotted in Figure 119 for a point located on the campus of California Institute of Technology. The pollution sources are divided into four categories: heating, incinerator, motor vehicles, and industry.

As a check of his model, Frenkiel calculated the expected zone concentration as a function of time over one day. He included the effect of the photochemical reaction which makes ozone concentration dependent on concentrations of nitrogen dioxide and hydrocarbons from pollution sources. His theoretical curves are plotted on the same scale as two experimental observations taken on the same day.[4] Notice that his agreement with either observation is as good as the observations with each other.

A somewhat similar analysis of New York pollution has recently been made by L. J. Shieh et al.[7] This work emphasized the SO_2 pollution rather than ozone. A comparison of their theoretical results with a daily observation at the Bronx High School Station is given in Figure 121.

Since atmospheric oxygen is such an important requirement for man's existence, it has been recommended that measurements of the oxygen abundance in dry air should be made world-wide at fairly frequent time intervals. As a consequence of such a recommendation in May 1966 by the late Lloyd

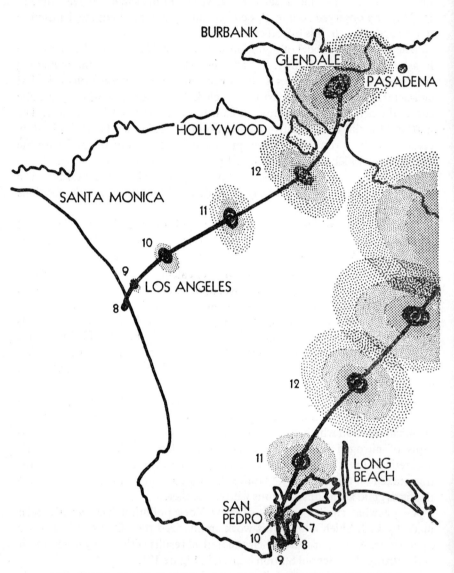

Figure 118 Hypothetical dispersion of smoke puffs released at two points of the Los Angeles Basin at 7 a.m. and 8 a.m., respectively.[4]

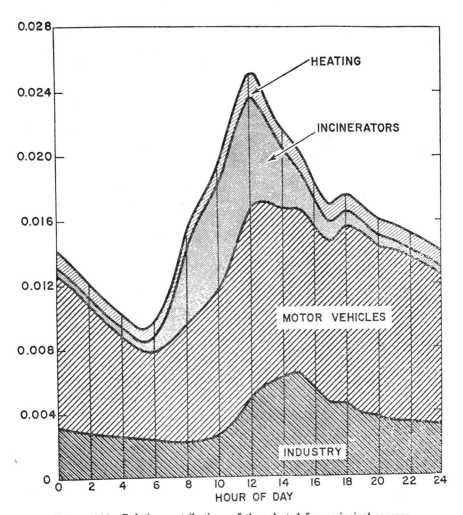

Figure 119 Relative contributions of the selected four principal sources to the mean concentration at the California Institute of Technology.[4] The data refer to a mathematical model of Los Angeles County in which the topographic features and inversion are taken into account. For this hypothetical model the relative proportion of the "important" pollutants (including acids, organics, and nitrogen dioxide) emitted by the four principal sources are based on the 1954 data for Los Angeles County. The meteorological conditions are based in large part on data for the month of September.

Berkner, several oceanographic vessels collected air samples over the oceans of the world in 1967 and 1968. These samples were analyzed and the results reported by L. Machta and E. Hughes in Reference 8. They reported that between the latitudes 50°N and 60°S, mainly over the oceans, dry air has an almost constant value 20.946 percent by volume (or, including error estimates

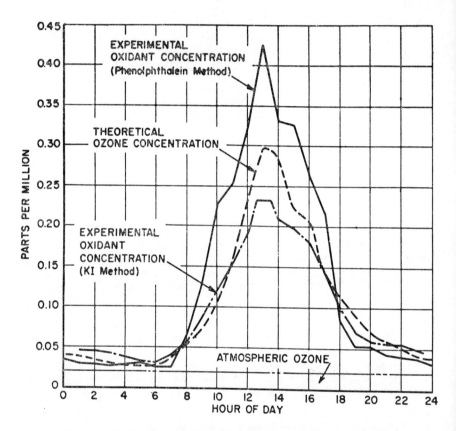

Figure 120 Measured and model concentrations of ozone—one day.[4]

in the measurements, 20.9458 ± 0.0017). These results are compared in Reference 8 to results of other large scale measurement programs undertaken since 1910. While the error estimates are not discussed so carefully in the earlier measurement series, the average values were very close to the figure given above. For example Shepherd of the National Bureau of Standards made six analyses of a large sample collected west of Washington, D.C. His results ranged from 20.935 to 20.950 with the average being 20.946. In 1910 Benedict analyzed air collected in the Boston area. Unfortunately, he first extracted the CO_2 from his samples so that his analysis was for CO_2 free air. However, his results are consistent with the modern ones when the observed

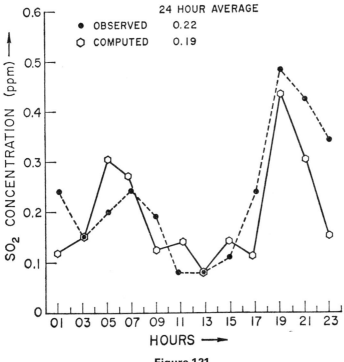

BRONX HIGH SCHOOL STATION 1

JAN. II, 1971

24 HOUR VARIATION OF SO_2 CONCENTRATION

Figure 121

abundance of CO_2 is combined with his figures. The general conclusion is that[8] "since 1910 changes with time over the globe appear to be either zero or smaller than the uncertainty in the measurements".

W. S. Broecker[9] has given an estimate of the effect of burning of the fossil fuel resources, the CO_2-oxygen conversion of photosynthesis, etc., on the oxygen content of the atmosphere. He concludes that the destruction of the oxygen balance is not one of the problems which should concern us.

REFERENCES

1. G. I. Taylor, Proc. *London Math. Soc.* **20**, 196 (1921).
2. O. G. Sutton, *Proc. Roy. Soc.* (London) **135A**, 143 (1932).
3. F. Gifford, Jr., p. 117 in *Advances in Geophysics* Vol. 6 (Academic Press, 1959, ed. F. N. Frenkiel and R. A. Sheppard). This volume is rich in papers relevant to this section.
4. F. N. Frenkiel, Ann. Reports of Smithsonian Institution (Washington, 1956), p. 269.
5. F. N. Frenkiel, Proc. of 7th Hydraulics Conference, 1958 (David Taylor Model Basin Report 1418 (1960)).
6. F. N. Frenkiel, *Advances in App. Mechanics* **3**, 61 (1953).
7. L. J. Shieh, P. K. Halpern, B. A. Chemens, H. H. Wang, and F. F. Abraham, IBM *J. Res. Develop.* **16**, 162 (1972).
8. L. Machta and E. Hughes, *Science* **168**, 1582 (1970).
9. W. S. Broecker, *Science* **168**, 1537 (1970).

CHAPTER VII

On The Development of Countries and the Growth of Cities

1 Change in Character of Countries

PEOPLE have been concerned about the problems of the city from almost the earliest days of written history. Perhaps most of us are complainers to some degree and the complaints of those who write are louder and more publicized than others. Furthermore, few of the world's great writers were country folk. Hence, excellent historical records of complaints exist about the problems of cities of almost any period in the past 3,000 years or more. Remedies have been eloquently presented and those offered a hundred years ago do not differ much from those of 500 years ago and those proposed today. A common plea has been to limit the size of cities.

Several quotations from Reference 1 summarize the classical attempts on limitation. Incidentally, Weber's book on "The Growth of Cities in the Nineteenth Century" is one of the great Ph.D. theses of all time. It is a statistical work strongly recommended to all students of quantitative aspects of social phenomenon.

Plutarch's warning against the overgrowth of the great cities, and Cicero's constant effort to turn back the current of emigration from the country, alike came to naught. Justinian tried to stop the current by legal measures, and medieval statesmen and monarchs followed a similar course. The extension of Paris beyond certain limits was prohibited by law in 1549, 1554, 1560, 1563, 1564, and 1672. In the time of the late Tudors and Stuarts, proclamation after proclamation was issued forbidding the erection of new houses in London and enjoining the country people to return to their homes. There were many good reasons for such action—the difficulties of municipal government, the fear of local pressure on Parliament, the difficulty of providing an adequate food supply and water supply, the danger of fires, and, especially, the danger of plagues and epidemics arising from unsanitary conditions. The evils enumerated in the Act of 1593 are almost identical with those depicted in a report of the New York Tenement House Commission of the late 1890's.

There have been many schemes to make farming more attractive and more remunerative with the help of the development of scientific methods, allotments for laborers, and government subsidies. All that are successful, generally have the effect of driving more people to the city. The reason for this is that they make the farm more productive, thus requiring less people to produce the same crop. They generally lead to larger and more efficient farms which provide larger yields and profits with a smaller and more mechanized labor force.

Another scheme of stopping migration city-ward is to make village life more attractive . . . so long as the present industrial organization endures, no amount of village improvement will keep ambitious youths at home for the reason that all the opportunities for rising in the world are in the cities.[1]

One can also say that the least ambitious who wish to free themselves from parental and neighborhood restrictions can find more exotic entertainment and company in the cities.

The attractions of the cities can be summarized in the following items:

(1) Broad educational opportunities.
(2) A greater variety of entertainment from the most cultured to the most base.
(3) A greater variety of job opportunities.
(4) A higher standard of living.
(5) Intellectual associations.
(6) The gregariousness of people.

Of the four classes of activities of man, (1) Extractive (agriculture and mining), (2) Distributive, (3) Manufacturing, and, (4) Service, the second and third have become enterprises of the city. Less than 7% of the people in the United States are all that are needed to feed the rest of us; (in the Soviet Union, about 40% are in agriculture). Since service work is performed where the people being served are located, it has also become a city occupation. Hence the drift to the city cannot be reversed. On the other hand, the population density of a city does tend to decrease as it becomes older, and suburbia and city transportation systems develop. The conversion of the US from a rural to an urban economy is presented in Figure 123 where we have plotted the fraction of working people doing non-agricultural labor.

There has been a replacement of agricultural activity by non-agricultural activity. The situation is analogous to the replacement of one type of material by another, say replacement of soap by detergent, or the Bessemer process by the open hearth for the production of steel. For some reason, economic or otherwise, the new mode becomes more attractive than the old and grows at the expense of the old. J. C. Fisher and R. H. Pry[2] have recently made a detailed analysis of 17 such replacement processes. They find that they all obey the logistic law which we discussed for population growth (see Eq. (II.2.5)). The fraction of elements in the new mode is

$$f(t) = \frac{\exp k(t-t_0)}{[(1-f_0)/f_0]+\exp k(t-t_0)}$$

with $f(t_0) \equiv f_0$. The "takeover" time required for $f(t)$ to go from 0.1 to 0.9 is $\simeq 1.11\,k$. Note that

$$\log[f/(1-f)] = \log[f_0/(1-f_0)]+k(t-t_0)$$

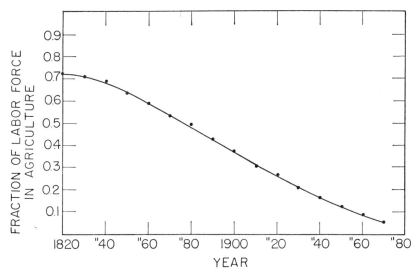

Figure 122 Decline of fraction of labor force in agriculture in U.S. since colonial times.

so that if $\log[f/(1-f)]$ is plotted as a function of time, one should obtain a straight line as is the case in Figures 123a–123d. All 17 cases which were analyzed are plotted in Figure 124. We have plotted the replacement of agricultural by non-agricultural activity in Figure 125.

While the flow of people from rural to urban areas and from agricultural to non-agricultural employment is interesting and important, it is still desirable to characterize a country by more than the fraction of its population still down on the farm. One way of refining the description is to consider n possible

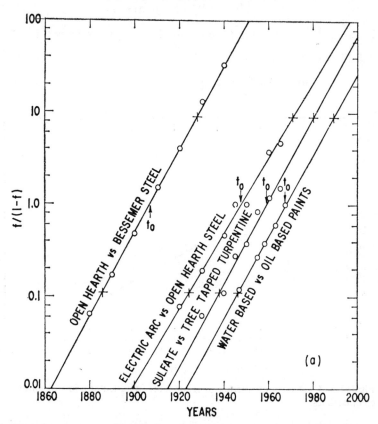

Figures 123 (a-d)   Substitution data and fit to model for a number of products and processes. All data U.S. except detergents for soap as noted.

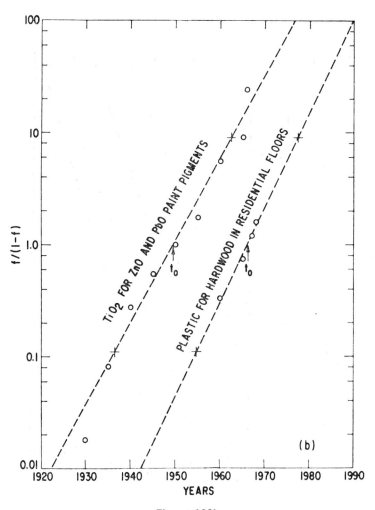

Figure 123b

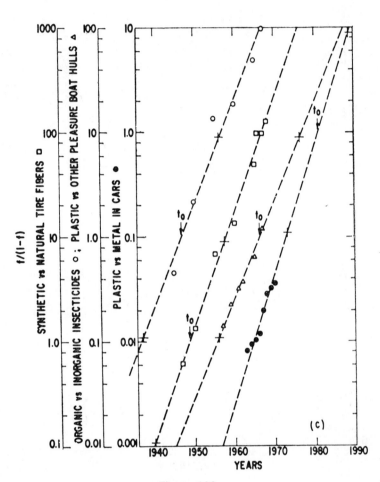

Figure 123c

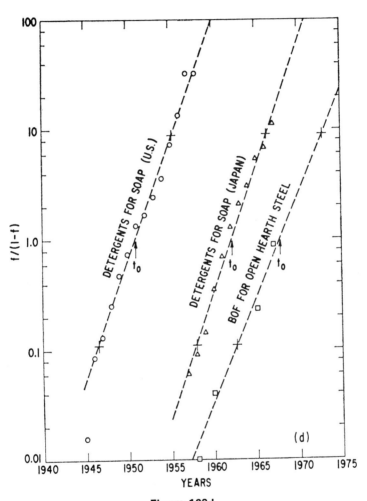

Figure 123d

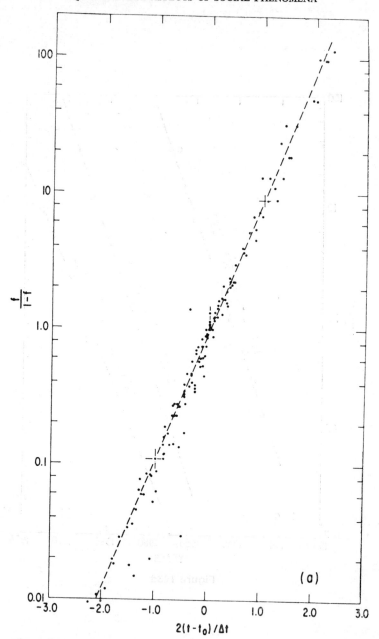

Figure 124a Fit of substitution model function to substitution data for all 17 cases vs normalized units of time.

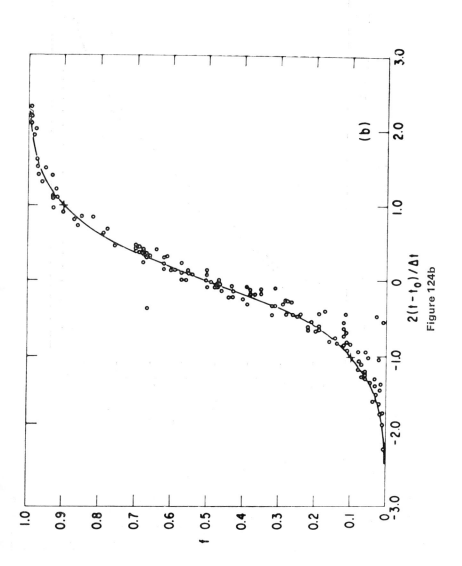

$2(t-t_0)/\Delta t$

Figure 124b

(b)

f

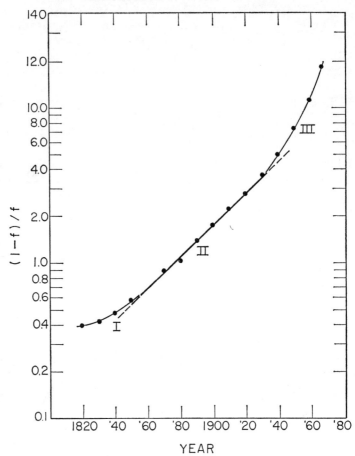

Figure 125 Replacement of agricultural activity by non-agricultural activity of U.S. labor force. Here f represents fraction of labor force in agriculture. The sharp rise in slope of $(1-f)/f$ at 1940 reflects the improvement of agriculture output per worker in response to World War II production demands with a limited supply of farm labor.

categories of employment of individuals (which are chosen to exhaust the entire employed population). Let, f_j represent the fraction of the population employed in category j. Then a "phase" point which might be used to define the nature of the country is the point $(f_1, f_2, ..., f_n)$ in an n dimensional Euclidian space.

Since such an n dimensional space is hard to visualize, it is desirable to consider an alternative two-dimensional representation of the phase point. Construct n rays emanating from the origin of a $2D$ rectangular coordinate system and let successive rays form an angle of $2\pi/n$ between them. A ray is then assigned to each category and the length of the jth ray is chosen to be f_j as indicated in Figure 126. If a polygon is formed by connecting the ends of successive rays by lines, one has a "snowflake" representation of a country as indicated in Figure 126. One might expect countries with similar snowflake representations to be similar to each other.

The simplest abstraction of a country is its representation by a point defined by the center of mass of the snowflake, i.e., the point whose x and y coordinates are respectively

$$x = (1/n) \, \Sigma f_j \cos(2\pi j/n)$$
$$y = (1/n) \, \Sigma f_j \sin(2\pi j/n)$$

The abstraction of the time development of a country would then be the

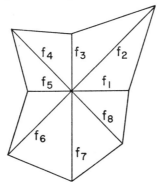

Figure 126 A snowflake diagram.

trajectory that was generated by the variation of (x, y) with time. Such points and diagrams have been discussed by R. Herman and E. W. Montroll in Reference 3.

The social history of the United States for the past 120 years has been abstracted in Figure 127. For simplicity we choose the basic number of categories to be the four areas of employment; agriculture, trade, manufacturing and service. The "phase points" in the figure which are exhibited by dots correspond to labor in the U.S. in the years, 1850, 1890, 1920, and 1960. The drop in the trajectory between 1930 and 1940 shows a diminishing of trade and growth of service during the great depression. The general character of shift of the working population from an agricultural to a service orientation is expressed in the graph. The corresponding trajectories for England and Sweden are given in Figures 128–9. In Figure 130 we have introduced a large number of phase points, each corresponding to a different country, the basic data being available in the U.N. demographic yearbooks.

L

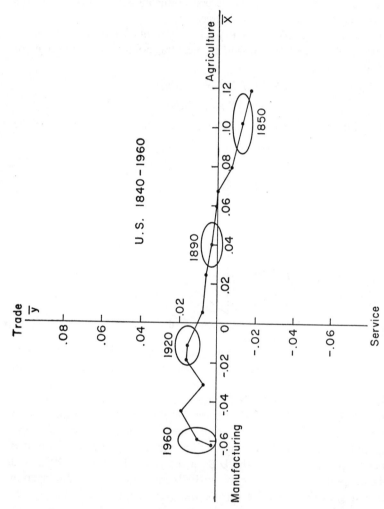

Figure 127 The shift of the U.S. from an agricultural to a manufacturing country. The downward trend of the last few points indicates the manner in which service is growing in importance.[3]

Countries whose phase points lie close to each other can be expected to be more similar to each other than to those whose phase points are widely separated.

If one wishes to relax the severity of the abstraction, each snowflake diagram might be replaced by an ellipse instead of a point. The semi-axes and the angular orientation can be expressed in terms of the second moments of the snowflake.

Let us consider the correlation matrix defined by

$$C = \begin{pmatrix} \langle(x-\bar{x})^2\rangle_{Av} & \langle(x-\bar{x})(y-\bar{y})\rangle_{Av} \\ \langle(y-\bar{y})(x-\bar{x})\rangle_{Av} & \langle(y-\bar{y})^2\rangle_{Av} \end{pmatrix} \equiv (C_{ij})$$

Our representative ellipse is determined by its semi-axes and the angle its major axis makes with the horizontal. The matrix C, being real and symmetric,

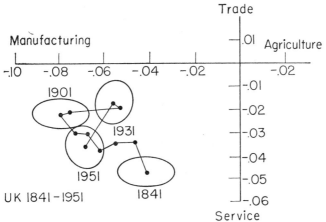

Figure 128 The trajectory[3] of the UK which was in the manufacturing service quadrant in the 1840's.

can be diagonalized by an orthogonal matrix Q such that

$$Q = \begin{pmatrix} \cos\theta & \sin\theta \\ \sin\theta & \cos\theta \end{pmatrix}$$

and (the λ's being the characteristic values)

$$Q^{-1}CQ = \begin{pmatrix} \lambda_1 & 0 \\ 0 & \lambda_2 \end{pmatrix}$$

If we let the λ's be the semi-axis and θ the rotation angle, the time variation of the elliptical representative of the labor force snowflake of the U.S. is given in Figure 127.

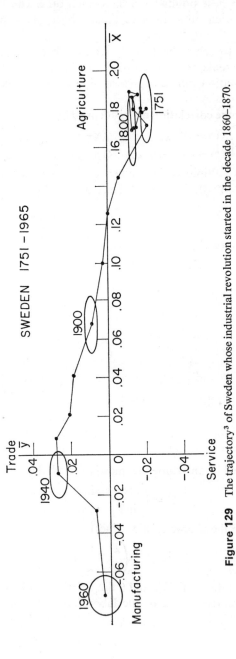

Figure 129   The trajectory[3] of Sweden whose industrial revolution started in the decade 1860–1870.

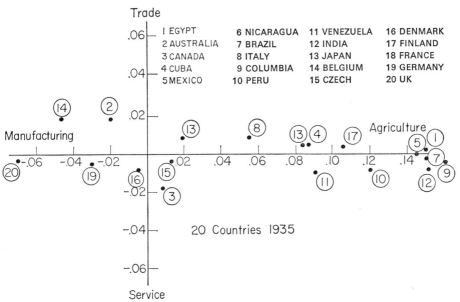

Figure 130 Phase points of 20 countries, 1935.

The explicit formula for θ is obtained from

$$\cos \theta = [\tfrac{1}{2}(1 + |C_{11} - C_{22}|d^{-1})]^{\frac{1}{2}}$$

$$d = [(C_{11} - C_{22})^2 + 4C_{12}^2]^{\frac{1}{2}}$$

Also,

$$\sin \theta = \text{sign}[C_{12}(C_{11} - C_{22})]\{\tfrac{1}{2}(1 - |C_{11} - C_{22}|^{\frac{1}{2}}d^{-1})\}$$

The significance of the ellipse can be understood if we consider a typical case; for example, the 1960 ellipse whose center is close to the $\lambda = 0$ axis. A phase point near the $\lambda = 0$ axis corresponds to the case of trade and service having essentially the same importance. The vertical major axis means that both trade and service are large, compared with manufacturing and agriculture.

REFERENCES

1. A. F. Weber, *The Growth of Cities in The* 19th *Century*, (MacMillan, 1899; Cornell Paperback Reprints of Urban Studies, 1963).
2. J. C. Fisher and R. C. Pry, *Practical Applications of Technological Forecasting in Industries* (Ed. M. J. Cetron, Wiley, 1971).
3. R. Herman and E. W. Montroll. *Proc. Nat. Acad. Sci.*, **69**, 3019 (1972).

2 On the Growth of Cities

Weber[1] displayed, in a dramatic way, the preference for urban over rural life as it had already developed by the 1890's. He noted that the population of the seven colonies of Australia in 1891 was 3,809,895 as compared with that of the U.S. in 1790, which was 3,929,214.

The Australia of today (1891) has the population of America of 1790; it is peopled by men of the same race, it is liberal and progressive and practical, it is a virgin country with undeveloped resources; it is to an equal extent politically and socially independent of Europe.

However, the population of the U.S. in cities over 10,000 was 123,551 (3.14%) in 1790 while 1,264,283 Australians (33.20%) lived in such cities in 1891. This pattern was characteristic of the change observed almost everywhere in the 19th Century. It has developed even further in the 20th Century.

Certain of the unpleasant aspects of this flow to the cities have motivated the currently fashionable Zero Population Movement. If history is to help our intuition, it is doubtful that the success of the movement will have more than a secondary effect on the problems; and that effect may be to worsen the situation if certain political and industrial actions are not taken. During the 19th Century, France was the European continental country with the smallest rate of population growth. The growth of the French cities and the ensuing problems were not significantly different from those in other European countries.

The country which showed the greatest *population decline* in modern times is Ireland whose population drop is plotted in Figure 4. The population flow to the larger cities was even greater in Ireland than in some other countries whose population was increasing. The total population and the urban population of Ireland at various decades between 1841 and 1891 is given in Table XIII.

TABLE XIII   Total and urban population of Ireland 1841–1891

	Total population	Urban population
1841	8,196,587	1,143,674
1851	6,574,278	1,226,661
1861	5,798,967	1,140,771
1871	5,412,377	1,201,344
1881	5,174,836	1,245,503
1891	4,704,750	1,244,113

The most dramatic effect is not the change in rural-urban ratio nor the general movement to the cities, but it is the movement to the *largest* cities at the expense of the rural areas *and the smaller cities*. The population change in various classes of cities as taken from Reference 1, p. 65, is shown in Table XIV.

TABLE XIV Population, in thousands, or various classes of cities.

	1841	1891	Increase or decrease %
19 cities (10,000+)	671.1	908.5	+35
Dublin	266.4	342.3	+28
Belfast	73.3	255.9	+240
Dublin + Belfast	341.7	598.3	+75
4 cities 20,000 to 100,000 in 1891	167.5	166.5	−0.6
13 remaining cities having $<2 \times 10^4$	161.9	143.6	−12

Incidentally, these figures do not include the tremendous movement to even larger cities than Belfast and Dublin, namely New York, London and Boston, which occurred during the period considered.

One can argue that certain special problems existed in Ireland such as relations with England, considerable rural poverty, etc., which stimulated this migration. However, we wish now to suggest that a decline in the population of the U.S. would not abate urban migration and, indeed, it might accelerate the present trend of movement to the largest cities. It has already been mentioned that the improvement of agricultural technology reduces the need for farmers. In the same sense, a reduction in population would reduce the demands on agricultural production and, therefore, the need for farmers. This would induce continued migration to the cities. The widely known welfare programs of the largest cities would make them more attractive to migrants than the smaller cities. One looking for new work opportunities would argue that even if a position is not immediately available in the larger cities, he could remain on welfare until one appeared.

Since economic growth is closely correlated with population changes, one would have to be very careful during a population decline to prevent a serious depression in the economy. Such a depression would affect the poor and the young more than the older, more settled component of society because there would be fewer new positions available. Unless the economy would be developed to provide more material or services per person, the demands for productivity would diminish, as would the number of employed. Since this would discourage investments in new production facilities, foreign producers who were not coupled with this movement might, through improved technology, underprice domestic producers who operated older equipment, stimulating a further decline in the local economy. An analysis of a mathematical model of these processes is now in progress.

While the intellectuals and the middle class generally of New York, London, Mexico City, etc., are finding their lives more oppressive and intolerable, the message has not reached the poor of Puerto Rico, Georgia, Jamaica, the Mexican hinterlands, etc. The future of these people at home looks bleak while their limited experience, and education prevents them from comprehending the problems which they must face when they reach the megalopolis. It is interesting to note in passing that many of the mass migrations have been stimulated by the aggressive ticket salesmen of expanding transportation firms. There was an expansion in the steamship lines during the last half of the 19th Century. Ticket salesmen of the Cunard and other lines plied their wares through the pubs of Ireland in that period. After a few drinks, the exotic descriptions of life in America stimulated the imagination of many a young Irishman and sold many steerage passages. The ticket salesmen of the Illinois Central Railroad[2] were especially successful with the young Swedes who bought tickets to take them to the end of the line, Minnesota. The Pan-American airlines were just as aggressive in developing the emigration route from Puerto Rico to New York.

According to the 1970 census, 70% of the population of the U.S. live on 2% of the land. Furthermore, in the last ten years, the rate of growth of the U.S. population was less than in any other decade except for the depression one, but the movement to the larger cities was accelerated over the previous decade with half the counties losing population and the other half gaining.

A feeling for the change in population of the larger cities is exhibited in Table XV. It contains some information[1] on population changes in the 49 cities which were the largest in the world outside of Japan and China in 1891. The populations are given in a selection of periods before 1891. The change in order is quite evident. It is interesting that Constantinople headed the list in 1500 while that distinction shifts to Paris in 1600, to London in 1800, and to New York in 1970. Venice which was the 4th city in 1500 and 1600 does not appear on the list, nor do other Italian cities such as Palermo and Messina which were 6th and 7th at that time; nor does Antwerp which was 11th in 1600. Table XVI refers to the U.S.

The 24 largest cities in the U.S. are listed with their 1960 and 1970 populations as obtained from census reports. The plus and minus signs denote increase or decrease in population in the decade considered. The fact that of the 12 largest cities, 8 decreased in population, at first glance seems to contradict our statement that the larger cities grow at the expense of the small ones.

TABLE XV The growth of cities[1]

	Rank of European cities in the years: 1500	1600	1800	1800	Population in 1850 (oo omitted)	1890	Annual increase per cent 1800–90	1850–90
Group A.	2.	3.	4.	5.	6.	7.	8.	9.
1. London	..	9	1	958,8	2,362,1	4,211,7	3.77	1.96
2. New York	..	..	..	62,9	660,8	2,740,6	47.3	7.89
3. Paris	2	1	2	546,9	1,053,3	2,448.2	3.81	3.31
4. Berlin...........	..	..	10	173,4	378,2	1,578,8	9.08	7.94
5. Vienna	..	..	8	232,0	431,1	1,341,9	5.31	5.28
6. Chicago	..	..	..	0,0	30,0	1,099,9	..	89.21
7. Philadelphia	..	..	..	81,0	408,8	1,047,0	19.25	3.90
8. St. Petersburg	..	..	7	270,0	490,0	1,003,3	3.01	2.61
Group B.								
9. Constantinople....	1	2	5	300,0–1,000,0	ca 400,0+	873,6	?	ca 2.96
10. Moscow..........	..	14	6	ca 300,0	ca 360,0	822,4	?	ca 3.21
11. Bombay	..	..	..	ca 150,0	ca 560,0	821,8	4.97	ca 1.17
12. Rio de Janeiro	..	..	..	ca 125,0	ca 170,0	ca 800,0	ca 6.0	ca 9.30
13. Calcutta..........	..	..	..	ca 800,0	ca 400,0	741,1	0.	ca 2.10
14. Hamburg Altona ..	..	..	16	ca 120,0	205,0	711,9	5.48	6.18
15. Manchester-Salford	..	..	..	90,4	388,5	703,5	7.63	2.03
16. Buenos Ayres	..	..	..	ca 70,0	ca 120,0 (1895)	677,8	ca 9.6	ca 11.5
17. Glasgow	..	..	..	77,1	329,1	658,2	8.37	2.5
18. Liverpool	..	..	..	82,3	376,0	518,0	6.21	0.95
Group C.								
19. Budapest	..	..	..	ca 61,0	156,5	491,9	ca 8.0	5.36
20. Melbourne........	..	..	..	0,0	23,1	490,9	..	50.6
21. Warsaw	..	..	..	ca 65,0	ca 160,0	485,3	ca 7.2	ca 5.1
22. Birmingham	..	..		70,7	232,8	478,1	6.4	2.63
23. Madrid	..	..	12	156,7	281,2	470,3	2.2	1.68
24. Brussels	..	..	..	66,3	188,5	465,5	6.7	3.67
25. Naples	3	3	3	ca 400,0	ca 415,0	463,2	ca 0.19	ca 0.29
26. Madras	..	..	..	ca 800,0	ca 700,0	452,5	decr.	decr.
27. Boston	..	..	..	24,9	136,9	448,5	19.0	5.69
28. Baltimore	..	..	..	26,5	169,1	434,4	18.2	3.92
29. Lyons............	..	..	19	109,5	177,2	429,3	3.2	3.56
30. Hyderabad	..	..	..	ca 200,0	ca 200,0	415,0	ca 1.4	ca 2.6
31. Amsterdam	..	12	9	(1795) 217,0	224,0	408,1	0.92	2.16
32. Marseilles	..	..	18	111,1	195,3	403,7	2.94	2.67
Group D.								
33. Sydney	..	..	..	2,5	53.9	383,3	169.2	15.28
34. Copenhagen	..	..	21	101,0	ca 143,0	375,7	3.1	4.07
35. Cairo	..	..	..	250–700,0	ca 250,0	374,8	?	ca 1.3
36. Leeds	..	..	..	53,2	172,3	367,5	6.57	2.84
37. Leipzig	..	..	..	32,1	62,4	357,1	11.2	11.8
38. Munich	..	..	..	40,6	109,5	350,6	8.5	5.5
39. Pittsburg-Allegheny	..	..	..	1,6	67,9	343,9	251.6	10.16
40. Breslau	..	..	..	62,9	110,7	335,2	4.81	5.07
41. Edinburgh-Leith ..	..	..	..	81,4	191,2	329,9	3.4	1.81
42. Mexico	..	..	..	ca 137,0	ca 150,0	('89) 329,5	ca 1.6	ca 3.0
43. Sheffield..........	..	..	..	45,8	135,3	324,2	6.76	3.49
44. Milan	5	5	15	ca 134,5	ca 190,0	320,8	ca 1.4	ca 1.7
45. Odessa	..	..	..	?	('56) 101,3	313,7	?	ca 5.0
46. Dublin	..	..	11	ca 160,0	261,7	311,2	ca 1.05	0.47
47. Lisbon	6	10	4	350,0	275,0	307,7	decr.	ca 3.0
48. Minneapolis-St. Paul	..	..	..	0,0	1,1	302,3	..	680.0
49. Rome............	..	8	13	ca 153,0	175,9	300,5	ca 1.1	1.8

This false conception arises because the definition of the city has broken down. Suburbia, which has engulfed neighboring towns, should be considered now as part of the city and the losses indicated in the large cities generally represents the escape to suburbia while, if we had a table of similar losses for much smaller cities, they would represent a flight to more distant areas.

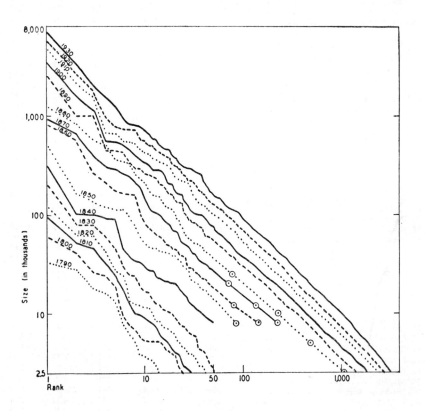

Figure 131   U.S.A. 1790–1930. Communities of 2500 or more inhabitants, ranked in the decreasing order of population size.[3]

Zipf has noted that if the cities of a given country are ordered by the integers 1, 2, 3, ..., then the fraction of people living in the nth city is roughly characterized by

$$f_n = k/n \qquad (1)$$

Hence

$$\log f_n = \log k \text{-} \log n \qquad (2)$$

so that if f_n and n are plotted on log-log graph paper, the slope of the curve should be -1 which is fairly well exhibited in Figure 131. Zipf has also found

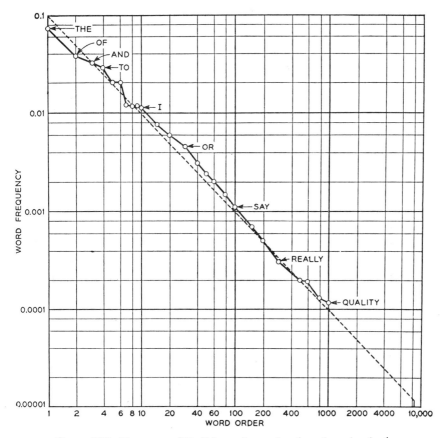

Figure 132   Frequency of English words as a function of word order.[4]

a similar relation for the frequency of the appearance of words in English prose. If f_n now represents the relative frequency of the nth word in the order of frequency, then (2) is again a fair fit to the data exhibited in Figure 132.

Most of the early cities in the U.S. were located along the eastern seaboard. The internal cities tended to develop around the lakes and rivers along which travel was easier than through the forests and mountains. Man-made changes in the terrain stimulated the development of cities in certain patterns. For example, after the construction of the Erie Canal in upstate New York, a linear array of cities grew along the canal. Cities often grew at intersection points of two railroads in a later period.

TABLE XVI   Largest cities in the U.S.; population from census reports

		April 1, 1960	April 1, 1970	
1.	New York	7,781,984	7,867,760	+
2.	Chicago	3,550,404	3,366,957	−
3.	Los Angeles	2,481,595	2,816,061	+
4.	Philadelphia	2,002,512	1,948,609	−
5.	Detroit	1,670,144	1,511,482	−
6.	Houston	938,219	1,232,802	+
7.	Baltimore	939,024	905,759	−
8.	Dallas	679,684	844,401	+
9.	Cleveland	876,050	790,903	−
10.	Washington	763,956	756,510	−
11.	Milwaukee	741,324	717,099	−
12.	San Francisco	740,316	715,674	−
13.	San Diego	573,224	696,769	+
14.	San Antonio	587,718	654,153	+
15.	Boston	698,080	647,071	−
16.	Memphis	497,524	623,530	+
17.	St. Louis	750,026	622,236	−
18.	New Orleans	629,525	593,471	−
19.	Phoenix	439,170	581,562	+
20.	Columbus	471,316	539,677	+
21.	Seattle	557,087	530,831	−
22.	Jacksonville	455,411	528,865	+
23.	Pittsburgh	604,000	520,117	−
24.	Kansas City	475,539	507,087	+

As the American pioneers moved westward, each developed as large a block of land as he could buy or manage by himself or with his family. Each of these early pioneers lived with his family on his own block of land. Villages only developed when the population in a given area reached a magnitude that could support various specialists—millers, blacksmiths, carpenters, trades-men, etc.—who tended to live close to each other. In Europe, villages grew around the old manor houses or in regions in which the land was divided into small farms and the farmers tended to live in a village close to each other. Their homes were sometimes separated from the land which they cultivated. With time, these villages grew into larger towns. It has been observed that if the locations of these centers of the towns are considered as a set of points, the set is somewhat similar to the lattice points of a hexagonal lattice.

An interesting megalopolis, which is sometimes called a "ring city", has without special planning developed in The Netherlands. The old cities of Rotterdam, The Hague, Haarlem, Amsterdam and Utrecht, have grown so that the boundary of any one of them is not very far from that of its nearest

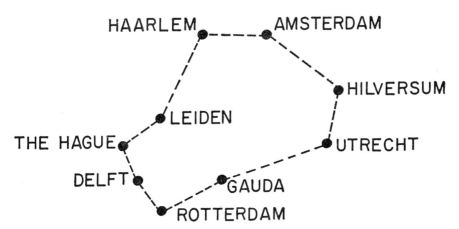

Figure 133   The great ringed city of The Netherlands.

neighbors. The complex might be considered as a single larger ring city, as is indicated in Figure 133. The railroad, bus, and road system is excellent between these cities so that it is not uncommon for residents of one to work at another. Living in one of these cities has the attractive feature that one is close to the rural area in the middle of the ring. Every resident of the city is close to the country, while everyone who lives in the country in the center or around the outskirts of the ring is close to one or more high population density regions on the ring so that he can easily participate in the cultural activities of the city. This population pattern seems to the authors to be more attractive to them than the more common arrangement (which is discussed in the next section) of a city with high population density in the center with a monotonic decreasing density as one proceeds to the outskirts.

REFERENCES

1. A. F. Weber, The Growth of Cities in the 19th Century, (MacMillan, 1899; Comill Paperback Reprints on Urban Studies, 1963).
2. S. H. Holbrook, *American Railroads*, Crown (New York, 1947).
3. G. K. Zipf, *Human Behavior and the Principle of Least Effort*, Addison-Wesley (Cambridge, 1949).
4. C. Shannon, *Bell Tel. Tech. J.* **30**, 53 (1951).

3   Population Density Distribution in Cities

The many attractive features of cities which draw people to them, e.g., the wide variety of employment and trading opportunities, the availability of social intercourse, and the presence of cultural and educational activities, are inevitably accompanied by overcrowding, noise, dirt, pollution, etc. While the former tend to concentrate people, the latter tend to disperse them. Each family (or single individual) chooses a residential location on the basis of income, social status, a relative preference for residential space versus the convenience of a central location, the cost and time involved in commuting to work, the location of vacancies, etc. These factors plus an area's economic base and local geography (the location of rivers, steep slopes, etc.) determine the existing population distribution in a city.

Since the most important characteristics of a city are inextricably connected with the basic facts of how many people live where, population density distributions may be used as a very rough basis for classifying and comparing cities (or, more generally, metropolitan areas). Two pioneering investigations of population density distributions in a number of cities were made at the turn of the century by Mark Jefferson[1] (U.S. cities) and P. Meuriot[2] (European cities). The findings of both these investigations were summarized in a large number of density contour maps.

As important and satisfying as these maps are, one would hope to characterize urban population densities by some functional form $\rho(R, \theta)$ where R is the distance from the center of the core city and θ specifies direction relative to some arbitrarily chosen standard (e.g., north). Note that the third dimension (i.e., "up") is not used to specify residential location on the somewhat arbitrary grounds that man usually starts with a reasonably flat two-dimensional surface on which to build a city. Building heights (which potentially increases available residential space) are strictly determined by various technological and economic factors which we would like to absorb into the dependent density variable. While the angular dependence of $\rho(R, \theta)$

is usually quite marked we would, however, like to preliminarily restrict our attention to

$$\rho(R) = \int_0^{2\pi} \rho(R, \theta)\, d\theta \qquad (1)$$

where suitable modifications must be made if the city does not subtend a full 360 degrees. A fairly typical example of $\rho(R)$ is given in Figure 134. Because

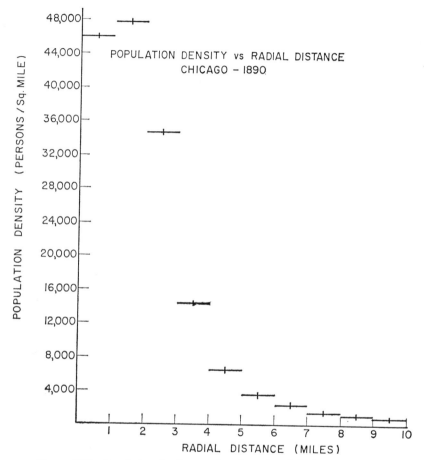

Figure 134 Population density as a function of radial distance from the center of a city—Chicago, 1890.

of the proximity of Lake Michigan, Chicago very nearly subtends 5/9th of a complete circle from its center at the intersection of State and Madison Streets. Except for the innermost areas inclusive of the central business district, the most prominent feature of such data is the monotonic decline in density (i.e., $(dp/dR) < 0$) after a certain distance from the center is reached. It should also be evident that the density drops off quite sharply for small R and then more gradually as we approach the suburbs. The functional form of $\rho(R)$ is then quite evidently concave upward (i.e., $(d^2\rho/dR^2) > 0$) for most values of R (e.g., for $R > 2$ miles in Figure 134) and also appears to get flatter and flatter (i.e., its curvature becomes progressively less or $(d^3\rho/dR^3) < 0$) as the rural periphery is approached.

Although Bleicher (1892)[3] must be credited with its initial introduction, Colin Clark's work[4,5] has provided most of the impetus for the study of the empirical relation

$$\rho(R) = Ae^{-bR} \tag{2}$$

which quite simply satisfies the conditions discussed above. Statistically significant fits to relation (2) have now been obtained for approximately one hundred cities which lends considerable substance to Clark's claim "that the falling of density is an exponential function . . . appears to be true for all times and all places studied, from 1801 to the present, and from Los Angeles to Budapest." (Clark, 1951, pp. 490–491.)

Most direct measurements of $\rho(R)$ have been made by drawing a series of concentric circles about what is considered to be a city's center. As long as the census tracts, wards, or other administrative areas used for classifying populations are reasonably small, the arbitrary apportionments that must be made when a circle cuts through one of them need not introduce any significant error. The size of these districts plus the time-consuming nature of the process has, however, limited most measurements to average densities over annuluses which are a mile or sometimes two miles wide. It should also be noted that available measurements are almost always of *gross* densities. No corrections to the area of an annulus have been made for uninhabited business space, parks, lakes, rivers, etc.

Having obtained a set of measurements, the most appropriate values of A and b are determined by means of the "best" straight line fit to a plot of $\log \rho(R)$ versus R. It is easily seen from (2) that the slope of this line can be identified as $-b$ and the y-intercept as $\log A$; although it should be emphasized that the values of A so obtained are extrapolated central densities and generally not indicative of the actual population density at the center of a city. This point and the considerable degree of approximation involved in assuming (2) are aptly illustrated in Figures 135 and 136. Table XVII lists a large number of the A, b pairs determined in this manner.

It is often said that cities can only grow in two ways, up and out. A can be considered a measure of the first mode (or, alternately, the degree of overcrowding) while b is characteristic of the second mode. A high value of b

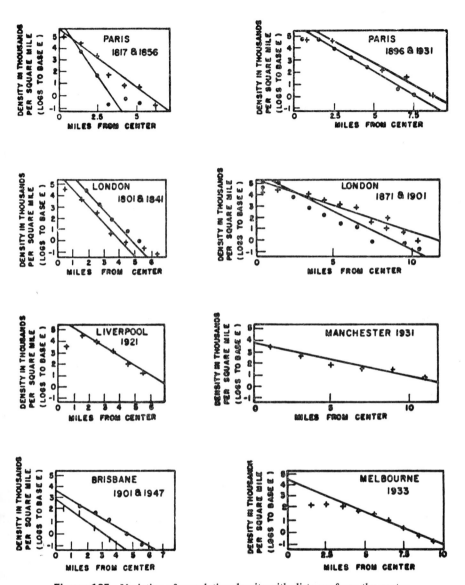

Figure 135   Variation of population density with distance from the center of a city for eight cities.[4]

M

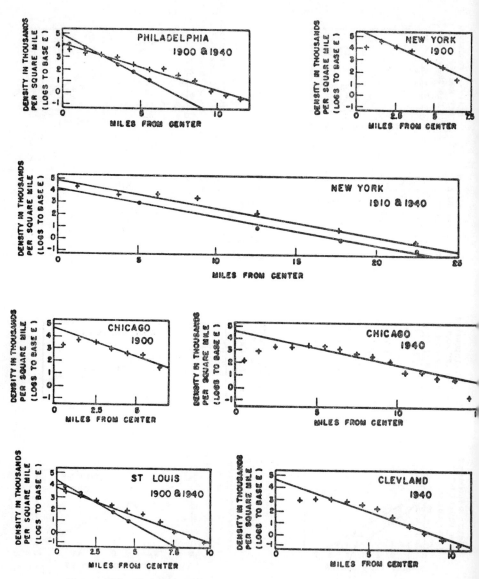

Figure 136 Variation of population density with distance from center of
city for seven more cities.[4]

TABLE XVII   Values of A and b coefficients. A measured in thousands per square mile; b in the fall of *natural* logarithm of density per mile of distance.

		A	b			A	b
	ASIA				CONTINENTAL EUROPE		
Colombo	1946	60	0.40	Berlin	1885	290	1.10
Hongkong	1931	800	1.27		1900	410	0.95
Nagoya	1950	30	0.44	Budapest	1935	280	0.90
Okayama	1939	360	2.83	Copenhagen	1940	60	0.59
	1953	240	2.12	Oslo	1938	80	0.80
Osaka	1950	32	0.20	Paris	1817	450	2.35
Poona	1822	75	1.90		1856	240	0.95
	1881	95	1.90		1896	370	0.80
	1953	200	1.36		1931	470	0.75
Rangoon	1931	200	1.15		1946	180	0.34
Singapore	1953	660	0.60	Stockholm	1940	110	0.78
Tokyo	1950	60	0.21	Vienna	1890	170	0.80
				Zurich	1936	85	0.46
AUSTRALIA AND NEW ZEALAND							
Brisbane	1901	17	0.93	UNITED STATES			
	1933	25	0.75	Allentown	1950	15	0.56
	1947	37	0.73	Baltimore	1950	100	0.78
Christchurch	1911	40	1.61	Birmingham	1950	10	0.19
	1936	40	1.35	Boston	1900	160	0.85
	1951	55	1.33		1940	45	0.30
Dunedin	1911	11	0.68	Bridgeport	1950	60	1.06
	1936	9	0.35	Buffalo	1950	50	0.41
	1951	8	0.19	Chicago	1880	76	0.60
Melbourne	1933	65	0.56		1900	110	0.45
	1954	35	0.35		1940	120	0.30
Sydney	1911	26	0.48		1950	68	0.18
	1947	35	0.30	Cleveland	1940	79	0.42
	1954	24	0.25	Dallas	1950	12	0.25
Wellington	1911	28	1.21	Detroit	1950	50	0.21
	1936	25	0.85	Hartford	1950	30	0.90
	1951	19	0.78	Indianapolis	1950	20	0.49
				Los Angeles	1940	29	0.27
BRITISH ISLES				Minneapolis	1950	20	0.37
Birmingham	1921	104	0.80	New Orleans	1950	60	0.64
	1938	52	0.47	New York	1900	178	0.32
Dublin	1936	70	0.85		1910	59	0.21
Leeds	1951	30	0.50		1925	81	0.21
Liverpool	1921	330	0.80		1940	110	0.21
London	1801	269	1.26		1950	240	0.17
	1841	279	0.94	Omaha	1950	14	0.43
	1871	224	0.61	Philadelphia	1900	112	0.66
	1901	170	0.37		1940	56	0.34
	1921	115	0.27	Rochester	1950	30	0.52
	1931	123	0.28	San Francisco	1950	90	0.36
	1939	83	0.22	Seattle	1950	40	0.72
	1951	62	0.20	St. Louis	1900	120	0.85
Manchester	1939	37	0.29		1940	35	0.43
					1950	40	0.37
				Washington	1950	30	0.26
				Youngstown	1950	60	1.24

Data extracted directly from Census volumes except where indirect sources used as indicated below:

ASIA

Hongkong Hughes, *Geographical Journal*, March 1951. Very approximate estimate. Data are for 1931 and density may be much worse now.
Okayama *American Journal of Sociology*, March 1955.
Poona *Social Survey of Poona* (Gokhale Institute).
Rangoon *Geographical Review*, 1942.
Singapore Private communication from City Planning Authorities.

AUSTRALIA

Melbourne Fooks, *X-ray the City!* (1933 only).

BRITISH ISLES

Birmingham *When we Build Again* (published in Birmingham, 1941).
Dublin Wilson, *Geographical Review*, 1946.
Liverpool Jones and Clark, *Journal of the Royal Statistical Society*, 1930.
London Earlier Census data summarised in 1871. *Census Population Tables*.
London and Manchester 1939 data from National Registration.

EUROPE Data up to 1901 from Meuriot, *Des agglomérations urbaines* (Paris). Very approximately estimated from shaded maps.
Budapest *Geographical Review*, 1943.
Copenhagen, Stockholm and Paris (1946) Grytzell, *Svensk Geografisk Årsbok*, 1951.
Zurich *Statistisches Amt der Stadt, Areal, Liegenschaft und Grundbesitz*, 1945.

U.S.A. Data up to 1900 from Jefferson, *Bulletin of the American Geographical Society*, 1909.
New York 1925, *Regional Planning Report*.

implies a compact city in which density falls off quite rapidly with distance, whereas a very small value of b can be associated with the "urban sprawl" which upsets so many present-day planners. We can relate A and b to the total metropolitan population by noting that the number of people living within a distance R_0 of the city's center is theoretically given by

$$N(R_0) = \int_0^{R_0} Ae^{-bR}(2\pi R)\, dR \tag{3}$$

Integrating by parts, this yields

$$N(R_0) = (2\pi A/b^2)\{1 - e^{-bR_0}(1+bR_0)\} \tag{4}$$

which reduces to

$$N(\infty) = 2\pi A/b^2 \tag{5}$$

as an estimate of total metropolitan population. This expression yields figures that are of the right order of magnitude, but is subject to at least two important qualifications. First, it tends to overestimate total population because it implicitly utilizes extrapolated densities at small values of R. Secondly, it fails to account for the fact that most cities do not spread out uniformly around their center because of lakes, rivers, swamps, mountains, other cities (enter "megalopolis"), state, or national political boundaries, etc.

These qualifications aside, we can in general say that a city can grow by increasing A (crowding together) or decreasing b (spreading out) and that the latter effect is squared. Sir Leonard Wooley has estimated that the ancient city of Uhr (which reached its mature phase about 2,000 B.C.) had an average density of 125,000 per square mile. Parts of fourteenth-century-Paris reached a density figure of 140,000 per square mile, as did the innermost parishes in London of 1700. Western cities flourished with the advent of industrialization and central densities increased far beyond anything that had previously been experienced. The worst areas of New York's Lower East Side reached densities of 350,000 per square mile by 1900.

Although rising central densities were important in accommodating an ever-increasing urban populus, rapidly falling b values were even more important. What little data is available for the early nineteenth century shows that the value of b for London was about 1.4 while the comparable figure for Paris may have been as high as 2.35 (see Table XVII). Available data for Western cities shows a steady temporal decline in b values from that time on, with certain exceptions such as New York where the value has remained nearly constant. These declines can primarily be attributed to advances in transport technology which reduced the cost (and usually time) of traveling relative to the average citizen's income. London and Paris were so very compact in the early nineteenth century because almost everyone walked; horsedrawn buses were not used extensively until later in the century. Consequently, between 1801 and 1841, the population of London grew by about the same proportion in all areas; b remained constant and A increased. With the introduction of steam transport, the nature of the growth of London fundamentally changed and, between 1841 and 1871, the value of b dropped from 1.41 to 0.66. This drop was sufficiently large so that London's population increased appreciably while the value of A actually fell. London exemplifies the fact that cheaper transportation to the outlying districts is usually the result of public policy. In the 1890's, the London County Council induced the railroads to improve their suburban morning and evening train service for workmen and to develop a complete network of underground, surface and suburban transit systems rather than dealing directly with the slum housing question.[6] Table XVII shows that this and subsequent decisions resulted in the continued decline of b and A while the population of London kept growing (see Figure 136).

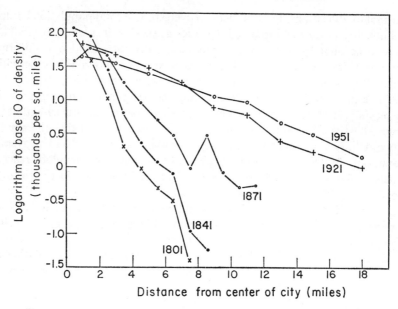

Figure 137   Variation in population density of London at various distances from the center of the city at different times.[4]

In direct contrast, the growth of the relatively new Australian city of Brisbane has been characterized by *increasing* values of A while b has declined, as is usually the case. An intermediate case is supplied by Chicago which was characterized by generally increasing central densities until 1900 or 1910, and decreasing values thereafter. (See Table XVIII.)

TABLE XVIII   Central densities and density gradients in Chicago* 1860–1950

Decennial census	Central density	Density gradient	Decennial census	Central density	Density gradient
1860	30.0	0.91	1910	100.0	0.36
1870	70.8	0.87	1920	73.0	0.25
1880	96.6	0.79	1930	72.8	0.21
1890	86.3	0.50	1940	71.1	0.20
1900	100.0	0.40	1950	63.7	0.28

* Urbanized area.

The smallest values of $b \approx 0.2$ are for one reason or another only found in the largest metropolitan areas, e.g., New York, London, Chicago, Sydney and Manchester. While the cities mentioned above can historically attribute their extremely dispersed forms to the efficiency of surface and underground railways, an equally dispersed city like Los Angeles has quite recently been built up at very low densities while its citizens depend almost exclusively on the automobile. Older American cities (e.g., Bridgeport, Baltimore, and New Orleans) are now also almost solely dependent on bus and auto transport. Yet the existence and continued viability of appreciable, older, closely-spaced housing stocks keeps the b values of these cities higher than one might otherwise expect. The timing of residential construction limits a city's future form.

Even though New York is characterized by the lowest known value of $b \approx 0.17$, this value has not changed much for many decades. Apparently the area is so large and densely populated that existing rail and automotive transport will not permit further spread of the type characterized by decreasing values of b. Instead, densities increase at roughly the same rate everywhere (with the exception of Manhattan and some of the immediately adjacent areas). The same sort of growth appears to have taken place in Paris during the latter half of the nineteenth century and the beginning of the twentieth, although b only decreased slightly during the same period.

The Metro has been electrified, but the fares are high in relation to Parisian wages; more important is the belief of the Paris worker that his two-hour lunch interval should be devoted to its proper purpose and not wasted in traveling; for him to have to live at such a distance from his work that he has to eat his lunch away from home is a real hardship. (Clark, 1951, pp. 495–496.)

This same mode of growth (A increasing while b remains constant) has until recently characterized almost all non-Western cities. Prolonged growth of this type has led to central densities which are orders of magnitude larger than anything found in Western cities. The worst areas in Hong Kong, which is built on a very restricted area between the mountains and the sea, reach densities of approximately 800,000 per square mile. While local transport technology and social customs (particularly the strong desire in the Latin countries to have lunch at home) have contributed to this pattern, the spatial inversion of non-Western socio-economic classes relative to their Western counterparts has been the determining factor.[8]

If in Western cities the poor live at the center and mobile rich at the periphery, in non-Western cities the reverse is true. The least mobile groups occupy the periphery. Any income improvements lead to greater demands for central locations, and increased over-crowding. Sprawl reflects projection of the overall surface outward as densities increase throughout, in a periphery of degrading and depressing slums.

(Berry, *et al.*, p. 404). Recent research[9] indicates the beginnings of a reversal of this socio-economic spatial pattern in Latin America as the elite move to more spacious peripheral areas and are easily able to reach traditional central areas by automobile.

REFERENCES

1. Mark Jefferson, *Bulletin of The American Geographical Society* **41**, 537 (1909).
2. P. Meuriot, *Des Agglomérations Urbaines dans l'Europe Contemporaine* (Paris, 1898), Berlin Fréres.
3. H. Bleicher, *Statistiche Beschreibung der Stadt Frankfort am Main and Ihrer Bevol-kerung* (Frankfort am Main, 1892).
4. Colin Clark, *Journal of the Royal Statistical Society* **114**, Series A, 490–498 (1951).
5. Colin Clark, *Bulletin de l'Institute Internationale de Statistique* **36**, Part 4, 60–68 (1958).
6. A. F. Weber, *The Growth of Cities in The Nineteenth Century*, (Cornell, 1899, Cornell University Press Reprint Edition, 1965), p. 354.
7. H. H. Winsborough, *A Comparative Study of Urban Population Densities*, unpublished Ph.D. dissertation, Department of Sociology, University of Chicago, 1961.
8. Brian J. L. Berry, James W. Simmons, and Robert J. Tennant, *The Geographical Review* S3, 389–405 (1963).
9. Peter W. Amato, *Journal of the American Institute of Planners* **36**, No. 2, (March, 1970), pp. 96–105.

4   Cities and Countries as "Organisms"

If one wishes to make a systems analysis of a country or a city, he starts with a diagram of boxes each representing a component or function. Then flow lines are introduced connecting various boxes which influence each other. It is sometimes suggestive to make an analogy of a new system being investigated with another which has been well studied. While such an analogy should not be taken too seriously, it generally aids one's intuition. A number of people have compared countries and cities with organisms.

Weber[1] stated

... we may liken industrial society of today—embracing all countries within the circle of exchange of products—to a great organism composed of heterogeneous parts. This organism, however, is the product of ages of slow growth. Originally, in place of one all-embracing social organism, where there were myriads of small social units, each complete in itself and independent of the others ... The history of civilization is simply the narrative description of the breaking down of the barriers that separated the primitive social units ... the most conspicuous and influential role in the process was played by the trader, working upon man's desires for what they did not possess or produce.

Neither war (conquest) nor religion has been so vital and far-reaching an influence in the integration and amalgamation of isolated social groups as trade and commerce.

A rather detailed description of a city as an organism has been made by John P. Eberhard[2] in an article in which he emphasized the need to analyze and plan cities as a system rather than as a patchwork of individual items and relations. Since we feel that his outline of structure might make a good framework for a mathematical description of a city, we review some of his ideas.

Systems generally are composed of interconnected elements of hardware whose functions might be guided by software (using computer system terms). A "hardware" component of a city might be a road, while an example of software would be the traffic regulations.

The four major hardware systems of an organism are: (i) the metabolic system which provides nourishment and arranges for waste disposal; (ii) the cardiovascular system which transports processed nourishment of the right type to the required points and carries waste to the points at which it is to be processed; (iii) the nervous system which transports information and arranges for the proper response to stimuli; and, (iv) enclosure system which keeps the organism in the proper compact form and which houses the various elements in their proper juxtaposition. The basic laws of molecular physics and biochemistry represent the software code, while the brain and certain muscular and nerve controls arrange for their proper management in the organism.

The metabolic function of the city involves inputs and outputs (both waste and productive outputs for which the city might have been organized). Some examples are given:

Inputs	Outputs
Food	Garbage
Water	Sewage
Fuel	Pollutants
Raw materials for production	Industrial Production

The processing and organization of these items is done through markets and distribution centers, sewers, factories, incinerators; even the atmosphere is a sewer for pollutants.

The city's cardiovascular system provides the movement paths and the driving force for these items, as well as for the people that shift about. The trucks, automobiles, buses, subways, elevators, etc., are the vehicles of transport (as the red cells and the blood proteins are vehicles of transport in the circulatory system). The roads, elevator shafts, sidewalks and subway tubes play the same role that the veins and arteries play in an organism.

The nervous system of a city is its communication and information distribution network. It is composed of the telephone and telegraph complex, the newspapers, radio, TV, and even the system of traffic signals. The electrical distribution system, as well as the various switching stations, are to be included.

The enclosure system is the collection of buildings which house both the people and the equipment included in the above systems. The schools, churches and amusement centers also belong in this system. Even functional areas such as parks belong here.

The software is not as easy to catalogue but four main systems are: the educational system, the economic system, the political system, and the life support system. The reader will have little difficulty filling out this bare software skeleton.

Clearly our four hardware and four software systems cannot be defined with tremendous precision. There are gray areas containing objects whose classification is debatable, as is the case in all classification schemes.

Now what should one strive for in understanding the organism we call the city? First, the world is full of a tremendous variety of cities, some large, some small, some sophisticated, some primitive, some a pleasure to live in, others to be avoided at all cost. All of these cities have had a history, each developing in its own way, sometimes looking at other cities and following or profiting from their successes and failures, and sometimes looking only within themselves and neglecting the lessons which might be learned from others. Hence one of the first things we should attempt is a classification of cities and an ordering of them in some manner (not necessarily linearly). Can the eight variables used above (the four hardware and four software variables) be brought into the classification?

One means of classification might be in the tree-like Linnaeus manner that has been used to classify organisms. We have not attempted to do this at all, but it would be worth considering. Another, which is more amenable to quantitative interpretation, is to consider the fraction of people involved in, or fraction of money spent on, each system. Once this is established, some scheme could be used to represent the city in some space, eight-dimensional or otherwise. Cities whose representative points are close to each other are then "similar", those far away from each other, "different". The "phase point" represented by each city would wander through the phase space when plotted as a function of time. It would be interesting to examine the trajectories followed and to see if there was a similarity of these trajectories for various cities. Is Budapest following Brussels but ten years behind? Or, are there a set of trajectories such that some cities follow type A trajectory and others type B? This is, of course, just the idea used in our discussion of the evolution and comparison of countries which was discussed in Section 1 of this chapter.

Since the data for cities has not yet been collected and processed to the same degree as that of countries, we cannot proceed further along this line at present. However, in order to give some idea of how one might develop the

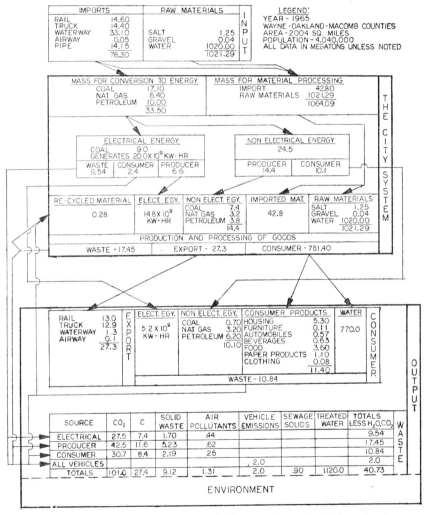

Figure 138   Mass balance[3] of material input and output of Detroit, 1965.

scheme sketched above, we briefly report on an analysis of part of the metabolic system of the Detroit area made recently by Ahn, Caldwell, and Piccirelli.[3]

Their exploratory study is a derivation of a rough mass balance of major input and output of material components of the tricounty Detroit area. Their results are summarized in the flow chart shown in Figure 138. Air and sunlight were omitted from their mass and energy balance. In a rural area, the influence of sunlight would of course be more important. The appropriate units for annual mass transfer of most significant items is megatons. Water is exceptional, being used in thousands of megatons per year. Of the 76.3 megatons of imports, 20 MT are used by consumers with the remainder being applied to production. An account of the manner in which the numbers in the chart were obtained will be published by Ahn, Caldwell and Piccirelli.

It would be interesting to obtain similar charts for other cities and to investigate the variation of the mass and energy flows for several cities as a function of time. Charts should also be prepared for the remaining seven systems of a city and to try to see how these influence each other. Perhaps one way of obtaining some feeling for the importance of various connection links and of the role played by each system as part of the whole is to assume that the budget of the items associated with one of the systems is decreased by 10% or increased by 10% and to try to estimate the effect this has on the operation of the affairs of the other systems.

Some intuition on the relative importance of our eight systems as a function of city size might be derived by starting with a city of population 10^5. Then consider the difference in budget and operation procedures of that city from one half as big, one twice as big, one ten times as big, and one with 1/10th the population.

After performing a number of the gedanken experiments, one should be in a better position to make a systematic investigation of the city as a system of subsystems.

REFERENCES

1. A. F. Weber, The Growth of Cities in the Nineteenth Century (Reprint Edition, Comill Univ. Press, 1965), p. 159.
2. J. P. Eberhard, International Sci. and Technology, p. 18, Sept. 1966.
3. K. Ahn, W. Caldwell and R. Piccirelli, Private Communication.

Subject Index

N

Author Index

343

Acknowledgments

MANY FIGURES and several quotations taken from other sources are reprinted in this book. We wish to thank the authors and publishers, the copyright holders, listed below for permission to reprint the following identified figures, tables, and qotations on the pages indicated.

Figures 1 (p. 3), 2 (p. 4) and 19 (p. 50). L. I. Dublin and A. J. Lotka, *Length of Life*, © 1936, The Roland Press Company, New York.

Figures 3 (p. 5), 15 (p. 43) and 17 (p. 46). W. S. Woytinsky and E. S. Woytinsky, *World Population and Production: Trends and Outlook*, © 1953, The Twentieth Century Fund, New York.

Table I (p. 8). J. Graunt, *Natural and Political Observations Made Upon the Bills of Mortality*, 1676 (Reprint © 1936, The Johns Hopkins Press).

Table II (p. 13). E. T. Newell, *The Numismatist* (Sept. 1916), © 1916, American Numismatic Society).

Figure 5 (p. 23). E. Montroll, *Lectures in Theor. Phys.* X A, 531, © 1967, University of Colorado Press, Boulder Col.

Figures 8 (p. 28) and 18 (pp. 48–9). W. D. Camp, *Marriage and the Family in France since the Revolution*, © 1961, W. D. Camp (Bookman Assoc.) New York.

Figure 10 (p. 33). S. G. Lasky, *Eng. Mining J.*, © 1955, Engineering and Mining Journal.

Figures 11 (p. 35) and 43 (p. 116). D. J. de Solla Price, *Little Science, Big Science*, © 1963, Columbia Univ. Press, N.Y.

Figure 13 (p. 38). C. S. Elton, *The Ecology of Invasions by Plants and Animals*, © Methuen & Co. Ltd., London.

Figures 20 (pp. 50–1) and 21 (p. 52). H. P. Jones, *Adv. in Bio. and Med. Phys.*, © 1956, Academic Press, New York.

Figure 22 (p. 53). G. H. Whipple, *Vital Statistics*, © 1923, Chapman Hall, London.

Figure 23a (p. 62). D. A. MacLulich, University of Toronto Studies, *Bio. Sci.* **43** © 1937, University of Toronto Press, Toronto.

Figure 23b (p. 62). C. S. Elton, *J. of Exp. Biol.* © 1924, Cambridge University Press, Cambridge.

Figures 24–7 (pp. 64–5, 67, 70). N. Goel, S. Maitra, and E. Montroll, *Rev. Mod. Phys.* © 1971, American Institute of Physics, New York.

Figure 28 (p. 80). L. F. Richardson, *Arms and Security* © 1960, The Boxwood Press, Pacific Grove Cal.

Figure 34 (p. 92). D. Wechsler, *The Measurement and Appraisal of Adult Intelligence* © 1958, The Williams and Wilkins Co., Baltimore.

Figure 35 (p. 93). Yule and Kendall, *Introd. to Theory of Statistics*, (14th Ed.), © 1950, Chas. Griffin & Co. Ltd., London.

Table VI (p. 98). R. Rothery, Ph.D. Thesis, Brussels (1968).

Figure 38 (p. 101) and Table VII (p. 102). W. J. Horvath, *Behavioral Science* **13, 18,** © 1968, Behavioral Science Ann Arbor.

Figures 39, 40 and 41 (pp. 112–114). H. T. Davis, *The Theory of Econometrics,* © 1941, Trinity University Press, San Antonio, Texas.

Figure 42 (p. 115). A. J. Lotka, *J. Wash. Acad. of Sci.* **16,** p. 317, © 1926, Wash. Acad. of Sci., Washington D.C.

Figures 44 and 45 (pp. 117, 118). W. Shockley, *Proc. Of IRE* **45,** p. 282, © 1957, Inst. of Electrical and Electronic Engineers, New York.

Figures 46 and 47 (pp. 122, 123). E. J. Gumbel, *Statistics of Extremes,* © 1958, Columbia University Press, New York.

Figure 48 (p. 130). J. Davidson, *Transactions of the Royal Society of South Australia* **62,** 343, © 1938, Roy. Soc. of S. Australia.

Figures 50, 52–57, 61 and 62 (pp. 137, 146–50, 198–9). E. J. Gumbel, N.B.S. *Appl. Math. Series* No. 33, © 1954, U.S. Govt. Printing Office.

Figure 51 (p. 139). D. van Dantzig, *Proc. Int. Congress of Math.,* Series II, Amsterdam I, p. 218, © 1959, North Holland Publishing Co. Amsterdam.

Figures 59 (pp. 180–1) and 60 (p. 183). W. L. Thorp, *Business Annuals,* © 1926, National Bureau of Economic Research, New York.

Figure 65 (p. 207). Yale Hirsh, *The Stock Trader's Almanac and Record,* © 1969, The Hirsch Organization, Old Tappan, N.J.

Figures 66–69 (p. 209–11). H. V. Roberts, *Journal of Finance* **14,** 1, © 1959, Journal of Finance, New York.

Figures 70–75 (p. 213–19). M. F. M. Osborn, *Operations Research* **7,** p. 145, © 1959, Operations Research Society of America, Baltimore.

Figures 76 and 77 (pp. 221, 223). M. F. M. Osborn, *Operations Research* **10,** p. 345, © 1962, Operations Research Society of Amerca, Baltimore.

Figures 78 and 79 (p. 227). W. Owen, *The Metropolitan Transportation Problem,* Brookings Inst. Press Original Photographs from U.S. Bureau of Public Roads.

Figure 80 (p. 228). Gustave Doré, *Impressions of London,* Jerrold (1872).

Figure 81 (p. 229). © 1965, Jardin of Arts, Paris.

Figures 82 and 83 (pp. 230, 232). R. J. Smeed, *J. of Transport Economics and Policy* **2,** 1, © 1968, Journal of Transport Economics and Policy, London.

Figure 84 (p. 236). E. W. Montroll and R. B. Potts, Chapter II of *Introduction to Traffic Flow,* NRC Special Report 79, © 1964, National Research Council, Washington D.C.

Figure 85 (p. 237). R. Herman, E. Montroll, R. Potts and R. Rothery, *Operations Research* **7,** p. 86, © 1959, Operations Research Society of America, Baltimore.

Figure 86 (p. 237). R. Herman and R. Rothery, General Motors Technical Report 1964, Détroit.

Figure 88 (p. 248). D. Gazis, IBM Report, 1971.

Figure 90 (p. 254). D. Gazis, *Proc. of IEEE,* **59,** p. 1090, © 1971, Institute of Electrical Engineers, New York.

Figures 91–96 (p. 256–63). W. von Stein, *Theory of Traffic Flow* p. 68, © 1961, Elsevier Publishing Co., Amsterdam.

Figures 97–99 (p. 267–9). Committee on Air Pollution, Interim Report, H.M. Stationery Office, London, 1965.

Figures 100–104 (pp. 270, 272–4). M. E. Smith, *The Use and Misuse of the Atmosphere,* Brookhaven Lecture Series, © Gordon and Breach, New York.

Figures 106 (p. 276) and 115–120 (pp. 291–7). F. Frenkiel, Ann. Reports of Smithsonian Institution, p. 269, 1956, U.S. Govt. Printing Office, Washington D.C.

Figures 107–114 (pp. 280, 282–7). Lord Rothschild, *Proc. Roy. Soc. Lond.*, A 322, 147, © 1971, The Royal Society, London.

Figure 121 (p. 297). L. Shieh, P. Halpern, B. Chemens, H. Wang and F. Abraham, *IBM J. Res. Develop.* **16**, p. 32, © 1972 by International Business Machine Corp. Armonk, **N.Y.**

Figures 123 and 124 (pp. 302–7). J. C. Fischer and R. H. Pry, *General Electric Report* 1970, General Electric Co., Schenectady, N.Y.

Figure 131 (p. 318). G. K. Zipf, *Human Behavior and the Principle of Least Effort*, © 1949, Addison-Wesley Publishing Co., Reading, Mass.

Figure 132 (p. 319). C. Shannon, *Bell Tel. Tech. J.* **30**, 53 © 1951, Am. Telephone and Telegraph Co., New York.

Figures 135–137 (pp. 325–6, 330). C. Clark, *JRSS*, Series A, p. 114 © 1951, Royal Statistical Society, London.

Figure 138 (p. 335). K. Ahn, W. Caldwell and R. Piccirelli, *Private Communication.*

QUOTATIONS

p. 163. M. Beard, *A History of Business*, Vol 1 (Univ. of Mich. Press, 1963).

p. 183. F. J. Allen, *Only Yesterday* (Harper, 1931; Reprint Bantam, 1946).

pp. 187–8, 191–5. J. K. Galbraith, *The Great Crash* (Houghton Mifflin, 1954).

p. 208. M. G. Kendell, *Trans. of Roy. Stat. Soc.* **96**, p. 11 (1953).